# Lecture Notes
# in Business Information Processing    143

Series Editors

Wil van der Aalst
  *Eindhoven Technical University, The Netherlands*
John Mylopoulos
  *University of Trento, Italy*
Michael Rosemann
  *Queensland University of Technology, Brisbane, Qld, Australia*
Michael J. Shaw
  *University of Illinois, Urbana-Champaign, IL, USA*
Clemens Szyperski
  *Microsoft Research, Redmond, WA, USA*

João Falcão e Cunha
Mehdi Snene
Henriqueta Nóvoa (Eds.)

# Exploring Services Science

4th International Conference, IESS 2013
Porto, Portugal, February 7-8, 2013
Proceedings

 Springer

Volume Editors

João Falcão e Cunha
FEUP – University of Porto
Porto, Portugal
E-mail: jfcunha@fe.up.pt

Mehdi Snene
University of Geneva
Geneva, Switzerland
E-mail: mehdi.snene@unige.ch

Henriqueta Nóvoa
FEUP – University of Porto
Porto, Portugal
E-mail: hnovoa@fe.up.pt

ISSN 1865-1348                              e-ISSN 1865-1356
ISBN 978-3-642-36355-9                      ISBN 978-3-642-36356-6  (eBook)
DOI 10.1007/978-3-642-36356-6
Springer Heidelberg Dordrecht London New York

Library of Congress Control Number: 2013930014

ACM Computing Classification (1998): J.1, H.3.5, H.4.1, D.2

*Typesetting:* Camera-ready by author, data conversion by Scientific Publishing Services, Chennai, India

Printed on acid-free paper

Springer is part of Springer Science+Business Media (www.springer.com)

# Preface

Writing these words means that we have reached the end of a long road, and that in some way all the obstacles and problems have been overcome. We can now say that it is a great pleasure to welcome you to IESS 1.3.

IESS 1.3 is the 4th in the series of International Conferences on Exploring Service Science. The IESS conferences provide a forum for the presentation and exchange of exploratory research results and practical experiences within the field of service science. In the year 2013, the conference was hosted by FEUP, Faculty of Engineering of the University of Porto, Portugal, during February 7–8, after having been very successfully held for the past three editions in UNIGE, University of Geneva, Switzerland.

Service science is an interdisciplinary approach to the systematic innovation in service systems, integrating management, social, legal, and engineering aspects to address the theoretical and practical aspects of the challenging services industry and its economy. Service science leverages methods, results, and knowledge stemming from these disciplines toward the development of its own concepts, methods, techniques, and approaches thus creating the basis for true transdisciplinary gatherings and the production of innovative results.

The conference theme of IESS 1.3 was "Enhancing Service System Fundamentals and Experiences." Complex multi-technology-based service systems are now being deployed covering most aspects of life in our society. The sustainability of service systems involves technical, economic, and social responsibility issues, and therefore its fundamentals need to be better understood. Opportunities for radical innovation arise in this environment, and new transdisciplinary exploratory work is deemed essential to address all the challenges being faced. Service system value co-creation also requires an improved understanding of the experiences that are being designed for the benefit of everyone. Service science needs to explore enhanced methods, approaches, and techniques for a more sustainable and inclusive economy and society.

This challenging proposal of IESS 1.3 attracted scientists and practitioners from all over the world to submit their contributions. Up to 78 submissions were received from 22 countries, out of which the Program Committee selected 19 top-quality full papers and 9 short papers (starting from p. 279). This strong concurrence has given an acceptation rate of 28%, what explains by itself the hard selection process of the conference. All the submissions where reviewed by at least three members of the IESS 1.3 Program Committee, composed by well-known and relevant scientists related to the different topics. The resulting program reflects the fact that Exploring Service Science encompasses human and organizational issues as well as technical issues. This includes different issues related to the innovation, services management, services engineering and services discovery.

We would especially like to devote a special thanks to the members of the Program Committee and referees for doing an excellent work in reviewing the submitted papers. Their dedicated work was instrumental in putting together another high-quality IESS conference. We also wish to give special thanks to the local organizers at FEUP for their commitment, in particular Isabel Horta and Vera Miguéis. Thank you very much!

Finally, the IESS 1.3 organizers would also thank the main conference sponsors that made possible the success of the conference, and also the keynote speakers.

We wish you a very pleasant reading, and a fruitful use of these results in your research and applications.

February 2013

João Falcão e Cunha
Mehdi Snene
Henriqueta Nóvoa

# Organization

## General Chair

Joao Cunha

## Program Chairs

Mehdi Snene
Henriqueta Novoa

## Program Committee

Ana Sasa
Andy Rindos
Anelize Biljon
António Brito
Arash Golnam
Bernardo Almada Lobo
Bruno Prata
Camille Salinesi
Claudia Roncancio
Claudio Pinhanez
Davor Meersman
Dimitri Konstantas
Dominique Rieu
Dorith Tavor
Eric Dubois
Geert Poels
George Pavlou
Gerhard Satzger
Gil Regev
Isabel Horta
Jaap Gordijn

Jaelson Castro
Jean-Henry Morin
Jelena Zdravkovic
Joan A. Pastor
Joao Cunha
Jolita Ralyté
Jonas Manamela
Jorge Cardoso
José António Faria
José Palazzo M. De
    Oliveira
Lia Patrício
Malgorzata Spychala
María Valeria De Castro
Marion Lepmets
Marite Kirikova
Mark Shlomo
Mark Davis
Michel Leonard
Miguel Mira Da Silva
Monica Dragoicea

Natalia Kryvinska
Olivier Zephir
Paul Maglio
Paul Lillrank
Pere Botella
Petra Komarkova
Pieter De Leenheer
Regina Frei
Riichiro Mizoguchi
Ruth Raventos
Selmin Nurcan
Sergio Mancini
Soe-Tsyr Yuan
Taro Kanno
Theodor Borangiu
Tomas Pitner
Vera Migueis
Vicente Pelechano
Victoria Torres

# Table of Contents

Strategic Reorientation and Influences on Business-IT Alignment:
Case Study of a Luxembourgish Financial Services Provider . . . . . . . . . .   1
   *Dieter De Smet and Wolfgang Molnar*

A Service Oriented Simulation Architecture for Intelligent Building
Management . . . . . . . . . . . . . . . . . . . . . . . . . . . . . . . . . . . . .   14
   *Monica Drăgoicea, Laurenţiu Bucur, and Monica Pătraşcu*

Capabilities in Systems Engineering: An Overview . . . . . . . . . . . . . . . . .   29
   *Gonçalo Antunes and José Borbinha*

Applying the Lead User Method for Designing e-Services - Practical
Techniques and Experiences . . . . . . . . . . . . . . . . . . . . . . . . . . . . . . . .   43
   *Martin Henkel, Erik Perjons, and Anders Thelemyr*

Theory of Constraints in the Service Sector: Characterization for
Banking and Analysis of the Factors Involved in Its Adoption . . . . . . . . .   58
   *Julian D.M. Castaño, Maria R.A. Moreira, Paulo S.A. Sousa, and
   Raquel F.Ch. Meneses*

Service Innovation Analytics: Towards an Approach for Validating
Frameworks for Service Innovation Capabilities via Text Mining . . . . . . .   73
   *Niels Feldmann, Marc Kohler, Steven O. Kimbrough, and
   Hansjörg Fromm*

Modeling ITIL Business Motivation Model in ArchiMate . . . . . . . . . . . . .   86
   *Marco Vicente, Nelson Gama, and Miguel Mira da Silva*

Service Science: A Service System Design Science Research Method? . . .   100
   *Eric Dubois and Anne Rousseau*

Modeling Service Relationships for Service Networks . . . . . . . . . . . . . . . .   114
   *Jorge Cardoso*

Evaluating the IT Strategic Plan for the Public Administration in
Portugal . . . . . . . . . . . . . . . . . . . . . . . . . . . . . . . . . . . . .   129
   *Diogo Nunes, Isabel Rosa, and Miguel Mira da Silva*

Open Semantic Service Networks: Modeling and Analysis . . . . . . . . . . . . .   141
   *Jorge Cardoso, Carlos Pedrinaci, and Pieter De Leenheer*

Ontological Representation and Governance of Business Semantics in
Compliant Service Networks . . . . . . . . . . . . . . . . . . . . . . . . . . . . . . .   155
   *Pieter De Leenheer, Jorge Cardoso, and Carlos Pedrinaci*

Simulation-Based Quantification of Business Impacts Caused by Service
Incidents . . . . . . . . . . . . . . . . . . . . . . . . . . . . . . . . . . . . . . . . . . . . . . . . . . .   170
*Axel Kieninger, Florian Berghoff, Hansjörg Fromm, and
Gerhard Satzger*

IT Governance Mechanisms: A Literature Review . . . . . . . . . . . . . . . . . . . .   186
*Rafael Almeida, Rúben Pereira, and Miguel Mira da Silva*

A Model-Driven Environment for Service Design, Simulation and
Prototyping . . . . . . . . . . . . . . . . . . . . . . . . . . . . . . . . . . . . . . . . . . . . . . . . . .   200
*Biljana Bajić-Bizumić, Claude Petitpierre, Hieu Chi Huynh, and
Alain Wegmann*

Towards a Taxonomy of Service Design Methods and Tools . . . . . . . . . . . .   215
*Rui Alves and Nuno Jardim Nunes*

A Survey of Tool Support for the Animation of IT Services Process
Models Execution . . . . . . . . . . . . . . . . . . . . . . . . . . . . . . . . . . . . . . . . . . . . .   230
*Marco Roque and Fernando Brito e Abreu*

Factors Influencing the Internationalization of Services Firms:
The Case of Design, Engineering and Architecture Consulting Firms . . . .   246
*Maria R.A. Moreira, Miguel A.S. Maia, Paulo S.A. Sousa, and
Raquel F.Ch. Meneses*

A Proposal for a Mobile Ticketing Solution for Metropolitan Area of
Oporto Public Transport . . . . . . . . . . . . . . . . . . . . . . . . . . . . . . . . . . . . . . .   263
*Marta Campos Ferreira, Maria Henriqueta Nóvoa, and
Teresa Galvão Dias*

Benchmarking as a Development Tool in Healthcare . . . . . . . . . . . . . . . . . .   279
*Paulus Torkki and Paul Lillrank*

Towards an Ontology and Modeling Approach for Service Science . . . . . .   285
*Geert Poels, Griet Van Der Vurst, and Elisah Lemey*

Extended DEMO-Based SLAs to Specify Customers' Expectations . . . . .   292
*Mário Almeida, Carlos Mendes, and Miguel Mira da Silva*

Exploring the Drivers of E-Commerce through the Application of
Structural Equation Modeling . . . . . . . . . . . . . . . . . . . . . . . . . . . . . . . . . . .   299
*Andre F.G. Castro, Raquel F.Ch. Meneses, and Maria R.A. Moreira*

A Model for Open, On-Demand, Collaborative Education for Service
Science . . . . . . . . . . . . . . . . . . . . . . . . . . . . . . . . . . . . . . . . . . . . . . . . . . . . . .   306
*Theodor Borangiu, Monica Drăgoicea, Ecaterina Oltean, and
Iulia Iacob*

Factors Influencing Purchase Intention of Private Label Products:
The Case of Smartphones ........................................... 313
    Dany C. Coelho, Raquel F.Ch. Meneses, and Maria R.A. Moreira

Media Sharing in Situated Displays: Service Design Lessons from
Existing Practices with Paper Leaflets ............................. 322
    Ana Melro, Bruno Silva, and Rui José

Towards a Personal Relationship-Based Assignment of Client
Representatives to Accounts ....................................... 329
    Johannes Kunze von Bischhoffshausen and Jeffrey T. Becker

Future Deployment of Technology in Healthcare Services - A Delphi
Approach .......................................................... 336
    Benedikt Brenken, Arno Schmitz-Urban, and Gerhard Gudergan

Author Index ...................................................... 343

The Discriminating Power of the Distribution of Service-Time Profiles
in Cloud and Grid Resource ........................................... 89
Tiana Gonsalez-Rogue, I. Chiola, and Marco J. C. Perron

Dynamic Fault-Tree Tolerant Algorithm in Service-Based
Applications with Fuzzy Evaluation ................................... 108
Xudong Wang, Fengyu Tian, and Jun Ma

Location-Based and Relationship-Based Assignment of Cloud
Services ............................................................. 125
Siqiang Luo and Haofen Wang

Constraint-Aware and Throughput-Optimization and Green E-Buffer
Aware the Approach of Business to Business Service Selection .......... 139
Cloud ...

# Strategic Reorientation and Influences on Business-IT Alignment: Case Study of a Luxembourgish Financial Services Provider

Dieter De Smet and Wolfgang Molnar

Public Research Centre Henri Tudor, Avenue John F. Kennedy 29,
1855 Luxembourg, Grand Duchy of Luxembourg
{Dieter.Desmet,Wolfgang.Molnar}@Tudor.lu

**Abstract.** This research aims to provide a concrete description of the influences from a financial services provider's strategic orientation on its business-IT alignment practices. Adopting an in-depth, qualitative case study design, several semi-structured interviews were conducted. Interview data was analysed by using a customized reference framework for the governance and implementation of business-IT alignment initiatives. The case study induced insights about the influences of (1) the IT legacy, (2) the existence of more opaque business goals or an unclear definition of them and (3) a low level of inter-departmental collaboration. The expertise of an external partner favoured streamlining the provider's service delivery, yet influenced the existing practices which are more focused on customer service. The new strategic focus is based on the need for growth and the dependence on external know-how. This is the first business-IT alignment study from a financial services provider offering pivotal services in the Grand Duchy of Luxembourg.

**Keywords:** Financial services, case study, business-IT alignment.

## 1 Introduction

Information systems and technology play a paramount role in the financial services industry because it was one among the first to adopt it [1]. Furthermore it can be considered as a clear example of a service industry because its core business is the processing of information [2, 3] and its use of information technology was also reported to be relevant as a competitive advantage [4, 5].

This research will provide in-depth insights into the impact strategic reorientation has on business-IT alignment practices and explore its influence on the co-creation of new (financial) services. This is possible through case study research and this study relies on an established typology in strategic management, the Value-Discipline Model [6], to characterize the company's context.

The strategic focus of the involved company (before strategic change) is more "customer intimate", due to its central and unique position in the past (i.e. cooperative structure for the local market with fewer customers). The shift in strategy caused its focus to evolve towards "operational excellence", in order to operate in the EU

J.F. e Cunha, M. Snene, and H. Nóvoa (Eds.): IESS 2013, LNBIP 143, pp. 1–13, 2013.
© Springer-Verlag Berlin Heidelberg 2013

market and work with many customers. Following the Value-Discipline Model, a company will not be able to excel in all value disciplines (i.e., product, process and customer) because the fundamental culture, structures, people, processes and business activities lead to an excellence in only one discipline, creating difficulties to achieve excellence in the others [6]. Within financial services there is a need for balance between operational excellence and customer intimacy as they cannot be excluded from each other [7, 8]. This research will deal with a context where this balance is being tipped in favour of operational excellence.

To the best of our knowledge, this research's contributions are threefold. Firstly, past research into business-IT alignment for financial services did not focus on Luxembourg, but on several other countries (cf. section 2). Secondly, the influence from the growth requirements, followed by a strategic repositioning, also wasn't researched in those countries. Lastly, the resource dependency theory [9] hasn't been used as a theoretical lens in business-IT alignment research involving financial services companies.

The rest of this research will be structured as follows: the second section will provide a literature review of business-IT alignment within financial services and its link with service science. The third section will describe the research site, approach and methods for data collection and analysis. The actual findings from this case study will be presented in the fourth section and its discussion with implications will be discussed in the fifth section.

## 2    Literature Review

Business and IT leaders need to align their respective strategies to ensure advancement of the company. Possible reasons for its importance can be found in the dynamic environment, both from a business and technological point of view, thereby creating many opportunities and challenges [10]. Business-IT alignment can be viewed as a process or as an outcome [11], complementing this dynamic environment [12]. Technology and information systems are able to operationalize the strategy but they can also build new ones [13, 14]. Disposing of a companywide, strategic alignment model is therefore paramount to adapting and implementing changes [15-17] in the service system.

Service science research is oriented towards the co-creation of new services [5] and business-IT alignment fits into this, because it's a collaborative effort in financial services companies [2]. Operational efficiency was found to be complementary with a profound customer knowledge within financial services [7]. Hence changes in the strategic focus of these companies can influence the co-creation of new services [8]. The latter requires an alignment between the value for the customer and strategic value for the company [18] through a systematic approach [19]. Appropriate valuation is an integral part of this approach, yet conventional financial methods are not sufficient for investments into these longer term strategic alignment initiatives. Thus various value-based analytical methodologies are being explored, still requiring a reinforcement of their theoretical grounds and integration into a crisp concept [20].

Previous research dealing with business-IT alignment in financial services covers several countries. Mutual financial companies were researched in order to find the drivers for adopting an IT governance framework [21]. This also implies business-IT alignment since the goal of IT governance is to improve it [22]. Large financial institutions in the USA were investigated to gather insights into the reasons for alignment gaps [5, 23]. Australian financial institutions were also targeted in order to find practices that enhance alignment [4] or describe the use of an alignment model in custody services [3]. The effects on organizational performance were also explored in the Indonesian financial services industry [24]. Exploratory research in the Belgian financial services industry provided insights into the practices needed to be put into place, to favour business-IT alignment [25]. The Dutch financial services industry was used to test a business-IT alignment maturity model. Financial services companies were found to have a higher degree of maturity compared to public or professional services companies [26]. The retail sales process of a German financial company was also explored and alignment within the business itself was found to be an important driver for an effective, overall business-IT alignment [27]. The Swiss financial services industry was also studied but from a value management perspective, hence focussing on the anticipated results of the business-IT alignment process [28]. The enterprise IT architecture's evaluation has also been studied before, empirically researching investment criteria within larger Austrian companies [29]. Another method for evaluating the service value for business-IT alignment was also proposed and explored within the Chinese financial services industry [30]. Next to the structural elements in business-IT alignment, social elements and human interactions between its actors are also relevant. Communication, trust and knowledge are social elements to take into consideration [31] and the possible influences from national cultures were also explored [32]. Communication issues between business and IT experts in financial services companies were also reported and possible solutions involve the use of sufficiently precise (not the same as detailed) abstract models to enhance understanding [33].

Table 1. Business-IT alignment research within financial services companies

| Country | Research focus | Reference |
|---|---|---|
| Austria | Investment criteria and enterprise architecture evaluation. | [29] |
| Australia and Canada | IT governance choices for financial companies and regulatory differences. | [21] |
| Australia | Explore business and information strategy alignment in banking. | [4] |
| Australia | Determine if the strategic alignment model (SAM) is useful as a management tool to create, assess and sustain strategic alignment. | [3] |
| Belgium | Triangulates research strategies to explore how companies are implementing IT governance and to analyse the relationship between these implementations and business/IT alignment. | [25] |

**Table 1.** (*Continued*)

| | | |
|---|---|---|
| Belgium and the Netherlands | Influence of the cultural dimensions of Hofstede on the variables of business-IT alignment maturity. | [32] |
| China | Uses Business Aligned IT Strategy (BAITS) architecture which evaluates service processes and assesses its value based on the perspectives of stakeholders. | [30] |
| Europe | Identity major alignment issues and attempt to determine the relationships between these issues. | [2] |
| Europe | Use of international standards to understand and facilitate interactions between business and IT experts and the organization. | [33] |
| Germany | Case study in four branches, the back office, and the IT department of a retail bank. | [27] |
| Indonesia | Survey on the impacts of strategic alignment on organizational performance. | [24] |
| Indonesia (Manufacturing) | The influence of employee alignment orientations on successful implementation of business-IT alignment is investigated. | [31] |
| Scotland | The aim of the study was to ascertain the effects of technological developments on the traditional branch network of the banking industry by researching employees and customers | [7] |
| Switzerland | Survey studying the expected benefits from IT projects and hence alignment initiatives. | [28] |
| The Netherlands | Overview of theory development business-IT alignment and reports on the issues, based on a number of focus group discussions. | [26] |
| USA | Reasons for alignment gaps between business and IT strategy. | [23] |
| USA | Investigates differences in strategies at smaller and larger banks. | [5] |

To the best of our knowledge, the resource dependency theory [9] and the influence of external partners haven't been investigated before. The resource dependency theory was reported to serve as a framework for researching the interactions between complementary (or competing) organizations [34] and should therefore provide a good basis for this research where strategic change was stimulated by an external partner. It states that external partnerships and alliances are needed to acquire key resources for an organization's growth and survival. This theoretical framework is interested in the effect of external constraints and doesn't view organizations as fully autonomous or self-supporting. Hence tensions are unavoidable due to a certain degree of external control.

Our goal is to provide a concrete example of this and its influences on business-IT alignment practices within a financial services company. Therefore the following research questions (RQ) are formulated.

RQ1: What are the influences of strategic change on the business-IT alignment practices within a financial services firm in Luxembourg?

RQ2: How do these influences shape the business-IT alignment practices within a financial services firm in Luxembourg?

# 3      Research Approach

Understanding the business-IT alignment practices within a financial services company requires rich data. Qualitative research is therefore appropriate since it obtains insights into the specific processes and practices that exist within a location and its context [35]. This qualitative research chose a case study approach [36] with several semi-structured interviews within a financial services company to create an in-depth case study [37]. It's well suited when there are interactions between people and the organization [38], and it generates insights and rich descriptions [39]. This fully corresponds to our needs to explore the influence of strategic change on business-IT alignment practices.

## 3.1      The Case Study Site: FiSCo

The fictitious name FiSCo (i.e., Financial Service Company) will be used to describe the involved company. It was founded as a cooperative structure in Luxembourg with operating services providing back-office activities, such as clearing of stock markets, transactions and payments, internet payment transactions, etc. The company is confronted with new EU regulations which opened up a larger EU market with more potential competitors, but also business opportunities.

**Table 2.** Overview of research interviews

| Number of interviews | Position of the interviewee | Responsibility of the interviewee |
|---|---|---|
| 1 | Program Manager | New service development and company transformation |
| 1 | Head of Department | Business Unit |
| 1 | Chief Operating Officer | Service to end users |
| 1 | Head of Department | Business Unit |
| 1 | Team Manager | Operational Control |
| 1 | Chief Executive Officer | Overall Management |
| 1 | Head of Department | Business Unit |
| 1 | Head of Department | Support Department |
| 1 | Head of Department | Support Department |
| **Total: 9** | | |

In total 9 persons participated to the interviews (cf. Table 2) which lasted between 45-70 minutes each, conducted between January and February 2012. Nearly all the interviewees occupy strategic, leading positions in this organization, except for one which has an operational oversight role. The background of the interviewees was sufficiently diversified, with a mix of profiles having extensive in-company and previous experience in the industrial, consulting or financial services industry.

## 3.2    Method for Data Collection

The interview guide was pilot tested a few weeks before the interviews, in order to assess its clarity, sequence of questions, interpretations by interviewees and overall design. The identification of FiSCo as a case study site was done through purposive sampling and the identification of the interviewees was done through reference sampling. Therefore the case selection technique was based on the likely importance of FiSCo and the influence of the interviewees within that organization [40]. This facilitated in-depth discussions on business-IT alignment and the meaningful selection of interviewees allows our interview data to be reliable reflection of its context. There were always two interviewers and every interview was tape recorded, except one where very sensitive information was shared, requiring enhanced confidentiality.

## 3.3    Methodology for Data Analysis

Careful judgments are needed about determining which interview data is meaningful and significant [41]. It's essential to have uniform criteria that describes a category in order to justify the inclusion of interview data within that category [42]. The Val IT™ framework developed by the IT Governance Institute [43, 44] was used as a starting point to meet this requirement. There are three groups of processes in the Val IT™ framework: Value Governance (VG), Portfolio Management (PM) and Investment Management (IM). The VG group of processes deals with the control and strategic direction. The alignment with the organization's strategy is discussed in the PM process group. Finally the IM process group focuses on the formulation of a business case.

Business-IT alignment is part of this framework since it tries to optimise the new service developments by proposing various processes and a governance structure. It supports the executive management in focusing on the strategic contributions and fosters an adequate service system through a set of principles, processes and management practices [43]. It was used before as a basis for research in another financial services context [45] and it's part of the COBIT® framework [46] which is practiced by experts in the financial services industry.

Inspired by Val IT™, an analysis framework was developed for the interview data. It was organized in two major groups: a governance layer (decision-making and monitoring of business-IT alignment) and a management layer (implementation of business-IT alignment). The governance layer was subdivided into the following elements: (G1) leadership, containing hierarchical and cultural characteristics of the company, (G2) strategy and value formulation, (G3) formulation of the IT-investment portfolio and alignment possibilities, and (G4) monitoring the strategy and value contribution. The implementation layer was subdivided into the following elements: (I1) available means for implementation like budget and time, (I2) available IT and business resources, including their skills and competences, (I3) monitoring the implementation. The interview questions were linked to these various elements and in turn provided a common point of reference.

# 4 The Case Study

## 4.1 General Description

FiSCo is engaged in the financial industry in Luxembourg, a business field known for major influences from both national and international organizations (e.g. competing companies, legislation). A few years ago, a company in the international financial industry became shareholder (representing now half of the shares). FiSCo consists of three business units: unit A serves merchants and companies, unit B serves the retail customers and finally unit C is dedicated to its historical business partners and founders. Although the new shareholder structure was introduced a few years ago, FiSCo is still in transition and migration projects are ongoing resulting in causing changes to all the established tools and processes. According to the interviewees, the transition involves several issues, such as an operational alignment with the service offer of the international shareholder.

## 4.2 Findings

The business model of FiSCo has to evolve from a "cost-sharing center" towards a "profit-driven center" due to the new shareholder structure. This implies an increased attention to international expansion. FiSCo perceives itself to be less independent than before due to the shareholder changes and was still adapting at the time of interviews. The executive management has a very central role and disposes of a lot of decision power. Customer orientation is believed to be very important and omnipresent, perhaps even too present according to some interviewees. The operations are nearly all IT enabled and their nature requires compliance with many regulations and standards. The formulation of the strategy is based on a longer term goal (5 years) but its realization is perceived as difficult with the current set-up of the company. In order to execute the revised strategy and a new IT platform, new competences are also recruited since certain competences for its realization, operation and maintenance are unavailable.

A new governance structure was implemented and the company is in full adaptation to those changes at the time of the interviews. Therefore the actual use of the new structures and rules was still being subject to a process of testing and exploration, causing tensions or unexpected results. Several interviewees recognize that the current situation is not optimal. The technical complexity was underestimated by many actors and led to delays (specifically related to the need to dispose of a new platform). Consensus building took a lot of time and unfortunately nobody is fully satisfied nor fully prepared for the (unexpected) impacts. Steering committees for projects and regular meetings exist in which the executive management participates. A new project management office was introduced for follow-up and FiSCo was experimenting with the newly designed governance and alignment processes. The business devised its own business management board to discuss the business-IT projects. It's unclear if this was part of the new governance structure.

The implementation of the chosen strategy encountered difficulties. There are several parallel functions, making its implementation more complex due to the influence of the new shareholder. In general the atmosphere of significant, compelling changes is cited by all the interviewees, often coupled with communication and internal organizational challenges. Mixed project teams exist, yet it's perceived as difficult to adequately collect business requirements. Teamwork is deemed important but several examples were given regarding good intradepartmental, yet moderate interdepartmental teamwork. Business people were used to have a direct contact with IT, something which was reduced. Common language issues were also reported.

**Table 3.** Interview analysis

| Governance Layer | |
|---|---|
| **G1**<br>Leadership, containing hierarchical and cultural characteristics of the company. | - Reduced independence<br>- Orientation towards international growth<br>- Strong influence of past management practices and habits such as a very strong customer orientation<br>- Their business is actually an IT service |
| **G2**<br>Strategy and value formulation. | - Formulation of the (company) goal may be perceived differently<br>- Top-down formulation of strategy<br>- Company transformation is the main driver |
| **G3**<br>Formulation of the IT-investment portfolio and alignment possibilities. | - Recent introduction of a governance framework, new rules, structures and other significant changes<br>- Consensus building takes time and is not always successful<br>- Important legacies |
| **G4**<br>The monitoring of the strategy and value contribution. | - New project management structure<br>- Less clear communication of the new governance framework |

Table 3. (*Continued*)

| Implementation Layer | |
|---|---|
| **I1**<br>Available means for implementation like budget and time | - Many things change at the same time causing time issues<br>- Dedicated change program |
| **I2**<br>Available IT and business resources, including their skills and competences | - Mixed project teams<br>- Cross-unit collaboration is difficult yet teamwork is deemed as important<br>- Difficulties with the formulation of business requirements |
| **I3**<br>Monitoring the implementation through its progress and performance | - Processes in the governance framework are not yet fully known or understood<br>- IT function pushes certain projects |

# 5    Discussion and Implications

The reorientation of the FiSCo's strategy affects the organization in different ways organization (cf. RQ1). The new shareholder was actually sought by FiSCo because it offered unparalleled know-how and expertise to support FiSCo's growth. The different practices and required competences caused change management challenges, resulting in several new (executive) hirings, process modifications and Board Member changes. These elements were reported to be a tactic for managing the uncertainty of external induced changes within the resource dependency theory [47]. The following elements emerged as additional areas that influence business-IT alignment practices, which should also be addressed to reduce uncertainty: (1) the IT legacy, (2) the existence of more opaque business goals or their unclear definition and (3) difficulties regarding teamwork.

The influences on FiSCo's business-IT alignment practices are multiple (cf. RQ2). They could be enhanced due to the external control of the new shareholder, but FiSCo shows that this is not readily achieved by deciding on a new strategy, new processes and the required adaptations to infrastructure. The new processes and structures for FiSCo's operations and governance are the clearest example of compelling modifications to their practices. The instauration of these aimed at realizing the new strategy and streamline existing habits and processes. The reported difficulties to find consensus and the resulting (non-optimal) solutions are illustrations of the underlying power struggle due to FiSCo's past customer integration, and the need for more operational excellence to compete at an international level. Power within the resource dependency framework is situational [9], clearly observable at FiSCo since they are dependent on the know-how of the new shareholder for growth, causing the power to shift along with the adapted strategy. The changes in business-IT practices can even influence the final customer, something which was perceived as being unacceptable.

This research also has implications for the co-creation of new financial services. First of all the new shareholder detains vital resources, while at the same time offering the possibility to streamline its operations to be abreast of international competitors. This resulted in the creation of a dedicated change management program and new organizational structures, also influencing the established business-IT alignment practices. This was illustrated by an interviewee who stressed the importance of having a new service development process with a clear governance framework.

Secondly, FiSCo's belief that processes induce the needed changes is partly true. The new structures and processes also require effective communication to reduce human resistance and foster teamwork. The latter is needed at the executive level but must also be promoted at the operational level. The co-creation of services can be enhanced by the external know-how but those benefits are conditional upon an adequate take-up by FiSCo.

Thirdly, a sustainable innovation is multidisciplinary and attention to customer preferences shouldn't be neglected too much [48]. FiSCo should be aware that their investments shouldn't be exclusively focused on service exploitation but also pay attention to service exploration, since customer know-how is needed in the co-creation of services [49]. This means that the strategic change towards more operational excellence could actually sap the customer's willingness in sharing his know-how and tacit knowledge during the co-creation of new services [50].

## 6    Conclusion

With regard to future research, these results could be transferred to different contexts of similar smaller, central financial services providers. Future research could also enlarge the sample of interviewed persons in order to obtain richer insights, in different contexts. However saturation was deemed to be reached during the interviews, indicating that closure was appropriate [51]. Another caveat relates to our research design, a single in-depth case study might not always be transferrable to other service companies. However the research results are trustworthy [42] since they provide credible results on the impacts of a strategic reorientation on the business-IT alignment practices within a Luxembourg financial services provider.

**Acknowledgements.** This research was financed by the ASINE (Architecture-based Service Innovation in Networked Enterprises) project, part of the PEARL research program of the Luxembourg National Research Foundation (FNR). The contributions and availability of the interviewees at the involved company are gratefully acknowledged.

## References

1. Chiasson, M.W., Davidson, E.: Taking Industry Seriously in Information Systems Research. MIS Quarterly 29, 591–605 (2005)
2. Baets, W.R.J.: Some empirical evidence on IS Strategy Alignment in banking. Information & Management 30, 155–177 (1996)

3.  Avison, D., Jones, J., Powell, P., Wilson, D.: Using and validating the strategic alignment model. The Journal of Strategic Information Systems 13, 223–246 (2004)
4.  Broadbent, M., Weill, P.: Improving business and information strategy alignment: Learning from the banking industry. IBM Systems Journal 32, 162–179 (1993)
5.  Tallon, P.P.: A Service Science Perspective on Strategic Choice, IT, and Performance in U.S. Banking. Journal of Management Information Systems 26, 219–252 (2010)
6.  Treacy, M., Wiersema, F.: Customer Intimacy and Other Value Disciplines. Harvard Business Review 71, 84–93 (1993)
7.  Curry, A., Penman, S.: The relative importance of technology in enhancing customer relationships in banking: A Scottish perspective. Managing Service Quality 14, 331–341 (2004)
8.  Tallon, P.P.: A Process-Oriented Perspective on the Alignment of Information Technology and Business Strategy. Journal of Management Information Systems 24, 227–268 (2008)
9.  Pfeffer, J., Salancik, G.R.: The External Control of Organizations: A Resource Dependence Perspective. Stanford University Press, Stanford (2003)
10. Luftman, J.N.: Key Issues for IT Executives 2004. MISQ Executive 4, 269–285 (2005)
11. Reich, B.H., Benbasat, I.: Factors that influence the social dimension of alignment between business and information technology objectives. MIS Quarterly 24, 81–113 (2000)
12. Venkatraman, N.: Five Steps to a Dot-Com Strategy: How To Find Your Footing on the Web. Sloan Management Review 41, 15–28 (2000)
13. Luftman, J.N., Lewis, P.R., Oldach, S.H.: Transforming the enterprise: The alignment of business and information technology strategies. IBM Systems Journal 32, 198–221 (1993)
14. Henderson, J.C., Venkatraman, H.: Strategic alignment: Leveraging information technology for transforming organizations. IBM Systems Journal 38, 472–484 (1999)
15. Venkatraman, N.: The Concept of Fit in Strategy Research: Toward Verbal and Statistical Correspondence. The Academy of Management Review 14, 423–444 (1989)
16. Venkatraman, N., Camillus, J.C.: Exploring the Concept of "Fit" in Strategic Management. The Academy of Management Review 9, 513–525 (1984)
17. Henderson, J.C.V.N.: Understanding strategic alignment. Business Quarterly 56, 72 (1991)
18. Golnam, A., Regev, G., Ramboz, J., Laprade, P., Wegmann, A.: Systemic Service Design: Aligning Value and Implementation. In: Morin, J.-H., Ralyté, J., Snene, M. (eds.) IESS 2010. LNBIP, vol. 53, pp. 150–164. Springer, Heidelberg (2010)
19. Kreuzer, E., Aschbacher, H.: Strategy-Based Service Business Development for Small and Medium Sized Enterprises. In: Snene, M., Ralyté, J., Morin, J.-H. (eds.) IESS 2011. LNBIP, vol. 82, pp. 173–188. Springer, Heidelberg (2011)
20. Kryvinska, N., Auer, L., Strauss, C.: An Approach to Extract the Business Value from SOA Services. In: Snene, M., Ralyté, J., Morin, J.-H. (eds.) IESS 2011. LNBIP, vol. 82, pp. 42–52. Springer, Heidelberg (2011)
21. Robb, A., Parent, M.: Understanding IT Governance: A case from two financial mutuals. Journal of Global Information Technology 17, 59–77 (2009)
22. Van Grembergen, W., De Haes, S., Guldentops, E.: Structures, processes and relational mechanisms for IT governance. In: Van Grembergen, W. (ed.) Strategies for Information Technology Governance, pp. 1–36. Idea Group Publishing, Hershey (2003)
23. Rathnam, R.G., Johnsen, J., Wen, H.J.: Alignment of business strategy and IT strategy: A Case Study of a fortune 50 financial services company. Journal of Computer Information Systems 45, 1–8 (2005)

24. Iman, N., Hartono, J.: Strategic alignment impacts on organizational performance in Indonesian banking industry. Gadjah Mada International Journal of Business 9, 253–272 (2007)
25. De Haes, S., Van Grembergen, W.: An Exploratory Study into IT Governance Implementations and its Impact on Business/IT Alignment. Information Systems Management 26, 123–137 (2009)
26. Silvius, A.J.G.: Business & IT Alignment in Theory and Practice. In: Proceedings of the 40th Annual Hawaii International Conference on System Sciences (HICSS-40), p. 211b (2007)
27. Beimborn, D., Franke, J., Wagner, H.-T., Weitzel, T.: The Influence of Alignment on the Post-Implementation Success of a Core Banking Information System: An Embedded Case Study. In: Proceedings of the 40th Annual Hawaii International Conference on System Sciences (HICSS-40), p. 234b (2007)
28. Schwabe, G., Banninger, P.: IT-Benefits-Management in the Swiss Financial Sector. In: Proceedings of the 41th Annual Hawaii International Conference on System Sciences (HICSS-41), p. 456 (2008)
29. Auer, L., Belov, E., Kryvinska, N., Strauss, C.: Exploratory Case Study Research on SOA Investment Decision Processes in Austria. In: Mouratidis, H., Rolland, C. (eds.) CAiSE 2011. LNCS, vol. 6741, pp. 329–336. Springer, Heidelberg (2011)
30. Jun, Q., Kecheng, L., Jingti, H.: Service valuation in business and IT alignment: with a case study in banking in China. In: 5th IEEE International Conference on Management of Innovation and Technology (ICMIT 2010), pp. 390–395 (2010)
31. Wong, T.C., Ngan, S.-C., Chan, F.T.S., Chong, A.Y.-L.: A two-stage analysis of the influences of employee alignment on effecting business–IT alignment. Decision Support Systems 53, 490–498 (2012)
32. Silvius, A.J.G., De Haes, S., Van Grembergen, W.: Exploration of Cultural Influences on Business and IT Alignment. In: Proceedings of the 42nd Hawaii International Conference on System Sciences (HICSS-42), pp. 1–10 (2009)
33. Kilov, H., Sack, I.: Mechanisms for communication between business and IT experts. Computer Standards & Interfaces 31, 98–109 (2009)
34. Chen, J., Roberts, R.: Toward a More Coherent Understanding of the Organization–Society Relationship: A Theoretical Consideration for Social and Environmental Accounting Research. Journal of Business Ethics 97, 651–665 (2010)
35. Connolly, P.: Dancing to the wrong tune: Ethnography generalization and research on racism in schools. In: Connolly, P., Troyna, B. (eds.) Researching Racism in Education: Politics, Theory, and Practice, pp. 122–139. Open University Press, Buckingham (1998)
36. Yin, R.: Case Study Research, Design and Methods. Sage Publishing, Beverly Hills (2003)
37. Walsham, G.: Interpretative case studies in IS research: nature and method. European Journal of Information Systems 4, 74–81 (1995)
38. Crowston, K., Myers, M.D.: Information technology and the transformation of industries: three research perspectives. The Journal of Strategic Information Systems 13, 5–28 (2004)
39. Siggelkow, N.: Persuasion with case studies. Academy of Management Journal 50, 20–24 (2007)
40. Gerring, J.: Case Study Research: Principles and Practices. Cambridge University Press, New York (2007)
41. Patton, M.Q.: Qualitative Evaluation and Research Methods. Sage Publications, Thousand Oaks (2001)
42. Lincoln, Y.S., Guba, E.G.: Naturalistic Inquiry. Sage Publications, Newbury Park (1985)

43. ITGI: Enterprise Value: Governance of IT Investments, The Val IT Framework 2.0. IT Governance Institute, Rolling Meadows (2008)
44. ITGI: Enterprise Value: Governance of IT Investments, Getting Started with Value Management. IT Governance Institute, Rolling Meadows (2008)
45. De Smet, D., Mention, A.-L.: Inducing Service Innovations through the Governance of IT-enabled Projects. Journal of Management Research 4, 1–16 (2012)
46. ITGI: COBIT® 4.1: Framework, Control Objectives, Management Guidelines, Maturity Models. IT Governance Institute, Rolling Meadows (2007)
47. Peng, M.W.: Outside Directors and Firm Performance during Institutional Transitions. Strategic Management Journal 25, 453–471 (2004)
48. Spohrer, J., Maglio, P.P.: The Emergence of Service Science: Toward Systematic Service Innovations to Accelerate Co-Creation of Value. Production & Operations Management 17, 238–246 (2008)
49. Ordanini, A., Pasini, P.: Service co-production and value co-creation: The case for a service-oriented architecture (SOA). European Management Journal 26, 289–297 (2008)
50. Chesbrough, H.: Bringing open innovation to services. MIT Sloan Management Review 52, 85–90 (2011)
51. Eisenhardt, K.M.: Building Theories from Case Study Research. The Academy of Management Review 14, 532–550 (1989)

# A Service Oriented Simulation Architecture for Intelligent Building Management

Monica Drăgoicea[1], Laurenţiu Bucur[2], and Monica Pătraşcu[1]

[1] University Politehnica of Bucharest
Dept. of Automatic Control and Systems Engineering
313 Splaiul Independenţei, 006042-Bucharest, Romania
{monica.dragoicea,monica.patrascu}@acse.pub.ro
http://acse.pub.ro
[2] University Politehnica of Bucharest
Dept. of Computer Science and Engineering
313 Splaiul Independenţei, 006042-Bucharest, Romania
laur.bucur@gmail.com

**Abstract.** This paper introduces a proposal on developing a service oriented modelling and simulation architecture related to intelligent building management based on an existing open platform that is intended to allow different people to participate and contribute at developing a intelligent building management service ecosystem. In this way, both users and developers can compose new services, while the developer can focus on the most effective use of devices and data, instead of getting lost in upgrading to the latest device driver. The novelty of the proposed framework is the integration in the simulation loop of a Smart Building Controller that can control the real and virtual devices at the facility level. Therefore, the simulation model of the smart building integrates both real as well as simulated devices. The web-based service oriented software application allows to *simulate* the *device-level* and *facility level* behaviour of an intelligent building. It demonstrates a strategy to define an Intelligent Building Management solution that includes scenario simulation, testing of the functionality of the Smart Building Controller (SBC), device monitoring and control, report generation, and implementation of device web services.

**Keywords:** intelligent building management, modelling and simulation, web services, service composition, service ecosystem.

## 1 Introduction

Today, novel modelling and simulation techniques reveal a completely new perspective on evaluating Intelligent Building Management solutions. State-of-the-art perspective on available Smart Building Simulation reveals the following most specific development directions.

Relating to Smart Building Simulation, in [1] the **Performance Framework Tool** suite for simulating a smart building's energy performance is described, as a

J.F. e Cunha, M. Snene, and H. Nóvoa (Eds.): IESS 2013, LNBIP 143, pp. 14–28, 2013.

set of applications that interoperate and exchange **Building Information Model** data. It is shown that the existing state of the art focuses on the **B**uilding Information Model 's Industry **F**oundation **C**lasses (**IFC**) standard (see [2] and [3]), and that in the building lifecycle a great amount of information is lost at various design phases because the **BIM** model is not used consistently. In [1] the proposed PFT tool suite addresses these shortcomings by using the BIM IFC model for simulation and virtual reality visualization with multi–user "avatar" capabilities in the Pudecas Smart Building Simulation and Visualisation software.

In [4] the Interactive Smart Home System (ISS) is described, as an interactive smart home simulator. In this research, the smart house is considered as being an environment made up of independent and distributed devices interacting to support user's goals and tasks. Therefore, by using ISS, the developer can realize the relationships between virtual home space, surrounded environment, users and home appliances.

Smart Energy Solutions' Smart Energy simulator [5] is a cloud-based simulator for smart buildings. Its main features refers to energy analysis and thermal load simulation (Smart Energy web-application). The Smart Energy application includes a powerful thermal simulation engine that facilitates the web based simulation, it requires no installation, it includes the building model in simulation, schedule simulation, air flow simulation, occupant-based analysis, predefined inputs based on real-world data (temperature), and user friendly visual reports.

Other approaches are oriented towards the adaptation of computer games and related technologies to create virtual and mixed reality intelligent environments (an extended discussion can be found in [6]).

Along with ensuring comfortable and green living environments, special attention should be given to sustaining structural integrity. The main danger to buildings' lifespan is caused by earthquakes and other natural disasters that can interact negatively with the purpose of Smart and/or Intelligent Buildings. Researche of the past decades reveals new damping technologies (see for example [7],[8]) and control strategies (see for example [9],[10],[11],[12]) that consistently ensure structural safety prior, during and post seismic activity.

This present research proposes a service-oriented approach of creating and using simulation models based on real and virtual devices integrated in a building model in order to a) test the functionality of intelligent building control components (like smart building controllers) and b) to estimate and evaluate power consumption at the facility level. The real and virtual device models are hosted and exposed by a Simulation Engine web service and optionally by a Simulation Bridge web service. The fundamental advantage of this approach over related references (see [13], for example) is a unitary description of the devices based on web services and their integration in a Service Oriented Architecture for Intelligent Building Management (section 2). These device web services can be composed with a Smart Building Controller in order to test policies and schedules (section 4), without the need of a dedicated building infrastructure. In addition, the proposed approach integrates both human and structural safety (seismic events and response to natural disasters are considered), making the architecture extensible and flexible. Thus, considering its pertinence to a large range of buildings (regardless of infrastructure), its ability to incorporate a variety of devices (from elevator controllers and ventilation systems to seismic dampers and fire protection), the approach that is discussed in this paper is extensive and has a wide applicability expanse.

Therefore, in this proposed framework a *service ecosystem* dedicated to the Intelligent Building Management solution development could be eventually created, both for *control* and *monitoring*, as well as for *utilities cost estimation*. Such a service ecosystem would comprise a group of users within the industry *sharing* their *services* for use across the group for *testing* or *training*.

This paper is organized as follows. Section 2 presents a novel service oriented perspective on developing Intelligent Building Management solutions. Section 3 introduces the main contribution of this work, the proposed service oriented framework for smart building modelling and simulation that can integrate virtual device models (through web services) and real devices. Section 4 presents working results of the proposed strategy that uses simulation models integrating virtual device models and real devices for testing the SBC behaviour. Section 5 presents conclusions and further directions of development.

## 2   A Perspective on Service Orientation for Intelligent Building Management

This section shortly describes the service-oriented approach to control and manage building facilities via intelligent controllers and a web-based portal [14] that consists on an infrastructure for people to share their building control services using a service-oriented platform (Fig. 1), so that:

1. users could define, search and compose building services according to their facility needs through a portal, **Environment Manager**;
2. users can define working policies and schedules using a **Policy Editor** as explained in section 3;
3. users can execute simulation before deployment accessing through a portal a **Simulation Engine** by help of a **Simulation Console**.

The operation of the whole service-oriented framework is based on specific service composition mechanisms, as follows:

1. Composition between the web-based building control application (**Environment Manager**) and a **Smart Building Controller** (WCF web service). The Environment Manager consumes the Smart Building Controller (SBC) service to enumerate devices, classes of devices, schedules and operation timetables. At the same time, it allows to visualize the state of the devices in the SBC, their direct control, as well as to edit the SBC's schedules and operation timetables;
2. Composition between a **Smart Building Controller** (WCF web service) and the **Simulation Engine** (RESTful web service). This mechanism allows to include real devices from the SBC in a simulation, and to test the

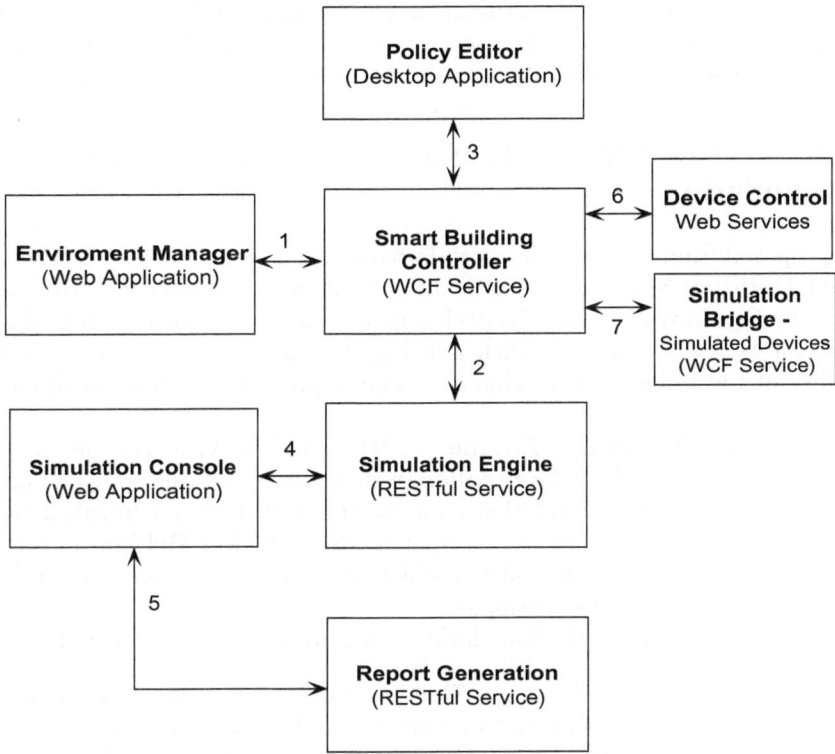

**Fig. 1.** The Service-Oriented Approach for Intelligent Building Management

Smart Building Controller in different operation scenarios. In this respect, the controls and events are sent directly from the simulation scenario to the SBC, to be processed. In this way, the functioning of the devices and the policies defined in the SBC which are triggered by the events can be tested;

3. Composition of a **Policy Editor** (desktop application) with a **Smart Building Controller** (WCF web service). This will allow to manage and edit the functioning policies of the Smart Building Controller;

4. Composition of the **Simulation Console** (web application) with the **Simulation Engine** (RESTful web service). This allows to expose the functionality of the Simulation Engine as a web application to develop simulations;

5. Composition of the **Simulation Console** (web application) with the **Report Generation Service** (RESTful web service). This allows to generate standard (PDF) simulation reports and to estimate power consumption and operation costs of the devices present in a building;

6. Automated composition of a **Smart Building Controller** (WCF web service) with the device control web services. This allows to control real devices by using the corresponding web services and to automatically compose these services with the Smart Building Controller web service;

7. Composition of a **Smart Building Controller** (WCF web service) with the virtual device control web services, through the simulated device control web service, i.e. the **Simulation Bridge** (WCF web service) [15].

## 3   A Service-Oriented Framework for Smart Building Simulation

The proposed Simulation Framework is based on a *service-oriented, web-based* **Smart Building Simulator (SBS)**. In fact, the SBS is obtained by the *composition* of a **Simulation Console** (web application) with a **Simulation Engine** (RESTful web service), see branch 4 in Fig. 1. This allows to expose the functionality of the Simulation Engine as a web application to develop simulation scenarios.

Further, the **Simulation Engine** (RESTful web service) can be *composed* with the **Smart Building Controller** (web service) and this composition will allow to include in the simulation scenario the real devices controlled by the SBC, and virtual device models through the **Simulation Bridge**, in order to test the Smart Building Controller in different scenarios (see branch 2 in Fig. 1 and section 4 for a detailed example).

The two main goals of the Simulation Framework are the following:

1. *testing* the response of a Smart Building Controller (SBC) in various simulation scenarios (see section 4 for example and simulation results);
2. *estimating* the utility bill for a real building or a virtual building (whose model integrates virtual device models) based on the definition, composition and simulation of a simulation model.

The Simulation Framework Architecture that integrates the Smart Building Simulator (SBS) is outlined in Fig. 2.

The **Simulation Console** communicates with the **Simulation Engine** to create, manage and execute *smart building simulations*. The **Simulation Engine** manages one or more *simulation scenarios* in a simulation [16].

On the perspective of the Simulation Framework proposed in this paper, we use the following definition of a **simulation scenario**:

**Definition 1.** A *simulation scenario* is a perspective created in the Simulation Console by the composition of the following elements:

1. a set of time ordered *events* that are processed by the Simulation Engine and visualised in the Simulation Console in the timeline of the simulation scenario. They can be exchanged between the Simulation Engine and the Smart Building Controller, in both directions, such as: a) *External events* can be sent from the simulation scenario (by the Simulation Engine) to be processed by the Smart Building Controller, and b) The events from the SBC can be imported into the simulation, instantiated and visualized through the EventTypes window in Simulation Console;

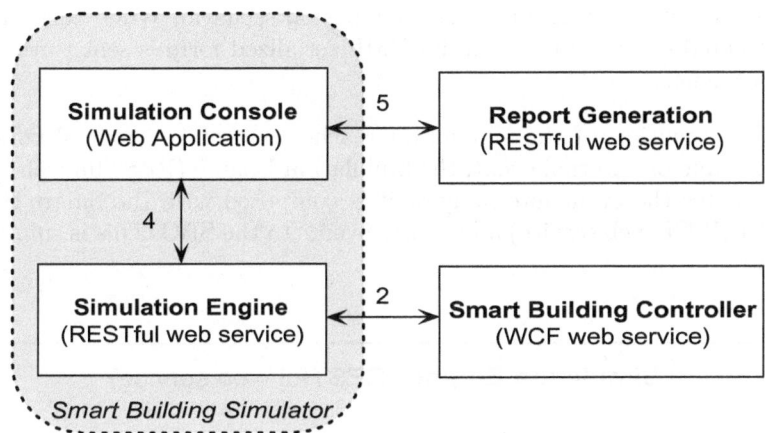

**Fig. 2.** The Smart Building Simulator in the Service-Oriented Simulation Framework

2. a set of *virtual devices*, that means virtual objects hosted, created and managed in the Simulation Engine, as instances of virtual device classes defined by the user for a given simulation. Virtual devices hosted by the Simulation Engine are used for energy estimation only;
3. a set of *real devices*. The real devices are the devices installed at the facility level. They can be recognized and **controlled** by the Smart Building Controller through the corresponding web services. Real device models imported from the SBC in the simulation console are used by the Simulation Engine to send commands to real devices during simulation.

The Simulation Framework allows the user to define one or more simulation scenarios that can include three different types of *events*:

1. *Control Command* events. The *CommandEvent* is related to the Start/Stop operations for virtual and real devices. These commands are used to start and stop devices and are mainly used during energy consumption simulation;
2. *Change Of Value* (CoV) events. The *ChangeOfValue* event can be used to change the value of a device property in the simulation. The user may choose to place a *ChangeOfValue* event on the simulation scenarios timeline that changes the power consumption or any parameter of a device to a specific value. These events are related to virtual and real devices in a simulation. In case of virtual devices the events are executed internally by the Simulation Engine while for real devices the events are routed and executed to the SBC, thus **controlling** real devices during simulation;
3. *External events*. They are asynchronous user-defined event types that are defined in and recognized by the Smart Building Controller as XML serializable object types. Through the Simulation Console, the Simulation Engine imports the definitions of all the external event types defined in and recognized by the Smart Building Controller. External events can be instantiated

on the simulation timeline of the simulation scenario. When such an event is executed during simulation, its XML serialized form is sent to the SBC's event queue.

When the execution of the simulation reaches one of the control command, change of value or external event, the Simulation Engine (RESTful web service) either executes the event internally or it is composed with the Smart Building Controller (WCF web service) and routes events to the SBC. This is summarized in Fig. 3.

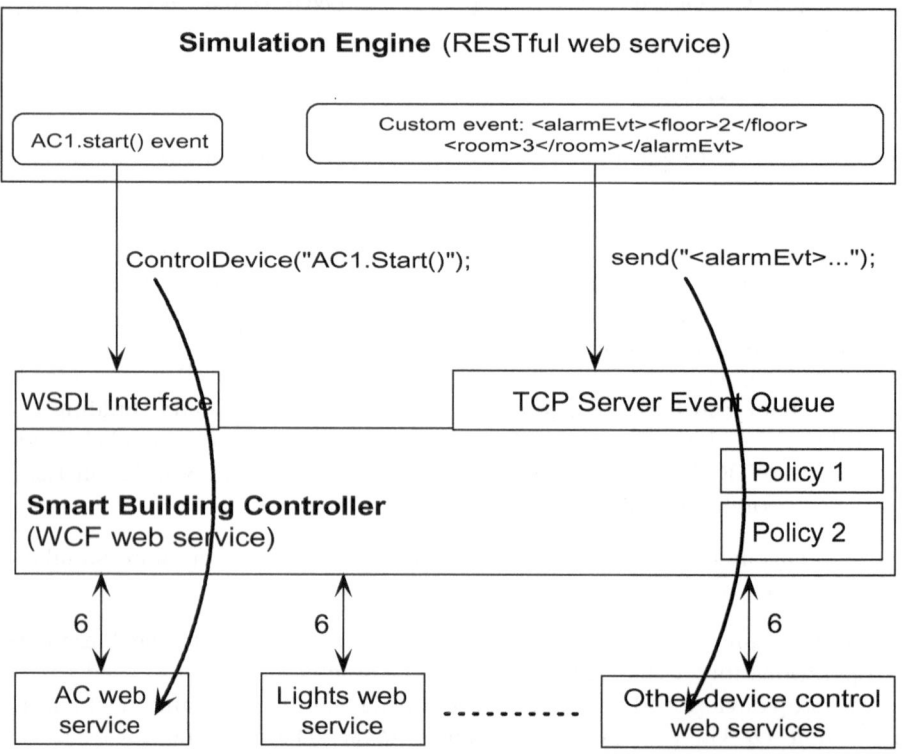

**Fig. 3.** Composition of the Simulation Engine and the Smart Building Controller

## 4   Testing the Response of a Smart Building Controller

The Smart Building Controller is the client-side service orchestration component of the Service-Oriented Architecture [14]. Its role is to manage the operation of physical building devices that are controlled by web services. The SBC, as an orchestrator, manages the execution of device control web services by different sets of user-defined operating *schedules* and *policies* [17].

Specific *policies* apply for the real-time behaviour of the Smart Building Controller, using a specific set of rules combining *event triggers, conditions* and *actions* to be executed if certain conditions are fulfilled or exceptions occur.

**Definition 2.** A Smart Building Controller *policy* is a set of rules of the form:

**ON** (Trigger) **IF** (Condition) **THEN** (Execute block of actions)
**ELSE** (Execute block of actions)

where:

- *Trigger* specifies the name of the rule trigger. It can be set to `true` or it can take the name of an event type registered in the Smart Building Controller, such as `EarthquakeEvent` (see section 4.1);
- *Condition* is an expression recognized by the Smart Building Controller at runtime and evaluated as a `boolean` value.

*Note:* A condition can be composed from a set of web service call expressions, device property reads, using a special Smart Building Controller calling convention.

The behaviour of the Smart Building Controller can be tested in various scenarios. A Smart Building Controller test scenario may include real, as well as virtual devices through the Simulation Bridge. Testing the Smart Building Controller operation implies two aspects:

1. Sending *ChangeOfValue* events for various *real devices* to the Smart Building Controller, as one or more web service calls and observing the response of the Smart Building Controller in the real environment (the event is executed and the device is controlled by altering its operating parameters);
2. Sending asynchronous events (external events in simulation) to the SBC's event queue and observing the results of the Smart Building Controller executing the event-triggered policy in the real environment.

In this case, the composition between the Simulation Engine and Smart Building Controller, through the Simulation Console, is performed as follows:

1. The communication from the Simulation Engine to the Smart Building Controller consists of:
   (a) Establishing the connection to the SBC and create a blank simulation scenario in the Simulation Console;
   (b) Sending external events defined in the simulation scenario (in the Simulation Console) to the SBC;
   (c) Listing available devices defined in the SBC in the Simulation Console;
   (d) Sending *ChangeOfValue* commands to the devices installed in the SBC.
2. The communication from the Smart Building Controller to the Simulation Engine consists of:

(a) Importing the events defined in the SBC in the Simulation Console. The SBC is ready to receive events through the external events mechanism of the Simulation Engine;

(b) Visualizing the event types in the EventTypes window in the Simulation Console.

In order to test the behaviour of the Smart Building Controller, the following steps should be fulfilled in order to define and execute the corresponding simulation scenario:

1. Define the events in the simulation scenario to be sent to the Smart Building Controller. They are defined as external events and correspond to the events list defined in the SBC (section 4.1);
2. Define the simulation scenario in the Simulation Console. It may include real devices in the building infrastructure recognized and controlled by the SBC and models of the virtual devices through the Simulation Bridge (section 4.2);
3. Define the policies and schedules for the Smart Building Controller operation, through the Policy Editor (section 4.3);
4. Execute simulation scenario in the Simulation Console and inspect the SBC's execution logs (section 4.4).

The following subsections present results that concern testing the SBC operation in a earthquake scenario using models of dedicated virtual devices through the web service definition mechanism in the Simulation Bridge. Previous work on this direction is related to the definition of the way in which emergency response protocols can be combined at a microscopic level with a Smart Building Controller such as a high level of performance in what concerns comfort could be assured [18].

## 4.1   Testing: Define a Set of Events

We define an EarthquakeEvent as a SBC serializable class containing the following fields:

1. Magnitude_min: a double representing the minimum estimated magnitude of the earthquake;
2. Time_to_earthquake: is a number (double) expressing the estimated number of seconds until the earthquake actually occurs (see for reference [19]);
3. Geographical_area: specifies the area in which the earthquake will occur. For example, *Vrancea*.

The event type is registered in the Smart Building Controller. This means compiling the class in a shared .NET assembly and placing it in the SBC EventTypes folder. At startup, the Smart Building Controller will register this event by enumerating all public serializable classes from the EventTypes folder shared assemblies.

## 4.2   Testing: Define a Simulation Scenario

The simulation scenario for the earthquake event management is presented in
Fig. 4. A blank simulation is created in the Simulation Console by connecting to
the SBC. A simulation scenario is defined spanning one day. The list of events
recognized by the SBC is automatically imported in the simulation model.

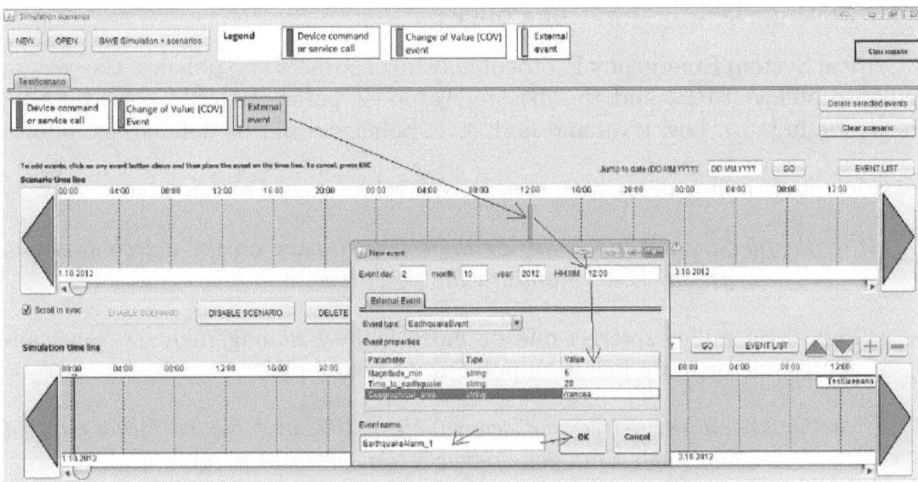

**Fig. 4.** Simulation scenario - Smart Building Controller earthquake testing scenario

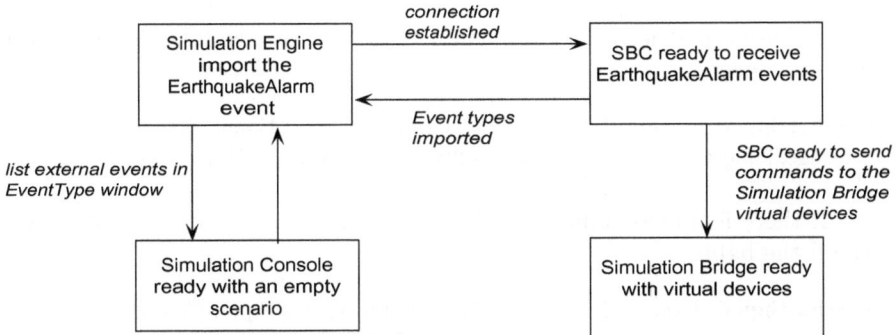

**Fig. 5.** List of connections - Smart Building Controller earthquake testing scenario

The Simulation Bridge [20] is started and a virtual building device configuration is created with the following components (see also the connection configuration in Fig. 5):

1. GasSwitch: a virtual device that controls the gas distribution in the building
   exposed with a single parameter: state = 0 ot 1

2. `Light1`, `Light2`, `Light3`: 3 virtual lights, exposed with a single parameter: state = 0 or 1
3. `EarthquakeAlarm`: a virtual earthquake acousting alarm exposed with a single parameter: running = 0 or 1
4. It is assumed the building is situated in `Vrancea` geographical area or Romania.

### 4.3   Testing: Define a Set of Policies

A Critical System Emergency Protocol may incorporates two policies: the seismic response policy (SRP) and the disaster response policy (DRP) (see a detailed discussion in [18]). Low level and high level policies could be defined, as follows:

– a low level policy deals with executive level actions. For example:

*If earthquake magnitude is higher than 4, then turn on the active damping system. Else, maintain the passive damping system.*

– a high level policy queries one or more facility management systems and executes one or more low level policies. For example:

*If earthquake alarm active and occupancy > 40% and security understaffed, then apply emergency evacuation protocol number 6.*

A three rule policy named `EarthquakeAlarmPolicy` is defined using the Policy Management System [21] as follows:

*Rule 1:* If there are at least 10 seconds until the earthquake hits Vrancea, start the acoustic alarm:

ON(EarthquakeEvent) IF (message.Geographical_area.Equals(Vrancea) and (message.Time_to_earthquake >=10) THEN [[EarthquakeAlarm.running=1]];

*Rule 2:* If there is an earthquake in this area, if the magnitude is greater than 4, turn off the lights:

ON(EarthquakeEvent) IF (message.Geographical_area.Equals(Vrancea) and message.Magnitude_min >=4.0) THEN [[GasSwitch.state=0]];

*Rule 3:* No matter how large the magnitude, if the earthquake hits Vrancea, turn off the three lights:

ON(EarthquakeEvent) IF (message.Geographical_area.Equals(Vrancea) THEN  [[Light1.state=0]]; [[Light2.state=0]]; [[Light3.state=0]];

## 4.4    Testing: Execute Simulation Scenario

The goal of this step was to test this policy in 3 earthquake alarm scenarios:

*Behaviour 1:* On a magnitude 5 earthquake hitting Vrancea within the next 20 seconds, this policy would activate the virtual acoustics alarm, stop all lights and turn off the gas distribution installation.

*Behaviour 2:* On a magnitude 3 earthquake alarm hitting Vrancea in the next 5 seconds, this policy would turn off the Lights.

*Behaviour 3:* On a magnitude 4 earthquake alarm hitting Vrancea in the next 8 seconds, this policy would turn off the gas installation and the lights.

Three custom events of the type `EarthquakeEvent` were created on the simulation time line, with the following fields (time expresses in seconds):

*Event 1:* At simulation time 12:00 – Magnitude_min = 5, Time_to_earthquake = 20, Geographical_area =Vrancea. Desired behaviour: **Behaviour 1**

*Event 2:* At simulation time 14:00 – Magnitude_min = 3, Time_to_earthquake = 5, Geographica_area = Vrancea. Desired behaviour: **Behaviour 2**.

*Event 3:* At simulation time 16:00 – Magnitude_min = 4, Time_to_earthquake = 8, Geographical_area = Vrancea. Desired behaviour: **Behaviour 3**.

An excerpt of the obtained results are present in the following figures and tables.

Table 1 depicts the policy execution in the SBC and the event log when the event 1 is received in the SBC.

**Table 1.** Events log in the Smart Building Controller - policy execution

| Date | Time | Device ID | Logged actions | Type |
|------|------|-----------|----------------|------|
| 14.09.2012 | 00:31:37.545 | 0 | EarthquakeEvent: Magnitude_min=5 Time_to_earthquake=20 Geographical_area=Vrancea | event |
| 14.09.2012 | 00:31:37.590 | 1211008 | EarthquakeAlarm: running=1 | Earthquake Alarm Policy |
| 14.09.2012 | 00:31:37.608 | 1211004 | GasSwitch: state=0 | Earthquake Alarm Policy |
| 14.09.2012 | 00:31:37.617 | 1211005 | Light1: state=0 | Earthquake Alarm Policy |
| 14.09.2012 | 00:31:37.626 | 1211006 | Light2: state=0 | Earthquake Alarm Policy |
| 14.09.2012 | 00:31:37.638 | 1211007 | Light3: state=0 | Earthquake Alarm Policy |

The earthquake event `Event 1` is sent by the Simulation Engine, a Single Step simulation is executed and the event is correctly received by the SBC (Fig. 6).

**Fig. 6.** The earthquake event is received in the SBC

The Event Manager window depicts the SBC log (Fig. 7).

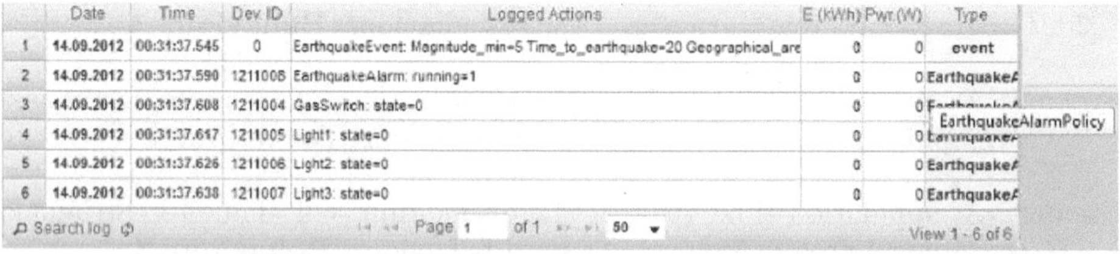

| | Date | Time | Dev ID | Logged Actions | E (kWh) | Pwr (W) | Type |
|---|---|---|---|---|---|---|---|
| 1 | 14.09.2012 | 00:31:37.545 | 0 | EarthquakeEvent: Magnitude_min=5 Time_to_earthquake=20 Geographical_are | 0 | 0 | event |
| 2 | 14.09.2012 | 00:31:37.590 | 1211006 | EarthquakeAlarm: running=1 | 0 | 0 | EarthquakeA |
| 3 | 14.09.2012 | 00:31:37.608 | 1211004 | GasSwitch: state=0 | 0 | 0 | Earthquake... |
| | | | | | | | EarthquakeAlarmPolicy |
| 4 | 14.09.2012 | 00:31:37.617 | 1211005 | Light1: state=0 | 0 | 0 | Earthquake... |
| 5 | 14.09.2012 | 00:31:37.626 | 1211006 | Light2: state=0 | 0 | 0 | EarthquakeA |
| 6 | 14.09.2012 | 00:31:37.638 | 1211007 | Light3: state=0 | 0 | 0 | EarthquakeA |

Search log — Page 1 of 1 — 50 ▾ — View 1 - 6 of 6

**Fig. 7.** The earthquake event is received in the SBC - SBC log

## 5   Conclusions and Further Development Directions

The Simulation Framework introduced in this paper serves two purposes. On one hand, it assist in testing the behaviour of a Smart Building Controller using simulation scenarios. This is achieved by creating a simulation scenario containing events to be sent to and processed by a real Smart Building Controller. On the second, it may further allow estimating the energy consumption in a building environment without real devices being installed. This option will be developed in future experiments. Optionally, the simulator can also estimate the energy consumption of real devices by creating a simulation from the set of devices installed in a Smart Building Controller.

Apart from the already mentioned advantages of this solution, this work introduces the notion of *policy*, that means a set of rules that govern device control according to user preferences. The novelty of this work consists on the extension of the service oriented mechanisms at the policy level, that means the definition of the conditions for the Smart Building Controller policies based on web service composition and testing their proper execution using a service-oriented simulation framework. Due to the service oriented nature of the Smart Building Controller, a condition can be composed from a set of web service call expressions, device property reads, using a special Smart Building Controller calling convention.

Further developments of the proposed service oriented infrastructure would approach an openly integration of functionalities, devices, simulation and operation scenarios, related to different operation and security aspects for intelligent building management. An example referring to earthquake monitoring and response is included that depicts testing the behaviour of the Smart Building Controller in simulation scenarios that include virtual devices control.

Also, this strategy can be used to provide users with practical and research experience with HITL (hardware-in-the-loop) technique for training and testing of Intelligent Building Management solutions.

**Acknowledgments.** This work was supported by INSEED - Strategic Grant POSDRU/107/ 1.5/S/76903, Project ID 76903 (2011), co-financed by the European Social Fund – Investing in People, within the Sectoral Operational Programme Human Resource Development 2007 – 2013.

# References

1. McGlinn, K., Corry, E., O'Neill, E., Keane, M., Lewis, D., O'Sullivan, D.: Monitoring Smart Building Performance Using Simulation and Visualisation. In: Proceedings of the Ubicomp 2010 Workshop - Ubiquitous Computing for Sustainable Energy, UCSE 2010, pp. 41–47 (2010)
2. International Alliance for Interoperability. Industry Foundation Classes, http://www.buildingsmart.com/ (accessed April 2009)
3. InfoComm BIM Taskforce. Building Information Modelling, http://www.infocomm.org/cps/rde/xbcr/infocomm/Brochure_BIM.pdf (accessed April 2009)
4. Van Nguyen, T., Kim, J.G., Choi, D.: ISS – The Interactive Smart Home Simulator. In: 11th International Conference on Advanced Communication Technology (ICACT), pp. 1828–1833 (2009)
5. Smart Energy, Web-based Energy Modelling Software, http://www.smartenergysoftware.com (accessed April 20, 2009)
6. Davies, M., Callaghan, V.: Towards Producing Artificial Humans for Intelligent Environments Research. In: Intelligent Environments 2011 (IE 2011), Nottingham, July 27-29 (2011)
7. Ma, H., Yam, M.C.H.: Modelling of a self-centring damper and its application in structural control. Journal of Constructional Steel Research (JCSR) 67, 656–666 (2011)
8. Bitaraf, M., Ozbulut, O.E., Hurlebaus, S., Barroso, L.: Application of semi-active control strategies for seismic protection of buildings with MR dampers. Engineering Structures (ES) 32, 3040–3047 (2010)
9. Ali, S.F., Ramaswamy, A.: Optimal fuzzy logic control for MDOF structural systems using evolutionary algorithms. Engineering Applications of Artificial Intelligence 22, 407–419 (2009)
10. Oates, W.S., Smith, R.C.: Nonlinear Optimal Control Techniques for Vibration Attenuation Using Magnetostrictive Actuators. Journal of Intelligent Material Systems and Structures (JIMSS) 19, 193–209 (2008)

11. Shook, D.A., Roschke, P.N., Lin, P.-Y., Loh, C.-H.: GA-optimized fuzzy logic control of a large-scale building for seismic loads. Engineering Structures (ES) 30, 436–449 (2008)
12. Neelakantan, V.A., Washington, G.N.: Vibration Control of Structural Systems using MR dampers and a 'Modified' Sliding Mode Control Technique. Journal of Intelligent Material Systems and Structures (JIMSS) 19, 211–223 (2008)
13. Virtual Device Technologies. Techniques for Developing Virtual Device Models, `http://virtualdevicetech.com/technologies/hdvd.php` (accessed at September 12, 2012)
14. Tsai, W.T., Petrescu, S., Bucur, L., Chera, C.: A Service-Oriented Approach for Intelligent Building Management. In: 18th International Conference on Control Systems and Computer Science, CSCS 18, Bucharest, Romania, vol. 2, pp. 676–681 (2011) ISSN 2066-4451
15. FCINT Specification for Web Services, `http://www.fcint.ro/portal/Documents/`
16. FCINT Simulator Tutorial, `http://portal.fcint.ro/Simulator/Simulator.html`
17. Bucur, L., Tsai, W.T., Petrescu, S., Chera, C., Moldoveanu, F.: A Service-Oriented Controller for Intelligent Building Management. In: 18th International Conference on Control Systems and Computer Science, CSCS 18, Bucharest, Romania, vol. 2, pp. 665–670 (2011) ISSN 2066-4451
18. Drăgoicea, M., Pătraşcu, M., Bucur, L.: Service Orientation for Intelligent Building Management: An IoS an IoT Perspective. In: UNITE 2nd Doctoral Symposium R & D in Future Internet and Enterprise Interoperability, Sofia, Bulgaria, October 11-12 (2012)
19. NIEP – National Institute for Earth Physics, Romania. Seismic rapid early warning system for dangerous facilities, `http://www.infp.ro/real-time/ews`
20. FCINT Simulation Bridge, `http://www.fcint.ro/portal/Downloads/FCINT_SimulationBridge.zip/`
21. FCINT Policy Management System, `http://www.fcint.ro/portal/Downloads/FCINT_PolicyManagementSystem_kit.zip/`

# Capabilities in Systems Engineering: An Overview

Gonçalo Antunes and José Borbinha

INESC-ID, Rua Alves Redol, 9 1000-029 Lisboa Portugal
{goncalo.antunes,jlb}@ist.utl.pt
http://web.ist.utl.pt/goncalo.antunes

**Abstract.** The concept of capability has been deemed relevant over the years, which can be attested by its adoption in varied domains. It is an abstract concept, but simple to understand by business stakeholders and yet capable of making the bridge to technical aspects. Capabilities seem to bear similarities with services, namely their low coupling and high cohesion. However, the concepts are different since the concept of service seems to rest between that of capability and those directly related to the implementation. Nonetheless, the articulation of the concept of capability with the concept of service can be used to promote business/IT alignment, since both concepts can be used to bridge different conceptual layers of an enterprise architecture. This work offers an overview of the different uses of this concept, its usefulness, and its relation to the concept of service.

**Keywords:** capability, service, alignment, information systems, systems engineering, strategic management, economics.

## 1 Introduction

The concept of capability can be defined as "the quality or state of being capable" [19] or "the power or ability to do something" [39]. Although simple, it is a powerful concept, as it can be used to provide an abstract, high-level view of a product, system, or even organizations, offering new ways of dealing with complexity. As such, it has been widely adopted in many areas.

In economics and strategic management, capabilities are a part of the resource-based view of the organization [11,2], which built upon the idea that firms could have the same resource inputs available but they could differ on the capability to use those resources in the most productive way [27]. In that sense, capabilities can be seen as a factor of competitive advantage which differentiates firms [9], functioning as a means for organizations to adapt better than others to changing environmental conditions [5,22]. The concept of capability involves routines that are executed by the organization in a repeatable and often non-conscious way [22].

In the area of system engineering, capabilities are seen as a core concept [20]. Particularly in the military field, a capability is seen as the ability to achieve

J.F. e Cunha, M. Snene, and H. Nóvoa (Eds.): IESS 2013, LNBIP 143, pp. 29–42, 2013.

a determined military objective [37], requiring a combination of people, process and material [24]. In general, this notion is considered particularly relevant for the engineering of complex systems-of-systems (SoS), which relies on the combination of different systems for achieving a particular capability [18,4].

In software engineering, the first capability maturity model (CMM) was developed with sponsorship from the US Department of Defense with the aim of assessing the capability of software contractors [12,13]. For that purpose, it considers processes as capabilities, thus defining how to assess specific qualities of software engineering processes, providing a way to understand the current state of potentially complex software systems. The CMM has ever since been evolving and integrating several other models. Nowadays, it covers acquisition, development and delivery processes [6,7,8].

The concept was also embraced by the information systems field, namely by the Enterprise Architecture (EA) domain through its use, for example, on the US Department of Defense Architecture Framework (DoDAF) [38] and the UK Ministry of Defense Architecture Framework (MODAF) [36]. It has since then been also adopted by The Open Group Architecture Framework (TOGAF), a generic enterprise architecture framework where it is an integral part of the architectural practices described in its specification [35].

In the field of organizational design and engineering, which advocates the combination of organization theory and engineering practice in order to create computer-based artifacts that sustain economically relevant knowledge, capabilities and their underlying routines also are considered concepts of major research importance [17]. They are considered to provide a means of observing the drivers that underlie change in organizations and, according to that, steer the organization in the right direction.

In all, capabilities can be seen as a way of linking stakeholder intentions to the properties of a system [28], which obviously are closely related to the concept of service, making the bridge between intentions and actual implementation. It is a concept which can be linked directly into the drivers and motivation, being stable in face of change, similarly to the concept of service, albeit at a different abstraction level. This work offers an overview of the different uses of this important concept and its usefulness, and its relation to the concept of service.

This work is organized as follows. Section 2 provides an historical account of the usage of the concept in the areas of economics and strategic management, pioneers in the usage of the concept. Section 3 provides an historical account of the usage of the concept in the areas of systems and software engineering, which pioneered on the usage of the concept in systems where the technical aspect is evident. Section 4 provides an account of the usage of the concept in the area of information systems, which evidently was influenced by its usage in systems engineering. Section 5 provides a summary of the different definitions of capability provided in the aforementioned areas. Section 6 describes the relationships existing between the concept of capability and the concept of service, arguing for the importance of the joint use of the two concepts in service design and engineering. Finally, section 7 concludes this work.

## 2    On the Concept of Capability in Economics and Strategic Management

The concept of capability has been adopted in several areas of knowledge. The concept of *organizational capability* has been used for many years in economics and strategic management essentially to explain competitive advantage. Early mentions of the term, although not reified, include the ones by Penrose [27], in 1959, which indicated that the differences between firms could be explained by differences in the capabilities to deploy resources that were available to all firms, and by Richardson [30], in 1972, which pointed that those differences were explained by the fact that firms tend to specialize in activities for which their capabilities offer competitive advantage.

In their 1973 publication, Nelson and Winter introduced the idea that competitive advantage comes both from the internal and external search processes for enhanced production capabilities and the *"natural selection"* processes that influence the growth and contraction of organizations, resulting as an indirect consequence of the search [21]. As described later by the authors, the usage of the term *capability* in this work came from the involvement of the authors in the military field at the time, and not directly from the works cited above [40]. The same authors later presented their evolutionary theory that described organizational capabilities as consisting of the ability to "perform and sustain a set of routines" [22]. Those routines are "habitual reactions" that involve coordination among the actors of the organization and the usage of skills, organization and technology to respond to the demands of the environment. Routines can even be considered the building blocks of capabilities, since for a set of activities and associated resources and skills to be considered a capability, there is a need for repeatability [9]. In order to survive, organization should engage on search operations which involve the evaluation of the current situation and changes to the organizational capabilities, if needed [22]. Chandler described organizational capabilities as the "collective physical facilities and human skills", "carefully coordinated and integrated", as a means of achieving economies of scale and scope, highlighting their importance in the evolution of capitalism [5].

The concept of organizational capability promoted by Nelson and Winter was highly influential for the development of the concept of dynamic capability, initially developed by Teece and Pisano, in 1994 [33]. The former notion of capabilities can explain why firms attain competitive advantage in a determined market, but it fails to explain why some firms can adapt to highly disruptive changes in the environment prompted by technological change, critical timings, or even change in markets and competition [34]. Dynamic capabilities involve "reconfiguring the internal and external organizational skills, resources, and functional competences to match the requirements of a changing environment" [34]. The same work also describes the existence of factors that can be used to assess the distinctive capabilities of an organization (i.e., those which cannot be easily replicated by others), and that are classified in three categories: processes (i.e., the routines or other activities), positions (i.e., current technological infrastructure, intellectual property, customers, relation with suppliers, etc.), and paths (i.e., strategic alternatives available to the organization). The relationship between these three categories is explained by the fact that the essence of capabilities lies in the processes of the organization. However, competitive advantage is driven or constrained by the positioning of the internal and external assets of the organization and by the evolutionary path that the firm has chosen to adopt. In the words of the authors, "what a firm can do and where it can go are thus rather constrained by its positions and paths". Those factors can only deliver competitive advantage if the capabilities are based on a collection of routines, skills, and assets that are difficult to imitate.

The work in [10], published in 2000, argues that dynamic capabilities are not themselves sufficient for attaining competitive advantage, since their functionality can be duplicated by organizations. However, competitive advantage lies on the resource configurations deployed by those capabilities. Additionally, dynamic capabilities are important for achieving short-term advantages through reconfiguration of the resources in order to make the most out of an opportunity. In order to be effective, dynamic capabilities often need to rely on new knowledge, which might involve experimental activities, such as prototyping, real-time information, and experimentation. The evolution of these capabilities is guided by well-known learning mechanisms. Product development routines, strategic decision making, resource allocation routines, knowledge creation routines, alliance and acquisition routines are given examples of dynamic capabilities.

In order to explain the evolution of capabilities, the work in [11], published in 2003, describes a generic capability life cycle framework that can be applied to any type of organizational setting. The framework divides the life cycle of a capability in three plus six stages. The three first stages are: the *founding* stage, which marks the "birth" of a capability; the *development* stage, which represents the building up of the capability; and the *maturity* stage, which marks the ending of the capability building. The *maturity* stage can then be followed by any of the following six stages in different combinations or orders (or even simultaneously in some cases): *retirement*, which marks the death of a capability; *retrenchment*, which depicts the gradual decline of a capability; *renewal*, which depicts the improvement of the level of a capability, and which might involve minor or major modifications to a capability; *replication*, which depicts the transfer of a capability into a new market; *redeployment*, which represents another type of capability transfer, this time for producing a different but closely related result; and *recombination*, which aims to improve a capability through the combination of existing capabilities.

## 3   On the Concept of Capability in Systems and Software Engineering

The International Council on Systems Engineering (INCOSE)[1] defines Systems Engineering as being "an interdisciplinary approach and means to enable the

---

[1] http://www.incose.org/

realization of successful systems", focusing in the whole life cycle of the system, from the definition of stakeholders' requirements to the dismantlement of the system, considering the business and technical needs of customers in order to provide a quality product [31]. One of the origins of systems engineering is arguably the military field [31]. As such, much of the terminology used in the domain has been adopted from that origin, including the concept of (military) capability. A *military capability* is defined as the ability to achieve a determined military objective [37], requiring a combination of people, process and material [24].

It was precisely on the military field that the first capability maturity models (CMM) appeared. The Software Engineering Institution (SEI) of the Carnegie Mellon University, funded by the U.S. Department of Defense produced the first capability maturity model for assessing software engineering processes, in 1987 [12,13]. The main purpose of the CMM is to achieve a controlled and measurable software engineering practice that can be continuously improved [12]. In this specification, software engineering capability is divided in three areas: organization and resource management, software engineering process and its management, and tools and technology. Despite the fact that this segmentation seems to match the triplet of people, process and material, the term *process* is used throughout the specification as a synonym for capability.

CMM was launched in its 1.0 version in 1991 [25], and version 1.1 came out in 1993 [26], incorporating the feedback from the software engineering community. Soon, capability maturity models began being adopted by other areas, including the more general area of systems engineering, with the purpose of improving its processes. In the *A Systems Engineering Capability Maturity Model, Version 1.0*, issued in 1994, a capability is defined as a "measure of the system's ability to achieve the mission objectives, given that the system is dependable and suitable" and as a "systems engineering metric" [3]. Based on this work, the Electronic Industries Alliance[2] published standard EIA-731.1 - Systems Engineering Capability Model, which described capability as involving the attributes of people, technology, and process [1]. In an effort to unify capability maturity models, the SEI published the Capability Maturity Model Integration (CMMI) as a unifying model for three different process areas: acquisition, development, and services [6,7,8].

It was also in the military field that the idea that capabilities could be used as essential building blocks in engineering efforts was formed [24]. *Capability engineering* is a process which supports *capability management* throughout the life cycle of a capability. *Capability management* aims to manage capabilities through an integrating framework consisting of three inter-related functions: *capability generation*, which refers to the conception, development, planning, acquisition and management of a capability; *capability sustainment*, which refers to the sustainability of a capability at an appropriate level of readiness, for a determined time horizon; and *capability employment*, which refers to the planning for and conducting military operations which involve the use of the capability.

---

[2] Already extinct.

The concept of capability was also adopted in IBM's Rational Method Composer[3], more precisely the concept of capability pattern. The Method Composer allows the customization of the Rational Unified Process (RUP) for software engineering. RUP provides several disciplines which are collections of tasks which can be applied during the life cycle of a system. These tasks can be combined into workflows. A capability pattern is a reusable process which can be applied at any stage of the life cycle and prescribes a work breakdown structure (the workflow), the team allocated to the activities, and the work products produced from the activities.

# 4   On the Concept of Capability in Information Systems

An information system can be defined as "an information processing system, together with the associated organizational resources such as human, technical, and financial resources, that provides and distributes information" [15], a definition which in some sense presents some similarities with that of capability. One of the main research topics in information systems is *enterprise architecture*.

Enterprise Architecture (EA) is a holistic approach to systems architecture with the purposes of modeling the role of information systems and technology on the organization, aligning the enterprise-wide concepts, aligning the business processes and information with the information systems, planning for change, and providing self-awareness to the organization [32]. Despite the fact that it was first created with a more traditional company setting in mind, its practices where also adopted by the military field with the surfacing of two well known enterprise architecture frameworks: the US Department of Defense Architecture Framework (DoDAF) [38] and the UK Ministry of Defense Architecture Framework (MODAF) [36].

Both frameworks adopt the concept of capability, and explicitly model it through its inclusion on the meta-model and on the viewpoints provided by the framework. DoDAF defines capability as being an ability to achieve a desired effect under specified conditions through the combination of activities and resources [38]. In MoDAF, a capability is defined as a a classification of some ability that the enterprise possesses, and that it can be specified wether the enterprise is able to achieve it or not [36]. Capabilities in MoDAF can be represented through a composite structure entitled *capability configuration*, which us defined as "a set of artefacts or an organization configured to provide a capability", and involves physical, human, and software resources and the interactions between them.

The concept of capability is also making its cross to general enterprise architecture approaches. The Open Group Architecture Framework (TOGAF), a generic enterprise architecture framework where it is an integral part of the architectural practices described in its specification [35]. The concept is a part of the meta-model and a capability-based planning for business is included as one of the techniques provided by the specification. TOGAF defines capability as "an

---

[3] http://www-01.ibm.com/software/awdtools/rmc/

Table 1. The concept of capability in the analyzed domains

| Domain | Definition | Source |
|---|---|---|
| Strategic Management | The ability to perform and sustain a set of routines, involving coordination among the actors of the organization and the usage of skills, organization and technology to respond to the demands of the environment. | [22] |
| | The collective physical facilities and human skills, carefully coordinated and integrated, as a means of achieving economies of scale and scope. | [5] |
| | The essence of capabilities lies in the processes of the organization, driven or constrained by the positioning of the internal and external assets of the organization and by the evolutionary path that the firm has chosen to adopt. | [34] |
| Systems and Software Engineering | A (military) capability is defined as the ability to achieve a determined military objective, requiring a combination of people, process and material. | [37,24] |
| | Capability is divided in three areas: organization and resource management, software engineering process and its management, and tools and technology. | [12] |
| | A measure of the system's ability to achieve the mission objectives, given that the system is dependable and suitable. | [3] |
| | Involves the attributes of people, technology, and process. | [1] |
| Information Systems | An ability to achieve a desired effect under specified conditions through the combination of activities and resources. | [38] |
| | An ability that the enterprise possesses, and that it can be specified whether the enterprise is able to achieve it or not. Its configuration involves physical, human, and software resources and the interactions between them. | [36] |
| | An ability that an organization, person, or system possesses, typically requiring a combination of organization, people, processes, and technology. | [35] |

ability that an organization, person, or system possesses", and that it typically "requires a combination of organization, people, processes, and technology" [35].

## 5   Consolidation of Definitions

Based on the descriptions provided in the previous sections, Table 1 describes the different definitions for capability stemming from different areas of knowledge. It is clear that a capability is delivered by a determined configuration of the organization's resources and it is influenced (driven or constrained) by the surrounding environment. In that sense, the definition provided in [34] provides a sound and broad characterization of what constitutes a capability, and that is compatible with the other listed definitions. In detail, the factors that can be used to assess the instinctive capabilities of an organization are (i.e., those which cannot be easily replicated by others):

- processes (i.e., the routines or other activities)
- positions (i.e., current technological infrastructure, intellectual property, customers, relation with suppliers, etc.)
- paths (i.e., strategic alternatives available to the organization).

The relationship between these three categories is explained by the fact that the essence of capabilities lies in the processes of the organization. However, competitive advantage is driven or constrained by the positioning of the internal and external assets of the organization and by the evolutionary path that the firm has chosen to adopt. In the words of the authors, "what a firm can do and where it can go are thus rather constrained by its positions and paths". Those factors can only deliver competitive advantage if the capabilities are based on a collection of routines, skills, and assets that are difficult to imitate.

# 6   On the Concept of Capability and Services

The relationship between capabilities and services seems rather obvious, since capabilities aim to bridge stakeholders intentions to the properties of a system [28]. In fact, capabilities can be seen as functional abstractions decoupled from implementation, and exhibit properties similar to those possessed by services: low-coupling and high cohesion [29]. Given this, it becomes important to differentiate the concept of capability from that of service, something that is already done in enterprise architecture frameworks, although in some cases without providing a clear relationship between the two concepts (e.g., TOGAF), and on relevant service-related modeling languages, which relate the two concepts but do not provide a full enterprise model.

Concerning service-related modeling languages, two examples of such languages making use of the concept are BSDL and SoaML, the former more related to the business realm and the last more related to technical aspects. The Business Service Description Language (BSDL) has the purpose of describing business services from a pure business perspective, addressing specifically their decomposition and non-functional properties [16]. It aims to close the gap existing between more strategy and goal description languages and operational service description languages, and to model both functional and non-functional concepts related to business services. The concept of capability is modeled as a functional concept, representing a function that is performed by a business service. The SoaML modeling language is another example of the inclusion of the concept of capability in the meta-model of the language. The usage of this concept allows the expression of service architectures in terms of the logical capabilities of the services in a way that is agnostic to participants in the architecture, identifying a set of functions or resources that a service might provide or the abilities that are needed in order to provide a service [23]. Figure 1.(a) depicts the capabilities that a service interface provides, and Figure 1.(b) depicts the capabilities a participant has to provide a service.

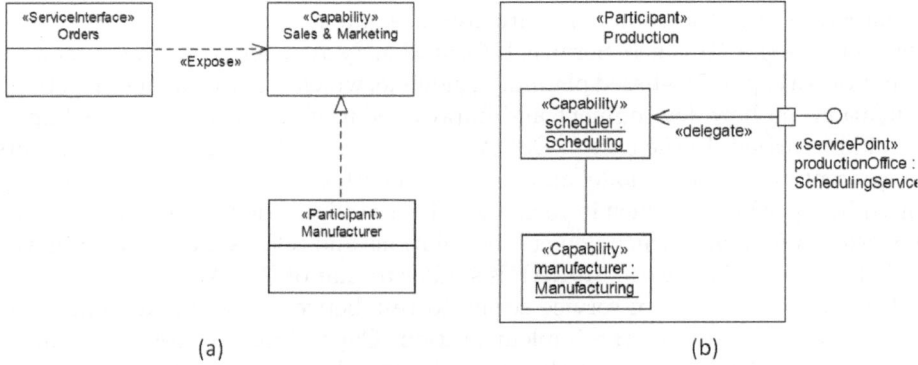

**Fig. 1.** Capabilities in SoaML

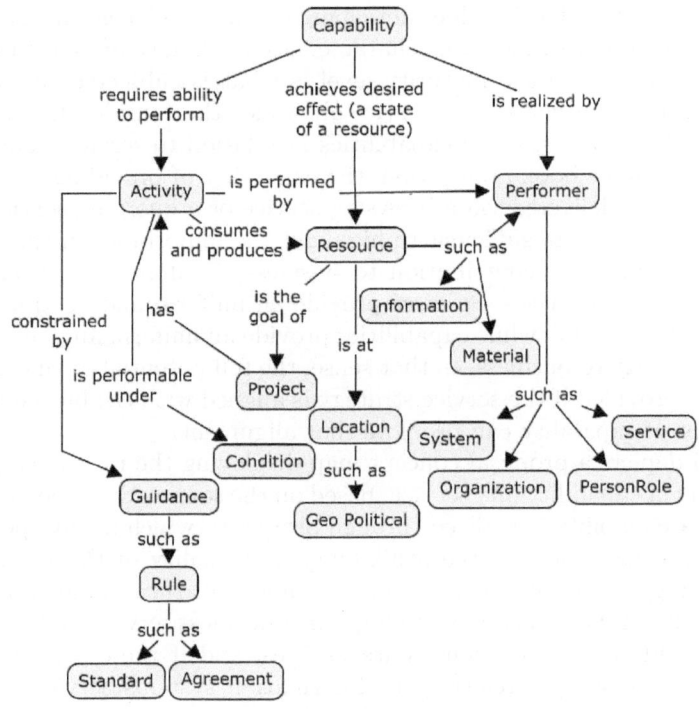

**Fig. 2.** Capability and associated concepts in DoDAF

In the case of the most relevant Enterprise Architecture frameworks, as already referred, the concept of capability is present, although in some cases not directly related to that of service. Concerning TOGAF, the concept is present in the meta-model although not directly related with other concepts belonging to the business architecture or to the application architecture, particularly the concepts related with services (i.e., Business Service, Information System Service). The framework also sports a capability-based planning guideline, which consists on high-level considerations on how development and improvement of organizational capabilities should be carried. In the case of DoDAF, as shown in Figure 2, the two concepts are present in the meta-model and are related with each other: a capability is realized by a performer, which in turn might be a service. The DoDAF also includes a *Services Viewpoint*, which depicts the solutions and relates these to capabilities and operations. The case of MoDAF is similar to that of DoDAF.

In fact, the concept of service seems to rest between that of capability and those directly related to the implementation. Capabilities are easier to link to the drivers and motivation of the business, thus becoming a useful concept to business stakeholders, in the sense that it is easier to understand than more technically oriented concepts. Similarly to the way the concept of service works concerning the technical implementation of a solution, the concept of capability creates an anchor model that does not change in face of changes in the way business is implemented. In fact, this characteristic is already present in capability maturity models, since the maturity level is what is subjected to change, not the capabilities themselves. As a service allows for the consideration of different implementation options, so do capabilities in relation to services. For instance, considering a phone book application, the capability of providing contact information might be delivered via a browsing service or a querying service.

These facts alone are sufficient to highlight the importance of the concept of capability as one more contribution to business/IT alignment, in articulation with the concept of service. Services provide an uniform and abstract interface from the business to IT, while capabilities provide an uniform and abstract interface from strategy to business. In that sense, the full potential of an organization will only be provided if the service strategy is aligned with the business strategy. The concept of capability can promote that alignment.

Figure 3 depicts a proposal concept map displaying the relationship between the concepts of capability and service, based on the sources described throughout this work. A capability is realized through processes (which involve people), and is driven or constrained by the availability and quality of the resources, and by the strategic decisions made. A process might in turn orchestrate business services[4] or might be a part of a larger grained business service. In turn, business services provide and/or consume data entities, and if these services are fully automated, then we are referring to information systems services, which are realized by application components and implemented on technology components.

---

[4] In line with the definition of service provided in [14], a business service consists in the performance of activities, work, or duties associated with a product. The term is used here to distinguish between fully automatized and (semi-)manual services.

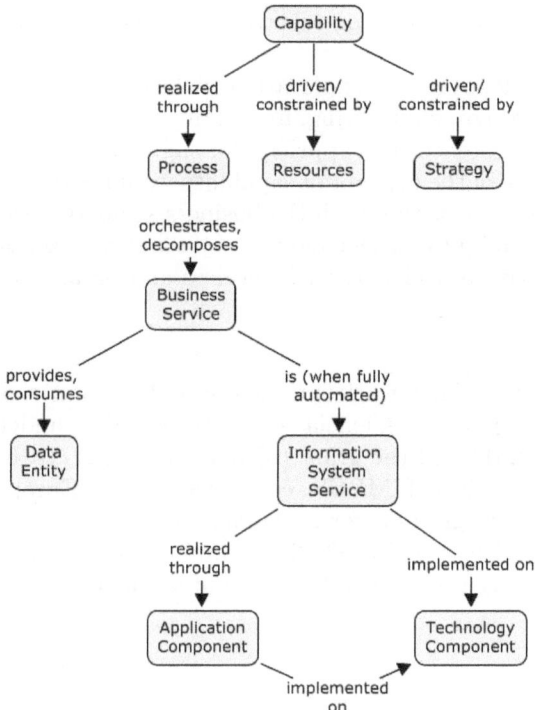

**Fig. 3.** Relationship between Capability and Service

## 7   Conclusion

This work provided an overview on usages of the concept of capability. It has been deemed useful by different knowledge communities, such as the examples of economics and strategic management, systems and software engineering, and information systems, and has been employed to describe products, systems, or even organizations.It can be described as being delivered by a determined configuration of the organization's resources and it is influenced (driven or constrained) by the surrounding environment.

The relationship existing between the concepts of capability and service is also described in this work. Capabilities seem to bear the similarities with services, namely their low coupling and high cohesion. However, the concepts are different since the concept of service seems to rest between that of capability and those directly related to the implementation. That fact can be deduced from different modeling frameworks already making use of the concepts.

In fact, the concept of capability can be used to promote business/IT alignment, in articulation with the concept of service. In fact, most of the works described make use of both concepts. However, either the direct relationships between the concepts are not present or no relationships are made with strategy concepts and/or with implementation concepts. Due to that fact, a concept map was elaborated (Figure 3) relating relevant concepts through the use of simple relationships.

Future work will focus on the exploration of the concept in methods and techniques for service design, engineering, management and governance. In methodological terms, the existence of an approach for engineering and governing services that takes advantage of the concept of capability would better promote the alignment of service implementation with the business strategy. Associated with this, the existence of techniques for the identification and representation of the capabilities and respective association with services and organizational goals would complement this work.

**Acknowledgments.** This work was supported by national funds through FCT - Fundação para a Ciência e a Tecnologia, under project PEst-OE/EEI/LA0021/2011 and the grant (SFRH/BD/69121/2010) to Gonçalo Antunes, and by the project TIMBUS, co-funded by the European Union under the 7th Framework Programme for research and technological development and demonstration activities (FP7/2007-2013) under grant agreement no. 269940. The authors are solely responsible for the content of this paper.

# References

1. Electronic Industries Alliance. EIA-731.1 - Systems Engineering Capability Model. Number EIA-731.1. Government Electronics and Information Technology Association

2. Barney, J.: Firm resources and sustained competitive advantage. Journal of Management 17, 99–120 (1991)

3. Bate, R., Garcia, S., Armitage, C., Cusick, K., Jones, R., Kuhn, D., Minnich, I., Pierson, H., Powell, T., Reichner, A., Wells, C.: A systens engineering capability maturity model, version 1.0. Technical Report CMU/SEI-94-HB-04, Software Engineering Institute, Carnegie Mellon University (1994)

4. Bernier, F., Couture, M., Dussault, G., Lalancette, C., Lemieux, F., Lizotte, M., Mokhtari, M., Lam, S.: CapDEM - towards a capability engineering process, a discussion paper. Technical Report TR 2004-230, Defence R&D Canada - Valcartier (2005)

5. Chandler, A.D.: Scale and Scope: The Dynamics of Industrial Capitalism. Harvard University Press (1990)

6. CMMI Product Team. CMMI for acquisition, version 1.3. Technical Report CMU/SEI-2010-TR-032, Software Engineering Institute, Carnegie Mellon University (2010)

7. CMMI Product Team. CMMI for development, version 1.3. Technical Report CMU/SEI-2010-TR-033, Software Engineering Institute, Carnegie Mellon University (2010)

8. CMMI Product Team. CMMI for services, version 1.3. Technical Report CMU/SEI-2010-TR-034, Software Engineering Institute. Carnegie Mellon University (2010)

9. Dosi, G., Nelson, R.R., Winter, S.G.: The Nature and Dynamics of Organizational Capabilities. Oxford University Press (2000)

10. Eisenhardt, K.M., Martin, J.A.: Dynamic capabilities: What are they? Strat. Mgmt. J. 21, 1105–1121 (2000)
11. Helfat, C.E., Peteraf, M.A.: The dynamic resource-based view: Capability lifecycles. Strat. Mgmt. J. 24, 997–1010 (2003)
12. Humphrey, W.S.: Characterizing the software process: A maturity framework. Technical Report CMU/SEI-87-TR-11, Software Engineering Institute, Carnegie Mellon University (1987)
13. Humphrey, W.S., Sweet, W.L., Edwards, R.K., LaCroix, G.R., Owens, M.F., Schulz, H.: A method for assessing the software engineering capability of contractors. Technical Report CMU/SEI-87-TR-23, Software Engineering Institute, Carnegie Mellon University (1987)
14. ISO/IEC. ISO/IEC 12207 - Systems and software engineering - Software life cycle processes. International Organization for Standardization and International Electrotechnical Commission (2008)
15. ISO/IEC/IEEE. ISO/IEC/IEEE 24765 - Systems and software engineering - Vocabulary. International Organization for Standardization and International Electrotechnical Commission and Institute of Electrical and Electronics Engineers (2010)
16. Lê, L.-S., Ghose, A., Morrison, E.: Definition of a Description Language for Business Service Decomposition. In: Morin, J.-H., Ralyté, J., Snene, M. (eds.) IESS 2010. LNBIP, vol. 53, pp. 96–110. Springer, Heidelberg (2010)
17. Magalhães, R., Silva, A.R.: Organizational design and engineering (ode). Technical report, INOV Centre for Organizational Design and Engineering, CODE (2009)
18. Meilich, A.: System of systems (SoS) engineering & architecture challenges in a net centric environment. In: Proceedings of the 2006 IEEE/SMC International Conference on System of Systems Engineering (2006)
19. Merriam-Webster. Merriam-Webster's Collegiate Dictionary. Merriam-Webster, Inc. (2003)
20. Neaga, E.I., Henshaw, M., Yue, Y.: The influence of the concept of capability-based management on the development of the systems engineering discipline. In: Proceedings of the 7th Annual Conference on Systems Engineering Research 2009, CSER 2009 (2009)
21. Nelson, R.R., Winter, S.G.: Toward an evolutionary theory of economic capabilities. The American Economic Review 63, 440–449 (1973)
22. Nelson, R.R., Winter, S.G.: An Evolutionary Theory of Economic Change. Harvard University Press (1985)
23. OMG. Service Oriented Architecture Modeling Language (SoaML) - Specification for the UML Profile and Metamodel for Services (UPMS). Number ptc/2009-12-09. Object Management Group, OMG Adopted Specification, Finalisation Task Force Beta 2 Document Edition (2009)
24. Pagotto, J., Walker, R.S.: Capability engineering - transforming defence acquisition in canada. In: Proceedings of SPIE (2004)
25. Paulk, M.C., Curtis, B., Chrissis, M.B., Averill, E.L., Bamberger, J., Kasse, T.C., Konrad, M., Perdue, J.R., Weber, C.V., Withey, J.V.: Capability maturity model for software. Technical Report CMU/SEI-91-TR-24, Software Engineering Institute, Carnegie Mellon University (1991)
26. Paulk, M.C., Curtis, B., Chrissis, M.B., Weber, C.V.: Capability maturity model for software, version 1.1. Technical Report CMU/SEI-93-TR-024, Software Engineering Institute, Carnegie Mellon University (1993)
27. Penrose, E.: The Theory of the Growth of the Firm. Wiley (1959)

28. Penserini, L., Perini, A., Susi, A., Mylopoulos, J.: High variability design for software agents: Extending tropos. ACM Transactions on Autonomous and Adaptive Systems 2(4) (November 2007)
29. Ravichandar, R., Arthur, J.D., Bohner, S.A., Tegarden, D.P.: Improving change tolerance through capabilities-based design: an empirical analysis. Journal of Software Maintenance and Evolution: Research and Practice 20, 135–170 (2008)
30. Richardson, G.B.: The organisation of industry. Economic Journal 82, 883–896 (1972)
31. SE Handbook Working Group. Systems engineering handbook: A guide for system life cycle processes and activities. Technical Report INCOSE-TP-2003-002-03.2, International Council on Systems Engineering (INCOSE) (January 2010)
32. Sousa, P., Caetano, A., Vasconcelos, A., Pereira, C., Tribolet, J.: Enterprise architecture modeling with the unified modeling language. In: Enterprise Modeling and Computing with UML. IRM Press (2006)
33. Teece, D., Pisano, G.: The dynamic capabilities of firms: An introduction. Working paper WP-94-103, International Institute for Applied Systems Analysis (1994)
34. Teece, D.J., Pisano, G., Shuen, A.: Dynamic capabilities and strategic management. Strategic Management Journal 18, 509–533 (1997)
35. The Open Group. TOGAF version 9.1. Van Haren Publishing (2011)
36. U.K. Ministry of Defence. MOD Architecture Framework, Version 1.2.004 (2010)
37. U.S. Department of Defense. Joint Publication 1-02: Department of Defense Dictionary of Military and Associated Terms (2001)
38. U.S. Department of Defense. DoD Architecture Framework, Version 2.02 (2010)
39. Waite, M., Hawker, S.: Oxford Paperback Dictionary and Thesaurus. Oxford University Press (2009)
40. Winter, S.G.: Developing evolutionary theory for economics and management. Working Paper WP 2005-01, Reginald H. Jones Center, The Wharton School, University of Pennsylvania (2005)

# Applying the Lead User Method for Designing
# e-Services - Practical Techniques and Experiences

Martin Henkel, Erik Perjons, and Anders Thelemyr

Department of Computer and Systems Science, Stockholm University
{martinh,perjons,thelemyr}@dsv.su.se

**Abstract.** The interest for creating new and innovative e-services is increasing in both the private and public sector. One promising approach is to make use of user innovation, that is, to let innovative users participate in the design process. However, in order to use user innovation for e-service design, organizations need to have a clear approach to identifying areas for improvement, as well as engage and utilize innovative users. In this paper, a practical approach for e-service design based on the concepts of user innovation is presented. The approach consists of a set of steps, and each step is supported by a practical technique. The techniques used in the approach are based on enterprise models such as business value network models and business use cases, and analysis techniques such as SWOT and Open-EDI service phase analysis. The approach is demonstrated by applying it to a real-world case from the Swedish tax agency, and it has been assessed by business and IT practitioners. Furthermore, experiences with applying the techniques are presented.

**Keywords:** Lead user method, user innovation, e-services, enterprise models.

## 1    Introduction

Designing e-services introduce many new opportunities for business and IT developers. E-services can support existing collaborations between service providers and consumers. E-services can also open up new opportunities for the identification of new and innovative services; services that might not be possible to design without the use of information and communication technology (ICT). For example, in many countries, organizations can already today use public e-services to automatically deliver tax declarations to the taxation agencies instead of filling in paper forms and sending them by mail. Such e-services can also automatically perform calculations in various parts within the declaration, which would not be possible without ICT and e-service solutions. Identifying new and innovative e-services is an important task for organizations both in the private and public sectors. This put pressure on business and IT developers to be creative, and understand the needs of users.

Understanding users and involving them in the design of software have been emphasized for many years in design approaches such as user-centered design [1]. Involving users in e-service design is even more important. In e-service design, the service provider and service user (i.e., service consumer) often belongs to different

J.F. e Cunha, M. Snene, and H. Nóvoa (Eds.): IESS 2013, LNBIP 143, pp. 43–57, 2013.

organizations; this is in contrast to traditional software design where system might be built for organization-internal use only. This means that a broader scope needs to be considered when designing e-services, preferably involving both the service provider organization and the organizations using the service [2]. Methods for involving users in the identification and design of e-service are therefore needed. User-centered design is one interesting approach in which the users give their opinions on the functionality and usability of the e-services. However, in user-centered design, the business and IT designer are still driving the design process. To fully make use of the users' creativity, another approach could be to let the users themselves drive the design process, and involve users that are especially innovative, so called lead users.

According to Eric von Hippel's findings in the 1980s, many products and business services are improved by innovations by individual end users [3], [4], [5]. Based on these findings, von Hippel created a method, called Lead User Method [4], [6]. A central theme of the method is to find, engage and support lead users, i.e., users being ahead of the trend in the domain of interest, in order to identify innovative solutions.

These ideas to involve lead users could also be applied in the e-service design process in order to create new and innovative services [7]. However, involving users in limited parts of the software and service design process is complicated and designers often underestimate the complexity and the heterogeneity of the user base in the domain of interest. To fully make use of the users' creativity in the design process, like involving lead users, is even more complex, and method support is needed.

In this paper, a practical approach for involving users in the design of e-services is presented. The foundation of the approach is Eric von Hippel's lead user method. To provide practical support the approach contains a set of *techniques*. These techniques are making use of enterprise models such as business value network models and business use cases, and analysis techniques such as SWOT and Open-EDI service phase analysis. We put special emphasis on enterprise models and analysis techniques as they are today a common and practical instrument for involving users in software and service design. Enterprise models are usually represented as diagrams, which makes them easy to understand and manipulate for any stakeholder, thereby facilitating shared understanding.

The approach is demonstrated by applying it to a real-life case from the Swedish tax agency, in the paper called the Swedish IRS case. The Swedish IRS was involved in a research project, SAMMET [8], which aimed to create methods for designing new and innovative e-services for public and private organizations. We account for the experiences of using the techniques in the IRS case.

Erik von Hippels user innovation method are used as the foundation for the approach, and well as existing techniques for enterprise analysis and modeling. The main contribution of this paper is the compilation of practical techniques that aims to aid in e-service design, their illustrated use in the IRS case, and resulting experiences of their application.

The structure of the paper is as following: Section 2 presents related research, Section 3 describes, motivates and demonstrates the approach. In Section 4 the result of an assessment of the approach is described. Finally, in Section 5 the conclusion, including suggested further research, is presented.

# 2    Related Research

## 2.1    Enterprise Modeling and Analysis Techniques for e-Service Design

Enterprise modelling and analysis is the process of using models to represent an organization's business processes, resources, people, information, constraints, and organizational structure. Much research based on enterprise modelling is used for requirements engineering, that is, the process in which functional and non-functional requirements on IT-systems are elicited, specified and validated. In this paper, we make use of business value network model, business use cases model, SWOT analysis model, and a model over the Open-EDI service phases.

In this paper a *business value network model* are employed to present the context as well as the scope of the tasks for the innovative user. A business value network model (also called just business model or value model) is a representation of a network of cooperating actors that together create value through resource transfers and conversions. Business value network models as a base for designing e-services are presented in several research papers, e.g., [9], [10], [11]. However, none of these are set in the context of user innovation.

In this paper, a *SWOT analysis model*, as defined in the Business Motivation Model, BMM [12] is used to survey an organizations position within a market. This enables us to further scope the context for the innovative users. *Business use cases* are then used for finding user roles of interest when identifying lead users. Business use case is an enterprise modeling technique related to UML use cases [13]. We also make use of a model of *Open-EDI service phase analysis* [14] to help innovative users find complementary services.

## 2.2    User Innovation Methods

The importance of involving users in product development was highlighted by Eric von Hippel in the mid-to-late 1980s [4]. The proposition was that users can be innovative, and therefore can aid in the development of innovative products. Since then, research work within this area, often called user innovation, has spread and includes finding methods for describing how to find, engage and involve users in product innovation. Several empirical studies support the claim that innovative users can produce innovations of high originality and high monetary value [1].

Central to user innovation methods is the concepts of Lead Users. In essence a lead user is a user that is ahead of a market trend, and thus is an important source for new needs and ideas on how to best serve those needs [6]. Furthermore a lead user can typically benefit from improvements in product or services.

In [4] von Hippel outlines a first proposal for how businesses could involve lead users in marketing research. This method was later refined [6][15]. The refined method includes four steps; (1) specifying lead user indicators, (2) identifying lead users, (3) generating concepts/products, (4) test concepts/products. The approach presented in this paper supports the three first steps with concrete techniques based on enterprise analysis and modeling.

The lead user method has been applied in different settings with promising results [6], [16], [17]. The innovations resulting from using the lead user method were favorably received by the non-lead users evaluating them.

Even though there is no similar approach that combines user innovation methods with enterprise analysis and modeling, there exists empirical research on the effect of applying user innovation to e-service design. Kristensson, et al. [7] set up an experiment in order to examine the ability of idea creation among three test groups: ordinary users, users trained in innovation techniques, and a product expert group. The authors showed that the most innovative group was the group of users trained in innovation techniques. The expert group ended up the least innovative. Although the experiment was small, it shows the power of engaging users in the innovation process.

### 2.3    General Service Development and User Involvement

The areas of service design and innovation originally stems from the areas of business services that not necessarily need to involve IT. This area of service development is sometimes referred to as new service development, NSD [18][19]. While service development can be seen as a way to support product development, such as the development of customer services support the delivery of goods, it can also be performed with the purpose to create new standalone services. Within the NSD field it has been shown that user involvement has a positive effect of the speed of development and the quality of the final service [20]. However is has been pointed out that there is a lack of strategies to reach the positive results [21]. The approach presented in this paper should be seen as what is referred to as a supportive technique for NSD [22], that is, it is a complement to new service development approaches, with special focus on the use of enterprise modeling and user innovation.

## 3    Overview of the Approach

The general idea of applying a user innovative method is to engage the users in the creation of new and innovative products. Thus there are of course a need of finding and collaborating with lead users. However before engaging the users there are a need to set the scope of the development and the area of innovation. There is also a need to define metrics of how the new product ideas should be evaluated. To cover these areas we propose to use six steps in the approach, see table 1. These steps are based on Eriks von Hippels lead user method [6][15]. The general structure of the approach is to first widening the scope, looking for new markets and areas of improvements (step 1-2). The goal is to "broaden the innovation space", that is, to minimizing the risk of missing good innovation potential. To guide the work indicators of success are set up (step 3). In steps 4-5 the lead users are identified by finding important users roles and searching for innovative individuals acting in these roles. Finally, in step 6, there is a need to support the collaboration with the users.

**Table 1.** The steps of the approach

| Step | Technique used |
|---|---|
| 1. Clarify organizational context | Business value models |
| 2. Identify market and trends | SWOT analysis |
| 3. Find indicators for measuring success | Goal models |
| 4. Profile lead users | Profile template and Business use cases |
| 5. Identify lead users | Data mining |
| 6. Support the work of innovative users | Open EDI complementary service model |

Eriks von Hippels lead user method [6][15] contains four main steps, while the method we outline in table 1 contains six. The difference is that we have broken down Eriks Von Hippels first step (named "Specify lead user indicators") into three distinct steps (1-3) to have a more elaborated analysis of the business context and indicators.

# 4    Step 1- Clarify the Organizational Context

The first step of the approach is to clarify the organizational context, that is, broaden the perspective so that the entire network of actors, and the transfer of resources among them, is visualized. Broadening the contextual perspective, in order to push the limits of the innovation space, can be done in several ways. One well-known technique is to utilize *business value network models*, which is what we apply in this step. Business value network models visualizes the network of suppliers and customers that the organization is part of, as well as the resources involved, including the services transferred between the different actors [9]. It can often be useful to also identify the organization's customers' and business partners' own suppliers and customers, to further broaden the analysis. The business value network model describes central and existing business services and e-services together with other central resources. Note also that other resources, such as goods, are usually bundled with services, such as e-services. Therefore, analyzing other resources than e-services can be useful as a base for identifying innovative e-services.

A demonstration of applying this step in the Swedish IRS case is shown in Fig. 3. The e-service in focus is e-tax declaration aiming at supporting automated tax declarations for organizations via the web. The business value network model shows the context in which the e-service operates. Visible here are the various actors and the exchanges of resources of interest between the actors. This enables us to gain a better understanding of the e-tax declaration service and its context, and, thereby, suggests additional e-services, supporting the usage of e-tax declaration service.

Additionally, shown in Fig. 3, the IRS offers an e-tax account service, which can be used for inspecting the status of the organization's tax account. There is also an external book-keeping service available for the organizations, if they want to outsource the task of handling the declarations. Furthermore, the model shows that there are IT system developers that sell book-keeping systems to organizations, and that the government is funding the IRS. As mentioned above, the IRS offers an alternative to e-tax declaration service, namely a manual paper-based declaration service.

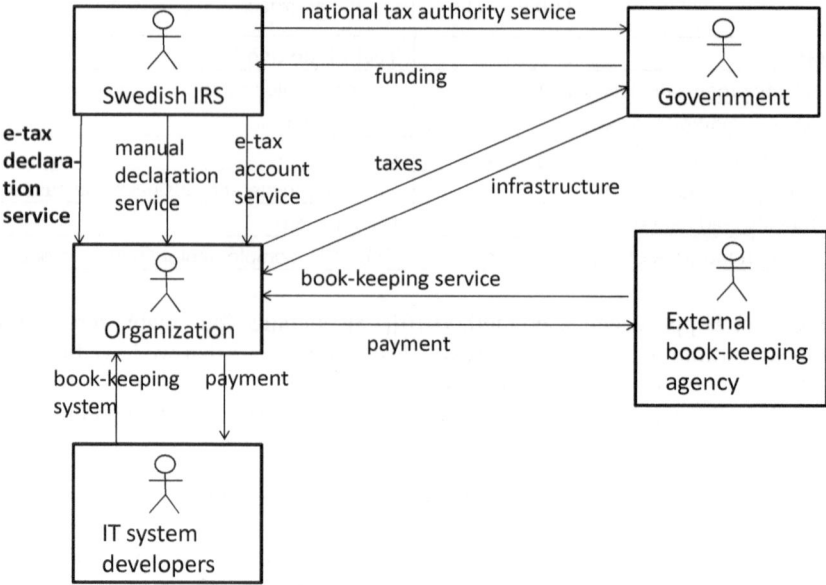

**Fig. 1.** A business value network model from the Swedish IRS case that shows the context in which the e-tax declaration service operates

*Our experiences with applying the business value network* technique for clarifying the organizational context concerns both the use of actors in the models, as well as how to best use the resources exchanges to depict the business context. We here describe the experiences in three simple guidelines that we found useful in this step in the approach:

*Include second level actors.* When it comes the identification of actors it is simple to not look further than the ones that are directly related to the business under study. To avoid this, also include the 2nd level actors – that is, actors that collaborate with consumers of your services. For example in Fig.3, we included the IT system developers and external book keeping agencies.

*Include reciprocal transfers.* For each transfer in the business value network model is good to think about possible transfers in the other direction. A simple example is that for rendered services there should be a payment in return. Another, maybe not so obvious example of reciprocity is that the organization using the tax agency services in turn get to use the infrastructure (roads, juridical system etc) as given by the government.

*Include "soft" resources if needed.* Everything is not services, goods and money. In areas such as healthcare it could be important to extend the business network model to also include softer resources such as trust and knowledge. We have not done this in the model shown in Fig 3, however an example would be to include the legitimacy and trust that properly using the IRS services gives an organisation.

# 5    Step 2 - Identify Markets and Trends

The second step of the approach is to decide which part of the market that should be focused on during the continued process of identifying innovative e-services, and which trends that is of interest to pursue further.

For this step we propose to use a SWOT analysis as a technique. A SWOT analysis identifies an organization's internal strengths and weaknesses, as well as the external opportunities and threats, i.e., the two external categories being out of control for the organization. Possible internal strengths and weaknesses could be, for example, the already existing infrastructure, the culture within the organization, resources, and management capabilities. Possible opportunities and threats could be existing, as well as future, laws and regulations, emerging technologies, services and products.

Finding strengths, weaknesses, opportunities, and threats for the organization gives a good foundation for identifying not only the optimal market and trends, but also promising e-services. Since e-services are about exchanging resources with an external part, extra focus could be put on the external parts of the SWOT-analysis, i.e., the opportunities and threats in the SWOT analysis. Since e-services are executed in IT applications, special focus could also be on new devices such as tablets and smartphones in the SWOT analysis.

A demonstration of applying this step in the Swedish IRS case is shown in Fig. 4. The SWOT-analysis model shows IRS's internal strengths and weaknesses, and its external opportunities and threats. In supporting the performance of the SWOT analysis, statistics of the usage of e-services within the IRS can be used. Another possibility is to interview personnel from organizations that perform their tax declarations manually or electronically, respectively.

| Strength (internal) | Weaknesses (internal) |
|---|---|
| The Swedish IRS is well-known to be a forgoer regarding e-government | Lack of method support for identifying and designing innovative e-services |
| **Opportunities (external)** | **Threats (external)** |
| Suppliers of book-keeping systems could collaborate better with IRS in order to better integrate those systems with the e-tax declaration service. Swedish employees traditionally have good skills in using computers, and in using public e-services. | The book-keeping systems used today by the organizations do not support the automatic insertion of tax declaration data into the e-tax declaration service. This insertion must currently be performed manually. |

**Fig. 2.** A SWOT analysis model from the Swedish IRS case

We express our experience with using SWOT models for identifying markets and trends using the following three guidelines:

*Make use of the business network model.* The previously defined actors are a good start for finding external opportunities and threats.

*Seek information from external actors.* By talking to the external actors it is possible to gain a deeper understanding of what they perceive as the current trends/opportunities. In the IRS case we performed structured interviews with organizations and their external book keeping agencies.

*Put priorities/weights on the SWOT items.* Each threat and opportunity is not equal. To discern the possible impact of changing the IRS services we made statistical analysis of past tax declarations. It turned out that most of the companies that used the manual paper-based declaration service was small companies (1-5 employees), thus targeting threats and opportunities for this group would have the highest impact on raising the level of e-service use.

# 6     Step 3 - Find Indicators for Measuring Success

The third step of the approach is to finding indicators that can guide the work with finding or improving e-services.

In this step of we suggest to use the goal model technique to define measurable indicators. Using indicators and measurable goal values is a common way of measuring projects or processes. An indicator is a property of a project or a process, e.g., the properties "income from the projects or process", "costs of the projects or processes", "number of satisfied customers", and so on. Upon deciding about goal values for indicators, the organization must know which market and trends that the identified e-services should support.

To guide the further work in the approach, indictors from different perspectives can be used. Two perspectives that can be of use are to measure the ongoing activities in the project, and to measure the projects result. Examples of measuring the results of the project includes posting using indicators like "How many innovative e-services were discovered within the project?", "How profitable are these e-services projected to be for the organization, both short-term and long-term?" and "How successful the organization's customers or clients consider the new e-services to be?".

A demonstration of applying this step in the Swedish IRS is shown in Figure 5, where one indicator and its related target value to be used for measuring the success of the project are shown.

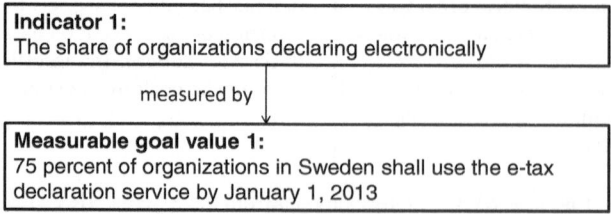

**Fig. 3.** A goal model, depicting an indicator and measurable goal value from the Swedish IRS case

In our experience goal models are very useful for having a structured approach to finding indicators. Based on our experiences we suggest the following guidelines:

*Work both top-down and bottom up.* Taking existing goals is a good way to start the goal modeling top-down. The top-level goal can then be broken down into sub-goals. However, in order to not only re-iterate well-known organizational goals it is also useful to bring in new goals in a bottom-up fashion, for example related to the threats and opportunities as identified in the previous steps.

*Be prepared to change goals.* Be aware of that predefined goals can be difficult to use for measuring innovations. For example, during the IRS case we found service improvements that could raise the quality of the provided services, however these changes can not only be measured by the increased number of users (measurable goal value 1 in Fig. 5).

# 7    Step 4 - Profile Lead Users

The fourth step of the approach is to create a profile for lead users. The motivation for the step is to make the search for lead users more effective, i.e., to find the best candidates given some limited amount of resources. The profile is generally based on the properties of lead users that von Hippel has identified. Here, we propose to first use a technique based on a *profile template* with general and predefined properties. The possible lead user roles could moreover be profiled/identified by using Business Use Case models. To start with a lead user could be characterized using this simple template, based on von Hippels lead user characteristics:

- A lead user should have *experience and knowledge* of the market and trends in question.
- A lead user should have an *intrinsic interest* for new and innovative e-services, within the market in question, earlier in time than other users.
- A lead user should anticipate *great value* in finding new and innovative e-services that solve their needs, within the market in question.
- A lead user should be known for having come up with new ideas and solutions for e-services, within the market in question.

While the template above defines desired properties of lead users, it is also helpful to examine in which roles the lead users should or could have. We here propose to use the technique of business use cases for identifying user roles in e-services. This enables discussion about in which business situations users can use the e-service, and thereby works as a tool for identifying new roles that can be of interest to find lead users. Thus, each service could be seen as a business use case, and the process of finding the related users of the use cases will lead to the identification of the link between user roles and services.

A demonstration of applying this step in the Swedish IRS case is shown in Fig. 6, showing some business use cases and related roles.

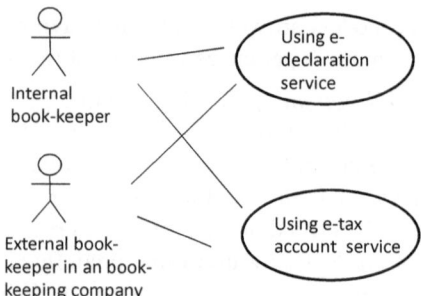

**Fig. 4.** Business use cases in a business use case model from the Swedish IRS case

Our experiences with using business use cases to profile lead users are summarized in two guidelines below.

*Use the business network model (step 1) as input.* The business value network model is a good input for finding roles, as it contains the main organizations in the business context.

*Focus on individuals, not organizations.* Finding lead users is about finding individuals, not organizations. Thus when specifying the use case model, it is important to think about roles that individual can cake. This will later help in finding the individuals.

# 8     Step 5 - Identify Lead Users

The fifth step of is about finding lead users who satisfy the properties of the lead user profile and the roles from the previous step. The two most common instruments for identifying lead users is *pyramiding* and *screening* [23]. Pyramiding is about asking customers, clients and other stakeholders whether they know someone who either satisfies the profile's properties directly, or knows someone who satisfies the profile's properties. Screening is about finding lead users among a large group of customers or clients in various registers.

In the Swedish IRS case there was several different ways of identifying lead users. One way that was considered was to contact the users that previously had put forward changes request on the existing services. The idea here was to find users that had the properties of the previous described profile template - users that had interest in improving services. Moreover by cross-referencing this data with information about their role (users of e declaration service and/or user of tax declaration services. see Fig. 6), it should be possible to screen out the right lead users. Members of the IRS personnel could also have personal knowledge about potential lead users from contacts gathered through the years. This is an example of *pyramiding*.

However these two options turned out to be difficult in the IRS case due to restrictions on the handling of user information. We describe our experiences in the following guideline:

*Be sure that you will not put off the users by contacting them.* IRS, being and governmental organization had very strict rules on how they are allowed to handle user data. Basically, the user data can be processed to aid in the IRS main mission, to collect taxes. However to cross-process data for other purposes, or to hand out user information to external parties is not allowed. In the end this dilemma was solved by contacting users in the IRS information days. During these information days the participating users had the option to freely participate in the project ("opt-in").

# 9    Step 6 - Support the Innovative Work of Lead Users

In this step the lead users are offered supporting techniques to be used during their innovative work. The techniques should facilitate a creative environment. According to von Hippel, lead users should produce ready-to-use products. This is usually not possible when dealing with e-services, since few users are skilled at software development. Rather, for e-services, the lead users' work is about producing innovative ideas for new e-services, or producing further requirements for existing e-services. To help in the creative process we propose to use the OPEN-EDI services phases as a technique. The service phases of OPEN-EDI are described as a set of complementary services to a main service [14]. The standard can be used to support the lead users to identify new innovative complementary services around the main service.

A demonstration of applying this step in the Swedish IRS is shown in Fig. 7, in which a template of OPEN-EDI complementary services is shown on the right-hand side. In this step, the IRS could, for example, arrange focus groups where lead users meet and together discuss problems and solutions based on the complimentary services. For example the problem of how to find, or even know about the tax declaration service could be discussed, since identification is one of the four complimentary services (see Fig 7).

In the IRS case, due to practical reasons, we ended up with having an individual dialogue with the identified users. It was simply very difficult to find a suitable time for a group of users to meet, and when we set up a time the number of users that could actually participate was too low. Based on these experiences we outline the following guidelines:

*When contacting users, time is not the issue, calendar time is.* It turned out to be quite time consuming to contact the users, not in actual man-hours, but in calendar days. The reason for this problem was the bookkeepers (see step 4) that we contacted was very busy at the end of each month (due to internal bookkeeping) and at in the first days of the month (due to the deadlines for sending the tax information to the IRS). Moreover it was more or less impossible to get in contact with the bookkeepers in January-February, due to the annual economic revisions. Thus it took a lot of calendar time to get in touch with the users.

*Use a structure to gain creativity when talking to users.* When discussing the possible extensions to the existing e-services with the users we used a structure similar to what is shown in Fig. 7. This proved very helpful, as is gave the users the opportunity to see the problem/e-service from different perspectives. Thus, in this case, we perceived that imposing a structure actually gave a good variety in the outcome, rather than limiting the outcome. A similar process structure is also useful when identifying bottlenecks in the users processes [24].

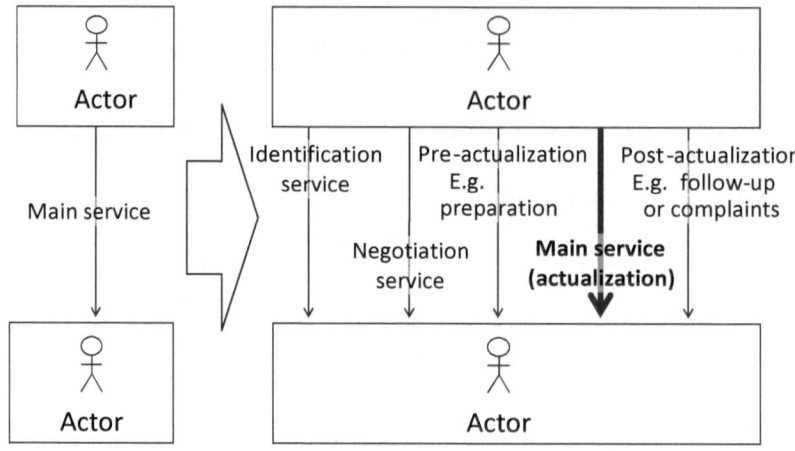

**Fig. 5.** Using the OPEN-EDI to find complimentary services

## 10    Assessment of the Approach

Our experience with using the approach and each technique was collected while the approach was applied and designed. To review the end result we performed an assessment of the approach once it was completed. This assessment is a first step towards a more exhaustive evaluation and was made in order to collect new ideas for forthcoming development of the approach.

The assessment was performed by interviewing experts within the areas of innovative methods and e-service development. The experts were identified using py-ramiding. In essence pyramiding are based on that experts know other experts. In total, three experts were identified, and subsequently individually interviewed. The interviewees were sent a combined slideshow presentation of the approach, and the demonstration, by e-mail a day before the interview. Included in the presentation was a set of questions that the interviewees were expected to give their comments to during the interview, although not necessarily in strict order.

Since we aimed for a practically applicable approach the interviews focuses on the *understandability*, *efficiency* and *coherence* of the approach. Understandability is the degree to which the approach is understood or comprehended by the users of the approach, effectiveness is the degree to which the approach supports creation of innovative ideas from innovative users of e-services, and coherence is the degree to which the approach and its parts are logically, orderly and consistently related. The interviewees were also asked to suggest method improvements, both in general, and for each step in the method. We below summarize the results from the interviews.

In the analysis of the assessment of the approach, it was found that the *understandability* of the method was good in general. However, question marks were raised regarding the intended target groups of using the method. One interviewee considered the method somewhat complex in nature. On the other hand, another interviewee believed that the method was well suited for business analyst and similar target groups.

Regarding the *effectiveness* of the method, the conclusion was that there was not any reason to believe that the method would not be effective in general. However it was pointed out that that the first two steps concerning the modeling of the organizational context could be time consuming. Furthermore it would be necessary to align the method to existing development methods for e-services.

Regarding *coherence*, one interviewee thought that steps 1 and 2 where on a somewhat different level, less detailed, than the other. Otherwise the steps were deemed to follow in a coherent way, i.e., the parts of the method are logically, orderly and consistently related. Another interviewee did not see any problems with the coherence. The third interviewee saw an interesting possibility to group the steps together to enhance the understanding, and thus clarify the coherence further.

Several improvements were suggested during the interviews:

▪ Steps 1 and 2 of could be enhanced by specifying in more detail, which kinds of model that are recommended to use (interviewee 1 and 3).
▪ For step 6 the organization should define which incentives they can offer the lead users when discussing contractual agreements. The reason for this is that people, including lead users are driven by different interests, and the right incentives have to match with the right lead users (interviewee 3).
▪ In step 6 it is important for most markets, especially governmental, to make sure that innovations are aligned with existing laws and regulations (interviewee 2). It is also important to not only describe and align the innovative e-services themselves, but also the existing service processes and architectures, as well as the delivery capacity (interviewee 3).

## 11    Conclusion

In this paper, an approach for e-service design based on the concepts of user innovation is presented. The approach is based on Eric von Hippel's Lead User Method, but in this paper we focus on how the methods can practically applied to design e-services. To support the use of the approach for the design of e-services each of the six steps of the approach is accompanied with easy-to apply techniques.

The approach has been assessed by business and IT practitioners. The assessment shows that the approach is promising; it is gives organizations a consistent structure when applying user innovation to e-service design. The assessment also resulted in several proposals for further enhancements.

Further research include evaluation of the method, by for example using an extended set of practitioners (i.e., domain experts), but also researchers in the area of user innovation. More important is also to gain more insights by applying the method in real-life organizations. As it is now the approach could give organizations that are to start their initial user-innovation driven project an initial toolbox.

# References

1. Gulliksen, J., Göransson, B., Boivie, I., Blomkvist, S., Persson, J., Cajander, Å.: Key principles for user-centred systems design. Behaviour & Information Technology 22(6), 397–409 (2003)
2. Goldkuhl, G.: Socio-instrumental Service Modelling: An Inquiry on e-Services for Tax Declarations. In: Persson, A., Stirna, J. (eds.) PoEM 2009. LNBIP, vol. 39, pp. 207–221. Springer, Heidelberg (2009)
3. Bogers, M., Afuah, A., Bastian, B.: Users as innovators: A review, critique, and future research directions. Journal of Management 36(4), 857–875 (2010)
4. von Hippel, E.: Lead Users: A Source of Novel Product Concepts. Management Science 32(7), 791–805 (1986)
5. von Hippel, E.: Democratizing innovation. MIT Press, Cambridge (2006)
6. Urban, G.L., von Hippel, E.: Lead User Analyses for the Development of New Industrial Products. Management Science 34(5), 569–582 (1988)
7. Kristensson, P., Magnusson, P., Matthing, J.: Users as a Hidden Resource for Creativity - Findings from an Experimental Study on User Involvement. Creativity and Innovation Management 11(1), 55–61 (2002)
8. SAMMET, SAMMET Project site (2010), http://www.dsv.su.se/sammet (accessed December 05, 2012)
9. Gordijn, J., Yu, E., van der Raadt, B.: e-Service Design Using i* and e3 value Modeling. IEE Software 23(3), 26–33 (2006)
10. Hruby, P., Kiehn, J., Scheller, C.: Model-Driven Design Using Business Patterns. Springer, Heidelberg (2006) ISBN 978-3540301547
11. Henkel, M., Johannesson, P., Perjons, E.: An Approach for E-service Design using Enterprise Models. International Journal of Information System Modeling and Design 2(1) (2011)
12. OMG. Business Motivation Model (BMM), version 1, ormal/2008-08-02, Object Management Group (2008), http://www.omg.org/spec/BMM/1.0/PDF (retrieved December 2012)
13. Cockburn, A.: Writing Effective Use Cases. Addison-Wesley (2001)
14. Open-EDI, UN/CEFACT Modeling Methodology User Guide (2012), http://www.unece.org/cefact/ (last accessed December 2, 2012)
15. Lüthje, C., Herstatt, C.: The Lead User method: an outline of empirical findings and issues for future research. R&D Management 34(5), 553–568 (2004)
16. Herstatt, C., von Hippel, E.: From Experience: Developing New Product Concepts Via the Lead User Method: A Case Study in a "Low Tech Field". Journal of Product Innovation Management 9, 213–221 (1992)
17. Lilien, G.L., Morrison, P.D., Searls, K., Sonnack, M., von Hippel, E.: Performance Assessment of the Lead User Idea-Generation Process for New Product Development. Management Science 48(8), 1042–1059 (2002)
18. Johne, A., Storey, C.: New service development: a review of the literature and annotated bibliography. European Journal of Marketing 32(3/4), 184–251 (1998)
19. Edvardsson, B., Olsson, J.: Key Concepts for New Service Development. The Service Industries Journal 16(2) (1996)

20. Carbonell, P., Rodríguez-Escudero, A.I., Pujari, D.: Customer Involvement in New Service Development: An Examination of Antecedents and Outcomes. Journal of Product Innovation Management 26, 536–550 (2009)
21. Kristensson, P., Matthing, J., Johansson, N.: Key strategies for the successful involvement of customers in the co-creation of new technology-based services. International Journal of Service Industry Management 19(4), 474–491 (2008)
22. Matthing, J., Sandén, B., Edvardsson, B.: New service development: learning from and with customers. International Journal of Service Industry Management 15(5), 479–498 (2004)
23. von Hippel, E., Franke, N., Prügl, R.: Efficient Identification of Leading-Edge Expertise - Screening vs. Pyramiding. In: PICMET Proceedings, Istanbul, Turkey, July 9-13 (2006)
24. Henkel, M., Perjons, E.: E-Service Requirements from a Consumer-Process Perspective. In: The 17th International Working Conference on Requirements Engineering: Foundation for Software Quality (REFSQ 2011), March 28-30. Springer, Essen (2011)

# Theory of Constraints in the Service Sector: Characterization for Banking and Analysis of the Factors Involved in Its Adoption

Julian D.M. Castaño[1], Maria R.A. Moreira[1], Paulo S.A. Sousa[1,2], and Raquel F.Ch. Meneses[1]

[1] Faculty of Economics, Universidade do Porto, Portugal
R.Dr. Roberto Frias, s/n, 4200-464 Porto, Portugal
julidamo@hotmail.com, {mrosario,paulus,raquelm}@fep.up.pt
[2] LIAAD-INESC Porto LA, Portugal

**Abstract.** In this research we represent the major elements of the Theory of Constraints (TOC) in a services environment, specifically for the banking sector, and we analyze the factors involved in the decision to adopt the TOC by companies in this sector.

It was identified that the four elements of the TOC theory, throughput, inventory, operating expenses and constraints, correspond to, respectively, the money coming from financial services rendered, the money required to generate this profit, the money to fund the expenses, and the limitations to the normal activity. Regarding the constraints, the most common are mainly administrative (regulations and policies) and the lack of technological resources associated to the scarcity of capital flow and the environment imposed by the state of the economy at a specific time.

The main factors that influence the decision to adopt the TOC by the banking sector reside, first, in the tool's current level of development; second, in the nature and the characteristics of the banking service that are very far from the original industrial reality and, finally, in organizational factors such as the attitude towards change, the leadership of the administration and the commitment of the entire institution.

**Keywords:** Services, Banking sector, Theory of Constraints.

## 1    Introduction

The services sector accounts for 67.01% of the gross domestic product (GDP) of the total world economy and 55% in the more developed economies [1]. In the case of the countries belonging to the OECD, the services sector has become a driving force in the growth of employment, accounting for over 70% of the current total. However, in most of these countries, productivity growth in services continues to be slow, which is why the OECD has drawn attention to the importance of adopting new policies, the use of information technologies, and innovation in products and processes, to match the countries that went through this process successfully, such as Australia and the United States [2].

J.F. e Cunha, M. Snene, and H. Nóvoa (Eds.): IESS 2013, LNBIP 143, pp. 58–72, 2013.

For its part, the Theory of Constraints (TOC) is one of the most widely recognized methods of optimization and continuous improvement by the industry in recent years. Initially developed by Dr. Eliyahu M. Goldratt, in the 1980s, TOC is often used by various industrial companies worldwide, intent on the continuous improvement of their processes and increasing efficiency [3-4]. Examples include Ford Motor Company, General Motors, Motorola, Pharmacia or Unilever, which have obtained positive results related to significant increases in production flow (throughput) and significant reduction in inventory, defects associated with quality, cycle time and lead time [4-5].

The historical success of TOC and the tertiary sector's need to increase its productivity serves to highlight the importance of further investigations that combine these two areas. Although there is a stark shortage of TOC developments specifically for the sector, compared to the vast number of existing studies in industry [6-14], some studies related to the area have shown the relevance of and current interest in the matter, which deserves to be more fully explored from new and different perspectives, the main aim of this study. Actually, the TOC is providing a process of centering the attention on the critical areas' improvement [7], and thus has the potential for much faster improvement. Another contribution for services of TOC method is that it provides techniques of dealing with change [10].

This paper begins with a brief review of the relevant literature on the areas involved in the research (services, banking, TOC and TOC in services). Subsequently, the methodology used is described, followed by the results of a multi-case study (aim 1) and the statistical analysis (aim 2). The paper ends with the conclusion, describing limitations and future topics of study.

## 2    Literature Review

### 2.1    Services

A generic, basic and simple definition of the term was proposed by Zeithaml and Bitner [15], which defines services as events, processes and performances. Grönroos [16] defines them as activities that are characterized by their intangible properties, and classifies their production based on the interaction, or not, of consumers, service providers, physical resources or systems.

In addition to the intangible properties, Parasuraman *et al.* [17] highlight heterogeneity as a property of services, related to the instability of the results in the production of services, which depend on a number of variables, such as service providers, the method used, and the same consumer, among others. The same authors explain the characteristic of inseparability in relation to the inability to break down the different elements that make up a service, as is possible in the case of goods. Meanwhile, Fitzsimons and Fitzsimons [18] state that experiences are perishable, intangible and produced by the same consumer, who necessarily becomes a co-producer. Later, Rubalcaba [19] explains that, in addition, services are a whole dimension of activities and not just one sector, noting, first, that the end result is achieved as a joint achievement between the parties involved and, second, the same properties were described by the authors mentioned above.

Regarding the classification of services within the existing set of proposals on the subject, this study used the classification of Schmenner [20], as used by Siha [10] in her study, which is considered the forerunner to the present research. The matrix classification of service processes, originally developed by Schmenner [20], proposes four categories based on the variables of work intensity and the degree of interaction and customization: Service factory (low labor intensity and low degree of customer interaction and customization), Mass Service (high labor intensity and low degree of customer interaction and customization), Service shop (low labor intensity and high degree of customer interaction and customization), and Professional service (high labor intensity and high degree of customer interaction and customization).

## 2.2    Banking Sector

Within the universe of existing service organizations, the banking sector was chosen as the focus for this study, since it is extremely regulated, with little variability in processes and highly concentrated (in the European case). A specified unit of analysis (Portuguese banks) would serve as the basis for analysis, as well as allow us to extrapolate the findings. The factors that Santillan-Salgado [21] considered as explanatory of this growth in concentration in the European banking industry are: first, the inclusion of high technology developments in banking activities and the rapid increase of competition linked to the deregulation of the sector and state intervention in times of crisis; second, the process of restructuring the EU region to achieve the creation of a single financial market in 1993; and third, the introduction of the euro from 1999, as the official currency of the majority of the EU countries.

In the Portuguese case specifically, the banking sector has been characterized by strong changes in both its structure and its system, resulting from a process of profound transformations over the last few decades: nationalization of banks in 1974, financial market liberalization in 1984, and recharged growth of competition in the sector [22]. This environment, resulting from the re-privatization of the sector, required a modernization of the traditional banking institutions so that they could remain profitable and competitive in the market. Thus, the Portuguese banking sector adopted the Universal Banking model, which is characteristic of those financial institutions that are able to offer, compared to the traditional bank, a more innovative range of financial services directly or indirectly related to its core business [23-25].

Honoban [26] explains how this process in Portugal, with the adoption of the universal banking model, the re-privatization of banks and the removal of limits on growth for loans [22], has endowed the Portuguese banking system with high levels of liberalism [27], being in fact one of the most drastic regulatory liberalizations in Europe [28].

## 2.3    The Theory of Constraints

At the end of the 1970s, Eliyahu Moshe Goldratt developed a scheduling algorithm for industrial production known as Optimized Production Schedule [29]. It was characterized by fixed rules and parameters designed for use in a computer program. Years later, it was named the Optimized Production Technology (OPT) [4].

In 1984, Goldratt published the book The Goal [30], which explains the concepts of OPT but does not delve into the details of its implementation. This information would be the central theme of his sub sequent The Race [31], in which he developed a new system to manage the flow of material called Drum-Buffer-Rope (DRB). But it was only in 1988 that the term "Theory of Constraints" was referred to explicitly, while Goldratt listed the results of all his previous work: "(...) *The second, and probably the most important result was the formulation of what I consider an overall theory running an organization. I call it Theory of Constraints and I regard everything I've done before as just a mere derivative of this theory* (...)" [32]. At the end of the 1980s, this theory became a tool for continuous improvement focused on processes, which, in the 1990s, would be complemented by the use of logic and Thinking Processes (TPs) as the bases for the resolution of the scenarios on which it is focused. No existing systems can have unlimited resources, because if they did, companies could increase profits without limit [4], [9] and [33-34]. These authors also frame a TOC in the area of continuous improvement and define its goal as the scope of improved organizational performance.

Among the variety of concepts involved in this theory and the extension of the philosophy on which it is based, the term 'restriction' is established as the starting point for all TOC philosophy. In the same publication that first referenced TOC, Goldratt (1988, P.453) defines the constraint as "*anything that limits a system from achieving higher performance versus its goal*". Regarding performance measurement systems, and based on the assumption that the goal of any business is to generate money, he defines three TOC indicators [3]: throughput (T) is the rate at which the system generates money associated with sales; inventory (I) is the money invested in the system to generate the Throughput; and Operating Expenses (OE) is the money the system spends in turning inventory into throughput [4], [6] and [9].

### 2.4    The Theory of Constraints in Services

TOC is a theory created mainly for industrial process optimization [4], [6-7], [9-10], [12-13] and [35-37]. The terminology used, its indicators, the tools for managing problems, the kind of thinking, their premises and, in general, all the elements involved, were developed according to the specific characteristics of the processes to transform raw material into tangible products [9-10] and [14].

Subsequent to the success of this methodology in the secondary sector and the increasing prominence of the service sector in the world economy, the idea arose of extending the application of TOC beyond traditional borders for which it had been designed [6-7]. Table 1 systematizes the TOC literature with relevance to services.

With respect to the relevant literature, as seen in Table 1, the first countries to publish studies on the application of TOC in various areas within the services sector were the United States, England, Australia and Israel, demonstrating the effectiveness of this philosophy in other areas besides the industrial. Although in recent years the literature related to the topic has significantly increased, the approaches are still too incipient to match the large number of studies on TOC developed for industry [6-7] and [13-14].

**Table 1.** Theory of constraints in services: literature review

| Theory of Constraints in Services | | | | |
|---|---|---|---|---|
| Authors | Country | Type | Sector | Objetives |
| [46] | Israel | Case Study | Education | To applying TOC to improve the quality of school education and productivity. |
| [47] | UK | | Health - Consulting | To modernize mental health services of the UK population through the merger of the only two service providers. |
| [35] | | | Unspecified | Study the impact of TOC concepts in administrative functions, applying performance indicators. |
| [42] | | | Health | Improving performance indicators identified in the system TOC. |
| [6], [7] | | | | Application of TOC for optimization and increased productivity of nonprofit organizations. |
| [43] | | | Construction | Support improved performance and productivity of the delivery of the service provided by the company. |
| [13] | USA | | Banking | To improve credit approval processes and overcome the constraints of the system. |
| [44] | | | Restaurants | To evaluate the possibility of the successful use of TOC TP tools to improve the performance of a small business. |
| [11] | | | Public Services | To consider using TOC TP in a public service organization for service and optimization of the processes. |
| [37] | | | Food | To evaluate the implementation, benefits and feasibility of TOC as a tool for planning and control of production in the service. |
| [45] | | | Consultancy | Improving the performance of billing system for increased business productivity. |
| [10] | | Theoretic | Service Sector | To create a classification model for implementing TOC in different service organizations. Adequacy of vocabulary TOC to services and developing solutions to potential problems TOC. |
| [8] | Australia | Exploratory | Banking | A classified model for Applying the Theory of Constraints to Service organizations |
| [36] | Australia / New Zelanda | | Operational Research OR/MS | To study TOC TP tools in relation to traditional methodologies OR / MS for building multi methodological tools. |

Based on the three elements (services sector, banking sector and TOC) and as a result of the analysis of the information extracted from the literature analyzed, this paper aims to, firstly, examine the implementation of the Theory of Constraints in the banking sector, and more specifically, the main TOC concepts (inventory, throughput, operating expenses and restrictions), based on the model to implement TOC for service organizations [9] and the study of the application of TOC in banks [8]. The research of Bramorski *et al.* [8] was the first one to show how banks can apply the principles of constraint management to improve their processes to obtain competitive advantage. However, it was made using a single bank example and not testing the importance of the several factors. Later on, Reid [13] proposed a five-step sequential process for implementing the TOC concepts. The approach is mainly descriptive and only an example is used to illustrate the framework. Therefore, further studies on the main performance indicators for specific services would be relevant, as they would facilitate the search for more effective solutions to typical problems of these services.

Next, an analysis is conducted of the factors involved in the decision to adopt TOC by companies in the banking sector, as supported in the literature review.

# 3    Methodology

This research can be considered a mixed study inspired by the different approaches and methodologies that were identified during the literature review on TOC in services. In Table 1 we can see the methodology used in several studies.

Initially, the study uses a qualitative methodology with a strong theoretical component and puts forward a proposal for future quantitative validation.

Given the lack of specific literature on the subject, this first theoretical approach is supported by the information extracted from reality through different instruments and it is framed in a multi-case study model. This approach provided the opportunity to include triangulation as a method aimed at achieving accuracy, precision and objectivity in answering the research question: How could TOC elements be characterized in banking?

Subsequently, as part of a quantitative approach to the second aim of the study, Table 2 presents the research hypotheses raised from the review of existing studies in the area. The total number of hypotheses are grouped into three categories according to the affinity of the issues that each addresses and involve some degree of influence on the decision to adopt TOC by banks, based on the level of current development of TOC for application in the banking sector (H1), the nature and characteristics of banking services (H2), and the internal management of sector institutions (H3).

Given the urgent need to increase productivity and optimize their processes to meet the many challenges that the global economy imposes, the banking sector was selected as the focus for this research. In addition, this sector remains highly regulated, and its operations and services have less variability among the institutions that compose it. Within this universe, Portuguese banks were chosen as the unit of analysis. With regard to the complete sample, the Bank of Portugal (BP) has records of 36 legally constituted and recognized banks, of which 24 are members of the Portuguese Association of Banks (APB), representing 94% of the banking system's total assets [38-39]. Given the default profile for the study, banks that are highly specialized business units of other banks, without participation in the commercial banking market or institutions without a minimum component of the universal banking concept, were excluded from the study. 24 banks were contacted via direct mail, e-mail and telephone in order to request their participation in the study. Following these contacts, four banks agreed to participate in the multi-case study. A fifth bank was included in the quantitative study, when it decided to participate only in this section of the research process due to time restrictions and internal priorities.

For the study of this sample, and according to the methodologies referred to when defining its two aims, three tools were used for data collection. To develop the multi-case study model, semi-structured personal interviews with predefined questions and issues were used. The interview script is divided into six sections (characterization of the interviewee, the bank, inventory, throughput, operating expenses and constraints), grouping 30 questions designed from the findings of the studies by Bramorski et al. [8] and Siha [10]. Also within the qualitative component, a tool was constructed in a matrix format, confronting the bank list for the Universal Banking model [18] with the four categories of services proposed by Schmenner [20], which reinforced the information obtained in the interviews, literature and details of the TOC elements within the model Schmenner. Four interviews were conducted in total (two in Lisbon and two in Porto) to high hierarchical level staff, corresponding to the commercial administration, management control and process improvement supervision.

**Table 2.** Research hypotheses

| Research Hypothesis | | Author |
|---|---|---|
| **H1: The level of development of TOC for application in the banking sector negatively influences their adoption by the banking sector.** | H1.1: The existence of TOC indicators for services influences the application of this theory in the banking sector. | [7-8] |
| | H1.2: The existence of TOC vocabulary for services influences the decision to adopt this theory in the banking sector. | [8], [37] |
| | H1.3: The existence of a formal method for implementing TOC in services influences their application in the banking sector. | [7], [13-14] |
| | H1.4: TOC is not a recognized tool in the banking sector. (*) | Exploratory |
| **H2: The nature and characteristics of banking services hinder the adoption of TOC by the banking sector.** | H2.1: The difficulty in determining the restrictions on banking processes, negatively influences the adoption of TOC in the banking sector. | [7-8], [44] |
| | H2.2: Creating TOC as a unique tool for the industrial sector, negatively influences their adoption by the industry. | [13], [37] |
| | H2.3: The particular characteristics of the services are crucial to the decision to apply TOC in the banking sector. (*) | [6-8], [10], [13-14], [37] |
| | H2.4: The nature of restrictions on services difficult to detect and thus, negatively influences the decision to apply TOC in the banking sector. (*) | [6-8],[13], [44] |
| **H3: The adoption of TOC in the banking sector depends on the internal management of sector institutions.** | H3.1: The organizational commitment of banking institutions determines the success of the application of TOC in the sector. | [40], [42] |
| | H3.2: Resistance to change in the organization, hinders the implementation of TOC in banking sector companies. | [45], [47] |
| | H3.3: The adoption of TOC in banks depends on motivation and leadership generated by management. | [40], [47] |
| | H3.4: The innovative culture of the bank determines the adoption of TOC to optimize their processes. | [37], [42], [44] |
| | H3.5: The absence of systematic, disciplined and with attention to detail processes in the banking companies, hinders the application of TOC in improving their processes. | [44], [45] |
| | H3.6: Banks do not have a formal policy of continuous improvement. | Exploratory |
| | H3.7: Banks do not consider that their systems are limited and, therefore, they do not consider the need for the use of tools such as TOC | [33] |
| | H3.8: Professional skills of banking employees determines adoption of TOC. (*) | Exploratory |
| | H3.9: The bank management provides the resources needed to drive continuous improvement programs. (*) | [40] |

*(*) These hypotheses will be tested only through the analysis of descriptive statistics. The results obtained on these hypotheses, did not allow an analysis of inferential statistics.*

Regarding the analysis of the determinants of adopting TOC by banks, which corresponds to the quantitative component of the study, we used an online survey format with 26 questions directly related to the research hypotheses presented in Table 3. This questionnaire was subject to a pre-test with two professionals in the area of continuous process improvement and the services sector, a statistician and a director of continuous improvement in a bank. 41 responses were obtained from banking employees from the five banks involved in the study, which are directly related to these institutions' area of continuous improvement and process optimization (51.3% response rate).

## 4     Multi-case Study

The multi-case study clearly showed that there are four main factors present in the dynamics of the current banking sector, also highlighted in the responses of the banks participating in the characterization of the TOC for the services sector. These are: the importance of technology resources and information systems, the need to increase the quality of their services, the use of human resources, and the current economic situation.

Based on these determinants, and in the case of the banks involved, the results obtained (see Table 3) served to relate the money needed to generate their profit (Inventory) with the use of economies of scale, the proper use of human resources, and capacity and efficiency in the production of services, because as one interviewee said, "the goal is to industrialize the banking business".

**Table 3.** TOC characterization by type of service in the banking sector

| Type of Service | Inventory | Throughput | Operating Expenses | Constraints |
|---|---|---|---|---|
| Service Factory | Financial resources required for the production of a service, whose minimum investment is maintained, although these are not sold in the expected amount. Example: outsourcing contracts, agency representation, technology applications. | The profit generated from the sale of banking services, mainly, the interests associated with home loans, deposits and trading fees. Gains from the sale of this service are related to the efficient management of customer relationships, management of prices, the bank's image, the efficiency of its business processes, streamlining expenses and any situation maximize the gain from the sale. | Capital invested in the creation and maintenance of the distribution network and the physical presence of the bank (agencies, branches, operations centers, etc.). | - Rigorous policies and excessive monitoring and control measures of the government audit institutions. - Hierarchical structure with insufficient control in the allocation, delimitation and compliance functions of each coworker. |
| Service Shop | Financial resources invested in production capacity and delivery of services provided (distribution network, physical presence and operations centers). | The profit generated from the provision of high quality perceived by the customer and which compels him to acquire (proximity, personalization, attention, etc.) | Capital invested in increasing the efficiency of processes based on systematic process creation and production of quality services, closer the ideal established standard. | - Manual processes without defining patterns and standards that facilitate the systematization of operations. - The variety of services offered and the complexity of its processes, problematize the most appropriate design method of work. |
| Mass Service | Financial resources invested in the efficiency of service production areas (backoffice operations center) and capital required for its management (maintenance, updating and automaización). | The profit generated by the responsiveness of the sales department and support areas, when producing a service requested by the demand. | Capital for the development of information technologies and systems. Automation of operations. | - Efficiency of the distribution network and sales force. - Efficiency of anti-fraud systems inside and outside the bank (ATM, credit and debit cards, virtual transactions, etc) - Automation of processes related to the current computing resource efficiency. |
| Professional Service | Financial resources required for personnel management in seeking to achieve the maximum utilization of human resources involved in the commercial and backofficede support areas (information systems, operations center). | The profit generated by the proper use of human resources (commercial department and support areas) for the provision of quality of its services. Gains associated with employees trained and constantly updated, optimization of existing resources and increased efficiency. | Capital invested in any aspect relating to the management of human resources in the production of services. | - Use of human resources and commercial department backoffice support. - Training of the sales force. - Demand management based on knowledge of its clients. |

Moreover, it was identified that the money generated by the bank (Throughput) is related to the profit that comes from the provision of these new services, being currently responsible for the profits of these institutions, among which the profits generated by trading and commission payment services. It should be noted that this generation of profits continues to liaise with the factors outlined at the beginning of this section and that, depending on the type of service, the weight of its influence varies. In relation to the costs incurred during the process of generating profits (Operating Expenses), the Portuguese banks analyzed continue to refer to the four factors presented at the beginning of the section (technology, human resources, quality, current economy), stating that their main expenses are borne by these situations.

Finally, the concept of constraint for the banks surveyed also corresponds to the claims identified in the literature, which explains that the constraints in services are generally not physical, they are self-imposed through policies and rules [13]. Three of the four banks attach great obstacles to the exercise associated with the existence of a large number of regulations and measures from the national government and the Portuguese central bank. In addition, the banks unanimously regard as restrictions those associated with current methods of work, to craft their processes, customer knowledge and the complexity of the systems. They also highlighted the obstacles imposed by limited technological resources and the influence of the state's economy.

# 5 Statistical Study

With regard to the sample, it is observed that most of the banking employees surveyed (75.6%) have a bachelor's degree, followed by those with completed secondary education (17.1%). The remaining percentage is distributed among staff with a master's degree (4.9%) and those who have no degree (2.4%). Analyzed in more detail, of the group of graduate employees, who represent the majority of the sample, 55% attended a degree in the area of administration, 33% in economics, and the remaining 11.1% are distributed in other areas, such as engineering, computing and marketing. Table 4 shows the results of the tests performed on the hypothesis presented in Table 2.

The statistical analysis shows that, globally, the claims made by the relevant theory are also present in the reality of Portuguese banks. In countries identified as pioneers in the study and application of TOC in services by the literature (USA and UK), the level of development of TOC for this sector is still classified as too young to spread in the same way as it did in the processing industry. Since its inception in 1980, the theory of constraints has evolved with the goal of becoming a highly efficient tool for optimizing the industrial sector; however, the existing theory does not verify the same trend for the tertiary sector. Based on this fact, it was expected that the level of development of TOC for services would influence banking sector companies to adopt this tool and make wide use of it in the financial business. The importance of the specific factors that support this claim (H1.1: Existence of indicators, H1.2: Existence of vocabulary, H1.3: Existence of a specific implementation method) was confirmed in the Portuguese banking reality. The importance of the specific factors that support this claim (H1.1: Existence of indicators, H1.2: Existence of vocabulary, H1.3: There is a specific implementation method) was confirmed in the Portuguese banking reality. However, it should be noted that, according to the responses from the banking employees surveyed, the majority (88.9%) attributed greater influence to the existence of a deployment method [7] and [13-14], while also recognizing the intervention of the other two. Regarding H1.4, it was observed that TOC is one of least well known continuous improvement tools among the banking employees surveyed with 7.3%, being surpassed only by Total Productive Maintenance with 4.9%.

**Table 4.** Compilation of the results of hypothesis tests

| Hypothesis | | | Statistical test | p-*value* | Decison |
|---|---|---|---|---|---|
| H1 | H1.1 | | Binomial | 0.000 | Reject |
| | H1.2 | | | 0.000 | Reject |
| | H1.3 | | | 0.018 | Reject |
| H2 | H2.1 | | Binomial | 0.002 | Reject |
| | H2.2 | | | 0.000 | Reject |
| | | | | 0.532 | Retain |
| H3 | H3.1 (*) | H3.2 | McNemar | 0.007 | Reject |
| | | H3.3 | | 1 | Retain |
| | | H3.5 | | 0.008 | Retain |
| | | H3.8 | | 0.000 | Reject |
| | H3.2 (*) | H3.1 | | 0.007 | Reject |
| | | H3.3 | | 0.001 | Reject |
| | | H3.5 | | 0.424 | Retain |
| | | H3.8 | | 0.000 | Reject |
| | H3.3 (*) | H3.1 | | 1 | Retain |
| | | H3.2 | | 0.001 | Reject |
| | | H3.5 | | 0.041 | Reject |
| | | H3.8 | | 0.000 | Reject |
| | H3.4 | | | 0.117 | Retain |
| | H3.5 (*) | H3.1 | | 0.078 | Retain |
| | | H3.2 | | 0.424 | Retain |
| | | H3.3 | | 0.041 | Reject |
| | | H3.8 | | 0.000 | Reject |
| | H3.6 | | Binomial | 0.000 | Reject |

Also related to the design of TOC according to industry, Parasuraman *et al.* [17] stated that the characteristics of services (intangibility, inseparability, heterogeneity and perish ability) should be carefully studied and taken into account when pursuing research in the area, as they are the conditions that make a significant difference between a service and product. Therefore, the fact that TOC have been designed to interact with characteristics totally contrary to those who own services clearly increases the challenge and, in turn, minimizes the intention of banks to try. Based on the above, it was not surprising to corroborate that the nature and characteristics of services (banking services in this case) are also involved in the decision to implement

TOC by Portuguese financial institutions (H2). Specifically, it was found that the fact that TOC has been created in the industrial context, also has some degree of influence on whether to adopt (H2.2), and that the degree of difficulty to detect restrictions on banking processes has a negative influence on the adoption of TOC (H2.1). The restrictions associated with service delivery systems (regulations, policies, measures, etc.) differ from those of typical industry (physical nature), i.e., being self-imposed and intangible, and they are thus difficult to clearly identify by bank management. With regard to the influence related to the difficulty in detecting the restrictions on services (H2.4), 61% of the population surveyed recognized that there was a "medium" degree of difficulty in identifying the real factors that limit the bank's processes, 24.4% consider it as "easy", while 14.6% reported feeling a "high difficulty". From the above, it should be noted that recognizing the existence of some degree of difficulty in detecting the restrictions by the respondents in this study, could also be a determining factor in the behavior of these banking institutions regarding the use of TOC.

Finally, despite being a statement reiterated by the literature, the responses of the Portuguese banking employees did not allow us to confirm, in general, that bank management is a factor in the adoption of TOC. In fact, 80.6% of the respondents reported feeling that their bank is committed to the implementation of continuous improvement tools; however, only 2.4% reported knowledge that TOC had been implemented, a situation that reinforces the independence of these two events (the bank's management and the decision to adopt TOC). However, the results indicate that there are specific factors within management which could become crucial in deciding to implement TOC, such as organizational commitment in implementing continuous improvement programs (H3.1), the attitude towards change (H3.2), motivation and leadership (H3.3), and existence of systematic processes (H3.5).

When relating academic background with knowledge of this instrument (H3.8), the results show that the recognition of TOC is concentrated among graduate banking employees (77.18%) in areas related mainly to management (50%), the remainder being distributed in areas of economics, information technology or marketing. Finally, it was considered important to determine the position of the banks on the availability of resources (not only financial) to drive continuous improvement programs, a crucial factor in the decision to adopt TOC according to Bessant et al. [40]. It is observed that 82.9% of the respondents recognize the existence of departments dedicated to the implementation of continuous improvement programs to operate processes within the structure of these banks, 36% of respondents stated that these programs are usually developed by the internal structure of the bank for its own use, 2.8% state that only existing continuous improvement programs are adopted, and 61% use both strategies.

# 6      Conclusion

This study proposed a characterization of the main TOC elements (Inventory, Throughput, Operating Expenses and Constraints) according to the different types of services defined by Schemenner [20] and based on studies by Bramorski et al. [8] and Siha [10]. It was found that these TOC elements in banking are closely linked to four factors identified in the current global financial sector and in Portuguese banks, which could also influence the results of the multi-case study used in reaching this goal. These are: the importance of technological resources and information systems, the need to increase the quality of their services, the use of human resources, and the current economic situation.

Through the quantitative component of the data analysis performed in this study, we analyzed, for the reality of the Portuguese banking sector, the factors considered by the theory as determinants for organizations to adopt TOC as one of their continuous improvement programs. Based on the responses from the Portuguese banking employees, it was concluded that the current development of TOC for services, and specifically for banking, is still insufficient to enable those companies to include it in their management. It was also possible to infer that the nature and characteristics of services is another factor which greatly limits the adoption of TOC by banks, as their particular properties make their associated restrictions more difficult to identify. Within this aspect, it was also possible to validate that, since TOC emerged within the industrial sector, the Portuguese banking organizations are suspicious of adopting this management tool. Unawareness of the existence of this tool beyond the boundaries of the industry could be one of the biggest obstacles to its spread and development in other fields.

Although the literature noted that the management of these companies is influential on the decision to adopt TOC, the sample did not confirm this assumption. Specifically, some elements in the management of these organizations are crucial in this decision (commitment, attitude towards change, commitment and organizational leadership). However some could not be confirmed (the innovative culture of the company) and others could not be part of the inferential statistical analysis due to the behavior of the responses. The process of this research and the results obtained were somewhat limited, mainly due to the reluctance of most active banks in Portugal to participate in the study. Furthermore, and considering that one of the advantages of conducting personal interviews is the possibility of examining the interviewee responses through additional factors, not only by consciously transmitted information [41], it was possible to detect that some of the banking employees interviewed refrained from responding, with details and faithfully, to questions they considered compromised the bank's privacy.

Also in connection with the information extracted from the Portuguese banking reality, the behavior of the responses was also identified as another limitation to this study. This limitation gives rise to the proposal of a topic for future research, to focus on determining which of these factors are more or less influential on the decision to adopt banking TOC. In this case, the fidelity of the process and results should be safeguarded, with more time for the development of the study, a broader number of participating banks and responses to the questionnaires. With regard to the characterization of the TOC in the sector, having only made a first exploratory approach (corresponding to qualitative multi-case study), the proposal is to compare these results with the reality of the banking sector overall, using the inferential statistical validation techniques similar to those used in the quantitative component of this research.

**Acknowledgement.** This work is funded by the ERDF through the Programme COMPETE and by the Portuguese Government through FCT - Foundation for Science and Technology, project PTDC/EGE-GES/099741/2008 and PTDC/EGE-GES/117692/2010.

# References

1. UNCTAD: World Investment Report-Transnational Corporations, Agricultural Production and Development. In: United Nations Conference on Trade and Development, New York and Génova (2009)
2. OCDE: Annual Report. The Organisation for Economic Co-operation and Development, Paris (2005)
3. Goldratt, E.M., Cox, J.: The Goal, 2nd edn. North River Press, Croton-on-Hudson (1992)
4. Mabin, V.J., Balderstone, S.J.: The Performance of the Theory of Constraints Methodology: Analysis and Discussion of Successful TOC Applications. Int. J. Oper. Prod. Man. 23(6), 568–595 (2003)
5. AGI: Overview of Results, Goldratt Institute, http://www.goldratt.com/ (accessed on September 26, 2012)
6. Motwani, J., Klein, D., Harowitz, R.: The Theory of Constraints in Services: Part 1 – the Basics. Manag. Serv. Qual. 6(1), 53–56 (1996a)
7. Motwani, J., Klein, D., Harowitz, R.: The Theory of Constraints in Services: Part 2 – Examples from Health Care. Manag. Serv. Qual. 6(2), 30–34 (1996b)
8. Bramorski, T., Madan, M., Motwani, J.: Application of the Theory of Constraints in Banks. The Bankers Magazine, 53–59 (1997)
9. Shostack, L.: Breaking Free from Product Marketing. J. Marketing 41(2), 73–80 (1977)
10. Siha, S.: A classified model for applying the theory of constraints to service organizations. Manag. Serv. Qual. 9(4), 255–264 (1999)
11. Shoemaker, T.E., Reid, R.A.: Applying the TOC Thinking Process: A case study in the government sector. Human Systems Manage. 24(1), 21–37 (2005)
12. Ku, E.K.-C.: An Investigation of Theory of Constraints (TOC) and Related Techniques in Health Care Operations. MSc Operations Management, University of Nottingham (2007)
13. Reid, R.A.: Applying the TOC five-step focusing process in the service sector: A banking subsystem. Manag. Serv. Qual. 17(2), 209–234 (2007)
14. Ellis, S.C.: A Theory of Constraints Service Systems Improvement Method: Case of the Airline Turnaround Problem. PhD in Industrial and Systems Engineering, Florida International University (2011)
15. Zeithaml, V., Bitner, M.J.: Service Marketing, 1st edn. McGraw-Hill, New York (1996)
16. Grönroos, C.: Service management and marketing: customer management in service competition. Chichester (2007)
17. Parasuraman, A., Zeithaml, V.A., Berry, L.L.: A Conceptual Model of Service Quality and Its Implications for Future Research. J. Marketing 49(4), 41–50 (1985)
18. Fitzsimons, J.A., Fitzsimons, M.J.: Service Management: Operations, Strategy, and Information Technology. McGraw-Hill, Boston (2011)
19. Rubalcaba, L.: The New Service Economy. Challenges and policy implications for Europe, Cheltenham, UK (2007)
20. Schmenner, R.W.: How can service businesses survive and prosper? Sloan Manage. Rev. 27(3), 21–32 (1986)

21. Santillán-Salgado, R.J.: Banking Concentration in the European Union during the Last Fifteen Years. Panoeconomicus 2, 245–266 (2011)
22. Canhoto, A.: Portuguese banking: A structural model of competition in the deposits market. R. Financial Econ. 13(s1-2), 41–63 (2004)
23. Bateson, J.E.G.: Do we need service marketing? In: Eiglier, P., et al. (eds.) Marketing Consumer Services: New Insights, Report no. 77-115, pp. 1–30. Marketing Science Institute, Cambridge (1977)
24. Lopes, J.M.G.: Direito Bancário Institucional, Lisboa (2001)
25. Martins, E.F.: Marketing Relacional na Banca. A Fidelização e a Venda Cruzada, Porto (2006)
26. Honoban, P.: Consequences for Greece and Portugal of the opening-up of the European banking market. Development Economics Group, The World Bank (1999)
27. Barth, J.R., Nolle, D.E., Rice, T.N.: Commercial Banking Structure, Regulation and Performance: An International Comparison, US Controller of the Currency. Economics Working Paper 97-6 (1997)
28. Decressin, J., Mauro, P.: The Portuguese banking system: Feeling its pulse on the eve of EMU membership. IMF Country Report 98/127 (1998)
29. Jacobs, F.R.: The OPT Scheduling System: A review of a new production scheduling system. P&IM J. 24(3), 47–51 (1983)
30. Goldratt, E.M., Cox, J.: The Goal. NorthRiver Press, Croton-on-Hudson (1984)
31. Goldratt, E.M., Fox, R.E.: The Race. NorthRiver Press, New York (1986)
32. Goldratt, E.M.: Computerized shop floor scheduling. Int. J. Prod. Res. 26(3), 443 (1988)
33. Rahman, S.U.: Theory of constraints. A review of the philosophy and its applications. Int. J. Oper. Prod. Man. 18(4), 336–355 (1998)
34. Lubitsh, G., Doyle, C., John, V.: The impact of theory of constraints (TOC) in an NHS trust. J. Manage. Development 24(2), 116–131 (2005)
35. Gillespie, M.W., Patterson, M.C., Bob, H.: TOC Beyond Manufacturing. Industrial Manage. 41(6), 22–25 (1999)
36. Davies, J., Mabin, V.J., Balderstone, S.J.: The theory of constraints: a methodology apart? - a comparison with selected OR/MS methodologies. Omega-Int. J. Manage. S 33(6), 506–524 (2005)
37. Spencer, M.S.: Theory of constraints in a service application: the Swine Graphics case. Int. J. Prod. Res. 38(5), 1101–1108 (2000)
38. BP Instituições Autorizadas: Banco de Portugal, http://www.bportugal.pt/pt-PT/Supervisao/Paginas/Instituicoesautorizadas.aspx#anchor (accessed on September 15, 2012)
39. APB Associados: Associação Portuguesa de Bancos, http://www.apb.pt/associados (accessed on March 11, 2012)
40. Bessant, J., Caffyn, S., Gallagher, M.: An evolutionary model of continuous improvement behavior. Technovation 21(2), 67–77 (2001)
41. Saunders, M.N.K., Lewis, P., Thornhill, A.: Research methods for business students, 3rd edn. FT Prentice Hall, Harlow (2003)
42. Gupta, M., Kline, J.: Managing a community mental health agency: A Theory of Constraints based framework. Total Qual. Manage. 19(3), 281–294 (2008)
43. Motwani, J., Vogelsang, K.: The theory of constraints in practice – at Quality Engineering. Manag. Serv. Qual. 6(6), 43–47 (1996)
44. Reid, R.A., Cornier, J.R.: Applying the TOC TP: A case study in the service sector. Manag. Serv. Qual. 13(9), 349–369 (2003)

45. Taylor III, L.J., Thomas, E.E.: Applying Goldratt's thinking process and the theory of constraints to the invoicing system of an oil and gas engineering consulting firm. Performance Improvement 47(9), 26–34 (2008)
46. Goldratt, R., Weiss, N.: Significant Enhancement of Academic Achievement through Application of the Theory of Constraints (TOC). Human Systems Manage. 24(1), 13–19 (2005)
47. Ritson, N., Waterfield, N.: Managing Change: the Theory of Constraints in the Mental Health Service. Strategic Change 14(8), 449–458 (2005)

# Service Innovation Analytics: Towards an Approach for Validating Frameworks for Service Innovation Capabilities via Text Mining

Niels Feldmann[1], Marc Kohler[1], Steven O. Kimbrough[2], and Hansjörg Fromm[1]

[1] Karlsruhe Institute of Technology, Karlsruhe Service Research Institute,
Englerstrasse 11, 76131 Karlsruhe, Germany
[2] University of Pennsylvania, The Wharton School, 3730 Walnut Street,
Philadelphia, PA 19104-6340 USA
{Niels.Feldmann,Marc.Kohler,Hansjoerg.Fromm}@kit.edu
Kimbrough@wharton.upenn.edu

**Abstract.** The importance of innovation for companies to gain competitive advantage is widely acknowledged. Realizing service innovations has shown to provide some particular challenges to organizations. Consequently, in recent years, several frameworks of capabilities for service innovation have been published; however, often not yet validated. Conventional empirical validation approaches are time and resource intense. In this research-in-progress paper we aim for indications that text mining can be applied to companies' documents written in natural language so that frameworks for service innovation capabilities can be validated. Building on established methods in text mining, we are working towards an approach to realize this. The paper outlines the approach and reports on the encouraging results from an exploratory study, which we have conducted by applying the approach to a single capability from a prominently discussed service innovation capability framework.

**Keywords:** Service innovation capabilities frameworks, text mining, framework validation, machine learning, innovativeness of companies, representations of service innovation capabilities

## 1    Motivation

In January 2011, Starbucks launched its mobile payment program: The previously existing Starbucks Card – a loyalty card with payment functionality – got integrated into a mobile app. The individual card's barcode got stored in the app in order to provide convenient and fast transactions at checkout. On December 6, 2011 Starbucks declared that 9,000 stores in the US had already implemented the program, accounting for 26 million mobile transactions in under a year. Consequently, Starbucks claimed to have the "nation's largest mobile payment program" [25]. Shortly after, in April 2012, the press reported 42 million transactions since the program's start [20].

J.F. e Cunha, M. Snene, and H. Nóvoa (Eds.): IESS 2013, LNBIP 143, pp. 73–85, 2013.

This example demonstrates some key characteristics of service innovation [30]: Many novelties are of architectural nature [10], i.e., they are new combinations of existing concepts. As the example suggests, such innovations are often created without an R&D program [26, 27]. Any employee, even without special expert knowledge, could have raised the idea of integrating an existing barcode into an app, and using it as an interface. Hence, entry barriers for players from other industries seem to be lower, in particular since the rise of Internet- and App-based services. In order not to be taken by surprise by developments of incumbents and new entrants, modern organizations are increasingly trying to take a proactive and more systematic approach to realizing service innovation [17, 29].

Several frameworks for service innovation capabilities have been published in recent years, one of the latest being a model by den Hertog et al. [8]. In this context, we define a Service Innovation Capabilities Framework as a set of capabilities that enable a company to realize service innovation. While these frameworks are often based on theoretical work, empirical validation of the latest models, including the den Hertog model, is lacking. Conventional empirical validation suggests methods such as expert interviews or experiments [4], all of which are time and resource intensive at best. In this work-in-progress paper, we are aiming at a novel approach, indicated in summary form by our research question:

**Research Question:** Is there an indication that text mining algorithms can be applied to documents written in natural language so that frameworks for service innovation capabilities can be validated?

We report here on an exploratory study, which has yielded very encouraging and positive results regarding our Research Question. The paper is structured as follows. In the subsequent chapter on related work we will select a service innovation capabilities framework, the validity of which is to be examined by our approach. In addition, we provide a brief overview of related literature on text mining and select the method we adopted in our research. Chapter three contains methodological descriptions of our approach, including the creation of a vocabulary to be used for the text mining tasks, document acquisition, and the method we used to evaluate our approach. The results of our exploratory study are presented in chapter four, followed by our conclusions, limitations and an outlook in chapter five.

## 2    Related Work

As pointed out in chapter 1, the motivation of this paper is to assess the feasibility of using text mining to empirically validate a service innovation capabilities framework. Firstly, this requires the selection of an appropriate service innovation capabilities framework. Secondly, we are covering related work in the area of "text mining for validating innovation capabilities frameworks".

### 2.1    Service Innovation Capabilities Frameworks

In recent years, several frameworks for service innovation capabilities have been published. Innovation capabilities in this sense are conceptualized as improving the productivity of resources and assets of the firm, specifically in facilitating the creation of innovation outputs [9, 18]. Amongst others, examples of these frameworks are the Innovation Capability Maturity Model (ICMM) of Essmann and du Prez [9], Müller-Prothmann and Stein's Integrated Innovation Maturity Model ($I^2MM$) [22], and the previously mentioned model of den Hertog et al. [8].

In this paper, as a test case, we consider the framework by den Hertog et al. [8], since it is one of the most recent frameworks, it is specifically designed for innovation management in service firms [15], and it is being advanced by members of the service science community. This framework is admittedly of a "conceptual" nature and without empirical validation heretofore [8:505]. The model itself encompasses six service innovation capabilities: *Sensing user needs and technological options[1]*, *Conceptualizing, (Un-) Bundling, (Co-) Producing and orchestrating, Scaling and stretching,* and *Learning and adapting.* It suggests that innovative firms will score high on these categories.

In our study, we focus on one of the six capabilities in the den Hertog framework: "(Co-) Producing and orchestrating". This represents an organization's aptitude to organize and leverage open innovation, an aspect of innovation management, the importance of which has been prominently demonstrated in the past decade [7, 12, 16].

### 2.2    Related Work in the Area of Text Mining

We have not found prior work that deals with the analysis of text to validate innovation capabilities frameworks, let alone any work on service specific innovation frameworks. However, there is literature on the application of text mining in the area of innovation management. The closest to our research goal is a study by Kabanoff and Keegan [13] (See citations therein to a body of relevant earlier work.). They use computer aided text analysis (CATA) to assess annual reports of Australian Stock Exchange (ASX) listed firms (2002-04) in order to measure indicators of the level of top-teams' attention to seven strategic dimensions (including innovation). They then examine the validity of these indicators by relating them to the Innovation Index Score (IIS), an independently derived indicator of firms' level of successful value adding innovation activity developed by the Intellectual Property Research Institute of Australia (IPERA). In terms of annual report contents, only the letter to shareholders from the CEO or managing director is included. The sample is based on a database of 117 firms in 2002, 775 in 2003, and 151 in 2004.

## 3    Methodology

Our motivating conjecture is that the vocabulary used to describe the capabilities in a framework can be employed to classify companies based on the framework. To illustrate schematically, let's assume a framework has capabilities A, B, and C and further predicts that companies scoring high in categories A, B, and C can be classified as X, Y, and Z. We call this a direct classification (see Figure 1). Based on

---

[1] In the original publication, this category is labeled 'Signaling user needs and technological options'. However, following the textual description of the capability we can conclude that 'sensing' was meant rather than 'signaling'.

this direct classification, we conjecture that the vocabulary describing capability A (B, C) will serve to classify companies as X (Y, Z), based on the match with documents of the companies in question. We call this an indirect classification (see Figure 1).

Let's apply this to the context of the previously selected service innovation capabilities framework. The den Hertog framework has six capabilities: A – F. Out of these capabilities we have chosen one, (Co-)Producing and Orchestrating, that is known to be a strong driver of innovativeness (see chapter 2.1). The model predicts that companies showing strengths with regard to this capability should be more innovative. Based on this direct classification we conjecture that a company is innovative, if the vocabulary used to describe the capability and the text the company uses in their documents show certain similarities, i.e., the vocabulary has a high matching score.

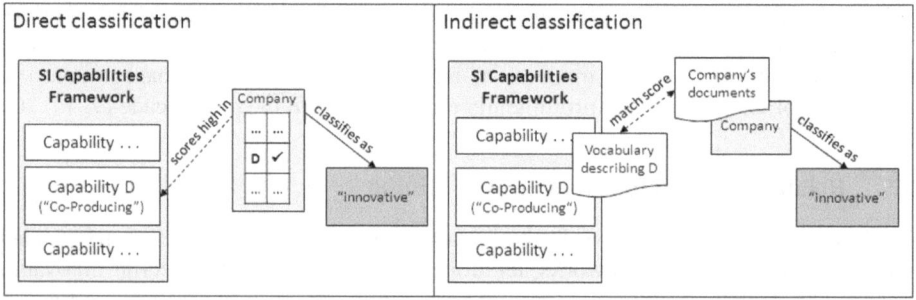

**Fig. 1.** Direct and indirect classification of an organization according to its innovativeness

With regard to the new approach to the validation of the selected capability of the framework, there is now only one step missing. When applying the indirect classification to a set of companies, it will suggest some of them as more innovative than others. Consequently, these results need to be compared to an externally available classification of the same set of companies in a confusion matrix (see Figure 2). If both sides match significantly, we can consider the vocabulary representing the selected capability to be significant. According to our conjecture above, this implies that the capability of the framework in question receives (a degree of) validation.

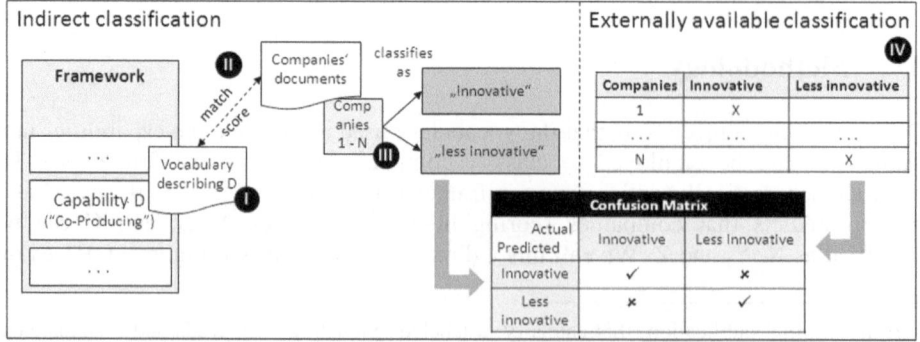

**Fig. 2.** Overview of the framework validation approach

Four major components are required in order to conduct the framework validation as described above. First, a vocabulary, sometimes also called a concept vector [19], describing the selected service innovation capability needs to be generated ("I" in Figure 2). Second, an appropriate text mining approach needs to be identified ("II"). Third, a set of companies ("III") is required that provides a satisfactory set of documents to analyze. Fourth, for each of the set's firms, an externally available classification needs to exist ("IV").

## 3.1    Vocabulary Creation

Chen et al. [6] describe two methods of obtaining a vocabulary, the ex-post and the ex-ante approach. Ex-post in our context means to learn which of the words in a collection of documents are most effective in telling whether an organization shows a high level of aptitude with regard to the selected den Hertog capability. Chen et al. point out that any ex-post mapping of predictive words to concepts is problematic for a number of reasons, and particularly because the predictive words are found entirely internally and so lack external validity. The ex-ante approach means generating a vocabulary based on external knowledge, such as existing literature or expert insight. This method is pointed out as more naturally interpretable and credible. Subsequently, we will follow this approach.

To create an initial vocabulary that represents den Hertog's service innovation capabilities and that is grounded in practice as much as possible, we undertook a series of interviews with five managers and executives from German knowledge-intensive business services firms. We conducted the interviews in May and June 2012 during a different study [15]. These approximately 60 minute long interviews were carried out in person and over the telephone. We presented the experts with the framework's six capabilities, including short textual descriptions. They were asked to "name assets that support or represent the individual SI capabilities in their organisation", sequentially for each of the capabilities. To ensure a wide collection of assets the interviewees were also provided with an overview on governance-oriented asset types, provided by Weill and Ross [32]. We transcribed the interviews and subsequently broke them up into a redundancy-free, cleansed list of words and phrases.

As mentioned above, in this exploratory study, we were interested in determining what might be learned by way of validating a single capability in the den Hertog framework, that of (Co-)producing and Orchestrating. In order to extend the initial vocabulary for this specific capability, we canvassed related literature [2, 11] for words and phrases representing it.

The resulting vocabulary (words and phrases) was translated (often breaking up a phrase into its component words) into the standard format used by our matching software (see Figure 3). This format allows regular expressions to generalize specific words and phrases into patterns, e.g., to allow singulars and plurals, or to permit a small number of intervening words in a given phrase.

## 3.2    Text Mining Approach EMCUT

According to our framework validation approach (Figure 2), the second required component is an appropriate text mining approach. In order to answer our research question, we wish to match a number of companies to classifications "innovative" and "less innovative", based on text documents associated with these entities. This approach has been termed EMCUT (entity matching [to] classification [schemes] using text) [6]. Chen et al. mention three different ways to solve EMCUT problems: Content analysis, a novel method called the "external approach", and machine learning.

```
1       \bcollaboration\b\W{1,}?\bplatform\b  collaboration_platform
1       \bopen\b\W{1,}?\binnovation\b open_innovation
1       \bcustomer\b\W{1,}?\bintegration\b    customer_integration
1       \bclient\b\W{1,}?\bintegration\b      client_integration
1       \bcustomer\b\W{1,}?\binvolvement\b    customer_involvement
1       \bclient\b\W{1,}?\binvolvement\b      client_involvement
1       \bexternal\b\W{1,}?\bexperts{0,1}\b   external_expert(s)
1       \bpartner\b\W{1,}?\bnetworks{0,1}\b   partner_network(s)
1       \bsharing\b\W{1,}(\w{1,}\W{1,}){0,}\bideas{0,1}\b    sharing_idea(s)
1       \bcrowdsourc\w{1,}\b    crowdsourc*
1       \brelationships{0,1}\b\W{1,}\bwith\b  relationship(s)_with
1       \blisten\w{0,}\b\W{1,}\bto\b  listen*_to
1       \binvolv\w{1,}\b        involv*
1       \bcollaboration\w{0,}\b\W{1,}\bwith\b collaboration*_with
1       \bco-{0,1}operation\w{0,}\b\W{1,}?\bwith\b    cooperation*_with
```

**Fig. 3.** Excerpt of the study's vocabulary in the standard format used by the matching software

Content analysis simply means reading the text documents and assigning them to the relevant capabilities manually. Validation techniques to support this method are ample and well established, e.g., voting among multiple readers to ensure readers understand and assign the sources correctly [14, 21, 23, 31]. On the other side, some disadvantages of content analysis are known: Obviously the approach is time-consuming, labor-intensive and therefore costly and does not scale favorably. In addition, skilled readers might be required and even they can miss important information, as a study by Pennebaker on the opacity of function words teaches us [24]. Thus, it appears to be an inefficient approach for validating a comprehensive capabilities framework.

Secondly, Chen et al. [6] present a novel method called the external approach. Applied to our study, this would mean providing a vocabulary as a representation for the capabilities, based on external knowledge, and using this vocabulary to classify documents. The vocabulary is built without empirical evidence that it actually does classify documents and the associated companies, according to the classifications. In other words, we would build a vocabulary for "innovative companies" and "less innovative companies" without any empirical evidence whether it may work or not. This setup does not apply to the conditions we are facing in our case. As described in the previous section, we derived our vocabulary from expert interviews and literature reviews, providing empirical evidence that the items of the vocabulary are appropriate indicators to tell "innovative companies" from less innovative.

This leaves us with the third way to address EMCUT problems: Machine learning. Chen et al. also point out that machine learning approaches have proven to be effective for large document collections, a condition that applies to our context, as we will demonstrate below. Hence, machine learning, in particular supervised machine learning, is the approach we are choosing for this study.

For matching documents associated with companies to a classification, the so-called "document classification using supervised learning" approach is an established method [1, 19]. In our context this means that we need to sample a list of companies and their documents and assign them to the classification "innovative companies" and "less innovative companies" by human judgment (see 3.3 for further information). We called this step "externally available classification" in Figure 2. Subsequently, a machine learning technique, such as 'classification trees', can be applied to learn about the classifiers, i.e., words and phrases, that help discriminate "innovative" from "less innovative" companies. In our case we start this machine learning with a given vocabulary derived via the previously explained ex-ante process and score all documents initially. Then, we use machine learning to learn about which words and phrases of our vocabulary need to occur how often and in which pattern in a company's documents to be able to assign it to the classifications "innovative" or "less innovative" ("indirect classification" in Figure 2).

For our explorative study, we employed MATLAB's classification tree implementation, with 10-fold cross validation, to find a robust, pruned tree (rule set) to classify the documents of the companies in question based on their match scores with the vocabulary described above.

### 3.3    Document Acquisition and Externally Available Classification

The third component of our validation approach is a set of companies providing documents to match with the previously created vocabulary (see "III" in Figure 2). In order to be able to carry out our validation approach as described above, we needed to identify companies who have been classified with regard to their innovativeness before, i.e., for which an externally available classification (component "IV" in Figure 2) was available. Since these two components are mutually interdependent, the acquisition of documents and the identification of a corresponding externally available classification are described jointly below. Also, document acquisition and identification of the externally available classification were done in cooperation with Chen et al. [6] since both studies required similar data (for a more detailed explanation on the document acquisition process see therein).

In 2010, BusinessWeek published a ranking of international firms according to their innovativeness [5]. The Boston Consulting Group (BCG), contracted by BusinessWeek, produced this ranking that we decided to use as a starting point for our company selection and document acquisition process.

Between November 2009 and January 2010, BCG conducted a survey [28], which was sent to a panel of senior management members of the BusinessWeek Market Advisory Board. 1,590 executives of the panel, from all major markets and industries, replied. Their result was subsequently complemented by the weighted average of three financial variables: three-year shareholder returns, three-year revenue growth, and three-year margin growth. While the panel's feedback accounted for 80 percent of the final ranking, shareholder returns represented another 10 percent and revenue growth as well as margin growth accounted for another 5 percent each.

The resulting BCG report ranks the 50 most innovative firms of which we selected all 22 US based companies. They form our list of "innovative companies". The primary reasons for this selection were homogeneity and availability of documents.

To compile a sample of "less innovative companies", we determined the industry of each of the previously chosen innovative companies and then randomly selected 5 other companies from the same industry that were not ranked as innovative in the BCG list. For the resulting 132 companies (innovative and less innovative), we then collected annual reports for four years, i.e. 2007 to 2010, in order to have a reasonable representation of recent behavior. Also, since text data is known to be noisy, we aimed for more than just a single year to gain more stability.

We primarily obtained those annual reports from the companies' websites. In case they were not available, as some companies used Form 10-K as requested by the SEC (U.S. Securities and Exchange Commission), we retrieved those Form 10-K filings from the SEC (http://www.sec.gov/edgar/searchedgar/webusers.htm). Nevertheless, there was some attrition in the documents collected (e.g. industry sets too small or documents could not be converted into a suitable format). In the end, our sample comprised 455 annual reports, 78 from innovative companies and 377 from less innovative ones.

# 4    Results

We applied the approach described above to the 455 selected documents and found that indeed the vocabulary for the den Hertog '(Co-) Producing & Orchestrating' capability, derived from interviews and literature, successfully classifies firms as innovative or not based on a disjoint set of documents.

Our results are embodied in two data structures: A listing of the discovered classification rules, which we present in tree form, and a confusion matrix that indicates the number of correct and incorrect classifications with the discovered classification rules.

Figure 4 shows the discovered classification tree that is robustly produced from multiple runs of 10-fold cross validation trials by pruning the full tree found by the classification tree program. The numerical scores shown in the tree are the breakpoints discovered by the classification tree algorithm in fitting the model to the data. For example, the top (root) node is "people" with branches labeled "< 2.6047" and ">= 2.6047". Scores for individual documents were obtained, using our software, by counting the number of "hits" (occurrences) of a term in the vocabulary (e.g., "people") in the company documents. The score for a given document for a given term is the number of hits times 100,000, divided by the length of the document in characters. The 100,000 is the value we gave to the program variable `normalizer`. It is there simply to scale the scores to numerically convenient ranges. Continuing with the example of the "people" entry in the vocabulary, the scores for the 455 documents ranged from 0 (no occurrence of the term) to a maximum of 53.62217813. The mean and median scores were 3.433276676 and 0.842969529, respectively.

What Figure 4 indicates is that the classification tree algorithm found that splitting the 455 documents at 2.6047 occurrences on "people" is highly effective at separating the corpus into innovative and less innovative firms. In fact, if we simply limit the tree to this top node only, it would split the sample into two groups: "Innovative", said to be innovative if the "people" score (number of occurrences) is >= 2.6047, and

"Less Innovative", said to be less innovative if the score is < 2.6047. The confusion matrix for this extremely simplified tree is shown in Table 1:

**Table 1.** Confusion Matrix for node "people"

| Actual<br>Predicted | "Innovative" | "Less Innovative" |
|---|---|---|
| Innovative | 49 | 80 |
| Less innovative | 29 | 297 |

Remarkably, this extremely simplified tree scores (49+297)/455 (76%) correct. The scores for the other nodes in the tree in Figure 4 have a corresponding interpretation.

Proceeding now to the pruned best tree emerging from cross validation (Figure 4), Table 2 constitutes the confusion matrix associated with that tree.

**Table 2.** Confusion matrix for best tree (as depicted in Figure 4)

| Actual<br>Predicted | "Innovative" | "Less Innovative" |
|---|---|---|
| Innovative | 72 | 24 |
| Less innovative | 6 | 353 |

The main points arising are as follows. (1) The numbers in the confusion matrix are very encouraging. Of the 455 documents, 72+353 or 93.4% are classified correctly. (2) Precision, i.e. the share of correctly predicted classifications, was at least 75% (= 72/(72+24) = 75%). Recall, i.e. the share of documents, the actual classification of which was 'discovered' by our approach, was at least 92% (= 72/(72+6) = 92%). Both impressive in the context of Information Retrieval numbers commonly encountered [3, 19]. (3) In general, given how the words and phrases of the vocabulary were chosen, we might expect that documents having comparatively higher mentions of these terms would score comparatively more innovative. (4) Quite remarkably, there are 277 documents (annual reports) in which "people" scores < 2.6047, "discussion(s)" scores < 8.79336, "partner network(s)" scores < 0.318633, "innovator(s)" scores < 0.0985975, AND "relationship(s) with" scores < 9.66926. Of these 277 documents, all predicted by the classification tree to be associated with less innovative firms, in fact 4 are from innovative firms and 273 are from less innovative firms. Further, this intuitively fits very well with point (3). (5) The richest leaf for innovative firms has "people" scores >= 2.6047, "involve*" < 3.38444, "stakeholder(s)" < 2.50445, AND "strategy" or "strategies" < 19.1911. Firms at this leaf are predicted to be innovative. From the sample corpus, 65 firms are so classified, of which 44 are indeed innovative firms and 21 not. Thus, while the tree classifier is very accurate at detecting less innovative firms (see (4)), it is less accurate, but still very good, at detecting innovative firms. (6) With one other exception ("board(s)" < 8.33161), all innovative leaves of the tree branch to the right, that is come from the >= branch of the parent node. (7) The tree in Figure 4, found as best under 10-fold cross

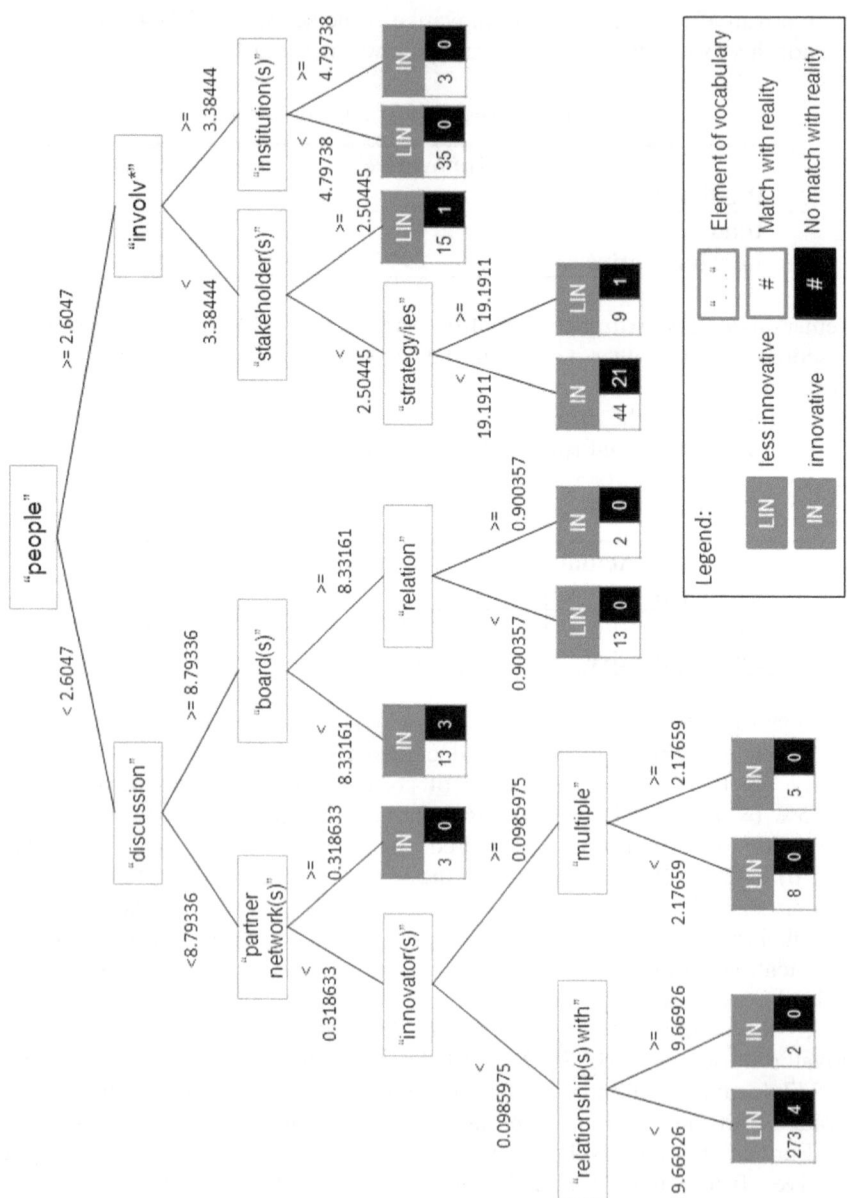

**Fig. 4.** Classification tree for den Hertog's capability "(Co-)Producing & Orchestrating"

validation, has 13 leaf nodes. The full tree found by the regression tree algorithm produced a much larger tree, with 28 leaf nodes, that is extremely accurate in classifying the training data. As is standard practice, we must assume that the full tree over fits the data and will predict poorly on out of sample case. Therefore, we applied 10-fold cross validation as a way to find a smaller tree that performs well on randomly drawn samples of the training data. The tree in Figure 4 is the result. It constitutes a considerable trimming of the full tree found by the classification tree program, which has 28 leaf nodes, and is very reassuring in the face of worries about over-fitting the data.

# 5    Conclusion and Outlook

Building on existing research in the fields of service innovation capabilities frameworks and applications of text mining to learn more about companies' innovativeness, this research in progress paper contributes to finding ways to analytically validate those frameworks. In our exploratory study we have found an indication that text mining algorithms can be applied to companies' documents in natural language so that frameworks for service innovation capabilities can be validated. For this, we selected a capability called "(Co-)Producing and Orchestrating" from the recent framework of den Hertog et. al. [8]. By involving experts on service innovation, as well as analyzing corresponding literature, we created a vocabulary representing this capability. By employing machine learning approaches, the vocabulary was matched with documents of companies, the innovativeness of which was given by an external ranking. The vocabulary demonstrated to serve well to classify companies according to their innovativeness. On the assumption that the vocabulary is a strong representation of the selected capability, we can conjecture that the capability is a strong determinant of innovativeness itself. The latter means that we have validated the capability in question. If, in subsequent steps, we could demonstrate the same for the remaining five capabilities of the den Hertog framework, an important step towards validating or rejecting the framework would have been taken.

Although the initial outcome is promising, current results can only be considered an indication, rather than hard evidence. First, the framework of den Hertog suggests that all capabilities together determine a company's innovativeness. Whether the contribution of capabilities to the innovativeness is additive can be questioned. Second, the matches of our study's vocabulary are not yet validated with regard to the context they appear in within the documents. Hence, as a subsequent research task, the matches in the documents shall be evaluated, for instance via a KWIC (Key Word in Context) index. A third limitation refers to the documents used in our exploratory study. So far, we have shown that our text mining algorithms and an expert-based vocabulary applied to annual reports can classify companies according to their innovativeness. This does not mean that the same method applied to different documents, e.g. newspaper articles or blog posts, leads to similar results. Furthermore, annual reports are supposedly designed rather to be effective publicity material than as a neutral representation of the company. Hence, a high matching score of the documents with a vocabulary in question could result from excellent public relations skills, rather than actual capabilities of the company. Forth, one might want to use the method described above to predict companies' innovativeness rather than validating a framework based on past reports. In this case, those who write up reports may use the vocabulary deliberately, i.e. they would make their organization appear more innovative than it probably is.

Nevertheless, the study shows encouraging outcomes, which open opportunities for further application: In case we are able to validate a Service Innovation capabilities framework and find ways to prevent misuse of the vocabulary, we will then be able to conclude from a company's self-representation in form of published documents on its actual innovativeness. What is more, text mining could contribute to the monitoring of a company's service innovation capabilities, e.g. updating a corresponding scorecard. Regularly analyzing internal documents could be a rather feasible solution to assess capabilities than frequent internal surveys. Finally, in case our text mining approach demonstrates to be applicable to the validation of a service innovation capabilities framework, it could be applied to further business frameworks addressing other management issues, for instance quality management or other areas.

# References

1. Bird, S., Klein, E., Loper, E.: Natural Language Processing with Python. O'Reilly, Sebastopol (2009)
2. Bjelland, O.M., Wood, R.C.: An Inside View of IBM's 'Innovation Jam'. MIT Sloan Management Review 50(1), 32–40 (2008)
3. Blair, D.C., Maron, M.E.: An Evaluation of Retrieval Effectiveness for a Full-Text Document-Retrieval System. Communications of the ACM 28(3), 289–299 (1985)
4. Bortz, J., Döring, N.: Forschungsmethoden und Evaluation für Human- und Sozialwissenschaftler, 4th edn. Springer, Berlin (2006)
5. Businessweek: The 50 Most Innovative Companies 2010 (April 2010), http://www.businessweek.com/magazine/toc/10_17/B4175innovative_companies.html and http://www.businessweek.com/interactive_reports/innovative_companies_2010.html
6. Chen, Y.-T., Chou, C., Kimbrough, S.O., Lin, H.: Developing Indicators for Multilingual Text Analytics. University of Pennsylvania, working paper (August 2012)
7. Chesbrough, H.W.: Open Innovation - The New Imperative for Creating and Profiting from Technology. Harvard Business School Press, Boston (2003)
8. den Hertog, P., van der Aa, W., de Jong, M.W.: Capabilities for managing service innovation: towards a conceptual framework. Journal of Service Management 21(4), 490–514 (2010)
9. Essmann, H.E., du Preez, N.: An Innovation Capability Maturity Model – Development and initial application. Engineering and Technology 53, 435–446 (2009)
10. Gadrey, J., Gallouj, F., Weinstein, O.: New modes of innovation: How services benefit industry. International Journal of Service Industry Management 6(3), 4 (1995)
11. Hemp, P., Stewart, T.A.: The HBR Interview: Samuel J. Palmisano – Leading Change When Business Is Good. Harvard Business Review 82(12), 60–70 (2004)
12. IBM: Expanding the innovation horizon: The global CEO study 2006. Technical Report, IBM Global Business Services (2006)
13. Kabanoff, B., Keegan, J.: Studying strategic cognition by content analysis of annual reports: A validation involving firm innovation. In: Chapman, Ross (eds.) Proceedings of Managing Our Intellectual and Social Capital, 21st ANZAM 2007 Conference, Sydney, Australia, pp. 1–14 (2007)
14. Krippendorff, K.: Content Analysis: An Introduction to Its Methodology, 2nd edn. Sage Publications, Thousand Oaks (2004)

15. Kohler, M., Feldmann, N., Habryn, F., Satzger, G.: Service Innovation Analytics: Towards Assessment and Monitoring of Innovation Capabilities in Service Firms. In: Proceedings of the 46th Annual Hawaii International Conference on System Sciences. Computer Society Press (forthcoming, 2013)
16. Laursen, K., Salter, A.: Open for innovation: the role of openness in explaining innovation performance among U.K. manufacturing firms. Strategic Management Journal 27(2), 131–150 (2006)
17. Maglio, P.P., Spohrer, J.: Fundamentals of service science. Journal of the Academy of Marketing Science 36(1), 18–20 (2008)
18. Makadok, R.: Toward a Synthesis of the Resource-Based and Dynamic-Capability Views of Rent Creation. Strategic Management Journal 22(5), 387–401 (2001)
19. Manning, C.D., Raghavan, P., Schütze, H.: Introduction to Information Retrieval. Cambridge University Press, Cambridge (2008)
20. Mobile Commerce Daily, http://www.mobilecommercedaily.com/2012/04/11/starbucks-reaches-42m-mobile-payment-transactions-as-app-gains-momentum
21. Morris, R.: Computerized content analysis in management research: A demonstration of advantages & limitations. Journal of Management 20(4), 903–931 (1994)
22. Müller-Prothmann, T., Stein, A.: I$^2$MM – Integrated Innovation Maturity Model for Lean Assessment of Innovation Capability. In: XXII ISPIM Conference 2011: Sustainability in Innovation, Hamburg, pp. 1–11 (2011)
23. Neuendorf, K.A.: The Content Analysis Guidebook. Sage Publications, Thousand Oaks (2002)
24. Pennebaker, J.W.: The Secret Life of Pronouns: What Our Words Say About Us. Bloomsbury Press, New York (2011)
25. Starbucks Coffee Company, http://news.starbucks.com/article_display.cfm?article_id=598
26. Sundbo, J.: The tied entrepreneur: On the theory and practice of institutionalisation of creativity and innovation in service firms. Creativity and Innovation Management 1(3), 109–120 (1992)
27. Sundbo, J.: Management of Innovation in Services. The Service Industries Journal 17(3), 432–455 (1997)
28. The Boston Consulting Group: Innovation 2010 (2010), http://www.bcg.com/documents/file42620.pdf
29. Tidd, J., Hull, F.M.: Managing service innovation: the need for selectivity rather than 'best practice'. New Technology, Work and Employment 21(2), 139–161 (2006)
30. Vermeulen, P., van der Aa, W.: Organizing Innovation in Services. In: Tidd, Hull (eds.) Service Innovation, pp. 35–53 (2003)
31. Weber, R.P.: Basic content analysis, 2nd edn. Sage Publications, Newbury Park (1990)
32. Weill, P., Ross, J.W.: IT governance: How top performers manage IT decision rights for superior results. Harvard Business School Press, Boston (2004)

# Modeling ITIL Business Motivation Model in ArchiMate

Marco Vicente[1], Nelson Gama[1,2], and Miguel Mira da Silva[1]

[1] Instituto Superior Tecnico, Av. Rovisco Pais, 1049-001 Lisboa, Portugal
[2] CINAV-PT Navy Research Center, Escola Naval, 2810-001 Almada, Portugal
{marco.vicente,nelsongama,mms}@ist.utl.pt

**Abstract.** According to Enterprise Architecture (EA) approaches, organizations have motivational concepts that are used to model the motivations that underlie its design or change, which represent the organization's Business Motivation Model (BMM). Likewise, this BMM is also present in the organizations who provide IT services. ITIL has become a reference for IT service providers, but is commonly modeled as a process-oriented approach to IT Service Management, often disregarding the remaining EA domains or its motivational elements. Conversely, we believe that like EA, ITIL has an important motivation model that should be formally represented.

**Keywords:** IT Service Management, ITIL, Enterprise Architecture, Business Motivation Model, ArchiMate, modeling.

## 1 Introduction

Enterprise Architecture is a coherent whole of principles, methods, and models that are used in the design and realization of an enterprise's organizational structure, business processes, information systems, and infrastructure [1].

The Open Group Architecture Framework (TOGAF) [2] is a freely available standardized method for EA that has become a worldwide and broadly accepted standard [3].

In the view of TOGAF, EA is divided into four architecture domains: business, data, application and technology. These domains describe the architecture of systems that support the enterprise and correspond to the "How, What, Who, Where and When" columns of the Zachman framework [4]. In turn, they dont cover the elements which motivate its design and operation which corresponds to Zachman's "Why" column [5].

In fact, these elements belong to what is called the Business Motivation Model defined by the Object Management Group (OMG) as a "scheme and structure for developing, communicating, and managing business plans in an organized manner" [6].

The BMM provides a small set of important concepts to express motivation: means, ends, influencers and directives. The model was initially created to provide the motivations behind business rules, but can also be used to find the

J.F. e Cunha, M. Snene, and H. Nóvoa (Eds.): IESS 2013, LNBIP 143, pp. 86–99, 2013.

motivation for architecture principles [3]. Accordingly, TOGAF version 9.0 also includes a business motivation model that is simpler than the OMG one and is based on the concepts of drivers, goals, objectives, and measures.

On the other hand, IT Service Management (ITSM) evolved naturally as services became underpinned in time by the developing technology. In its early years, IT was mainly focused on application development, but as time went by, new technologies meant concentrating on delivering the created applications as a part of a larger service offering, supporting the business itself [7].

IT Infrastructure Library (ITIL) [8] is the *de facto* standard for implementing ITSM [9]. It is a practical, no-nonsense approach to the identification, planning, delivery and support of IT services to the business [10]. The ITIL Core consists of five publications: Service Strategy, Service Design, Service Transition, Service Operation and Continual Service Improvement. Each book covers a phase from the Service Lifecycle and encompasses various processes which are always described in detail in the book in which they find their key application [11].

Across these books, ITIL is presented through textual definitions of concepts and its relationships, while its processes are usually depicted as well defined sequences of activities by flow charts.

However, the motivation behind why we need ITIL, why those were the chosen processes, the drivers, assessments, goals, principles and requirements, when not described through text, are loosely depicted by adhoc graphical diagrams that lack a formal notation and representation.

That doesn't surprise us, because as opposed to engineering disciplines (where modeling a system consists of constructing a mathematical model that describes and explains it), in the fields of enterprise and software architecture, it is usual to see diagrams as a form of structure that helps in visualizing and communicating system descriptions. In other words, in architecture there is a tendency to replace mathematical modeling by adhoc visualizations [1].

Unfortunately, the lack of a strong symbolic and semantic model often leads to some drawbacks: there isnt a clear, uniform representation of the concepts; each diagram has concepts of different conceptual levels; it is not clear which are the elements represented or its attributes and its hard to check for coherence across the several diagrams.

This paper goal is therefore to enhance ITIL with a formal representation of its business motivation model, for knowledge sharing, stakeholder communication and to aid discussion and validation by the ITIL community itself.

To achieve this, we chose ArchiMate's Motivation extension as the modeling language for reasons that we shall later address. This work's contribution isn't just a theoretical concept map between ITIL and the ArchiMate notation, but an actual set of ITIL models demonstrating the proposal value and feasibility.

The methodology applied across this paper is Design Science Research, where we develop and validate a proposal to solve our problem [12]. The following sections follow the methodology's steps: "Related Work" covers aims and objectives as the awareness and recognition of a problem from a state of the art review giving us the issues that must be addressed. The following section, "Research Problem", exposes the main problem while offering a tentative idea to how these issues might be addressed. Afterwards, "Proposal" presents a proposal as an attempt to solve the previously described problem. Next, we present a "Demonstration" followed by the "Evaluation" comparing the results with the research questions and to conclude we show our proposal applicability and themes for further work.

## 2   Related Work

The Business Rules Group (BRG) developed the Business Motivation Model which was later accepted as an OMG specification. BMM identifies factors that motivate the establishing of business plans, identifies and defines its elements and indicates how all these factors and elements inter-relate. In fact, there are two major areas of the BMM.

First we have Ends and Means, where Ends are things that the enterprise wishes to achieve (as goals and objectives) and Means things that will be used to achieve these Ends (as strategies, tactics, business policies and business rules). The second is the Influencers that shape the elements of the business plans, and the Assessments made about the impacts of those Influencers on Ends and Means (eg strengths, weaknesses, opportunities and threats).

On the other hand, TOGAF defines a simpler BMM through a motivation extension, with concepts as Driver (factors generally motivating or constraining an organization), Goal (strategic purpose and mission of an organization), Objective (near to mid-term achievements that an organization would like to attain) and Measure (performance criteria).

TOGAF recommends to use this extension when the architecture needs to understand the motivation of organizations in more detail than the standard business or engagement principles and objectives that are informally modeled within the core content metamodel [2]. Likewise, ArchiMate 2.0 has a motivation extension which is closely linked to the developments of TOGAF, as ArchiMate does not provide its own set of defined terms, but rather follows those provided by the TOGAF standard [5].

As for service management, ITIL is a collection of five books with the best practices related to the effective and efficient management of IT [13]. As already mentioned, there is an effort on these books to illustrate concepts, its relationships, framework lifecycle, processes, information management, information systems and databases through visual representations. However, it is mainly in process modeling (by flow charts or BPMN) that we see a formal representation, with a known symbolic and semantic model. The other representations to describe the remaining ITIL domains seem to lack a common, clear and formal notation and semantic.

Besides these official books, we searched for other ITIL graphical representations. We found several adhoc diagrams from distinct organizations with different notations. These were mainly in-house sketches, diagrams and flowcharts expressing the ITIL views of its authors. Because they are so many and so distinct, its description would be lengthy and hardly noteworthy. Additionally, we have also come across with some commercial solutions. Thus, we have chosen three of the most popular ones to include here as an example on how ITIL is usually represented[1].

**ITIL Process Map** [14] from IT Process Maps, is announced as "a complete reference process model, designed to serve as a guideline and starting point for your ITIL and ISO 20000 initiatives". The product is a set of process models mapped in the Business Process Model and Notation (BPMN) [15], with processes, artifacts and events. The diagrams have drill-down capabilities and it also has a responsibility assignment matrix (RACI) to illustrate the participation of the ITIL roles in the various ITIL processes. It is available for several platforms, as Microsoft Visio, IDS Scheer's ARIS, and iGrafx Flowcharter/Process.

**foxPRISM** [16] from foxIT is a tool that consists of "a fully interactive web based process knowledge base that assists in the design and management of Service Management processes and the implementation of Service Management tools (...) provides a customizable framework onto which organizations can map and build their own process models". This web tool uses flowcharts in swimlane format and text to describe ITIL processes. The elements are processes, activities, roles and events. It also uses a RACI matrix to map roles to processes.

**Casewise Online Visual Process Model for ITIL** [17] is a web tool described as "the world's first diagram-only view of all guidance for each of the five new ITIL v3 books providing organizations with the insight to simplify the alignment of business processes ensuring all ITIL standards are met by using simple frameworks and mapping tools". It has all the ITIL processes mapped in BPMN, with processes, activities and events. Also has drill-down capabilities and in each process it is possible to check each process according to Critical Success Factors (CSFs), Key Performance Indicators (KPIs), Best Practice Tips and Hints, Risks and Controls.

It is noticeable from these representations that ITIL is often depicted as just a process architecture, hence the use of flowcharts or BPMN.

The BPMN standard is restricted to process modeling, not covering application, infrastructure or motivation issues. Its main purpose is to provide a uniform notation in terms of activities and their relationships [1]. We acknowledge the added value of these tools and models and are not claiming they are incorrect, but pointing out instead they lack completeness, because they limit themselves to the representation of business and informational concepts, not considering other domains.

## 3    Research Problem

As we have tried to bring forth in the last section, there seems to be a void when it comes to representing ITIL on other realms than the processes' one. In fact,

---

[1] IT Process Maps, ITIL Process Map, Microsoft, Microsoft Visio, IDS Scheer's ARIS, iGrafx Flowcharter/Process, foxIT, foxPRISM and Casewise are all registered trademarks.

and as Sante [18] points out, the earliest versions of ITIL hardly contained any references to architecture as a concept, method or framework.

However, in ITIL V3 references are made to architectural concepts, which are usually only found in publications about architecture. He also states that the main structural differences between ITIL V3 and TOGAF 9 is that ITIL doesn't change the organization's own business processes while, on the other hand, it runs IT operations and delivers IT services.

This difference is minimal, and it is still an heritage from both frameworks early versions, where ITIL was just about service delivery and support and TO-GAF just about EA.

Additionally, Gama [13] also related the core EA artifacts and the EA five architecture layers to ITIL artifacts and management processes, showing there is in fact a link between ITIL and EA in all these domains and not only on the business and information ones.

On the other hand, there is also an overall lack of representation when it comes to the elements that motivate ITIL design and operation. Indeed, we can easily find out *who* should perform the ITIL processes, *what, how, where* and *when* they should be executed, but we can't find representations that address *why* do we actually need them in the first place. Actually, this lack of a formal representation of the ITIL motivation model may even impair ITIL communication and implementation, because if stakeholders are not fully aware of ITIL motivations, concerns, benefits, goals, objectives or requirements, resistance to change will probably increase.

Therefore, we strongly believe that like EA, we can also look at ITIL as a composition of architectures, namely business, information, application and infrastructure. And, since ITIL is about service providing and shares so many similarities to EA, it should also share the same motivation elements as defined in TOGAF: "drivers, goals and objectives that influence an organization to provide business services to its customers. This in turn allows more effective definition of service contracts and better measurements of business performance" [2].

Hence, we define our problem as the lack of a formal, coherent, consistent, concise and complete model of the motivation aspects of ITIL. Thus, our work will try to contribute for the development of a ITIL business motivation model, along with its formal representation.

## 4   Proposal

To address our problem we needed the right language. Here we'll explain why we have chosen ArchiMate and propose a concept and relationship mapping from ITIL to it.

### 4.1   ArchiMate

It was our purpose, since the beginning, to use an EA modeling language, because this work is also part of a wider effort to specify an enterprise architecture for organizations that need to manage IT services.

In fact, EAs don't dwell on specific issues because their goal is to be able to represent every organization. On the contrary, our goal is to narrow it down, and restrict the architecture to organizations that have the management of IT services as an architectural driver. Thus, we wish to define an EA specification that uses ITIL principles, methods, processes and concepts to perform IT service management, and general EA principles, methods and models to the design and realization of the remaining organizational structure.

Therefore, the work presented in this paper will be later used as the definition of the motivation model of that architecture, and we will later relate our motivation models to the other EA domains, in order to show which of those domain's elements realize and implement the BMM requirements.

Hence, a BMM modeling language was not enough, we actually needed something wider that embraced several architectures while allowing to create an ITIL holistic organizational view.

In effect, Lankhorst [1] enumerates several languages for modeling IT and business. There's IDEF (Integrated Computer- Aided Manufacturing (ICAM) DEFinition), a group of methods for functional, process and data modeling; BPMN, which is restricted to process modeling; Testbed, a business modeling language and method that recognizes the domains *actor*, *behavior* and *item*; ARIS (Architecture of Integrated Information Systems), a business modeling language (supported by a software tool) known as event-driven process chains and finally UML (Unified Modeling Language) for software systems.

However, Lankhorst also identifies common issues among them all, like poorly defined relations between domains, models not integrated, weak formal basis and lack of clearly defined semantics, and the fact that most of them miss the overall architecture vision being confined to either business or application and technology domains.

ArchiMate, on the other hand, provides a uniform representation for diagrams that describe EAs. It offers an integrated architectural approach that describes and visualizes the different architecture domains and their underlying relations and dependencies [5].

The domains of business, application and infrastructure are connected by a "service orientation" paradigm, where each layer exposes functionality in the form of a service to the layer above. Besides this layered structure, ArchiMate also distinguishes between active structure elements, behavior elements and passive structure elements (where the passive ones represent the architecture information domain), having also another distinction between internal and external system view.

On top of this, ArchiMate is a formal visual design language, supports different viewpoints for selected stakeholders and is flexible enough to be easily extended. In fact, since version 2.0, it has a Motivation extension that introduces the elements that "provide the context or reason lying behind the architecture of an enterprise" [5].

Actually, this extension recognizes the concepts of stakeholders (persons or organizations that influence, guide or constrain the enterprise), drivers (internal or external factors which influence the plans and aims of a enterprise), assessments (an understanding of strengths, weaknesses, opportunities, and threats in relation to these drivers), goals (desired result to achieve) and requirements, principles and constraints (desired properties to realize the goals).

Therefore, it seemed to fill all the other languages' gaps and stood out as the one we were looking for to model ITIL business motivation.

## 4.2    Mapping ITIL Motivation to ArchiMate

Before starting modeling we needed to map ITIL motivational concepts in the languages metamodel. Motivational concepts are used to model the motivations, or reasons, that underlie the design or change of some enterprise architecture. These motivations influence, guide, and constrain the design [5].

On Table 1 we present a map with the summary of ITIL motivational concepts and relationships to ArchiMate's Motivation extension.

**Table 1.** Mapping concepts and relationships

| ITIL concept | ArchiMate |
| --- | --- |
| Role, Department, Business unit, Service Owner, Responsibility | Stakeholder |
| Concern, driver, scope, process introduction, process definition | Driver |
| Benefit, problem, mistake, risk, opportunity, SWOT analysis | Assessment |
| Mission, goal, objective | Goal |
| Requirement, policy | Requirement |
| Principle, implementation guideline | Principle |
| Constraint | Constraint |
| **ITIL relationship** | **ArchiMate** |
| Is related to, assessment resulted in, stakeholder is concerned with | Association |
| Makes possible, implements | Realization |
| Benefits, prejudices | Influence |

ArchiMate's Motivation metamodel has motivational elements that are realized by *requirements* which in turn are realized by core concepts. *Stakeholders* are structure elements assigned from *Business Actors*. The Motivation elements are *driver, assessment, goal, principle* and *constraint*.

In ITIL there are roles, departments, business units and service owners that have interests and concerns in the outcome of the architecture. These are ArchiMate's *stakeholders*. Then, factors that influence the motivational elements, are usually presented in the process introduction or definition, sometimes in the scope or otherwise referred as drivers or stakeholders concerns. These elements represent the ArchiMate concept *driver*. Later on, it is common for enterprises to take *assessments* of these drivers. In ITIL these are represented as a SWOT or driver analysis that is used to identify benefits, problems, mistakes, risks and opportunities. The desired results that a stakeholder wants to achieve is referred in ITIL as the organization mission, goal or objectives. This matches ArchiMate's *goal* concept. Next we have desired properties of solutions or means to realize the goals. In ITIL we have requirements, policies, implementation and guidelines that correspond to ArchiMate's *requirement*. Likewise, we have in ITIL principles and implementation guidelines that map to *principle* and finally there's *constraint* that maps to its ArchiMate homonym counterpart.

## 5  Demonstration

Although we already had this concept mapping, we wanted to go further on and demonstrate that it really could be used to model ITIL BMM in the ArchiMate language.

Thereby, we started to analyze the official ITIL books, going through all its processes' and functions' descriptions. In fact, we had already done this on a first iteration when we were identifying the ITIL BMM concepts. This time, however, we weren't looking for the concept's class, but for its instances. For example, instead of looking up for concepts that resembled ArchiMate's "goal", we were now searching for references of its ITIL counterparts "mission, goal, objective" and gathering its instances like "detect service events" or "ensure only authorized users can use services" in Service Operation.

Following this procedure, we eventually compiled a set of elements which are, in our opinion, the most relevant motivation items for every ITIL process.

This assumption is based on the elements' own relevance through the official books and general ITIL sources. However, being ITIL a set of best practices, built upon IT service providers different opinions and experiences, we also concede that some practitioners could include other elements or leave some of these out.

Thereby, we don't want to claim that this is the only motivational representation of ITIL, but instead to demonstrate that based on our mapping, on the identified concepts and on our perception, this is our proposed ITIL BMM model and its ArchiMate representation. We therefore welcome (and encourage) that these BMM proposals are revised by the ITIL community itself and may eventually be adapted to reflect, as ITIL does, the majority of its practitioners' opinions.

With these concepts' instances we produced several models. In this paper we shall only focus on three of them. The first (Figure 1) represents an ITIL overview with all its five books.

Its utility is to understand in a glance why there was the need for creating ITIL in the first place. What was it overall motivation, the industry concerns, the outcomes of the assessments about those concerns, what were the set goals to solve the identified issues, the needed requirements to fulfill the goals, and, at last, which of the books implements those requirements.

In (Figure 2) we zoom into one of the ITIL books, the Service Operation one. Here we can see an expanded set of drivers, assessments, goals and requirements that are related to the Service Operation book.

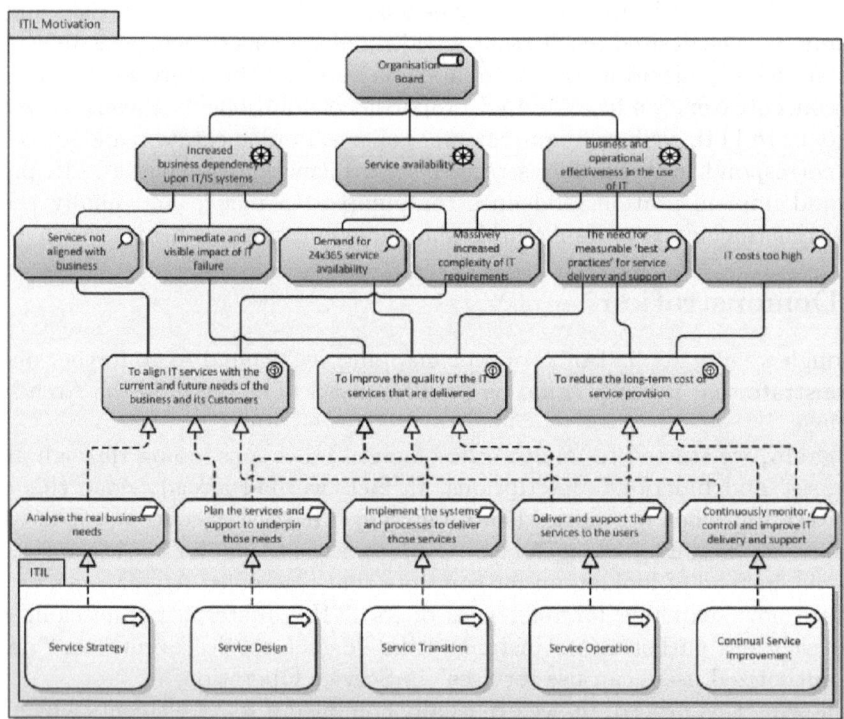

**Fig. 1.** ITIL business motivation model overview (https://dl.dropbox.com/u/13096223/IMG_itil_overview.pdf)

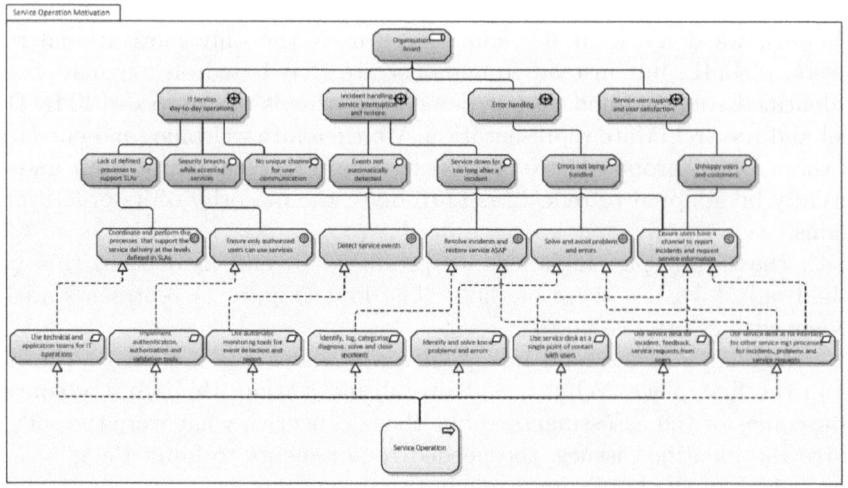

**Fig. 2.** Service Operation business motivation model https://dl.dropbox.com/u/13096223/IMG_service_operation.pdf

Finally, on (Figure 3) we aimed for a deeper fine-grained representation and focused on the Incident Management process. This allows us to look to this process and see again which are its motivational elements and how are they realized by requirements, now in a process scope.

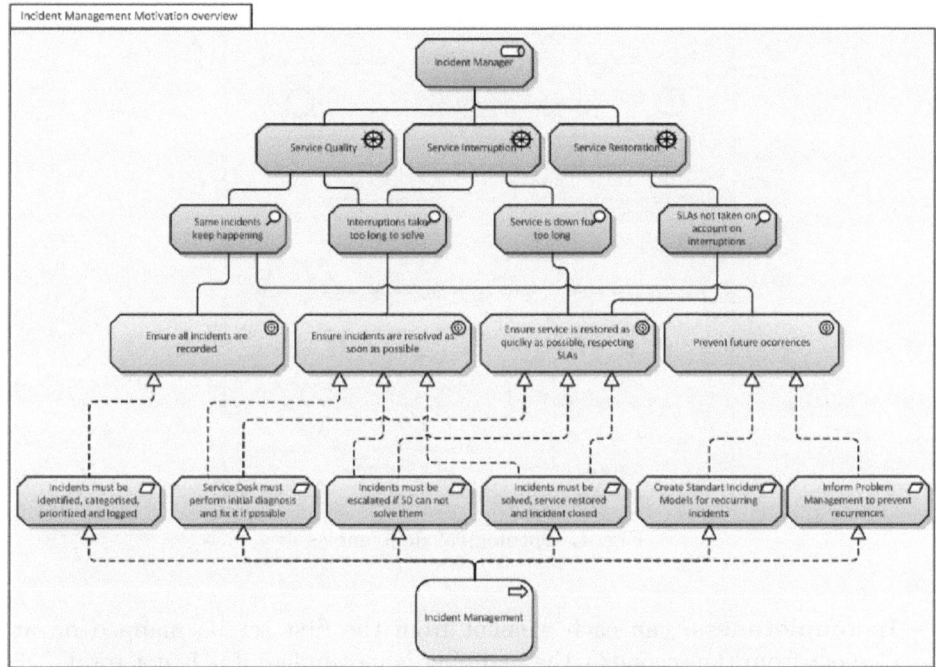

**Fig. 3.** Incident Management business motivation model `https://dl.dropbox.com/u/13096223/IMG_incident_management.pdf`

These models were chosen to demonstrate how ArchiMate can be used to show different ITIL views, directed to different stakeholders with own concerns. Yet, the three models remain consistent, since the elements are similar but on different granularity levels.

Besides these, we produced other models (not included due to paper size restrictions) representing the remaining ITIL business motivation model. Together, our work consists on a set of models with the whole ITIL 26 processes and 4 functions motivation model.

## 6  Evaluation

Since the main purpose of this paper is to contribute with a formal representation of the ITIL BMM, here we analyze the mapping of ITIL motivation concepts into ArchiMate's motivation extension. This analysis is based on the Wand and

Weber ontological analysis method [19] and compares the mapping of both sets of concepts by identifying the following four ontological deficiencies (Figure 4):

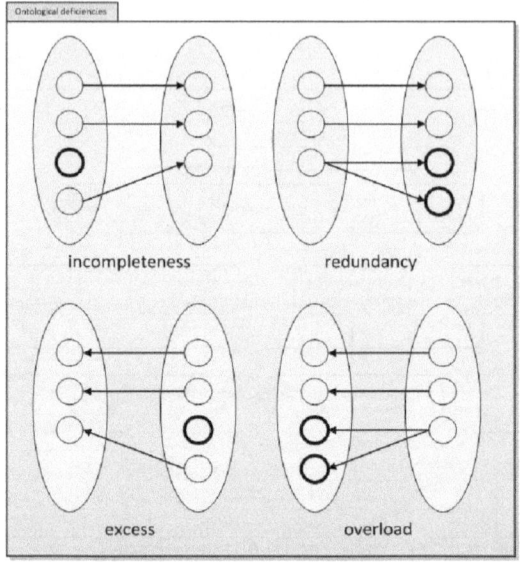

**Fig. 4.** Ontological deficiencies

- **Incompleteness:** can each element from the first set be mapped on an element from the second? - the mapping is incomplete if it is not total.
- **Redundancy:** are the first set elements mapped to more than a second set element? - the mapping is redundant if it is ambiguous.
- **Excess:** is every first set element mapped on a second set one? - the mapping is excessive if there are first set elements without a relationship.
- **Overload:** is every first set element mapped to exactly one second set element? - the mapping is overloaded if any second set element has more than one mapping to a first set one.

It should be again noted what we are mapping. In fact, we have on one hand ArchiMate, which is a formal modeling language, with a closed set of clearly defined concepts and, on the other, textual descriptions of IT best practices. There isn't in ITIL a clear definition of a motivational elements' set that would clearly ease our task, so our identification is based on ITIL textual references of concepts that, in the context where they are used, have business meanings which are similar to business motivation model elements.

Having that, we can then say that our mapping is **complete**, as every ITIL motivation element found has a mapping on ArchiMate's motivation extension elements, which means we can completely represent ITIL BMM on ArchiMate.

As for **redundancy**, since ArchiMate's motivation elements is a small, closed set, as opposed to ITIL richness of textual descriptions, it was expectable that there was only one ArchiMate element to represent any ITIL concept. This means it becomes straightforward to model ITIL BMM in ArchiMate as we don't have to choose between several elements to model a ITIL one.

We also didn't find **excess**, as ArchiMate concepts are all present on ITIL. This was also expected since the ArchiMate motivation elements are aligned with the TOGAF ones, which we used as guidelines when searching in ITIL.

Finally, we found one deficiency: **overload**, because there are several ITIL concepts to only one from ArchiMate. This happens because, as we have mentioned before, ITIL doesn't explicitly define a BMM or identifies its concepts. Therefore, since we have to derive motivation elements from ITIL textual descriptions, it was predictable that several ITIL concepts would match an ArchiMate one. This deficiency can lead to problems if we ever wanted to do the opposite process: to go from an ArchiMate ITIL motivation model back to ITIL again. To avoid this, while modeling, we should include in ArchiMate's object attributes a reference to the original ITIL concept it was mapped from, to allow an eventual reverse mapping.

To sum up, we can conclude that our mapping is complete, not ambiguous and not excessive. It is indeed overloaded, but this actually derives from the intrinsic nature of the problem we want to solve: the lack of a formal BMM for ITIL. Furthermore, by identifying and mapping these concepts, we believe we are also contributing with a tool that can help to identify and define the motivation model of future ITIL releases and to update our models accordingly.

# 7   Conclusion

We began this research work with the conviction that like EA, ITIL had a business motivation model and there was a need to define and model it through a formal graphical language.

For that task, we chose ArchiMate's Motivation extension and mapped ITIL motivation to it. The result was a set of consistent models with the whole ITIL motivation model in its 26 processes and 4 functions, with the inclusion of roles, drivers, assessments, goals and requirements. Furthermore, we added a ITIL overview to stress how we could zoom through the models' granularity levels.

Although our plans are to later use this work to represent the business motivation model of an enterprise architecture that uses ITIL to manage IT services, we also want to point out the contribution these models may offer today as standalone formal ITIL BMM representations.

In fact, they can be a tool to help organizations using ITIL, as they can use our models and mapping as templates to build their own models, according to their ITIL maturity levels and the processes they already support. They can assign people and departments to ITIL roles, and use the models to communicate to stakeholders what is ITIL, what problems does it solve and why are they using it.

Better yet, they could model their own organization motivation model and merge it with our ITIL models to provide a consistent organization view. This approach would be very useful on managing and communicating change, since AS-IS models could be produced with the current organization ITIL processes and TO-BE models would represent the ITIL level where the organization plans to stand in the near future. This would support phased, iterative ITIL implementations, supported by project planning and model driven milestones.

For future work, we believe the next step is to expose these models to the ITIL community where they can be validated, and, in particular, can be used to promote discussion about ITIL motivation model itself. Furthermore, we are currently working on modeling ITIL's business, application, information and infrastructure architectures in ArchiMate's core concepts, to answer the remaining Zachman's questions: the "How, What, Who, Where and When". Next, we plan to bridge both approaches using business motivation model requirements which are realized by core elements like processes, activities or databases.

Later on, we wish to validate both set of models on organizations with ITIL implementations to represent how ITIL fits in the organization EA, and to improve its implementation and communication. All these models will then be used as the representation of an enterprise architecture that uses ITIL motivation, principles, methods, processes and concepts to perform IT service management, and general EA principles, methods and models to the design and realization of the remaining organizational structure.

In short, IT has the goal to turn organizations more efficient and effective, and to achieve this, it is fundamental that each stakeholder is aware of change, its reasons and how he will be affected by it. Communicating change is therefore a key factor on agile, prone to change organizations. Furthermore, it is also our belief that when people are well informed about the whys, then resistance to change may be overcome and diminished.

Thereby, we hope this work can contribute to a better communication and representation of ITIL motivation concepts, to ITIL discussion in its own community and to help each stakeholder realize what is to be changed and why is it being changed through a set of complete, consistent and formal models.

# References

1. Lankhorst, M., et al.: Enterprise Architeture at Work. Springer, Berlin (2009)
2. TOGAF Version 9, The Open Group Architecture Framework (TOGAF). The Open Group (2009)
3. Greefhorst, D., Proper, E.: Architecture Principles: The Cornerstones of Enterprise Architecture. Springer, Berlin (2011)
4. Zachman, J.: A framework for information systems architecture. IBM Systems Journal 26, 276–292 (1987)
5. The Open Group, Archimate 2.0 Specification. The Open Group (2012)
6. Object Management Group, Business Motivation Model v1.1, Object Management Group (2010)
7. The Official Introduction to the ITIL Service Lifecycle. The Stationery Office (2007)

8. Hanna, A., Windebank, J., Adams, S., Sowerby, J., Rance, S., Cartlidge, A.: ITIL V3 Foundation Handbook. The Stationary Office, Norwich (2008)
9. Hochstein, A., Zarnekow, R., Brenner, W.: ITIL as common practice reference model for it service management: formal assessment and implications for practice. In: 2005 IEEE International Conference on eTechnology eCommerce and eService, vol. 21, pp. 704–710 (2005)
10. Arraj, V.: ITIL: The Basics White Paper. The Stationary Office (2010)
11. van Bon, J., et al.: Foundations of IT Service Management Based on ITIL v3. Van Haren Publishing (2007)
12. Hevner, A., March, S., Park, J., Ram, S.: Design science in information systems research. MIS Quarterly (28), 78–105 (2004)
13. Gama, N., Sousa, P., Mira da Silva, M.: Integrating enterprise architecture and IT service management. In: 21st International Conference on Information Systems Development (ISD 2012), Prado, Italy (August 2012)
14. ITIL Process Map (2012), `http://en.it-processmaps.com/` (Online accessed August 26, 2012)
15. Object Management Group, Business Process Model and Notation (BPMN) version 2.0. OMG (2011)
16. foxPRISM (2012), `http://www.foxit.net/pages/toolkits/foxPRISM.shtml` (Online accessed August 26, 2012)
17. The Casewise Online Visual Process Model for ITIL version 3 (2012), `http://www.casewise.com/itil` (Online accessed August 26, 2012)
18. van Sante, T., Ermersj, J.: TOGAF 9 and ITIL V3 (September 2009), `http://www.best-management-practice.com`
19. Wand, Y., Weber, R.: On the ontological expressiveness of information systems analysis and design grammars. Information Systems Journal 3(4), 217–237 (1993)

# Service Science: A Service System Design Science Research Method?

Eric Dubois and Anne Rousseau

Department of Service Science & Innovation
Public Research Centre Henri Tudor, Luxembourg
{eric.dubois,anne.rousseau}@tudor.lu

**Abstract.** Like 'Computer Science' a few decades ago, 'Service Science' deserves some attention today regarding the emergence of a possible new scientific discipline. In this paper, we explore the potential link existing between service science and design science, considering the service as the focus of the design. Our proposed contribution directly relies on the day-to-day work of our research and technology transfer institution regarding a science-based approach to service innovation. Our preliminary findings are formalized in a macro-process used for governing this type of innovation. The paper introduces and illustrates it.

**Keywords:** Service Science, design science, service system, service innovation, innovation governance process.

## 1 Introduction

According to Wikipedia, Service Science is a term introduced by IBM [29] to describe "an interdisciplinary approach to the study, design, and implementation of services systems". Since the introduction of the term around 2004, there have been several attempts, but not yet reaching a consensus, regarding the definition of service science. Different contributions present different perspectives on Service Science. Glusko [1] is discussing about the emergence of a new discipline in contrast to the design of a new curriculum. Like medicine is an integrative discipline of physical and biological sciences for the purpose of healing, Irene CL Ng & al. [2] considers service science as an "integrative discipline of engineering, technological and, social sciences (including business and law) for the purpose of value co-creation with customers". More recently, from the analysis of different service innovations enabled through IT artefacts, Becker et al. [3] advocate for further considering the role of design research in the service science discipline.

The article is willing to further investigating this last perspective by discussing: (1) the nature of the innovation artefacts associated with service systems and (2) the production of scientific knowledge associated with these artefacts through a rigorous design . Our view is that a design science research method (DSRM) is offering the adequate framework for the production of this knowledge. In particular, recent efforts

J.F. e Cunha, M. Snene, and H. Nóvoa (Eds.): IESS 2013, LNBIP 143, pp. 100–113, 2013.
© Springer-Verlag Berlin Heidelberg 2013

performed around the formalisation of the design science research in the domains of organisational studies and of information systems represent interesting avenues for service oriented artefacts, especially considering the important similarities between information systems and service systems domains.

The need for some scientific foundations related to the design of services is an important step towards the possible emergence of a service science discipline. In a more pragmatic way, it is also required for an institution like the Public Centre Research Henri Tudor (Tudor, in short) for accomplishing its mission related to a science based innovation. Like VTT, Fraunhofer Institutes, TNO and other RTO (Research and Technological Organisations), the role of Tudor is not only to design new innovative artefacts for the purpose of transferring them for the benefits of socio-economic actors but also to contribute to the advance of science. Regarding the specific topic of services, any consultancy company or private organisation can design new services and commercialize them. But this is not their usual role to produce scientific knowledge about them. In fact, a science-based approach offers a number of benefits: evidence based problem identification, demonstration and measures (whatever the kind), use of best available knowledge and technology... It doesn't concern just the knowledge about a problem/an issue but well a way of approaching and dealing with a problem. As a key differentiator, the role of a RTO is to contribute to this production through the application of an adequate scientific method. Regarding this last objective, the Service Science and Innovation department of Tudor is developing and experimenting the so-called "Science based and Sustainable Service Innovation Process" (S3IP in short) which aims at addressing requirements associated with the application of DSRM in the domain of service innovation following a multidisciplinary approach.

The rest of the paper is structured as follows. In Section 2, we discuss about the application of design science principles to the innovation of artefacts associated with service systems. Section 3 emphasises some principles associated with a specialization of a design science research method applicable to services. Then, in Section 4, we instantiate these principles in terms of the S3IP macro-process framework used by Tudor and illustrate its application on a real service innovation case.

## 2     Why a Design Science Research Method for Services?

As indicated in the Section 1, a RTO like Tudor has the twofold mission of producing technological innovations (T) in response to market needs and goals (M), as well as to contribute to the scientific theory (S) underlying these innovations (http://www.earto .org/). In Figure 1 these missions are summarised according to the interactions taking place between Science, Technology and Market. On the same figure, we provide an illustration of the STM concepts within the context of the innovation associated with steam machines (T): those have brought an answer to transportation problems (M) and their effect is explained through thermodynamics scientific principles (S).

According to the most traditional acceptance of the word "innovation", its ultimate objective is to contribute to the improvement of a production system, which also represents the targeted market for this innovation. In our domain of interest, production systems correspond to service systems which can be considered at different granularity levels: from a single company to a network of companies up to a national service system. [4] are defining a service system as "a configuration of people, processes, technology and shared information connected through a value proposition with the aim of a dynamic co-creation of value through the participation in the exchanges with customers and external/internal service systems". It is worth to note the close analogy existing between this definition and the one usually associated with Information System (IS) which also refers to the interactions between people, processes, data and technology. Major differences are associated to the concept of services with an emphasis on the nature of the new value propositions inherent of them as well as the importance of the co-construction of this value through interactions taking place between the service providers and the service users To summarise, a service system is supplementing the mission of an information system (support to the business) with an additional mission of making new businesses.

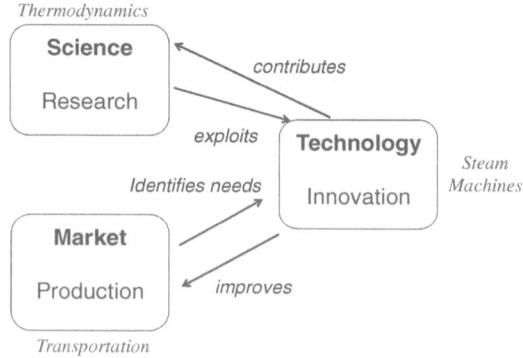

**Fig. 1.** STM (Science, Technology, Market) Interactions

Innovations are intended to improve the productivity of service systems. They are based on the identification of business goals and/or societal needs associated with these systems and result from the application of a problem solving process regarding the handling of these needs. Athtough the term technology is used for denoting these innovations, it should be understood in a broad sense, which also reflects the diversity of the components of a service system. According to OECD [5], innovations are not only associated with technological innovations but also encompass process innovations, organisational innovations and market (business models) innovations. For some authors, additional very interesting innovations should also be considered like those related to new people skills, regulations, or in the social economy.

In the domain of service innovation, there is a large variety of possible innovations. They are the result of a design and take the form of an artefact, i.e. a design not existing in the nature [6]. Examples of artefacts developed for improving service systems can be a new algorithm (technological innovation) that can optimize multimodal transportation in a complex eco-systems made from different individual tranport operators systems. It can be a method for measuring the maturity level of IT service management within an organisation (process innovation). It can be a model and a supporting IT platform enhancing the collaboration among the different actors involved in a construction project (technological and organisational artefacts). Finally, it can also take the form of a skills card associated with the characterisation of new competences  required by a new job profile. According to [30],  all these artefacts have to be instantiated into practical innovations. In our cases, most of them can be delivered as services according to different models: software as a service, method as service (provided by a consultant using perhaps a supporting IT tool), education as a service etc. Ultimately, all these services are plugged into service sytems in production for the purpose of improving them.  Conventionnaly in our case, we will use the words "artefact"  and "service" in an interchangeable way for the rest of this paper.

As also discussed in the Introduction, in the case of the service innovation performed  by a RTO, those innovative services have to scientifically grounded. There we need to consider two dimensions (see the top of Figure 1). On the one hand, the knwolegde that is exploited in the design of the artefact has to be grounded on scientifically established knowledge. On the other hand, while in most case, the existing knwoledge is not sufficient for building the artefact, additional knowledge has to be produced during the design process and this has to follow sound scientific research methods.

More traditional research methods are those associated with behavioural sciences. Their objective is to understand the real world through the formulation of theories regarding the behaviour of this reality and the validation of them through obervations. Natural sciences (physics, chemistry, etc) use these research methods but there are also other disciplines like social and management sciences  (observation of the behaviours of humans and of their organisations). Besides knowledge produced in the traditional scientific fields, authors like Simon [6] advocate that technological knwokedge has also to be produced in relation with artifical artefacts developed by humans. Design science aims at understanding the properties of the design of these artefacts: what are the problems that there are solving,  what are the properties of the proposed solutions, what are their values ?

Research methods founded on design science principles are a topic of growing interest in different fields, in particular in those related to I.S. (for example [7], [8]) and organisation studies(for example,[9],[10],[11]). In I.S., the work of Hevner is often quoted as a reference work introducing the guiding principles associated with scalability, repeatability and predictability of a given I.S. artefact. Those in particular emphasize the need for generalising the problem (instance vs type) as well as the proposed solution.  Hevner et al [7] describe the performance of design-science research via a concise conceptual framework and clear guidelines for understanding, executing, and evaluating the research (see Table 1).

**Table 1.** Hevner et al. Conceptual Framework

| Guidelines | | Description |
|---|---|---|
| 1. | Design as an Artifact | Design-science research must produce a viable artifact in the form of a construct, a model, a method, or an instantiation |
| 2. | Problem Relevance | The objective of design-science research is to develop technology-based solutions to important and relevant business problems. |
| 3. | Design Evaluation | The utility, quality, and efficacy of a design artifact must be rigorously demonstrated via well-executed evaluation methods. |
| 4. | Research Contributions | Effective design-science research must provide clear and verifiable contributions in the areas of the design artifact, design foundations, and/or design methodologies. |
| 5. | Research Rigor | Design-science research relies upon the application of rigorous methods in both the construction and evaluation of the design artifact. |
| 6. | Design as a Search Process | The search for an effective artifact requires utilizing available means to reach desired ends while satisfying laws in the problem environment. |
| 7. | Communication of Research | Design-science research must be presented effectively both to technology-oriented as well as management-oriented audiences. |

In the same way, but in the domain of organization studies, Van Aken et al. [11] present "Design Science Research (DSR) as a family of approaches to research that are driven by field problems, use a participant-observer instead of the independent observer perspective, and pursue a solution orientation. This implies design science researchers are not satisfied with describing field problems and analyzing their causes, but also develop alternative general solution concepts for these field problems." These authors suggest "the logic of the field-tested and grounded solution concept (...) called the CIMO-logic [12], a combination of problem-in-Context, Intervention, generative Mechanisms producing the outcome, and Outcome." Those phases are described in Table 2.

**Table 2.** Van Aken et al. Conceptual Framework

| | Phases | Description |
|---|---|---|
| 1. | Design problem formulation | Designers engage with principals and users to formulate the design problem and its specifications |
| 2. | Design the preferred solution | Designing then involves exploring alternative futures in close collaboration with various stakeholders |
| 3. | Creating an action net | This action net can be emergent in nature, occurring in an ad hoc, as-needed fashion. However, if an action net does not emerge spontaneously, design professionals need to deliberately develop it |

# 3    Some Features of a Service System Design Science

This section starts by consolidating our view regarding the relation that can be established between service science and design science. Then we discussed some distinctive features that should characterize the design of services. Those are related to the intrinsic nature of services, to their co-construction between service providers and external users, as well as the identification of the value proposition associated with the quality of the service.

As discussed in the previous section, design approach is first of all characterized by its problem-solving goal. Hevner et al. [7] argue that "a combination of technology-based artefacts (e.g., system conceptualizations and representations, practices, technical capabilities, interfaces, etc.) organization-based artefacts (e.g., structures, compensation, reporting relationships, social systems, etc.), and people-based arte-facts (e.g., training, consensus building, etc.) are necessary to address issues concerning the acceptance of information technology in organizations". We are convinced that we could not speak about value co-creation without taking into account this acceptance of the designed artifacts. Although Hevner et al. [7] argue that "the effective transition of strategy into infrastructure requires extensive design activity on organizational design to create an effective organizational infrastructure and information systems design activity to create an effective information system infrastructure. These are interdependent design activities that are central to IS discipline", but are not always taken it into account. Hence, it should be extended. Moreover these authors highlight also that "design-science research addresses important unsolved problems in unique or innovative ways or solved problems in more effective or efficient ways". That means that not only business needs could be the initiators for design research but as well IT as human/processes/knowledge resources could offer innovative opportunities. All this discussion is in relation with the design of I.S. artefact but also definitively applies to service systems. Thus we can argue that design science is well a legitimate research paradigm for service science.

The design of a service should result from intense interactions between the service designer and the different stakeholders, beneficiaries of this service. This requires at the level of a service research to establish close links between the researcher and the different interested parties. Thus we need to enrich principles associated with I.S. design research with organization studies design principles as discussed in the previous section. This concept is well illustrated in the work of Peffer et al. [8] who indicates the importance of better understanding the need to enrich Design Science Research with Action research principles: "DS research comes from a history of design as a component of engineering and computer science research, while action research originates from the concept of the researcher as an "active participant" in solving practical problems in the course of studying them in organizational contexts.". So action research could be a relevant strategy for design research to test (the validity of) the design in practice. This is illustrated by the Peffer research method process in Figure 2. Note that this process is a model consisting of six activities run in a nominal sequence. However, this is not a sequential process since the idea for the research could be various (resulted from observation of the problem or from suggested future research from a prior project,...) and Peffer added that researchers may start at almost any step and move outward.

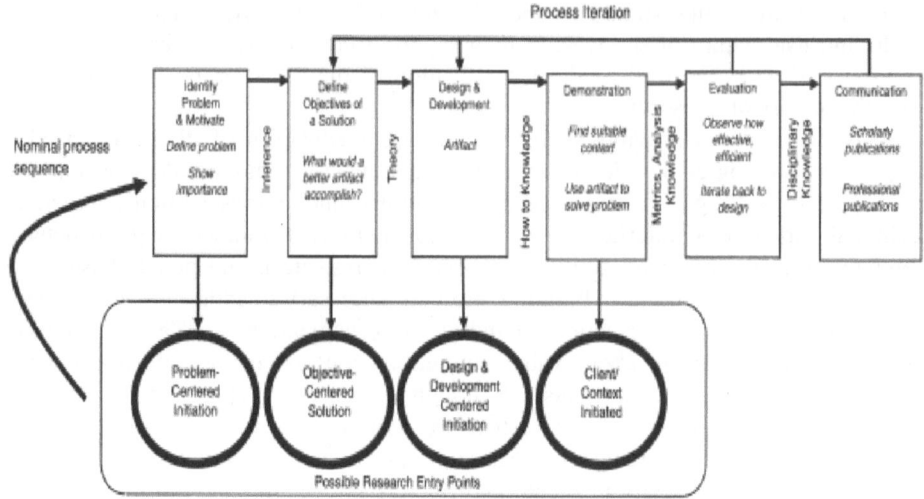

**Fig. 2.** The DSRM Process Model (Peffers et al.)

This work of Peffer et al. is a multidisciplinary response to the need of relevance in service science: design based approach can help bridging the gap between research and practice [13,14]. As emphasized by Andriessen [15] these authors also argue that "(...) researchers can draw from several different research methods to test the validity of the design, ranging from more positivistic quasi-experiments [16] to action research type interventions [17]. This implies that design-based research may make use of a variety of methodologies". As designing service systems implies to take into account the co-creation of the (service) value, that  means this latter is no longer the value-in-exchange but well the value-in-use [18,19].  This of course demands a major rethink of traditional disciplines in order to research service systems and to focus on producing knowledge on how a quality value could be co-created. Regarding the co-designing role of end users, [20] distinguishes between three approaches: 'what people say' in marketing research, 'what people do' in applied ethnography, and 'what people make' in participatory design.

Finally, a research method guaranteeing the quality of the resulting services is essential. Hevner et al. [7] argue that "the utility, quality and efficacy of a design artefact must be rigorously demonstrated via well-executed evaluation methods". This acceptance of the design artifact's quality tends to emphasize business needs and underestimate analysts' and customers' views as argued in [21].  In fact, "(...) quality is a multidimensional concept at least having four dimensions [22]: I. Excellence, II. Value, III. Conformance to specifications and IV. Meeting and/or exceeding customers' expectations. The first one is the general dimension. Different interested parties can be connected with three others as follows: II. Value (managers), III. Conformance to specifications (systems analysts) and IV. Meeting and/or exceeding customers'expectations (customers)."  In fact, as point out by [23,24] in their literature reviews one of the most relevant characteristics of service innovation is the need for different degree and means of user participation. A design approach implies that design and usages are firmly connected.

As a conclusion of this section, we plead that DSRM are both applicable to information and service systems because of their commonalities. For some authors, Information Science is discipline encompassing the design of I.S. [31]. Our proposal is to consider Service Science as the discipline related to the design of services.

# 4    A Science-Based Sustainable Service Innovation Process

Based on the considerations discussed in the previous section, we outline our proposal regarding a service system design science research method, adapted to the context of a RTO like Tudor, whose goal is to demonstrate a science based approach to service system innovation.  After having introduced the process framework underlying the proposed research method, we will illustrate its application on the specific case of a service system artifact associated with a software collaborative platform supporting project management in the building sector.

## 4.1    Introduction to the S3IP

Figure 3 presents the overall picture associated with our proposed Science-based Sustainable Service Process model framework (S3IP). Although the hereafter description could suggest that the S3IP is lifecycle oriented, the reality is that each box corresponds to a process that has to be performed and may be pursued in parallel with other processes in a non-strict sequence.

**Value:** This process covers the activities associated with the identification of an unsolved problem and/or an opportunity for a new service innovation. According to DSRM, the problem should not be characterized at the instance level but at a class level. In other words, there is the need for generalizing the problem associated with a very specific context. This identification is also coming with the identification of a gap in terms of technological/scientific knowledge associated with the proposed innovation. From a RTO perspective we are also carefully looking to state of the art technologies and scientific results that would play the role of enablers for the innovative service solution. Finally the identification of the innovative service should come with a preliminary identification of the business model and   of the value proposition.

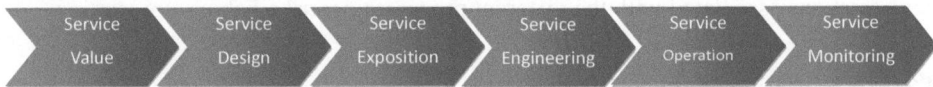

**Fig. 3.** The Science-based Sustainable Service Process model (S3IP)

**Design:** This process is associated with the definition of the service not only in terms of its business functional objectives but also in terms of all its required qualities. These activities required to elicit the strategies of the different early-adopters stakeholders involved in the final acceptance of the service as well as to understand the constraints associated with the environment (like specific regulations associated with the domain). From this initial elicitation, requirements have to be formally expressed in terms of properties of the services that can be organized in terms of a service contract (or a Service Level Agreement). These requirements should be sufficient characterize the service answering to the class of problems identified in the previous step, and not to a single instance of it.

**Exposition:** Once the service contract has been validated by early adopters, we consider that it is important to promote the service to other potentially interested parties. This can be done within an organization through some marketing regarding the socio-economical sustainability of the service. In a network of organizations or for a sector, this promotion can also include initiatives regarding the branding of the new service through some label definition and associated certification scheme. Ultimately standardization activities run for example at the national or international levels (like e.g. ISO) definitively help in a successful promotion of the service.

**Engineering:** This process is associated with the engineering of the solution meeting the requirements collected in the Design process. To be more precise, this solution should be a class of solutions bringing an answer to a class of problems, as mentioned earlier. At the level of our RTO role, we do not necessarily to have to develop the full service solution but rather to demonstrate the feasibility to do so. This can be achieved through some prototypes of the service and/or the production of complete specification of the service like an architecture model.

**Operation:** This is out of the scope of RTO's mission to deploy by itself the service within an organization or within a sector. This is where the market should play its role. However we define and provide tools that can be used by those that will deploy the service for checking and measuring the correctness of its implementation. In particular for each new service we propose metrics associated with the measurement of the quality of the service implementation as well as the degree of appropriation.

**Monitoring:** Once a services system is deployed within organizations, we can start to collect the feedbacks associated with the measures as well as from the assessment performed with the end-users. The analysis of this feedback indicates the needs for improvements and optimization of the service, as well as its possible evolutions of the service in terms of new requirements, new business model, etc. Thus this is where new iterations associated with the different processes described above are starting.

## 4.2    Application of the S3IP

As an exemplar for illustrating the application of the S3IP we would like to describe the Build-IT project and the resulting "CRTI-weB" platform.

CRTI-weB is a case of a service system innovation in the construction sector. The context is related to the management of Architecture, Engineering and Construction (AEC) projects. These projects are characterized by the fact that they are from a very different nature, involving a number of independent and heterogeneous actors and for short-lived time duration. The proposed innovation is based on a CSCW system as well as on innovative business practices defined in a consensual manner with business partners. More details on it can be found on www.crti-web.lu (in French). Hereafter we structure the different phases of the science-based innovation according to S3IP the framework introduced here above. More details can be found in different papers, a.o. [25,26].

**Value:** The original idea for the CRTI-weB service was coming from the following analysis based on a global survey and 8 long interviews with 2 architect offices, 3 engineering agencies, 1 contractor and 1 public owner. The resulting findings were: cooperation is essential in the construction sector but existing collaborative software platforms and tools are too rigid and lack from flexibility for supporting different cooperation situations (one different platform per situation!). Thus, the objective has been to develop a highly customizable and flexible platform of services that can be used in different cooperation situations. The validation of this idea was done by the CRTI-B (the national professional association promoting new usages of ICT in the construction sector, http://www.crtib.lu) in Luxembourg. The association clearly identifies the problem in terms of   (i) Human and organizational limits related to cooperative behaviors:   Structuring of documents not efficient, exchanges not enough described, too much documents/releases produced... and (ii) Technological/IT limits: No interoperability between tools, lack of flexibility and customization facilities, waiting times, no connection with internal management system... For the development of the CRTI-weB, regarding technology and scientific advances, the decision was to consider Model Driven Engineering approaches and Service Oriented Architectures for their support to flexibility and customization.

**Design:** The design activity was concerned with the elicitation and the modeling of requirements regarding the IT platform services to be developed. To this end, we decided to setup different working groups, involving person's representative of the major building trades (i.e. public owners, architects and engineers, contractors, manufacturers...) in order to let them define usual collaborative practices in a consensual way. During 2 years, 14 working groups were conducted, involving 10-15 persons in each session. These working groups then permitted the practitioners to debate and finally agree on standardized best practices and associated requirements for the CRTI-weB service. A total of 14 best practices were defined as well as the associated IT services (see below "service engineering". Two sets of best practices separately addressed "meeting report management" and "document management". We underline here that it is the role of the CRTI-B as a multi-trades representative body to standardize practices in a consensus requirements engineering methodology.

**Engineering:** As part of this process, six releases of a CRTI-weB demonstrator have been incrementally developed and regularly validated with different working groups. Through a prototyping approach we were also able to refine and/or revise some of the requirements collected during the previous Service Design stage, in particular the non-functional ones associated with the user interface. The development of the different successive prototypes was greatly enhanced by the use of model driven approaches as well as by a service oriented architecture. This facilitated the generation of the code associated with the successive prototypes as well as the flexibility of the architecture. Approximately one prototype (or sub-function of a prototype) was developed for one working group.

**Exposition:** Regarding the exposition of the CRTI-weB prototypes, two major challenges have been accomplished; on the one hand, the best practices and their associated requirements identified at the Service Design stage have been identified as standard best practices by the CRTI-B, and are promoted by key stakeholders of CRTI-B . On the other hand, an important department (APB) of the ministry managing the public construction projects has decided to promote the use of a platform like the CRTI-weB for its own projects. As a consequence, a partnership has been signed with a private software company for transforming the software prototype into a software product made commercially available.    Moreover the CRTI-weB® trademark has been registered for licensing purposes.

**Operation:** The CRTI-weB product has started to be commercially used in real construction projects in 2010, but CRP Henri Tudor experimented it through living lab projects early in 2006.

Through these projects, we have been available to study the end-users appropriation of the tool within a real context. We have considered three types of appropriation. On the one hand, the "technical" appropriation refers to a co-adaptation, in which the users adapt the tool to their frequent uses and adapt themselves to the characteristics of the new tool and to the norms (best practices) embedded in it. A good example in CRTI-weB is the standard name used for sharing documents between projects' participants. The tool "forces" them to agree on a standard naming of all documents at the beginning of the project. On the other hand the "social" dimension of appropriation focuses on the users as individuals, social actors whose behaviors are regulated by social norms. The CRTI-weB tool is a social construction, not only physically developed by humans but also socially built. Then the "socio-technical network" dimension targets how the actors network around the software service. One major point consists in appreciating the representativeness of the actors involved in experiments. We believe that experimental users have to represent most of the building sector profiles (owners, designers: engineers/architects and contractors) in order the appropriation be higher. In our case all profiles are represented. But we notice that designers (engineers and architects) are most involved in new demands and business service improvements. Finally appropriation also has a "managerial" dimension as the role of coordination in AEC projects is determining. Exchanges between the different actors of the project enables each of them to understand how important it is for the others, favoring motivation and trust.

**Monitoring:** At this date, Tudor is the responsible of the functional evolutions of the services platform and accompanies the construction practitioners in the specification of new requirements for future versions of these services. The satisfaction of users is collected by CRP Henri Tudor's team. Recently a questionnaire has been sent to all CRTI-weB users to ask them to provide their feedback on the various functionalities of the service. The "support service" provided by the private company as well as their "training service" was also assessed. This questionnaire has been followed by a working group session, with 8 representative users, dedicated to the improvements of CRTI-weB.

From interactions with stakeholders involved in these projects, we have been able to collect a set of requirements for new features to be included. Those are feeding new future cycles of the S2IP for the future, in the framework of ongoing and future research projects. Technical improvements of the platform are planned, such as multiple upload of documents. A mobile version is also under design at CRP Henri Tudor, with the aim to provide functions for mobile business situations as well as to discover new mobile usages supported by CRTI-weB enhanced with mobile technologies (geopositioning, multi-touch interfaces…). Finally a new service is under development in the framework of a new research project (CRTI-weB 2.0), and aims at improving the production of documents within and architecture or engineering firm (e.g. design and construction plans) and their sharing directly with CRTI-weB.

## 5    Conclusion

In this paper, we are advocating that service science is special case of design science. From a review of some design science research methods used in the I.S. and organizational studies, we can conclude that their underlying principles are also jointly applicable to service systems. However the specific nature of services has also to be considered and thus additional ingredients should be added in an adequate service system design science research method.

From this analysis, we propose a process reference model (S3IP) illustrating the application of this research method in the context of our Research and Technological Organisation (RTO) innovation mission. This process highlights the influence of the intensive networking, including the cross-functional collaboration within the organization and further emphasizes the downstream alliances with key beneficiaries and end-users of the generated innovations. In turn, these strong ties with users foster the sustainability of the innovation and through the capitalization phase, it is the innovation process itself that may be considered as sustainable, provided that all the capitalization mechanisms are actually put in place. Finally, this model captures the knowledge-intensiveness characteristic, which is also a common point with the 5th generation models [27].

To illustrate its application we consider a software intensive service system that we have developed in the construction context. Meanwhile we are also considering its application in other types of service innovation based on different artefacts. For example, in [28], the artefact is a method delivered as a service.

One of our further steps is to better related design science and natural science within the context of service science artefacts. As explained in [30] there are clear bridges between the two, which also apply to service innovation. Although service systems are artificial objects, once they are deployed, they are part of the real world. Thus, they can be the topic of observations and of theory formulation according to natural science research method. For example, in our S3IP process, the formulation of a problem could be based on such theory established during the service value process. At the stage of the service operation, observations of the deployed service could also result in theory associated with the performance of the service in a given context. Sustainability and openness are other research issues we intend to deal with regarding the specificities of the chosen approach in terms of DSRM in our Research Center working as a living lab [32]

# References

1. Glushko, R.J.: Designing a service science discipline with disciplinel. IBM Systems Journal 47(1), 15–27 (2008)
2. Irene, C.L., Maull, R.S.: Embedding the new discipline of Service Science: A Service Science Research Agenda. In: Proceedings of the Fifth IEEE International Conference on Service Operations, Logistics and Informatics (SOLI 2009), Chicago, USA, July 22 (2009)
3. Becker, J., Beverungen, D., Matzner, M., Müller, O., Pöppelbuß, J.: Design Science in Service Research: A Framework-Based Review of IT Artifacts in Germany. In: Jain, H., Sinha, A.P., Vitharana, P. (eds.) DESRIST 2011. LNCS, vol. 6629, pp. 366–375. Springer, Heidelberg (2011)
4. Spohrer, J., Maglio, P.P., Bailey, J., Gruhl, D.: Steps toward a science of service sytems. IEEE Computer 40, 71–77 (2007)
5. Manual, O.: The Measurement of Scientific and Technological Activities, Proposed Guidelines for Collecting and Interpreting Technological Innovation Data. In: OECD 2006 (2006)
6. Simon, H.A.: The Sciences of the Artificial, 3rd edn. MIT Press, Cambridge (1996)
7. Hevner, A., March, S., Park, J., Ram, S.: Design science in information system. MIS Quarterly 28(1) (2004)
8. Peffers, K., Tuunanen, T., Rothenberger, M., Chatterjee, S.: A design science research methodology for information systems research. Journal of Management Information Systems 24(3) (2008)
9. Jelinek, M., Romme, G., Boland, R.: Introduction to the special issue: Organization studies as a science for design: Creating collaborative artifacts and research. Organization Studies 29(3), 317–329 (2008)
10. Mohrman, S.A.: Having relevance and impact: The benefits of integrating the perspectives of design science and organizational development. Journal of Applied Behavioural Science 43(1), 12–22 (2007)
11. Van Aken, J.E.: Management research as a design science: Articulating the research products of Mode 2 knowledge production. British Journal of Management 16, 19–36 (2005)
12. Denyer, D., Tranfield, D., Van Aken, J.E.: Developing Design Propositions through Research Synthesis. Organization Studies 29, 393–413 (2008)
13. Romme, G.: Making a difference: Organization as design. Organization Science 14, 558–573 (2003)
14. Van Aken, J.E.: Management research based on the paradigm of the design science: The quest for field-tested and grounded technological rules. Journal of Management Studies 41(2), 219–246 (2004)
15. Andriessen, D.: Combining design-based research and action research to test management solutions. In: 7th World Congress Action Learning, Action Research and Process Management, Groningen (2007)
16. Cook, T.D.: Quasi-experimentation: Its ontology. In: Morgan, G. (ed.) Beyond Method: Strategies For Social Research, pp. 74–94. Sage Publishers (1983)

17. Susman, G.I., Evered, R.D.: An assessment of the scientific merits of action research. Administrative Science Quarterly 23, 582 (1978)
18. Payne, A., Storbacka, K., Frow, P.: Managing the co-creation of value. Journal of the Academy of Marketing Science 36(1), 83–96 (2008)
19. Prahalad, C.K., Ramaswamy, V.: The new frontier of experience innovation. MIT Sloan Mgtt. Review 44(4), 12–18 (2003)
20. Sanders, E.B.-N.: Design Research in 2006. Design Research Quarterly 1(1) (2006)
21. Järvinen, P.: Action research is similar to design science. Quality & Quantity 41, 37–54 (2007)
22. Reeves, C.A., Bednar, A.: Defining Quality: Alternatives and Implications. The Academy of Management Review 19(3), 419–445 (1994)
23. Menor, L.J., Tatikonda, M.V., Scott, E., Sampson, S.E.: New service development: areas for exploitation and exploration. Journal of Operations Management 20, 135–157 (2002)
24. Alam, I., Perry, C.: A customer-oriented new service development process. Journal of Services Marketing 16(6), 515–534 (2002)
25. Kubicki, S., Dubois, E., Halin, G., Guerriero, A.: Towards a Sustainable Services Innovation in the Construction Sector. In: van Eck, P., Gordijn, J., Wieringa, R. (eds.) CAiSE 2009. LNCS, vol. 5565, pp. 319–333. Springer, Heidelberg (2009)
26. Kubicki, S., Guerriero, A., Johannsen, L.: A Service-based Innovation Process for Improving Cooperative Practices in AEC. Journal of Information Technology in Construction (2009), http://www.itcon.org
27. Bernacconi, J.-C., Mention, A.-L., Rousseau, A.: Knowledge-based innovation in a service economy: An innovation management process governance model in a RTO. In: Proceedings of the 1st ISPIM Innovation Symposium (2009)
28. Barafort, B., Rousseau, A.: Sustainable Service Innovation Model: A Standardized IT Service Management Process Assessment Framework. In: O'Connor, R.V., Baddoo, N., Cuadrago Gallego, J., Rejas Muslera, R., Smolander, K., Messnarz, R. (eds.) EuroSPI 2009. CCIS, vol. 42, pp. 69–80. Springer, Heidelberg (2009)
29. Spohrer, J., Maglio, P.P., Bailey, J., Gruhl, D.: Steps Toward a Science of Service Systems. Computer 40(1), 71–77 (2007)
30. March, S., Smith, G.: Design and natural science research on information technology. Decision Support Systems 15(4), 251–266 (1995)
31. Ellis, D., Allen, D., Wilson, T.: Information Science and Information Systems: Conjunct Subjects Disjunct Disciplines. JASIS 50(12), 1095–1107 (1999)
32. Bergvall-Kåreborn, B., Ihlström Eriksson, C., Ståhlbröst, A., Svensson, J.: A Milieu for Innovation – Defining Living Labs. In: ISPIM Innovation Symposium (2009)

# Modeling Service Relationships
# for Service Networks

Jorge Cardoso

CISUC, Department of Informatics Engineering
University of Coimbra, Polo II, 3030 Coimbra, Portugal
jcardoso@dei.uc.pt

**Abstract.** The last decade has seen an increased interest in the study of
networks in many fields of science. Examples are numerous, from sociology to biology, and to physical systems such as power grids. Nonetheless,
the field of service networks has received less attention. Previous research
has mainly tackled the modeling of single service systems and service
compositions, often focusing only on studying temporal relationships between services. The objective of this paper is to propose a computational
model to represent the various types of relationships which can be established between services systems to model service networks. This work
acquires a particular importance since the study of service networks can
bring new scientific discoveries on how service-based economies operate
at a global scale.

**Keywords:** service relationship, service system, business service, open
service, service network, semantic Web.

## 1 Introduction

Many systems around us can be described by network models, which are structures consisting of nodes connected by edges. The examples available are numerous and range from social networks, to the Internet, to supply chains, and
to power grids. The global economy is itself a complex network composed of
national economies, which are themselves networks of markets, and markets are
also networks of providers, brokers, intermediaries, and consumers.

Understanding how services systems[1] evolve as networks and the risks and
gains of different topologies is becoming increasingly critical for society [1].
Vargo et al. [2], and others, have also perceived that society is moving into a
service-dominant system. Nonetheless, our knowledge on global service networks
is limited. Understanding the dynamics and laws governing service networks can
provide authoritative insights on *why* and *how* financial service systems fail. For
example, it can explain how the 2007–2012 global financial crisis propagated
throughout global service networks. It can also provide scientific grounds for the
engineering of efficient and robust service network topologies to resist adverse
environments.

---

[1] When no ambiguity arises, we will use the term *service* to refer to a *service system*.

J.F. e Cunha, M. Snene, and H. Nóvoa (Eds.): IESS 2013, LNBIP 143, pp. 114–128, 2013.

While service markets are ubiquitous, the study of service networks did not receive the needed attention. Research has been mainly done from a technical perspective by modeling single services as software components (e.g. Web services [3]). Business process and workflow management have also looked into how services can be composed to form process models by establishing temporal dependencies between services (c.f. [4]). The goal of the research conducted was not to model service networks as the representation of economic activities, but to model the technical interfaces that need to be in place to integrate information systems to operate in heterogeneous environments.

In [5,6] we proposed to model service networks by constructing what we call *Open Semantic Service Networks (OSSN)*. These networks are constructed by accessing, retrieving, and combining information from *service systems* and *relationship models* globally distributed. With respect to the modeling of services, we have developed a family of languages named *-USDL (the Unified Service Description Language)[7,8] to provide computer-understandable descriptions for business services. These languages[2,3,4] allow to formalize business services in such a way that they can be used effectively, for example, for dynamic service outsourcing and automatic service contract negotiation.

Since our previous work yielded suitable computational models to represent service systems, the objective of this paper is to propose a model to represent the various types of relationships which can exist in a service network. The model developed, and called *Open Semantic Service Relationship (OSSR)* model, is computer-understandable, is represented with semantic Web languages, and defines the main concepts and properties required to established rich semantic relationships between service models. We believe that the importance and expressiveness of relationships has been overlooked in many fields. Gradde and Snehota [9] also believe that existing studies on relationships in the field of business models usually oversimplify business representations. For example, we consider that the simple relations used by other modeling initiatives such Linked Data [10] to interconnect data – using rdfs:subClassOf, owl:EquivalentClass, and owl:sameAs – the relation foaf:knows from FOAF [11] to interconnect people, and the use of rdfs:seeAlso by SIOC [12] to interconnect documents are strict and limited relationships not suitable to connect service systems. Therefore, we developed a multi-layer relationship model which links services via multiple types of connecting perspectives (e.g. participating roles, interconnection level, and involvement strength [13,14,15,9]) capturing the richness, complexity, and characteristics of services. This goes well beyond the connection of service systems treated simply as unidimensional nodes.

This paper is organized as follows. In the next section, we present important definitions and illustrate application domains for service networks to serve as motivation scenarios. Section 3 describes the multi-level relationship model developed to connect service systems. Section 4 describes the evaluation and

---

[2] Linked-USDL = http://linked-usdl.org/

[3] $\alpha$-USDL = http://www.genssiz.org/research/service-modeling/alpha-usdl/

[4] USDL = http://www.w3.org/2005/Incubator/usdl/

implementation of the model. Section 5 presents the related work in this field of research. Section 6 is the conclusion.

## 2    Definitions and Motivation Scenarios

A *service network* is defined as a graph structure composed of service systems which are nodes connected by one or more specific types of service relationship, the edges. A *service system* is a functional unit with a boundary through which interactions occur with the environment, and, especially, with other service systems. Service networks are similar to social networks in their structure but connect service systems. They are different from process models since they do not place an emphasis on control-flow, temporal dependencies, and cases. We illustrate their possible use with two application domains.

*Regulation of Service Markets.* The analysis of service networks can detect topological patterns such as oligopolies, monopolies, or 'cartels' in service markets. For example, a power-law distribution pattern can be used to identify oligopolies since it implies that only a few large service providers exist, whereas the occurrence of small providers is extremely common. The identification of such network characteristics or anomalies are of importance for regulatory bodies such as the EU which routinely passes directives for European markets on laws to be followed.

*Supply Chain Management.* While supply-chain management is crucial for many companies, today, there is no practical and automated solution to analyze global supply-chain networks. The inexistence of global models only enables to study this type of networks from a local, reduced, and naïve view (c.f. [16]). The development of computational models will give firms a better understanding of the dynamic behavior of supply chain networks at a global scale.

## 3    Multi-layer Relationship Model

When examining previous approaches to model network structures by using semantic Web languages, relationships were often overlooked by placing the emphasis on nodes. For example, the use of simple primitives such as `foaf:knows`, `rdfs:subClassOf`, `owl:EquivalentClass`, `rdf:seeAlso` and `owl:sameAs` to connect people, data, and community generated documents (c.f. [10,11,12]) is limited for service networks. It only enables to create networks with one homogeneous layer thus limiting the types of analysis which can be made. The richness of service systems – which involve people, laws, resources, operations, processes, service levels, etc. – requires a different approach based on the use of multiple layers to construct service networks. For example, two service systems can be related by describing the roles they can take, by representing the strength of the relationship, and by establishing a comparison of the set of functionalities provided. This goes well beyond the connection of entities seen simply as unidimensional nodes.

To construct a comprehensive relationship model, we followed an inductive research approach. We conducted a literature review on work describing and discussing the types of relationships which exist in organizations applicable to the field of services. We electronically searched the titles, abstracts, keywords, and full texts of articles in GoogleScholar (`scholar.google.com`), SpringerLink (`link.springer.com`), Taylor & Francis (`www.tandf.co.uk`), and Google Books (`books.google.com`) for the main word string "relationship". The search included several variations of the original term like "service relationship", "service systems relationship", "business relationship" or "relationship model". Articles were read to determine there relevance for modeling relationships between service systems.

We identified propositions and generalized them in a theoretical multi-layer relationship model composed of six layers: 1) *role*, 2) *level*, 3) *involvement*, 4) *comparison*, 5) *association*, and 6) *causality*. OSSR comprises at total of 15 top level concepts, namely `Relationship`, `Service`, `Source`, `Target`, `Role`, `Level`, `Involvement`, `Comparison`, `Association`, `Causality`, `Cause`, `Link`, `Effect`, `Category`, and `KPI`. The layers are grouped together using the central concept `Relationship`. One of the endpoints of the relationship is the service source (`Source`) and the other one is the service target (`Target`). Both are subclasses of the concept `Service` which represents a service system possibly modeled with a language such as Linked-USDL (see §1 and §4).

The layers and concepts[5] are summarized in Table 1, illustrated in Figure 1, and described in the following sections. While the examples given are mainly from the field of Software-as-a-Service (SaaS), the model was designed to be applied to services that range from human-based services to fully automated software-based services.

**Table 1.** The multiple layers of the Open Semantic Service Relationship (OSSR) model

| Layer | Description |
|---|---|
| Role [14] | The role of the service sytems involved in a relationship. |
| Level [15] | The level (e.g. activity, resources, or people) at which a relation is established. |
| Involvement [9] | The strength of a relationship. |
| Comparison [17] | The comparison of service systems involved in a relationship. |
| Association [18] | An expression of the 'a part of' relation between two service systems. |
| Causality [19] | The influence that key performance indicators of one service system has in another service system. |

---

[5] The terms written using the `typewriter` font indicate a concept or property value of the OSSR model.

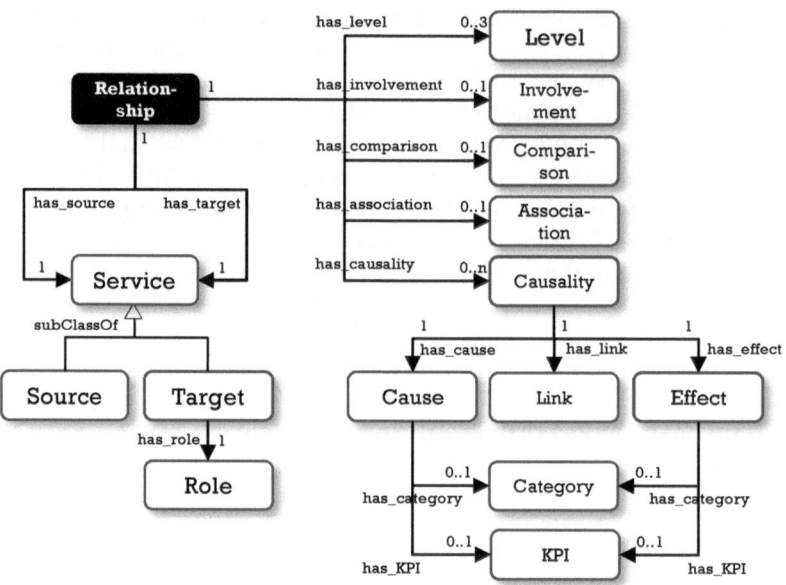

**Fig. 1.** The structure of the OSSR model

## 3.1   Participating Roles

Understanding roles is an important aspect to determine the position of a service system in a network. For example, a service can create alliances with complementors to differentiate itself from competition to deliver more value to customers. We rely on the work from Ritter et al. [14] to classify the role of the service systems involved in a relationship in four distinct types captured with the concept `Role`:

1. Customer,
2. Supplier,
3. Competitor, and
4. Complementor.

A service source which establishes a relationship with a service target with the role of `Customer` focuses on a good working mode with customers keeping always in mind the co-creation of value during service provisioning. A relationship with a service target of type `Supplier` focuses often on a durable stream of competitive advantage which maybe hard for others to imitate or break.

Complementors are the mirror image of competitors. In other words, customers value a service more when complementors exist whereas they value a service less when competitors exist [20]. A relationship with a target service of type `Complementor` enables a service source to increase its value by adding external operations to it. A service system $S_c$ is a complementor if customers value service system $S_i$ more when they have service $S_c$ than when they have service $S_i$ alone. One example is joining a flight transportation service, an accommodation service and a car renting service whereby services cooperate in reaching out to customers in the form of value added promotions. Finally, a service system can establish a relationship of type `Competitor` with a service target that belongs to a group of competing firms. In other words, service $S_c$ is a competitor if customers value service $S_i$ less when they have access to service $S_c$ than when they have service $S_i$ alone.

For example, the SaaS SugarCRM has several competitors including Sales-Force.com Sales Cloud, Microsoft On-Demand Dynamics CRM, and Oracle CRM OnDemand. Avis Scandinavia, a company providing rental services, is a customer of SugarCRM. Sage ERP and Sugar ERP Business Suite are complementors of SugarCRM. The SugarCRM service is a customer of Oracle and IBM since it relies on Oracle 11g or IBM DB2 database support services.

### 3.2   Interconnection Level

It is fundamental that a service system relates its activities, its actors, and its resources to those of other firms' services to streamline integration. Only the consideration of various levels can led to a sound integration of service system layers into networks. Håkansson and Snehota [15] showed that relationships can perform a variety of actions through:

1. Activity links,
2. Actor bonds, and
3. Resource ties.

This classification is captured by the concept `Level` which is associated with the concept `Relationship`. An activity link (modeled with the concept `ActivityLink`) refers to the integration of activities, tasks, or operations executed under the control of two service systems. Many arguments for closely integrating activities between manufacturers, suppliers, and customers originated from the fields of business process management and business process reengineering. In other words, this concept makes it possible to create cross-organizational workflows and business processes underlying a service network.

Actor bonds (modeled with the concept `ActorBond`) refer to the interaction among participants belonging to the human resource structure of distinct services. The objective of this concept is to enable the analysis and reasoning on social enterprise networks.

Resource ties (modeled with the concept `ResourceTie`) refer to the exchange of resources types. According to the resource-based view [21], service systems can differentiate themselves and increase their competitiveness by using heterogeneous, immobile, valuable, rare, inimitable, and non-substitutable resources. The concept of resource ties is aligned with the concept of value exchanged within companies in e$^3$value [22]. For example, the Progress Apama SaaS for complex event processing for capital markets establishes resource ties in the form of events with the stock exchange market service. This latter service executes trading operations and continuously sends events to Progress Apama.

These three levels of integration can benefit from extending the OSSR model by referencing Linked Data concepts to provide more information on the activities, actors, and resources exchanged among two service systems. For example, references using URI can be made to the type of resources being exchanged: 'US dollars' or 'BMW PART NR. 11127790052'.

### 3.3   Involvement Strength

The concept Involvement represents stakeholders willingness to establish a partnership. Gradde and Snehota [9] proposed to make a qualitative evaluation of relationships strength by using intensity properties. Higher levels of involvement usually mean that both parties are more interested to establish a long-term partnership while lower levels of involvement suggest that both parties choose for a more simplified relationship. The concept can take two forms:

1. Low-involvement and
2. High-involvement.

While High-involvement relationships are associated with investment logic, Low-involvement relationships can be handled with limited coordination, adaptation and interaction costs. For example, the SaaS SugarCRM establishes partnerships with technology partners such as Epicom Corporation[6], a company providing customization services, among others services. A relationship between these two service systems can be classified as low- or high-involvement depending on the number of customized business applications made by Epicom for SugarCRM, and the number of customers and users the customizations have.

### 3.4   Functional Comparison

Comparison consists in the identification of similarities and differences between service systems. A service system can be described by the functionalities and characteristics it provides (i.e. activities, operations, functions, options, etc.). Let us consider that the set of functionalities and characteristics provided by a service is represented by $fc(S_i)$. When comparing two service systems, we can identify five possible comparison cases (the cases were derived from set theory [17] and object-oriented programming [18]) expressing the degree of equivalence between two services:

1. $fc(S_i)$ is equivalent to $fc(S_j)$, $(fc(S_i) \equiv fc(S_j))$,
2. $fc(S_i)$ is a generalization of $fc(S_j)$, $(fc(S_i) \subsetneq fc(S_j))$,

---

[6] http://www.epicom.com/

3. $fc(S_i)$ is a **specialization** of $fc(S_j)$, $(fc(S_i) \supsetneq fc(S_j))$,
4. $fc(S_i)$ is **similar** to $fc(S_j)$, $(FC = fc(S_i) \cap fc(S_j), FC \neq \varnothing \wedge fc(S_i) \wedge FC \neq fc(S_i) \neq fc(S_j))$, and
5. $fc(S_i)$ is **different** from $fc(S_j)$, $(fc(S_i) \cap fc(S_j) \in \varnothing)$.

These cases are captured by the concept **Comparison**. Comparing two service systems cannot be viewed as a precise science and has often a high degree of subjectivity, especially when services involve sociotechnical subsystems. Subjectivity is an intrinsic aspect of the physical world. For example, the characteristics of an object in the physical world depends on the direction from which it is viewed. Therefore, all observations of physical characteristics are relative to the frame of reference of the observer, and the results reflect the state of observer.

Two service systems are **Equivalent** (full equivalence) when they are identical in their functionalities and characteristics. The specialization and generalization relationships are both reciprocal and hierarchical. The value **Generalization** (partial equivalence) expresses that a service has a narrower set of functionalities than another. The value **Specialization** (partial equivalence) expresses that a service has a broader set of functionalities than the other one. A **specialization** has the same semantics of the generalization relation but works in the opposite direction.

For example, the SaaS SugarCRM provides four packages: professional, corporate, enterprise, and ultimate. The base service is the same but the packages offer a different set of functionalities and characteristics. In other words, there is a implicit containment hierarchy $fc(S_{professional}) \subset fc(S_{corporate}) \subset fc(S_{enterprise}) \subset fc(S_{ultimate})$. The professional service has all the features that the corporate service has but does not include the option Sugar Mobile Plus; and the ultimate service is the only service providing 250GB Sugar On-Demand Storage. Therefore, the SugarCRM professional service is a **generalization** of the corporate service and the ultimate service is a **specialization** of all the others.

The value **Similar** (inexact equivalence) expresses that services are similar. Some functionalities intersect while others are disjoint.

A relationship of type **Different** indicates that two services do not have any functionality in common.

## 3.5   Service Association

The association of service systems enables to combine simpler services into more complex service systems. Associations are a critical building block of many fields of science (e.g. biology, physics, and programming). The concept **Association** can take the form of an:

1. Aggregation or a
2. Composition.

An association of type aggregation expresses 'a part of' or 'has a' relationship between two service systems. One of the services has the role of assembly and the other one has the role of component. The value `AggregationBy` indicates that the service source has the role of assembly and the service target has the role of component. The value `AggregationOf` is the inverse relation. It indicates that the service source has the role of component and the target service has the role of assembly. For example, an airline service is an aggregation of security, check-in, catering, handling, and cleaning services. Another example from the SaaS arena is the Internet self-service named IT Incident Management Service (ITIMS) adapted from ITIL best practices and described in [23]. The service is an aggregation which relies on three SaaS components to operate: the platform provider `Heroku.com`, the database provider `MongoDB.com`, and the email gateway provider `McAfee.com`. In other words, ITIMS establishes an `AggregationBy` with three other SaaS which take the role of role of components.

A composition is a specialized form of strong aggregation where component services cease to exist, or are not needed, if the assembly service ceases to exist. The value `CompositionBy` is the inverse of value `CompositionOf`. It indicates that the service source has the role of component and the target service has the role of assembly.

### 3.6    Causality between Services

A relationship has also associated a `Causality` concept. Causality or cause-effect describe how a *cause* event occurring in a service system has an *effect* in another service system. Causality is expressed using key performance indicators (KPI) of service systems which are connected. KPIs are often associated with service level (see *-USDL) and quality of service (QoS), and include parameters such as availability, cost, downtime, errors, response rime, etc. For example, the Invoice Accuracy KPI of a service provider to control the quality of service $S_p$ can be connected to the Time Delivery KPI of a service customer $S_c$. An increase of the first KPI will originate an increase in the second KPI since it will take more time to resolve errors. This cause-effect relation between KPIs enables to conduct the quantitative analysis of the propagation of changes or domino effect in a service network.

The system dynamics or systems thinking approach [19] is used to capture and enable the posteriori analysis of service networks. Instead of looking at causes (captured with the concept `Cause`) and their effects (captured with the concept `Effect`) in isolation, systems thinking enables to look at service networks as a system made up of interacting parts. The concept `Link` connects a cause to and sets the sign that a directed link can take: `Positive` or `Negative`. A positive link indicates that a change (increase or decrease) in a service KPI results in the same type of change (increase or decrease) in another service KPI. A negative link indicates that a change (increase or decrease) in a service KPI results in the opposite change (decrease or increase) in another service KPI.

By using the concept of causality it becomes possible to express and quantify the impact that one service system has in other service systems. This capability brings an important contribution to service networks. It enables to think about a service network as a complex dynamic system to study how a service behavior affects the provisioning of other services. Its application to global networks will make it possible to discover new scientific insights on global digital service economies.

Since KPIs are often domain dependent and their semantics may not always be clear to analysts, individual measures of performance in a cause-effects relation are classified with a schema composed of five elements (c.f. [24]) captured by the concept `Category`:

1. Quality,
2. Time,
3. Cost,
4. Flexibility, and
5. Other.

The use of this schema provides a level of abstraction which enables, for example, a time-based analysis of service network. Since the meaning of the elements that compose the schema is intuitive they will not be further explained.

## 4    Evaluation and Implementation

To evaluate the OSSR model from a user, expert, and ontology engineer point-of-view, we have followed the frame of reference proposed in [25]. It consisted in verifying several aspects of the model.

- *Consistency.* In this phase, we tried to identify possible design errors. We did not find circular definitions; the model was syntactically correct; it was validated using Protégé and Jena; several instances of the model were created; no contradictory knowledge was detected; and all concepts were consistent with the theoretical definitions of relationships.
- *Completeness, expandability, and sensitiveness.* In a second phase, we tried to locate concepts whose modeling was incomplete by reexamining the literature on relationships. We looked at the OSSR model from a holistic perspective and we have identified that the causality concept required an additional element to enable the dynamic analysis of service networks: the direction of the cause-effect link. We believe that the model is not complete and additional relations types will be added in the future as the model is experimented in industrial settings. The model is expandable since it is constructed based on the notion of layers: new relations can be added without altering the set of well-defined relations that are already guaranteed. The use of layers also make the model relatively insensitive to small changes.
- *Conciseness.* We proved the conciseness of the model by asserting that it did not contained redundant or unnecessary definitions. Redundancies could not be inferred using other knowledge.

The OSSR model was considered to be valid from a conceptual and formal point-of-view.

Our idea behind the implementation of service relationships is pragmatic and it is based on the objective to create a linked global service network using machine-readable descriptions [26]. Therefore, the model was implemented using the Resource Description Framework (RDF) which allows semantic information to be expressed as a graph. To improve the integration with other semantic Web initiatives, the model establishes links with various existing ontologies to reuse concepts from vertical and horizontal domains such as SKOS (taxonomies), Dublin Core (documents), Linked-USDL (service descriptions) and so on. The implementation is available at `http://rdfs.genssiz.org/ossr.rdf`.

The OSSR model was designed to integrate with Linked-USDL. In other words, a relationship connects two service systems which can be represented with Linked-USDL. Since the model references services using a URI, other service descriptions can be used (e.g. WSDL, OWL-S, and *-USDL [7,8]). Compared to the various choices available, the use of USDL has many benefits since it bridges a business, an operational, and a technical perspective to describe services. Once services and relationships are described in RDF with Linked-USDL and OSSR, respectively, it becomes possible to make queries over distributed service networks using the SPARQL RDF query language [27].

Listing 1 illustrates the use of the OSSR model. The relationship created, identified by `http://rdfs.genssiz.org/ossr/2012/10/`, relates two services: SurgarCRM and MySQL. The first service was modeled with Linked-USDL and its modeling is available at `http://rdfs.genssiz.org/SurgarCRM.ttl`. The model was based on the SaaS customer relationship management software available at `http://www.sugarcrm.com/`. The second service modeled was MySQL (`http://www.mysql.com/`). The relationship was modeled from the SugarCRM point-of-view since the OSSR model specifies that it is the source element.

```
 1  <ossr:Relationship rdf:about="http://rdfs.genssiz.org/ossr/2012/10/">
 2      <ossr:has_source>
 3          <ossr:Source>
 4          </ossr:Source>
 5              <ossr:has_service>http://rdfs.genssiz.org/SurgarCRM#
                    offering_SugarCRM</ossr:has_service>
 6      </ossr:has_source>
 7      <ossr:has_target>
 8          <ossr:Target>
 9              <ossr:has_service>http://rdfs.genssiz.org/MySQL#
                    offering_MySQL</ossr:has_service>
10              <ossr:has_role>Provider</ossr:has_role>
11          </ossr:Target>
12      </ossr:has_target>
13      <ossr:has_involvement>HighInvolvement</ossr:has_involvement>
14      <ossr:has_level>ActivityLink</ossr:has_level>
15      <ossr:has_comparison>Different</ossr:has_comparison>
16      <ossr:has_association>AggregationOf</ossr:has_association>
17      <ossr:has_causality>
```

```
18              <ossr:Causality>
19                  <ossr:has_cause>
20                      <ossr:Cause>
21                          <ossr:has_KPI>http://rdfs.genssiz.org/MySQL#
                                var_MySQL_Reliability </ossr:has_KPI>
22                          <ossr:has_category>Quality</ossr:has_category>
23                      </ossr:Cause>
24                  </ossr:has_cause>
25                  <ossr:has_link>
26                      <ossr:Link>
27                          <ossr:has_direction>Positive</ossr:has_direction>
28                      </ossr:Link>
29                  </ossr:has_link>
30                  <ossr:has_effect>
31                      <ossr:Effect>
32                      <ossr:has_KPI>
33              http://rdfs.genssiz.org/SurgarCRM#
                    var_SugarCRM_AvailabilityGuarantee_Value
34                  </ossr:has_KPI>
35                          <ossr:has_category> Quality </ossr:has_category>
36                      </ossr:Effect>
37                  </ossr:has_effect>
38              </ossr:Causality>
39          </ossr:has_causality>
40  </ossr:Relationship>
```

**Listing 1.** Example of an OSSR relationship relating two service systems

The relationship indicates that the MySQL service system is a provider of the SugarCRM service; the two services have a high degree of involvement; they establish a relation at the activity level; the service systems are different; and MySQL is a component of the SugarCRM service offering. Finally, a cause-effect relation on quality is established between the KPI `Availability` of the SugarCRM and the KPI `Reliability` of MySQL. This causality is positive since when the `Reliability` of MySQL increases/decreases the `Availability` of the SugarCRM service also increases/decreases. In this exercise, only one relationship was created, but several relationships can be created between two service systems, for example, to express more complex cause-effect relations.

## 5   Related Work

The work on relationships has mainly been carried out in the fields of business management, supply chain management, and operation management. The main contributions (e.g. [13,14,15,9]) have generally discussed the objectives, motivation, and benefits of relationships for businesses. While business relationships look at relationships from a macro perspective, service relationships look at relationships from a micro perspective. According to Jensen and Petersen [28], in service-based economies there is a fundamental need to move from a macro strategic business orientation to a fine-grained activity-based service analysis. Furthermore, previous work does not proposes conceptual models nor formalisms to build computer-understandable descriptions of relationships as described in this paper.

$e^3$service [22] provides an ontology to model e-business models and services. The model targets to represent very simple relations between services from an internal perspective, e.g. core-enhancing, core-supporting, and substitute. From an external perspective, the value chains proposed do not capture explicitly service networks across agents and do not try to analyze quantitatively the effect of relationships.

In [29], the authors look at service networks from a Business Process Management (BPM) and Service Oriented Architecture (SOA) perspectives and present the Service Network Notation (SNN). SNN provides UML artifacts to model value chain relationships of economic value. These relationships take the form of what we can call 'weak' relationships since they only capture offerings and rewards which occur between services. The notation is to be used to describe how a new service can be composed from a network of existing services. The focus is on compositions, processes, and on establishing how new services can be created using BPM to describe the interactions of existing SOA-based services.

Allee [30] uses a graph-based notation to model value flows inside a network of agents such as the exchange of goods, services, revenue, knowledge, and intangible values. In the same lines, Weill and Vitale [31] have developed a formalism, called the e-business model schematic, to analyze businesses. The schematic is a graphical representation aiming at identifying a business model's important elements. This includes the firm relationships with its suppliers and allies, benefits each participant receives, and the major flows of product, information, and money. Both approaches only take into account value flows and do not consider other types of relationships that can be established between agents.

In all these works, relationships can benefit from a deeper study to increase their expressiveness rather than simply connecting flows, cross-organizational processes, or calculating the global added value of distributed activities. Roles, categorization, KPI dependencies, and cause-effect relations also need to be considered. Furthermore, existing modeling approaches fail to adhere to service-dominant logic [2] and focus too much inward the company instead of the service network they belong to.

# 6    Conclusions

To provide theories and methods to analyze service networks there is the essential prerequisite to model service systems and service relationships. In this paper we addressed the latter: the modeling of service relationships. Our approach considers that service systems are represented with existing description languages, such as Linked-USDL, and derives a rich, multi-level relationship model – named Open Semantic Service Relationship (OSSR) model – from an extensive literature review process. Service relationships are very different from the temporal and control-flow relations found in business process models. They need to relate service systems accounting for various perspectives such as roles, associations, dependencies, and comparisons. After designing the OSSR conceptual model, it was evaluated and implemented. The encoding was based on Linked Data principles to retain simplicity for computation, reuse existing vocabularies to maximize compatibility, and provide a simple - yet effective - means for publishing and interlinking distributed service descriptions for automated computer analysis.

# References

1. Spohrer, J., Maglio, P.P.: Service Science: Toward a Smarter Planet, pp. 1–30. John Wiley & Sons, Inc. (2010)
2. Vargo, S.L., Lusch, R.F.: Evolving to a new marketing dominant logic for marketing. Journal of Marketing 68(1), 1–17 (2004)
3. Erl, T.: Service-Oriented Architecture: Concepts, Technology, and Design. Prentice Hall PTR, Upper Saddle River (2005)
4. Cardoso, J., Sheth, A.: Semantic e-workflow composition. J. Intell. Inf. Syst. 21, 191–225 (2003)
5. Cardoso, J., Pedrinaci, C., Leidig, T., Rupino, P., Leenheer, P.D.: Open semantic service networks. In: The International Symposium on Services Science (ISSS 2012), Leipzig, Germany, pp. 1–15 (2012)
6. Cardoso, J., Pedrinaci, C., De Leenheer, P.: Open Semantic Service Networks: Modeling and Analysis. In: Novoa, H., Snene, M. (eds.) IESS 2013. LNBIP, vol. 143, pp. 141–154. Springer, Heidelberg (2013)
7. Cardoso, J., Barros, A., May, N., Kylau, U.: Towards a unified service description language for the internet of services: Requirements and first developments. In: IEEE International Conference on Services Computing. IEEE Computer Society Press, Florida (2010)
8. Barros, A., Oberle, D.: Handbook of Service Description: USDL and Its Methods. Springer (2012)
9. Gadde, L.-E., Snehota, I.: Making the most of supplier relationships. Industrial Marketing Management 29(4), 305–316 (2000)
10. Bizer, C., Heath, T., Berners-Lee, T.: Linked data - the story so far. Int. J. Semantic Web Inf. Syst. 5(3), 1–22 (2009)
11. Brickley, D., Miller, L.: FOAF Vocabulary Specification (2005)
12. Bojars, U., Breslin, J., Peristeras, V., Tummarello, G., Decker, S.: Interlinking the social web with semantics. IEEE Intelligent Systems 23(3), 29–40 (2008)
13. Anderson, J.C., Narus, J.A.: Partnering as a focused market strategy. California Management Review 33(3), 95–113 (1991)
14. Ritter, T., Wilkinson, I.F., Johnston, W.J.: Managing in complex business networks. Industrial Marketing Management 33(3), 175–183 (2004)
15. Håkansson, H., Snehota, I.: Developing relationships in business networks. Routledge (1995)

16. Chen, C.-L., Lee, W.-C.: Multi-objective optimization of multi-echelon supply chain networks with uncertain product demands and prices. Computers & Cal Engineering 28(6-7), 1131–1144 (2004)
17. Hausdorff, F.: Set Theory. AMS Chelsea Publishing Series. American Mathematical Society (1957)
18. Booch, G.: Object-Oriented Analysis and Design with Applications, 3rd edn. Addison Wesley Longman Publishing Co., Inc., Redwood City (2004)
19. Forrester, J.: Industrial dynamics. MIT Press, Cambridge (1961)
20. Brandenburger, A., Nalebuff, B.: Co-opetition. A terrific book. Doubleday (1996)
21. Wernerfelt, B.: A Resource-Based View of the Firm. Strategic Management Journal 5(2), 171–180 (1984)
22. Gordijn, J., Yu, E., van der Raadt, B.: e-service design using i* and e3value modeling. IEEE Software 23, 26–33 (2006)
23. Cardoso, J., Miller, J.A.: Internet-based self-services: from analysis and design to deployment. In: The 2012 IEEE International Conference on Services Economics (SE 2012). IEEE Computer Society, Hawaii (2012)
24. Cai, J., Liu, X., Xiao, Z., Liu, J.: Improving supply chain performance management: A systematic approach to analyzing iterative KPI accomplishment. Decision Support Systems 46(2), 512–521 (2009)
25. Gómez-Pérez, A.: Evaluation of ontologies. International Journal of Intelligent Systems 16(3), 391–409 (2001)
26. Davies, J., Fensel, D., van Harmelen, F. (eds.): Towards the Semantic Web: Ontology-driven Knowledge Management. John Wiley & Sons, Inc., New York (2003)
27. Prud'hommeaux, E., Seaborne, A.: SPARQL query language for RDF (2005), http://www.w3.org/TR/2005/WD-rdf-sparql-query-20050217/
28. Ørberg Jensen, P.D., Petersen, B.: Global sourcing of services versus manufacturing activities: is it any different? The Service Industries Journal 32(4), 591–604 (2012)
29. Danylevych, O., Karastoyanova, D., Leymann, F.: Service networks modelling: An SOA & BPM standpoint. Journal of Universal Computer Science 16(13), 1668–1693 (2010)
30. Allee, V.: Reconfiguring the value network. Journal of Business Strategy 21(4), 1–6 (2000)
31. Weill, P., Vitale, M.R.: Place to space: migrating to ebusiness models. Harvard Business School Press (2001)

# Evaluating the IT Strategic Plan for the Public Administration in Portugal

Diogo Nunes, Isabel Rosa,
and Miguel Mira da Silva

Instituto Superior Tecnico, Av. Rovisco Pais,
1049-001 Lisboa, Portugal
{diogo.alexandre,darosa.isabel,mms}@ist.utl.pt

**Abstract.** Over the years ICT kept evolving and spreading. This vulgarization sparked numerous *ad hoc* technological projects inside ministries and public institutes which led to the creation of small scattered technological infrastructures and solutions. The Portuguese Government started taking action with the writing of a strategic plan (PGETIC) with two major goals: increase the quality and usefulness of IT services and reduce the IT spending. However the plan isn't really strategic. Hence we propose the comparison of PGETIC with recognized IT Governance frameworks to find out where it excels and fails. Our evaluation indicates that PGETIC as a strategic plan is incomplete, redundant, excessive and overly low-level.

**Keywords:** IS/IT governance, Strategic plan assessment, Value oriented organizations, Public administration's ICT.

## 1    Introduction

Over the years ICT kept evolving and spreading. Nowadays they play a major role on increasing the efficiency and quality of organizations' processes – public and private alike. On this research we'll address only the public sector, namely the public administration's ICT in Portugal.

This popularization of IT sparked numerous *ad hoc* technological projects inside ministries and public institutes which led to the creation of small scattered technological infrastructures (e.g. data centers) and solutions (i.e. software). These multiple – and sometimes duplicated – infrastructures increased the global maintenance costs and the number of information systems that aren't interoperable [1]. Without economies of scale and the reuse of existing resources the Portuguese State spent too much on these projects while not getting the maximum value they could yield.

The Portuguese government started recently taking action with two major goals: increase the quality and usefulness of IT services and reduce the IT spending. The will to act came from the decrease in financial resources' availability and the commitment of the Portuguese government to fulfill the measure 3.46 of the Memorandum of Understanding [1].

J.F. e Cunha, M. Snene, and H. Nóvoa (Eds.): IESS 2013, LNBIP 143, pp. 129–140, 2013.
© Springer-Verlag Berlin Heidelberg 2013

## 1.1    Research Focus

As a result in 2011 the Portuguese government wrote a strategic plan for the public administration's ICT called PGETIC. The plan comprises five strategic orientations: *"Improving Governance, Cost-cutting, Using ICT to foster change and modernization, Implementation of common solutions, Promote economic growth"* [1]. The plan started in 2012 and will be executed on each Ministry's IT department. It's forecasted to save 500 million Euros, in addition to the functional improvements, over the 4 years of its implementation.

In this research we evaluate PGETIC's completeness and efficacy as strategic plan using IT-CMF, *"an integrating framework that enables CIOs and business management to deliver more value from IT investments and practices"* [2].

## 1.2    Research Methodology

During the elaboration of this document the seven guidelines of Design Science [3] were taken into account. Our research followed the Design Science Research Methodology [4] and its six activities: Problem identification and motivation, Definition of the objectives, Design and development, Demonstration, Evaluation and Communication. The Communication activity is this document itself.

## 1.3    Structure of This Document

This document has the following structure: the first section (Introduction) gives context and also specifies the research's focus and methodology; the second section (Related Work) introduces IT Governance and IT-CMF, presents the UK's Strategy for ICT and distinguishes it from the Portuguese PGETIC; the third section (Problem definition) states what is the problem and why it is a problem; the forth section (Solution proposal) defines a solution and its main objectives; the fifth section (Solution demonstration) materializes the solution proposed; the sixth section (Solution evaluation) evaluates the solution results both theoretically and practically; and the eighth section (Conclusion) summarizes the main contributions of this research and the future work. Finally there's a References section.

## 2    Related Work

### 2.1    IT Governance, Frameworks and IT-CMF

IT Governance (ITG) is a somewhat new and growing concept so there's a lack of a shared understanding of the term [5], with several definitions across articles and books, although with minor differences [6]. Indeed there were attempts [7] in the past to create a definitive definition of ITG, whose result was:

*"IT Governance is the strategic alignment of IT with the business such that maximum business value is achieved through the development and maintenance of effective IT control and accountability, performance management and risk management."*

ITG is a major concern for CIOs during the last decade because it's seen as a tool to increase returns on IT investments and improve organizational performance [5]. An important milestone was the emergence of ITG's frameworks. Today, several frameworks – e.g. COBIT, ITIL, and CMMI – exist to align IT with business or improve the efficacy and efficiency of the organization's processes.

We use a framework called IT Capability Maturity Framework (IT-CMF). IT-CMF categorizes the essential capabilities of the IT organization into four macro-capabilities: managing the IT budget, managing the IT capability, managing IT for business value, and managing IT like a business [8]. Each macro-capabilities breaks down into critical capabilities that *"represent the key activities and procedures that must be defined and mastered to enable an IT organization to plan and deliver IT solutions, and to measure the business value outcomes of its initiatives"* [9]. In total there are 33 critical capabilities. IT-CMF then describes for each (macro and critical) capability five levels of maturity – from 1 (Initial) to 5 (Optimizing), just as CMMI's levels of maturity. Lastly the framework suggests *"building blocks"* that work as roadmaps to improve each capability's maturity.

## 2.2    United Kingdom's Strategy Plan for ICT

In 2011 the United Kingdom wrote a Strategic Implementation Plan for the Government's ICT. The plan was forecasted to save 1.4 billion pounds [10] over the 4 years of its implementation. It contained four programmes: *"Reducing waste and project failure, and stimulating economic growth; Creating a common ICT infrastructure; Using ICT to enable and deliver change; Strengthening governance"* [11]. The plan's objectives were to [12]:

- *Make government ICT more open to the people and organizations that use our services, and open to any provider – regardless of size;*
- *Reduce the size and complexity of projects, and better manage risks;*
- *Enable reuse of existing ICT systems and "off the shelf" components, reducing duplication, over-capacity and saving money;*
- *Move towards a common infrastructure in government, increasing efficiency and interoperability;*
- *Reduce procurement timescales and making it simpler for SMEs to compete for government business;*
- *Improving the implementation of big ICT projects and programmes.*

There are some similarities between Portugal's PGETIC and UK's ICT Strategy. Consequently the following question arises: "Should the Portuguese Government implement the UK's Strategy in Portugal instead of PGETIC?" The answer is

"No" because the starting point and objectives of UK's Strategy are totally unlike Portugal's. Also the ICTs of UK's public administration are more mature and modern than Portugal's. The following comparison points out the differences between the two plans:

| UK's Strategy aims to: | Whereas Portugal's PGETIC aims to: |
| --- | --- |
| • Save over one billion pounds; | • Save over 500 million Euros; |
| • Reduce projects' size and complexity, decreasing their risk; | • Establish criterions for project's prioritization, decreasing IT spending; |
| • Go towards a common ICT architecture; | • Start modeling current architecture and reduce ICT infrastructure; |
| • Simplify procurement for SMEs to compete for government business; | • Establish partnerships to create and export innovations; |
| • Improve the implementation of big ICT projects. | • Define projects which modernize public administration. |

## 3    Problem Definition

In general terms "*a strategic plan is not the same thing as an operational plan. The former should be visionary, conceptual and directional in contrast to an operational plan which is likely to be shorter term, tactical, focused, implementable and measurable*" *[13]*. According to this definition PGETIC is an operational plan. First, all PGETIC's projects are meant to be implementable with specific objectives, actions and deadlines. Second, certain projects are just an enforcing of a policy – like 3.11, 3.12, 3.13 and 3.21 – or local (operational) fixes – like 3.9, 3.10, and 3.20.

A recent review of the literature [14] identifies three main conceptions of Information Systems strategy, which further refine the above definition:

1. *IS strategy as the use of IS to support business strategy;*
2. *IS strategy as the master plan of the IS function;*
3. *IS strategy as the shared view of the IS role within the organization.*

The authors summarized the different conceptions and their characteristics into a single table. According to that table PGETIC matches the second conception because it was developed in isolation from business strategy, is IS-centric and focused on what IS assets are required and how to allocate the existing ones efficiently. However the authors found the third conception to be the best fit with their definition of IS strategy.

Finally, José D. Coelho commented at itSMF [15] that "*PGETIC is complex, with numerous projects whose final result set isn't coherent, there isn't a target scenario*". He also warned that deadlines were "*excessively optimistic*" and that IT shouldn't be regarded as an expense to reduce as much as possible.

Thus, *PGETIC is not a strategic plan*. This is a problem that must be addressed – by an improved plan or by a new one – as soon as possible because if it isn't then 500 million Euros won't be saved; public administration's ICT will continue to spread and multiply like mushrooms; maintenance costs will rise as real value stagnates or decreases; and opportunities for innovation will be lost.

Although not strategic, we can consider PGETIC a contingency plan – one that aims to solve operational problems which should have been addressed a long time ago. In that context, it's useful to *evaluate its completeness, efficacy and efficiency*. That way we can understand where PGETIC excels and fails. That's what our proposal aims to do.

# 4    Proposal

We propose the comparison of PGETIC with recognized IT Governance frameworks, in order to assess how much the plan is aligned with them. We consider that by mapping the plan with one of such frameworks – one whose objective is maximizing value creation for the business – we'll be able not only to benchmark PGETIC as a solution to the problem of public administration's ICT but also, and mainly, detect areas in need of further improvement and areas not addressed at all.

For that comparison we find IT-CMF an appropriate tool. We choose this IT Governance framework over others mainly because IT-CMF:

- aligns business' needs and strategy with the services and infrastructures which IT provides;
- is particularly focused on converting IT from a cost center to a value generator;
- structures the organization into well-defined capabilities which makes their management more objective;
- contains a wide variety of capabilities that covers most organizations' concerns;
- offers a quick way to audit with sufficient accuracy the capabilities' maturity and enables benchmarking;
- for each capability there's a roadmap of building blocks to improve its maturity;
- it's interoperable with other existing maturity frameworks (e.g. ITIL, CMMI);
- has proven its value to big and medium sized organizations and is backed up by academics and practitioners who continuously refine it.

Being PGETIC a strategic plan for IT with business needs in mind, we need a high-level and holistic view. IT-CMF provides that differentiated view by looking at IT services as high-level tools capable of creating value for the business. By focusing on service and not on technology, on the intersection of IT and business and not on both singly, IT-CMF enables a clear alignment between the two – and it does so in a simple, structured and holistic way, unlike other frameworks.

The mapping we suggest will uncover PGETIC's completeness, efficacy and efficiency. With all these insights we'll be able to pinpoint the plan's shortcomings, which will in turn increase the quality of future improvement suggestions.

## 5    Proposal Demonstration

Recalling section 2, IT-CMF describes five levels of maturity for each of its macro and critical capabilities. Each description details how a company with a capability on that level of maturity acts. Therefore by mapping the descriptions of PGETIC's projects with the descriptions of IT-CMF's maturity levels we can infer the level of maturity of each capability after the implementation of the plan.

First, to get the big picture, we map the five PGETIC's programmes into the four IT-CMF's macro-capabilities (see Table 1). We do so finding the best match between the expected result set of each programme and the maturity levels' description. We repeat the method for each of the macro-capabilities. This map shows which programme contributes the most to which macro-capability. The last column consolidates all programmes' contributions for each macro-capability and shows the highest maturity level attainable.

A full level is represented by a circle and an intermediate level by a semi-circle, so for example "Cost-cutting" programme contributes to attain a maturity level between level one and two for the macro-capability "Managing IT like a business". A dark gray cell indicates a serious problem that must be solved urgently (e.g. a project which doesn't improve any capability); a light grey cell also alerts for something needing revision/correction but less severe than the previous case (e.g. a project that scarcely improves a capability).

**Table 1.** Mapping PGETIC's programmes to IT-CMF's macro-capabilities

| | Improving Governance | Cost-cutting | Using ICT to foster change and modernization | Implementation of common solutions | Promote economic growth | | |
|---|---|---|---|---|---|---|---|
| Managing IT like a business | ●● | ●◖ | ●● | ●●◖ | ●●◖ | } | ●●◖ |
| Managing the IT budget | ● | ● | ● | ● | ● | } | ○ |
| Managing the IT capability | ●● | ●◖ | ●◖ | ●●◖ | ●●◖ | } | ●●◖ |
| Managing IT for business value | ● | ●◖ | ● | ● | ●◖ | } | ●◖ |

Second, to assess in greater detail PGETIC's improvements, we drill-down to projects and critical capabilities. Similarly, in Table 2 each cell contains the capability's (line) maturity level achieved after implementing a given project (column). Level 1 maturities were ignored whereas all the previous semantics remain.

## 6    Proposal Evaluation

### 6.1    Theoretical Evaluation

To clearly illustrate and classify PGETIC's flaws we analyze our previous mapping (Table 2) using the same mapping analysis used in [16], which is based on an ontological evaluation [17]. This analysis (Table 3) reveals projects which improve no capability (excess), multiple projects implementing the same maturity level of a specific capability (overload) and capabilities that aren't improved at all (deficiency).

**Table 2.** Mapping PGETIC's projects to IT-CMF's critical capabilities

* Level 3 is reached if projects 3.7, 3.8, 3.15 and 3.18 are successfully completed. Otherwise Level 2 is achieved instead.

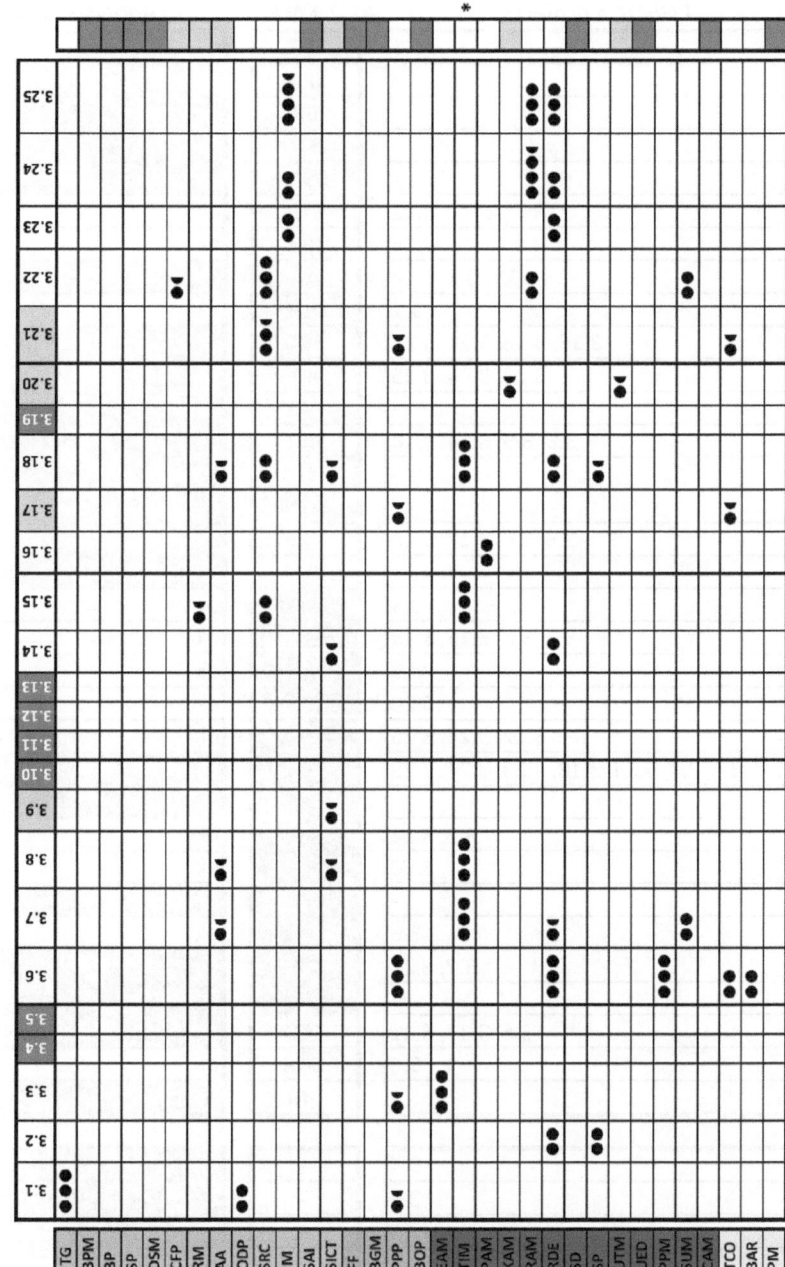

**Table 3.** Analysis of PGETIC's mapping into IT-CMF

| PGETIC's projects | IT-CMF | Analysis result |
|---|---|---|
| 3.1 | ITG | ok |
| - | BPM | deficiency |
| - | BP | deficiency |
| - | SP | deficiency |
| - | DSM | deficiency |
| 3.22 | CFP | ok |
| 3.15 | RM | ok |
| 3.7, 3.8, 3.18 | AA | overload ( ●◖ ) |
| 3.1 | ODP | ok |
| 3.15, 3.18, 3.21, 3.22 | SRC | overload ( ●● ) |
| 3.23, 3.24, 3.25 | IM | overload ( ●● ) |
| - | SAI | deficiency |
| 3.8, 3.9, 3.14, 3.18 | SICT | overload ( ●◖ ) |
| - | FF | deficiency |
| - | BGM | deficiency |
| 3.1, 3.3, 3.6, 3.17, 3.12 | PPP | overload ( ●◖ ) |
| - | BOP | deficiency |
| 3.3 | EAM | ok |
| 3.7, 3.8, 3.15, 3.18 | TIM | ok |
| 3.16 | PAM | ok |
| 3.20 | KAM | ok |
| 3.22, 3.24, 3.25 | RAM | ok |
| 3.2, 3.6, 3.7, 3.14, 3.18, 3.23, 3.24, 3.25 | RDE | overload ( ●● and ●●● ) |
| - | SD | deficiency |
| 3.2, 3.18 | SRP | ok |
| 3.20 | UTM | ok |
| - | UED | deficiency |
| 3.6 | PPM | ok |
| 3.7, 3.22 | SUM | overload ( ●● ) |
| - | CAM | deficiency |
| 3.6, 3.17, 3.21 | TCO | overload ( ●◖ ) |
| 3.6 | BAR | ok |
| - | PM | deficiency |

| PGETIC's projects | IT-CMF | Analysis result |
|---|---|---|
| 3.4 | - | excess |
| 3.5 | - | excess |
| 3.10 | - | excess |
| 3.11 | - | excess |
| 3.12 | - | excess |
| 3.13 | - | excess |
| 3.19 | - | excess |

It's positive that seven capabilities increase their maturity to level "Basic" and eight will reach level "Intermediate". In the end, almost half of the IT-CMF's capabilities will have a maturity level of 2 or higher. Nevertheless we must note some worrying negative aspects:

- *Excessively low-level to be strategic.* Some projects are simply an enforcing of a policy; others are local (operational) fixes. Not only they don't improve any capability, they are operational actions with no strategic value for the capabilities' maturity.
- *Incomplete.* Using the mapping analysis we find twelve deficiencies, meaning that 36% of IT-CMF's capabilities aren't improved at all. How can a strategic and cost-cutting plan ignore capabilities which, for instance, oversight and benchmark the IT budget or monitor projects for accurate data on money expenditure and value generation?
- *Redundant.* Using the same analysis we detect eight overloads, meaning that PGETIC has multiple projects to attain the same level of maturity for 24% of IT-CMF's capabilities. This shows the plan's lack of direction and its reactive nature. It also suggests that some maturity improvements may be indirect consequences.
- *Excessive.* More worrying we find seven excesses. This means there are seven projects that don't improve any capability. If this was an operational plan we could accept it – because it would be aimed to solve localized problems and not long term maturity improvements – but for a supposedly strategic plan this is a waste of time and resources.

### 6.2 Practical Evaluation

In order to validate that our solution met the objectives [18] and to get some feedback on our conclusions we decided to use *"User Opinion study"* [19]. We planned interviews with public bodies that are or will be implementing PGETIC. The interviews aimed to introduce them the research's results and collect their overall evaluation and feedback. In total we conducted three interviews.

The first public body interviewed was an entity of the State's business sector. We spoke with the entity's chief of Information Systems, who leads 21 collaborators and has a budget of quite a few million Euros. The department had ITIL in place and was attaining ISO 20000.

The second public body interviewed was a general directorate. We spoke with the chief of Planning, Documentation and Information Systems department, who leads 10 collaborators and has a budget of less than a million Euros. The department had no ITG framework in place.

The third public body interviewed was a public institute. We spoke with the institute's chief of Information Systems, who leads 15 collaborators and has a budget bigger than one million Euros. The department had no ITG framework in place.

We created a one page survey with a total of 26 statements[1]. The interviewee then selected his or her level of agreement – totally disagree, disagree, agree, totally agree

---

[1] The full version of the survey can be accessed online at http://goo.gl/u7OeZ

– with each statement. The statements were divided in groups: The first group of statements evaluated the relevance of the problems PGETIC aims to solve (e.g. cost-cutting); the second group evaluated the interviewee's opinion of PGETIC; the third, fourth and fifth group evaluated both the solution's quality and relevance and the framework's choice; the last group was a repetition of the second group but this time the interviewee's opinion took into account the research's results. In the end there were two open questions, one asking the interviewee's a global evaluation of the research and other asking his or her main concerns on PGETIC.

Comparing the interviews' results we found some patterns and reached the following conclusions:

• There's a need to implement common solutions and increase the value generated by public administration's ICT. It's not so unanimous the necessity of an aggressive cost-cutting plan;
• PGETIC has "good intentions" but is insufficient to fully achieve its objectives, thus the plan needs improvements;
• An evaluation of PGETIC's completeness, efficacy and efficiency was needed;
• Interviewees didn't know IT-CMF but after a short explanation they understood it and recognized that its usage didn't compromise their understanding about the evaluation;
• The results of this research are clear, objective, relevant and with practical utility;
• With this research it's easier to suggest and evaluate improvements to PGETIC;
• All three interviewees agreed that PGETIC is an operational plan, however two of them declared that the plan clearly defines ICT's priorities. Surprisingly one interviewee totally agrees with the statement *"PGETIC is a strategic plan that aims to increase ICT's maturity"*;
• The interviewees' opinion on PGETIC worsened after becoming aware of the research's results, acknowledging the plan's limitations or the need for improvements (or both).

## 7     Conclusion

By mapping the strategic plan (PGETIC) with an IT Governance framework (IT-CMF) we were able to evaluate the plan's completeness, efficacy and efficiency. In terms of completeness, we found that 36% of IT-CMF's capabilities won't be improved by the strategic plan at all. As for efficiency, we identified several redundant and excessive projects – 28% of PGETIC's projects improve no capability. As it is today the plan will hardly solve, in a sustainable way, the fundamental problems of public administration's ICT mentioned on section 1.

After analyzing the plan's content and the results mentioned above we consider PGETIC excessively low-level to be strategic. Most of the projects feel like local (operational) fixes. There are no clearly defined long-term strategic goals, so we are apprehensive on how the criterions for project prioritization will be defined. The Evaluation section provided valuable data that led us to one main conclusion:

*PGETIC isn't a strategic plan because it's aimed to solve localized operational problems. Frequently the improvement of certain capabilities' maturity is just an indirect consequence.*

It's important to note that PGETIC is relevant as a contingency plan, a plan that aims to fix several operational problems which should have been addressed a long time ago. We think that the plan can still be further improved to solve some of its shortcomings. Also it could be implemented with the support and guidance of an IT Governance framework, to make sure it's correctly aligned with value creation and standardized practices.

However if PGETIC can't be changed then it must be considered as mere a starting point, a preparation for an urgent broader strategic plan yet to come that defines strategic long-term goals for the public administration's ICT. This research, by pointing out the disregarded capabilities, will facilitate both the suggestion of improvements to this plan and the definition of a new plan.

As future work we plan to analyze in depth what caused some projects to be classified as "excess" on our mapping analysis: Do those projects map to an IT Governance framework other than IT-CMF? If not, then why were they created? Besides that analysis we aim to create a document with enhancements to the ongoing PGETIC, not to mention there's still a need for a strategic plan for the public administration's ICT.

## References

1. Diário da República. Resolução do Conselho de Ministros n.° 12/2012: Diário da República, 1.ª série - N.° 27 (2012)
2. IVI. Research and Development. Innovation Value Institute (June 15, 2012), http://ivi.nuim.ie/research-development.shtml
3. Hevner, A., et al.: Design Science in Information Systems Research. MIS Quarterly, Society for Information Management and the Management Information Systems Research Center 28(1), 75–105 (2004)
4. Peffers, K., et al.: A Design Science Research Methodology for Information Systems Research. Journal of Management Information Systems/Winter 24(3), 45–77 (2008)
5. Pereira, R., Mira da Silva, M.: A Literature Review: Guidelines and Contingency Factors for it Governance. In: 16th IEEE International EDOC, Conference on Enterprise Distributed Object Computing (2012)
6. Pereira, R., Mira da Silva, M.: Designing a new Integrated IT Governance and IT Management Framework Based on Both Scientific and Practitioner Viewpoint. International Journal of Enterprise Information Systems 8 (2012)
7. Webb, P., Pollard, C., Ridley, G.: Attempting to Define IT Governance Wisdom or Folly. In: Proceedings of the 39th Hawaii International Conference on System Sciences (2006)
8. Costello, T.: A New Management Framework for IT. IEEE Computer Society, IT Professional (2010)
9. Curley, M., Kenneally, J.: Using the IT Capability Maturity Framework to improve IT Capability and Value Creation: An Intel IT Case Study. In: 15th IEEE International Enterprise Distributed Object Computing Conference (2011)

10. Cabinet Office. ICT Strategy Strategic Implementation Plan to deliver savings of over a billion pounds. Cabinet Office, http://www.cabinetoffice.gov.uk/news/ict-strategy-strategic-implementation-plan-deliver-savings-over-billion-pounds (cited: September 14, 2012)
11. Cabinet Office. Government ICT Strategy. Cabinet Office, London (2011)
12. Cabinet Office. One Year On: Implementing the Government ICT Strategy (2012)
13. Issa-Salwe, A., et al.: Strategic Information Systems Alignment: Alignment of IS/IT with Business Strategy. Journal of Information Processing Systems 6(1) (2010)
14. Chen, D., et al.: Information Systems Strategy: Reconceptualization, Measurement, and Implications. MIS Quarterly 34(2), 233–259 (2010)
15. Coelho, J.D.: Considerações sobre a oportunidade e o impacto do PGETIC na AP: itSMF (2012)
16. Meertens, L.O., et al.: Mapping the Business Model Canvas to ArchiMate. In: SAC 2012 (2012)
17. Fettke, P., Loos, P.: Ontological Evaluation of Reference Models Using The Bunge-Wand-Weber Model. In: Ninth Americas Conference on Information Systems (2003)
18. Österle, H., et al.: Memorandum on Design-Oriented Information Systems Research. European Journal of Information Systems, 7–10 (2010)
19. Pries-Heje, J., Baskerville, R., Venable, J.: Strategies for Design Science Research Evaluation. In: 16th European Conference on Information Systems (ECIS), pp. 255–266 (2004)

# Open Semantic Service Networks: Modeling and Analysis

Jorge Cardoso[1], Carlos Pedrinaci[2], and Pieter De Leenheer[3,4]

[1] CISUC, Department of Informatics Engineering
University of Coimbra, Polo II, 3030 Coimbra, Portugal
jcardoso@dei.uc.pt
[2] Knowledge Media Institute, The Open University,
Milton Keynes, MK7 6AA, UK
c.pedrinaci@open.ac.uk
[3] The Network Institute, VU University Amsterdam,
1081 HV Amsterdam, The Netherlands
pieter.de.leenheer@vu.nl
[4] Collibra nv/sa, Brussels, Belgium

**Abstract.** A new interesting research area is the representation and analysis of the networked economy using Open Semantic Service Networks (OSSN). OSSN are represented using the service description language USDL to model nodes and using the service relationship model OSSR to model edges. Nonetheless, in their current form USDL and OSSR do not provide constructs to capture the dynamic behavior of service networks. To bridge this gap, we used the General System Theory (GST) as a framework guiding the extension of USDL and OSSR to model dynamic OSSN. We evaluated the extensions made by applying USDL and OSSR to two distinct types of dynamic OSSN analysis: 1) evolutionary by using a Preferential Attachment (PA) and 2) analytical by using concepts from System Dynamics (SD). Results indicate that OSSN can constitute the first stepping stones toward the analysis of global service-based economies.

**Keywords:** open services, service systems, service networks, system dynamics, services.

## 1 Introduction

Networks have been playing an increasingly important role in many fields. The Internet, the World Wide Web, social networks, and Linked Open Data (LOD)[1] are examples of some of the myriad types of networks that are a part of everyday life of many people. Service networks are another class of networks of emerging interest since worldwide economies are becoming increasingly connected.

To address the growing importance of service systems, we have introduced the concept of Open Semantic Service Network (OSSN)[2]. OSSNs are global service networks which relate services with the assumption that firms make the information of their service systems openly available using suitable models. Service

J.F. e Cunha, M. Snene, and H. Nóvoa (Eds.): IESS 2013, LNBIP 143, pp. 141–154, 2013.
© Springer-Verlag Berlin Heidelberg 2013

systems, relationships, and networks are said to be open when their models are transparently available and accessible by external entities and follow an open-world assumption. The objective of open services is very similar to the one explored by the linked open data initiative: exposing, sharing, and connecting pieces of data and information on the Semantic Web using URIs and RDF.

One limitation of OSSNs is that they were conceived without accounting for the dynamic behavior of service networks. In other words, they can only capture static snapshots of service-based economies. In this paper, our objective is to bridge this gap by bringing dynamic modeling capabilities to OSSNs. Our approach explores the General System Theory (GST)[3], a theory successfully applied in many fields of research (e.g. by John Von Neumann in computing and Ed Yourdon in structured analysis and structured design), to identify important requirements to model dynamic service networks. From these requirements, we studied the suitability of using USDL[1] (Unified Service Description Language) [4,5,6] and OSSR[2] (Open Semantic Service Relationship) [7] to represent dynamic service networks. USDL is a language which provides machine-processable descriptions for service systems. With the introduction of USDL there is a paradigm shift which sees that business services can be represented and controlled using guiding specifications. OSSR systematizes key elements to establish rich relationships between service systems such as the role of services (e.g. consumer, competitor, and complementor), the strength of relationships, and the level at which service systems are related (e.g. activities and actors).

Based on our study of GST, both USDL and OSSR models were extended with primitives to capture the dynamic behavior of open semantic service networks. Three extensions were identified: 1) attractiveness, 2) cause-effect relationships, and 3) time bounding. We validated our approach with two scenarios. One was based on an evolutionary analysis using a Preferential Attachment (PA)[8], while the second used System Dynamics (SD)[9] to forecast the behavior of an OSSN. The relations between the various theories and models explored in our work are illustrated in Figure 1. Our findings suggest that current developments – such as USDL, OSSR, and OSSN – have reached a maturity stage which enables the implementation of algorithms and simulation models to gain insights on the evolution of global service networks.

This paper is organized as follows. In the next section, we describe a motivation scenario for the application and relevance of open semantic service networks. Section 3 presents the related work. Section 4 describes the set of requirements which was identified after analysing the GST that is relevant to support dynamic service networks. Section 5 highlights the limitations of USDL and OSSR to model dynamic networks. Section 6 presents the extensions made to USDL and OSSR. Section 7 evaluates our approach by analysing dynamic networks using evolutionary and analytical methods. Section 8 provides the conclusion.

---

[1] When not otherwise stated, we will use the term USDL to refer to the service description language version named Linked-USDL (http://linked-usdl.org/)

[2] http://rdfs.genssiz.org/ossr.rdf

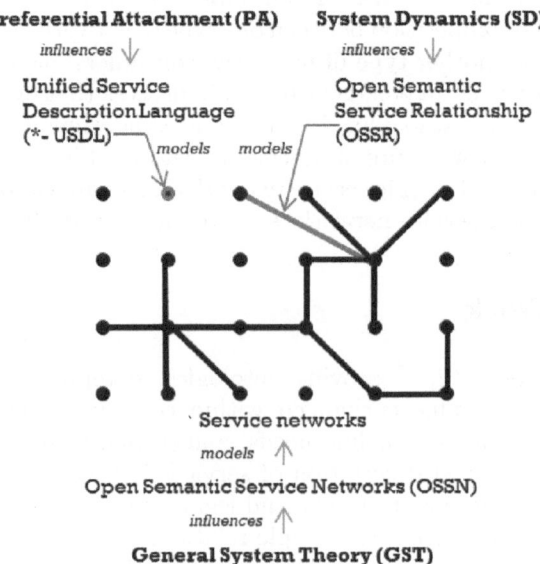

**Fig. 1.** Relations between theories (GST, PA, and SD) and service/relationship modeling languages (USDL and OSSR)

## 2    Motivation Scenario

A *service network* can be defined as a graph structure made up of service systems which are nodes, connected by one or more specific types of relationships. A *service system* is a self-contained representation of a repeatable business activity which typically aggregates people, processes, resources, consumables, regulations, and equipment that together create value to both consumers and providers. A service system can rely on other service systems to operate and are connected and interact via value propositions and shared information (language, laws, measures, etc.). Interactions that occur can be between people, information systems, businesses, or even nations.

The dynamic nature of service networks indicates that their topology might be shaped according to some intrinsic property, e.g. service cost, availability, or extrinsic property, e.g. perceived customer preference. This dynamic behavior has been verified in many fields. For example, the world-wide web forms a large directed graph with an apparent random character. Nonetheless, the topology of this graph has evolved to a scale-free network [10] by preferential attachment [8], i.e. when establishing hyperlinks, documents prefer the 'popularity' of certain documents (of 'popular sites') which overtime become hubs.

In service networks, we can hypothesize that a similar mechanism to the one describing the evolution of the web can also explain their evolution. Service networks are appropriate models of networked societies whereby consumers adopt a service system on the basis of its value proposition (e.eg a preferential attachment) since it was argued that networks are an implicit element of a service-dominant logic [11]. Thus, the competition between one type of network node, the providers, for the attention of another type of node, the consumers, mediated by a preferential attachment drives an emergent dynamic process that eventually leads the service network to some stable fixed point, to a cyclic, time-varying topology, or to a chaotic, unknown structure or stochastic pattern. Finding the mechanisms, laws, and properties of dynamic service networks can enable to better understand and explain why some service networks survive, prosper, decline or die.

## 3   Related Work

$e^3$service and $e^3$value [12,13] provide ontologies to represent e-business models, services, and the value exchanged within companies. The $e^3$value model places emphasis on wants, benefits, needs, and demand. Nonetheless, to model networks, a more detailed description of services is needed and should include aspects such as pricing, quality levels, and legal constraints. On the other hand, $e^3$service targets to represent very simple relations between services from an internal perspective, e.g. core-enhancing, core-supporting, and substitute. From an external perspective, the value chains proposed do not capture explicitly service networks across agents and do not try to analyse quantitatively the effect of relationships. Therefore, service network analysis is not possible. The $e^3$service and $e^3$value approaches fail to adhere to service-dominant logic and focus too much inward the company instead of the large-scale network they belong to.

In [14], the authors look at service networks from a Business Process Management (BPM) and Service Oriented Architecture (SOA) perspectives, and present the Service Network Notation (SNN). SNN provides UML artifacts to model value chain relationships of economic value. These relationships take the form of what we can call 'weak' relationships since they only capture offerings and rewards which occur between service systems. The focus is on composition, processes, and on establishing how new services can be created using BPM to describe the interactions of existing SOA-based services. On the other hand, OSSNs are not compositions of services, but rather a description of how services relate to each other in service markets.

Allee [15] uses a graph-based notation to model value flows inside a network of agents such as the exchange of goods, services, revenue, knowledge, and intangible values. The approach only takes into account value flows and does not consider other types of relationships that can be established between agents. Furthermore, the automatic machine-processing of services and flows was not a concern, hence limiting the applicability of the approach to the analysis of distributed large-scale networks.

While less related to our work, a number of researchers worked on formalizing models to capture business networks which also account for the representation of relationships. For example, Weiner and Weisbecker [16] describe a set of models addressing value networks, market interfaces, products and services, and financial aspects. Other research on value chains, value nets, and value networks (see

[17]) all attempt to represent business transactions using networks. Nonetheless, the emphasis is on textual or conceptual representations and the automatic machine-processing of networked models is not explored.

## 4   Theoretical Foundations

Due to its wide applicability to various domains, we used the General System Theory as a guiding framework to represent service systems and networks. We first analysed the properties proposed by the GST, i.e. wholeness, interdependence, hierarchy, self-regulation and control, interchange with the environment, balance/homeostasis, change and adaptability, and equifinality. Our analysis identified three important requirements: internal service relationships (R1), external relationships with other service systems (R2), and system dynamics and change (R3).

*Internal Relationships* (R1). A service modeling language needs to establish cause-effect relations between the internal elements of the machinery of a service system that range from participants, to information, to resources, to legal aspects, and to pricing. These elements are interdependent. For example, a change in the quality level of one activity of a service's business process can produce changes in the cost of another related activity.

*External Relationships (R2).* A comprehensive modeling requires facility in establishing cause-effect relations between internal- and external service systems. For example, if two services have established a relationship at the operational level and one service depends on the other, then the quality level delivered by one of the services depends on the quality level of the other.

*Understanding Change* (R3). To ignore the centrality of change overtime is to limit the modeling of service networks as snapshots that are alienated from reality. Time needs to be an integral modeling element. Another aspect is the attractiveness of a service (see Chapter 10 of [18]). It is relevant since it has been shown in other areas (e.g. the Web, business, and social networks) that a network may grow by adding relationships - not randomly, but by attraction or preference [8] to certain nodes.

## 5   Modeling Service Networks and Its Limitations

In our second activity, we made a literature review to investigate if existing work could be used to model service systems and service networks.

### 5.1   Service Modeling with USDL

Our research reviewed existing work from software-based service description languages (e.g. OWL-S, WSMO, SoaML, SML, SaaS-DL), business-oriented service descriptions (e.g. ITIL and CMMI for Services), and conceptual and ontology-based service descriptions (e.g. e³service [12], General Service Model [19], and Alter [20]). Our analysis yielded that, compared to previous developments, USDL provides a comprehensive model and a base to represent service networks for the following reasons (see Section 3 for a deeper comparison):

- It models the business, operational, and technical perspectives of service systems enabling to reason about the influence of pricing models, legal constraints, quality levels, business processes, and agents on service networks' dynamism.
- A version of the model based on Semantic Web principles, called Linked-USDL, was developed to provide the means for publishing and interlinking distributed services for an automatic and computer-based processing.

Nonetheless, requirement R1 identified in Section 4 is not supported. In other words, internal *cause-effect relationships* are not currently modeled with USDL. We propose to model them using KPI (Key Performance Indicator) as often recommended by ITIL and COBIT best practices, and suggested by Spohrer et. al. in [21]. Our idea is expressed in the following example. Two services – $s_a$ and $s_b$ – may establish a cause-effect relationship at the process level between the KPI error_rate of a process of service $s_a$ with the KPI redo_cost of a process of service $s_b$. When a positive variation of the KPI of $s_a$ occurs, it can be inferred that it will provoke an effect on the KPI of service $s_b$. In other words, an increase of the number of errors in $s_b$ originates an increase of cost in $s_b$. This is an important aspect since a service network is more than the sum of its parts only if the internal and external 'wiring' of services are established. To support requirement R3, and since *time-bounds* are a central variable in system theory and provides a referent for the very idea of dynamics, we propose an extension to USDL by using the formal time ontology proposed by Pan and Hobbs [22]. With respect also to requirement R3, since the concept of attractiveness [18] of a service may dictate the emergent topology of a network, we model this construct by allowing service systems to state their *attractiveness* to serve as the selecting rule (this is explained in Section 6).

## 5.2 Relationship Modeling with OSSR

As with the Web and the Semantic Web, the power of service systems is enhanced through the network effect produced as service systems create relationships to other service systems with the value determined by Metcalfe's law [23]: *the value of a network is proportional to the square of the number of connected service systems (n), i.e. $n^2$.* Our research also reviewed various proposals including value chains/nets/networks [17], and the service network notation [14] to evaluate their suitability to model service networks. Most work focuses on the business aspects of industries and do not take a close look at relationships. They are simply viewed as connecting elements which represent offerings and transactions. Furthermore, the modeling approaches are informal and, often, used as a communication tool.

What is needed is to be able to represent and identify richer relationships between services. This requirement goes well beyond what is offered by current approaches. While other types of relationships are also important, e.g. between services and actors, we follow the service-dominant logic [11] principal and consider that any other type of relationship is always mediated by services. This simplifies the construction and analysis of a network since all the nodes are homogeneous, i.e. they are services. Therefore, relations can occur between the actors that operate inside two service systems connected by a relationship.

We adopted the OSSR model, a multi-layer relationship specification composed of five layers: 1) role, 2) level, 3) involvement, 4) comparison, and 5) association. The model enables to interconnect services and indicate the properties of the connection. For example, it enables to indicate that two services maintain a relationship and one service is the consumer while the other is the provider. It also enables to indicate if a relationship represents a high or low involvement from its actors, or if a service is functionally dependent on another service.

While rich and comprehensive, a limitation of OSSR is that it does not model *cause-effect relationships* between services (requirement R2). To resolve this limitation, and to be consistent with the way we have addressed requirement R1, we rely on KPIs. For example, if a provider is competing by providing an efficient service, then internal KPIs related with activities' duration should be linked to KPIs of the same type present in other services of the same network. In other words, internal KPIs must be related to the KPIs of other service systems when forming service networks. Requirement R3 will also be addressed by including the modeling of time in relationships indicating that they are often *time-bounded*.

## 6   Modeling Dynamic Behavior

Based on the limitations identified in Section 5, we present three extensions to USDL and OSSR to model dynamic OSSN: 1) attractiveness, 2) cause-effect relationships, and 3) time bounding.

The attractiveness or preferential attachment is expressed by adding to USDL the concept `usdl-core:ValueProposition`. It allows service systems to state their value proposition by using a single KPI or a mathematical expression involving several KPIs. If should be noticed that more complex structures have been proposed (see [24]) to model a value proposition. Nonetheless, in our work, we are particularly concerned in showing that value propositions are a corner stone to simulate service systems dynamics rather than showing the completeness of value proposition. Therefore, we opt to explore the utility of measurable value propositions.

While USDL does not foresee the definition of KPIs, its model is organized into several clusters (e.g. service level and pricing) which provide a wealth of variables which can be used as KPIs. For example, service level and quality of service variables such as availability, reliability, and response time. The value proposition can refer to existing USDL concepts such as `usdl-price:Variable`, usdl-sla:Variable, usdl-core:Parameter, or to construct complex expressions using usdl-sla:ServiceLevelExpression. The calculation of the expression yields the value proposition. While the addition of a single concept to USDL seems simple, its implications are enormous. Preferential attachments [8] have been shown to be the main distinguishing feature which leads random networks to evolve into scale-free networks in particular domains such as the Web or social networks [10]. Thus, we can hypothesize that it can potentially be also a key factor which influences and determines the topological evolution of service networks.

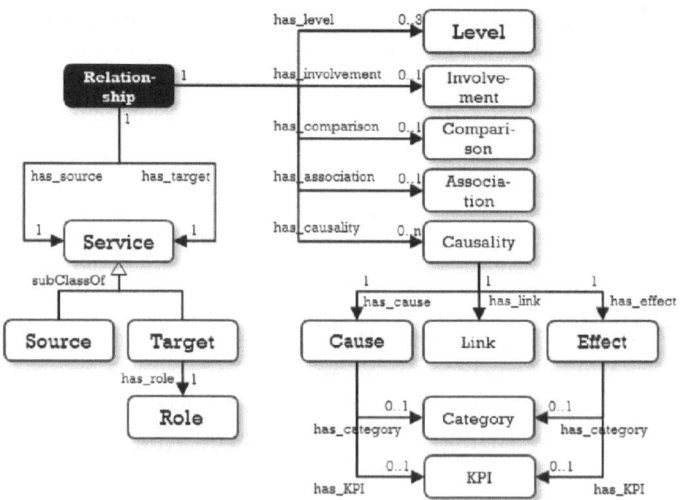

**Fig. 2.** The structure of the OSSR model

To model cause-effect relationships, we use the concept of causality from the area of System Dynamics (SD) [9] to express and quantify the impact that one service has in other services. Internal and external relationships of an OSSN are specified using the concept ossr:Relationship of the OSSR model (Figure 2). This concept involves the definition of two endpoints: the source service and the target service (for readability reasons, the prefix ossr: will be omitted from now on). When modeling an internal relationship, both source and target refer to the same service. A Relationship can capture several relations by using the concept Causality more than once. The concept can be thought as a 'wire' connecting two internal or external service system KPIs described with USDL. The concept Causality describes how a Cause event occurring in a service has an Effect in the same or in another service. The concept Link connects two KPIs and sets the sign of the link: Positive or Negative. A positive link indicates that a change in a service KPI (increase or decrease) results in the same type of change in another service KPI (increase or decrease). A negative link indicates that a change in a service KPI results in the opposite change in another service KPI. KPIs are described within the concepts Cause and Effect. For example, if a service provider uses Invoice Reliability as a KPI to control the quality of a service, it can be connected to the Response Time Delivery KPI of a service customer. An increase of the first KPI originates an increase in the second KPI since errors in the invoice require time to be resolved.

Since KPIs are often domain dependent and their semantics may not always be clear to analysts, individual measures of performance in a cause-effects relation are classified by the concept `Category` in one of five elements (c.f. [25]): quality, time, cost, flexibility, and other. The category 'other' was added to make the classification complete.

Time, one of the aspects identified by requirement R3, was modeled by using the time ontology `http://www.w3.org/2006/time` by adding the class `time:Interval`. This class contains the properties `time:hasBeginning` and `time:hasEnd` to define the beginning and the end of an interval in which a service specification is valid. While it is a simple concept, the time ontology provides a powerful mechanism to reason about the dynamics of service networks.

# 7  Evaluation of Dynamic OSSN

In this section, we evaluate the applicability of the extensions proposed to USDL and OSSR to model dynamic OSSN by using evolutionary and analytical approaches. The evaluation addresses the following two competency questions: 1) for a current service market share, what is the service market share forecast and 2) what is the effect that an increase of $KPI_a$, in service $s_a$, has on $KPI_b$ of service $s_b$?

## 7.1  Evolutionary Analysis of OSSN

In many scenarios, a service network contains two different types of service nodes: service consumers and services provided. Note that in our work customers are also seen as service systems. The network is bipartite and is represented by $SN$, such as $SN(t) = \{S(t), C(t), R(t), f(t)\}$, where $S(t)$ is the set of services provided, $C(t)$ is the set of service consumers, $S(t)$ and $C(t)$ are modeled with USDL, $R(t)$ is the set of relationships modeled with OSSR connecting consumers and services provided, and $f(t)$ is the mapping function $f : C \rightarrow S$. Network $SN$ is directed, such that a relationship from consumer node $c_i$ to service node $s_j$; $r : c_i \rightarrow s_j$, means that $c_i$ has adopted service $s_j$. Time is represented by parameter $t$. Customers alter the topology of a service network by diffusion when they adopt or abandon a service by adding or deleting an OSSR relationship to it.

To construct a service network $SN$, USDL and OSSR models are remotely accessed and retrieved (an overview description of the infrastructure to access and retrieve USDL and OSSR instances is described in [2]). OSSR models are mapped to relationship $R(t)$ and functions $f(t)$. By retrieving the `ossr:Role` concept of a relationship $r : c_i \rightarrow s_j$, the concepts `ossr:Source` and `ossr:Target` point to the USDL models to be mapped into services provided $S(t)$ and consumers $C(t)$.

The USDL model of each service system contains a value proposition communicated to customers (i.e, the attractiveness elements or preferential attachment). Service value is judged from the perspective of consumers as they compare services among the alternatives. For simplicity reasons, we assume that the value proposition is similar for all service systems and it is the price of the services calculated from a `usdl-price:PricePlan`[3].

Since our objective is to forecast the evolution of a service network over time, we use the following function to calculate the Market Share of each service provided $MS(s_i) = degree(s_i)/m$; where $degree(s_i)$ is the number of relationships established by service $s_i$ with service consumers and $m$ is the total number of relationships established between providers and consumers. Overtime, customers change preferences by changing from one service system to another service system. To monitor these changes in an OSSN, OSSR need to be regularly accessed and retrieved (since OSSR have a validity time stamp, optimization mechanisms can be implemented to reduce traffic and increase algorithms' efficiency.)

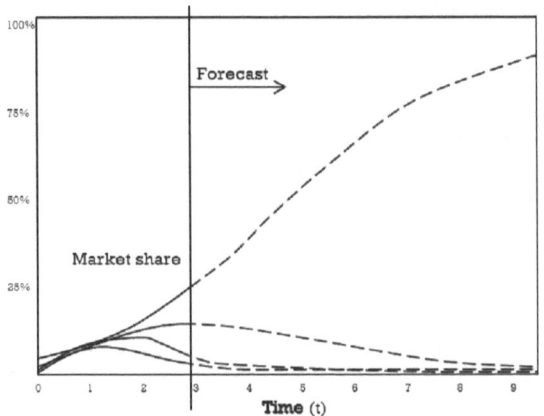

**Fig. 3.** Service market share evolution overtime

Let us assume that the (re)constructed $SN$ topology shows that overtime the market share is the one represented in Figure 3 at $t = 3$. The question to be answered is: what will happen to the market in the future if the conditions are not changed (i.e. the value propositions of $s_i$ remain the same and $m \not> c_i$). According to Bass model [26], the leading service system will reach a fixedpoint market share according to the following formula ($a$ and $b$ are constants):

$$MS(s_i, t) = \frac{1 - e^{-bt}}{1 + ae^{-bt}}; 0 \le t \le 9 \qquad (1)$$

Figure 3 illustrates that from the four services provided, three also rise in market share during the early stages, reach a peak, and then decline as the service

---

[3] For simplicity reasons, we consider that each service has only one pricing plan.

leader accelerates because of the increasing returns effect of preferential attachment. In this case, all but one service provided leaves the market, leaving one monopoly competitor. Such network forecast evolution is of utmost importance for regulatory bodies such as the European Commission which routinely passes directives for various markets to avoid monopolistic markets.

## 7.2   Analytical Analysis of OSSN

In our second evaluation, we explored the suitability of dynamic OSSNs to model system dynamics. Instead of looking at causes and their effects in isolation, we analyse service networks as systems made up of interacting parts (see Section 6). Once an OSSN is created from distributed service models, cause-effect diagrams can be derived for the network. For example, Figure 4 shows service systems $S_i$, $S_j$, $S_k$, and directed edges illustrating internal and external relationships.

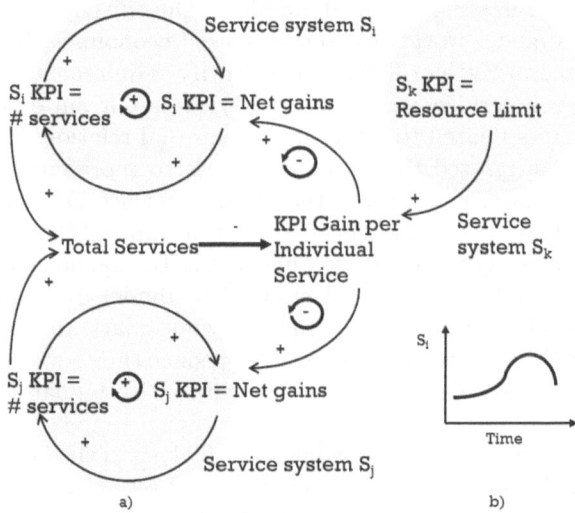

**Fig. 4.** Service networks and system dynamics

Looking closer, causal relationships connect KPIs from different services' and within services. The pattern represented by this OSSN is commonly known as the 'Tragedy of the Commons' archetype. It hypothesizes that if the two services $S_i$ and $S_j$ overuse the common/shared service $S_k$, it will become overloaded or depleted and all the providers will experience diminishing benefits. Service $S_i$ and $S_j$ provide services to costumers. To increase net gains, both providers increase the availability of service instances. As the number of instances increases, the margin decreases and there is the need to increase even more the number of instances available. As the number of instances increases, the stress on the availability of service $S_k$ is so strong that the service collapses or cannot respond anymore as needed. At that point, service $S_i$ and $S_j$ can no longer fully operate and the net gain is dramatically reduced for all the parties involved as shown in Figure 4.b).

To better understand the dynamics and the structure of the service network, the notions of stock and flow diagram, and causal loop diagram should be accounted for. They provide the basis for the quantification and the simulation of the behavior of the service network overtime. We refer the reader to [9] for a detailed description of dynamic systems and their representation.

While a deeper evaluation needs to be conducted, this first results show that the modeling of cause-effect relationships using the extensions proposed provides the required mechanism to execute an analytical analysis of dynamic OSSN.

## 8   Conclusions and Future Work

While network science has made contributions in the areas of social networks and the WWW, the concept of service networks is recent and presents new challenges. They are large scale, open, dynamic, highly distributed, and have the ambitious goal to model worldwide service-based economies. In this paper, we relied on the General System Theory to identify requirements to develop dynamic open semantic service networks (OSSN), an important extension to static OSSN. Requirements related to internal and external relationships between services, and change suggested that current models to represent networks should be extended. Therefore, we adapted the Unified Service Description Language (USDL) and the Open Semantic Service Relationship (OSSR) model to enable the representation of dynamic service networks. To demonstrate that the extensions to USDL and OSSR indeed enabled to model dynamic behavior, we evaluated their applicability to carry out an evolutionary and analytical analysis of dynamic OSSN. The results are promising since they constitute the first set of stepping stones for the development of algorithms to simulate and understand service-based economies.

For future work, we plan to complement the analysis of the GST with the analysis of the Viable System Model (VSM), proposed by Stafford Beer, to provide an additional theoretical conceptualization for OSSN. We also plan to conduct a more comprehensive validation by creating a working example to illustrate the applicability of the OSSN model and apply it in form of a case study with primary data. Action research will provide the foundations for validation and establishing a warranted belief that the OSSN model can contribute to the understanding, analyse, and design of service systems.

## References

1. Bizer, C., Heath, T., Berners-Lee, T.: Linked data - the story so far. Int. J. Semantic Web Inf. Syst. 5(3), 1–22 (2009)
2. Cardoso, J., Pedrinaci, C., Leidig, T., Rupino, P., De Leenheer, P.: Open semantic service networks. In: International Symposium on Services Science (ISSS 2012), Leipzig, Germany (September 2012)

3. Von Bertalanffy, L.: General System Theory: Foundations, Development, Applications. The International Library of Systems Theory and Philosophy. Braziller (2003)
4. Cardoso, J., Winkler, M., Voigt, K.: A service description language for the Internet of Services. In: First International Symposium on Services Science, Leipzig, Germany (2009)
5. Cardoso, J., Barros, A., May, N., Kylau, U.: Towards a unified service description language for the Internet of Services: Requirements and first developments. In: IEEE International Conference on Services Computing. IEEE Computer Society Press, Florida (2010)
6. Barros, A., Oberle, D.: Handbook of Service Description: USDL and Its Methods. Springer (2012)
7. Cardoso, J.: Modeling Service Relationships for Service Networks. In: Novoa, H., Snene, M. (eds.) IESS 2013. LNBIP, vol. 143, pp. 114–128. Springer, Heidelberg (2013)
8. Yule, U.: A mathematical theory of evolution based on the conclusions of dr. j. c. willis. Phil. Trans. Roy. Soc. Lond. 213(2), 21–87 (1925)
9. Forrester, J.: Industrial dynamics. MIT Press, Cambridge (1961)
10. Wang, X.F., Chen, G.: Complex networks: small-world, scale-free and beyond. IEEE Circuits and Systems Magazine 3(1), 6–20 (2003)
11. Vargo, S.L., Lusch, R.F.: Evolving to a new marketing dominant logic for marketing. Journal of Marketing 68(1), 1–17 (2004)
12. Gordijn, J., Yu, E., van der Raadt, B.: e-service design using i* and e3value modeling. IEEE Software 23, 26–33 (2006)
13. Akkermans, H., Baida, Z., Gordijn, J., Pena, N., Altuna, A., Laresgoiti, I.: Value webs: Using ontologies to bundle real-world services. IEEE Intelligent Systems 19(4), 57–66 (2004)
14. Danylevych, O., Karastoyanova, D., Leymann, F.: Service networks modelling: An soa & bpm standpoint. Journal of Universal Computer Science 16(13), 1668–1693 (2010)
15. Allee, V.: Reconfiguring the value network. Journal of Business Strategy 21(4), 1–6 (2000)
16. Weiner, N., Weisbecker, A.: A business model framework for the design and evaluation of business models in the internet of services. In: Proceedings of the Annual SRII Global Conference, Washington, DC, USA, pp. 21–33 (2011)
17. Basole, R.C., Rouse, W.B.: Complexity of service value networks: Conceptualization and empirical investigation. IBM Systems Journal 47(1), 53–70 (2008)
18. Sterman, J.: Business Dynamics: Systems Thinking and Modeling for a Complex World. McGraw-Hill Higher Education. Irwin/McGraw-Hill (2000)
19. Towards an Ontological Foundation of Services Science: The General Service Model (2011)
20. Alter, S.: Viewing systems as services: A fresh approach in the is field. Communications of the Association for Information Systems 26(11) (2010)
21. Spohrer, J., Maglio, P.P.: Service Science: Toward a Smarter Planet, pp. 1–30. John Wiley & Sons, Inc. (2010)
22. Hobbs, J.R., Pan, F.: An ontology of time for the semantic web. ACM Transactions on Asian Language Processing (TALIP) 3(1), 66–85 (2004)
23. Hendler, J., Golbeck, J.: Metcalfe's law, web 2.0, and the semantic web. Web Semantics: Science, Services and Agents on the World Wide Web 6(1), 14–20 (2008)

24. Kwan, S., Müller-Gorchs, M.: Constructing Effective Value Propositions for Stake-holders in Service System Networks. In: Academic Conference - Understanding Complex Services Through Different Lenses, Cambridge, UK (2011)
25. Cai, J., Liu, X., Xiao, Z., Liu, J.: Improving supply chain performance management: A systematic approach to analyzing iterative KPI accomplishment. Decision Support Systems 46(2), 512–521 (2009)
26. Bass, F.: A new product growth model for consumer durables. Management Science 15, 215–227 (1969)

# Ontological Representation and Governance of Business Semantics in Compliant Service Networks*

Pieter De Leenheer[1,2], Jorge Cardoso[3], and Carlos Pedrinaci[4]

[1] The Network Institute, VU University Amsterdam, The Netherlands
pieter.de.leenheer@vu.nl
[2] Collibra NV/SA & VUB STARLab, Brussels, Belgium
[3] CISUC / Dept. Informatics Engineering, University of Coimbra, Portugal
jcardoso@dei.uc.pt
[4] Knowledge Media Institute, The Open University, Milton Keynes, United Kingdom
c.pedrinaci@open.ac.uk

**Abstract.** The Internet would enable new ways for service innovation and trading, as well as for analysing the resulting value networks, with an unprecedented level of scale and dynamics. Yet most related economic activities remain of a largely brittle and manual nature. Service-oriented business implementations focus on operational aspects at the cost of value creation aspects such as quality and regulatory compliance. Indeed they enforce how to carry out a certain business in a prefixed non-adaptive manner rather than capturing the semantics of a business domain in a way that would enable service systems to adapt their role in changing value propositions. In this paper we set requirements for SDL-compliant business service semantics, and propose a method for their ontological representation and governance. We demonstrate an implementation of our approach in the context of service-oriented Information Governance.

## 1 Introduction

Given their essentially intangible nature, it is commonly believed that the Internet would enable new ways for creating, bundling and trading *services* as well as for analysing the resulting *value networks* on a world-wide scale with an unprecedented level of efficiency and dynamics [29]. Yet most economic activities related to online service trading, remain of a largely brittle and manual nature. Despite the initial assumption that *software-based services*[1] would be a core enabling technology supporting a highly efficient service-based economy at a global scale, we are still to witness a significant adoption of this technology on the Internet as a means to support service trading. Yet, from a computational perspective, a

---

* The research leading to these results has received partial funding from the European Commission's 7th Framework Programme under grant agreement no. 257593.
[1] As in Service-Oriented Architecture (SOA).

J.F. e Cunha, M. Snene, and H. Nóvoa (Eds.): IESS 2013, LNBIP 143, pp. 155–169, 2013.

large number of enterprise systems rely on a hierarchy of functional components encapsulated as Web services in order to support their activities or interact with third parties for data and/or functionality exchange and reuse [25]. Indeed electronic businesses implementations enforce *how* to carry out a certain business in a prefixed non-adaptive manner rather than an explicit understanding of the business (service) domain (read: *business (service) semantics*) in terms of assets and relationships that could enable a service system to adapt its role in changing value propositions.

*Service-orientation* is a promising paradigm to decompose inward-oriented organisational processes into outward-oriented business service components. SOA does not constitute business service components; they are about *functional decomposition* which is very distinct from business service decomposition. Thus the underlying conception of a service is not merely static: it is largely limited to request and response elements of software artefacts, which are disjunct from *value creation aspects* such as strategy, proposition, roles, resourcing, pricing, quality and regulatory compliance. This lack of ontological analysis of service as a first-class concept is also witnessed in business modeling. Only recently a commonly agreed service conception emerged from a *service-dominant logic* (SDL) in marketing [34]. SDL promotes a shift from goods to service as first-class citizen in economic exchange was required to understand and develop new ways of value creation in networked enterprises [21]. The immediate ontological consequence of this was to regard a service as a *perdurant* (value co-creation activity) rather than an *endurant* (value object). This has lead to the design of SDL-compliant upper-level models (e.g., [11,26]) that could play an important role in automated business service (de)composition.

The importance of services has triggered the idea to use more structured approaches to design and implement software-based services. For example, the ISE (Inter-enterprise Service Engineering) [4] methodology and workbench was one of the first attempts to devise a service engineering procedure for designing business services. While the approach was orthogonal to the domain for which services were engineered, ISE can benefit from agreed business semantics that can support meaningful decision making on the aforementioned value co-creation aspects of services.

In this paper, we give an overview of service perspectives in Sect. 2. Then, (in Sect. 3) we set ontological and (in Sect. 4) governance requirements for SDL-compliant business service semantics. Domain ontologies for the purpose of service automation must convey these business semantics in order to specifically account for the quality and compliance of functionality and data exchanged across the network. Obviously, this makes only sense if these ontologies are governed effectively. The adoption of an upper-ontology can also guarantee that the services developed follow an SDL paradigm. In Sect. 5, we set the background for our approach. In Sect. 6, we propose a method for the ontological representation and governance of business service semantics, and an application in the context of service-oriented Information Governance implemented in Collibra's software. We conclude with a discussion and future work in Sect. 7.

# 2   Service Science, Engineering, and Business Modelling

Maglio et al. [16] define Service Science as *"the study of the application of the resources controlled by one [service] system for the benefit of another [service] system in the context of an economic exchange"*. This study came along with a shift in marketing from goods-dominant to service-dominant logic [34] where *service* becomes this new unit of economic exchange. Hence, a *service* is conceived as a (value-providing or -integrating) action. This stands in strong contrast to goods-dominant logic in which a service is considered to be an object [11]. This paradigm shift was required to understand and develop new ways of value creation in networked enterprises [21]. From an operations management perspective, Unified Service Theory conceives service as a production process highlighting customer input and the differentiation from non-service processes [31]. The Gaps model captures the cross-functionality of service management and the inherent semantic mismatch between between divergent perceptions on service quality. It focuses strongly on the customer integration [24].

We distinguish at least two areas of service study important for our purpose. They have been developing largely independently from each other, resulting in divergent service conceptions.

1. The *business perspective* aims to understand why enterprises should innovate and trade services by considering value creation aspects. Yet most modelling approaches take an enterprise-centric perspective (e.g., [18,22]). As a consequence, they assume a *closed world*[2] and their business service semantics, i.e., shared understanding of value aspects, remains *tacit* [27]; hence unknown outside the organization. Also, these approaches classify a service as a *static* resource (i.e., endurant) rather than as an *occurrence* of actions (perdurant) in which resources are acted upon. Most *service network approaches* (see [29] for a survey) are process-based, hence focus on the problem of planning service delivery. Not many network-centric approaches exist that are value-based and therefore focus on the problem of automatically designing service value networks [28]. Only recently SDL-compliant service meta-models have been proposed (e.g., [11,26]) that may lead to sound ontological foundations, yet none account for governance.

2. The *IT perspective* adopts service-oriented modelling as a paradigm for functional decomposition and engineering of distributed systems. Prominent service description meta-models (i.a., WSMO and WSDL) conceive service as a static function, and fail to convey any value creation aspect. Web service engineering aims at the interoperability of communication protocols (e.g., SOAP, REST) and data formats between heterogeneous "service parks" (see [9]; and Sycara in [33]). Process languages (BPMN, BPEL, etc.) are adopted for choreography, control flows, events, and temporal dependencies to define valid sequences of service invocations. It may be the case that some business decision logic is cryptically embedded within some complex control flow

---

[2] A closed-world assumption is the logical presumption that what is not currently known to be true is false.

logic. In the worse case, the business logic is largely hidden within expert components or deferred to some manual decision steps.

In the networked Internet era, the ability to reactively (rather than proactively) and automatically (rather than manually) engage in service value networks is a key competitive advantage [21]. Yet it requires the ability to automate business decision making in a way such that computers do not only know a brittle prefixed operational procedure to carry out business but rather have embedded business semantics that shall enable them in adapting enterprises operational activities to maximise the business performance. The governance of business semantics and its embedding in ontologies that support the aformentioned value creation aspects of service networks entails many requirements that we cannot cover completely in this paper. Therefore, we focus on quality and compliance aspects of value interactions. This results in ontological requirements (*OR*s) (in Sect. 3) and governance requirements (*GR*s) (in Sect. 4).

# 3    Ontological Requirements

To overcome the issue of semantic alignment, peers usually create an ontology that is represented using a *knowledge representation* (KR) grammar (textually using SBVR or OWL , or visual using UML). The more aligned the ontology with the peer's individual perspectives, the easier it becomes to synchronize between business expectations and Web service solutions [5]. OWL-S$^3$ (in 2004) and WSMO$^4$ (in 2005) were first attempts to standardise operational semantics for a service, but the ontologies do not capture business semantics necessary to evaluate quality and compliance aspects of its constituting (action and content) commitments (Battle in [17]; [23,11]). Hence, our requirements constrain the foundation (*OR*$_1$ and *OR*$_2$) as well as representation (*OR*$_3$ and *OR*$_4$) of viable ontologies.

*Computational ontologies* for our purpose must convey domain-specific business service semantics in terms of upper-level categories and relations describing the nature and structure of service-dominant logic. Therefore, semantic alignment concerns requirements at the upper-level and domain-level, with each two types of validity. First, we require an upper-level foundation that accounts for SDL.

**Ontological Requirement 1.** An    SDL-compliant    upper-level    ontology accounts for an externally valid alignment of service conceptions such as action, service system, resource, and service.

By posing *external* validity, we require that an upper-level ontology should serve either (i) as a foundation for the development of domain ontologies; or (ii) as a common ground for aligning heterogenous domain ontologies. The latter requires domain ontologies to specialize upper-level concepts from SDL for a specific domain of value creation:

---

$^3$ http://www.w3.org/Submission/OWL-S/
$^4$ http://www.w3.org/Submission/WSMO/

**Ontological Requirement 2.** A domain-dependent specialisation of an SDL-valid upper ontology accounts for a descriptively valid alignment of business service semantics about value creation aspects in a specific domain.

By posing *descriptive* validity we require the domain terminology and rules to be a substantial description of the business service domain as perceived and *agreed* by a community. See [1] for more on ontological validity.

The intention of such a domain-dependent specialization is to provide a *service description*, i.e., a description of value-creation aspects, actions on these aspects, and peer roles entitled to realize these actions in a compliant way. In that respect, our conception lies close to the one proposed by Ferrario and Guarino [11]. They state that a service *commitment* needs to be distinguished from service *content*, i.e., what kind of action(s) the trustee commits to; and service *process*, i.e. how the service commitment is implemented. A trustee makes a service commitment to produce a certain content, i.e. set of actions. It is a temporal static event; a speech act documented in a contract among peers [11]. This corresponds largely to the business service semantics. A service content – while also defining the types of actions and roles, rather than merely pre-and postconditions – may well be close to the operational semantics; the latter which definitely corresponds to the service process. As a result, in order for a service description to make sense for both business and ICT, service commitment speech acts (hence business service semantics) are to be aligned with the service process (hence operational semantics) through domain-dependent specialisations that define service content. Doing so, we could possibly abandon the use of prefixed process-based languages and embrace instead declarative rules that capture *what* value aspects restrict our decision making, rather than *how* to actually honour these restrictions.

The Unified Service Description Language (USDL), and especially Linked-USDL, is a good example of such domain-specialization. The latter uses semantic Web principles to construct an ontology to describe services by establishing explicit links to other existing ontologies emerging from Linked Data initiatives. While the model was initially constructed to describe services, in [3], we conducted a study which revealed that it could also be used to model internal parts of service systems and service networks by describing rich, multi-level relationships. Representing this alignment between service commitment and content/process implies two additional requirements for the KR grammar.

**Ontological Requirement 3.** The ontology representation grammar must account for tracking of circumstances (e.g., state, event, process) that determine the relevance of value creation aspects across the service lifecycle.

Indeed, real-world entities, like services, are dynamic by nature [11]. Their possession of (i.e., *transient*) properties is not always persistent throughout their lifecycle; hence may change in function of different types of circumstances, including the form of the entities themselves. For example, it is possible that a service description is considered as possessing the property price only after having it passed all quality assurance tests during its production and it has been committed to by a provider. Moreover, the price of a service can have different manifestations (e.g., currency) depending on time and location of its integrator.

In an open-world assumption, functionality and users are not completely accounted for a priori. Hence, a sufficient level of implementation independence is required from the KR grammar and method. Ontologies that adopt these approaches will also have more potential for large-scale adaption by a wide variety of software-based service technologies; hence contribute to a generative service Web [36]. This all entails a dual utility for our ontologies.

**Ontological Requirement 4.** The adopted KR grammar and method allows to build a computational ontology that has a *dual* utility [1]:

- in an IT context, it serves as computer specification to realize semantic interoperability of data and functionality across systems;
- in a business context, it serves as a theoretical model referring to real-world objects aligning the strategic goals, values, and processes among (human) stakeholders.

The open-world assumption and dual utility puts additional constraints on new ways of governance as we will see next.

## 4    Governance Requirements

The need for ontologies that convey business service semantics to assess value aspects of business services such as *regulatory compliance* and *quality* has been hypothesised [30]. Only recently, it has become pertinent in the aftermath of the global financial crisis. Internationally agreed regulations such as *Sarbanes-Oxley* in the US, and *Basel* in the EU, enforce strict corporate governance policies that have primordial impact on the roles and responsibilities among peers in information management. Yet the issue has been more than often taken lightly as we witness from at best very poor information governance practice of many networked industries ranging from financial services to pharmaceuticals (see Gartner[5] and IBM[6]).

In order for business semantics to be useful in the assessment of regulatory compliance of services, they have to be defined and validated by relevant and trusted "stewards" from very different business functions (ranging from IT to business; with legal and compliance departments in particular). The industry's attempt to categorize this $GR$ is labelled as Information Governance[7] . Gartner defines IG as: *"the specification of decision rights and an accountability framework to encourage desirable behavior in the valuation, creation, storage, use,*

---

[5] Governance Is an Essential Building Block for Enterprise Information Management: http://www.gartner.com/id=777214 (last accessed on 29/10/2012)
[6] The IBM Data Governance Council Maturity Model: http://www-935.ibm.com/services/uk/cio/pdf/leverage_wp_data_gov_council_maturity_model.pdf (last accessed on 29/10/2012)
[7] See an overview of IG business drivers in MDM Institute's survey: http://www.the-mdm-institute.com (last accessed on 23/09/2012).

*archival and deletion of information. It includes the processes [actions], roles [actors], standards and metrics [actands] that ensure the effective and efficient use of information in enabling an organization to achieve its goals."* From this definition, we infer our first governance requirement:

**Governance Requirement 1.** In order to account for compliance and quality, an SDL-compliant upper ontology should additionally define governance concepts such as actors, roles and competencies.

Most scientific papers are directly inspired by traditional Data Quality Management and IT governance [14] and propose deterministic role patterns and decision domains with a predefined terminology. Yet, although best practices for so-called data stewardship are emerging, it is necessary that governance models need to be flexible at run-time, i.e. *contingent* upon issues [35]. E.g., in earlier work we analyzed individual contributions to an ontology. This behavioral analysis allowed us to roughly track user performance that could lead to a more effective assignment of roles in the governance model [7].

**Governance Requirement 2.** The configuration of roles and responsibilities among peers in governance of service descriptions must be adaptive and issue-driven.

# 5    Background in Ontology Representation

**Fact-Oriented Ontological Analysis.** In order to accommodate for $OR_4$, we adopt a *fact-oriented* approach for the following reasons. Its *natural-language* grounding closely relates to speech acts, and therefore it is easier for domain experts themselves to play a contributing role resulting in ontologies that clearly and accurately convey realistic business semantics. Furthermore, its *attribute-free* approach, as opposed to frame-based techniques (such as UML or ER), promotes *semantic stability* under change [13]. Fact-oriented methods include NIAM/ORM [13]. The key of conceptual analysis is to identify relevant object types, and the roles they play, so we can understand the facts of the business domain by minimizing the occurrence of lexical ambiguities.

Fact-orientation was repurposed for ontological analysis in the DOGMA project [19] and further extended with a method and system for community-driven ontology evolution, i.e. *Business Semantics Management* (BSM) [5] This method identified key ontology evolution processes and linked them to SECI, i.e. Nonaka's four community knowledge-conversion modes [20]). BSM is now commercially exploited via Collibra's Data Governance Center product[8]. Fact-orientation is currently also part of OMG's Meta-Object Facility for platform-independent modeling of business rules with modal logic capabilities using the SBVR[9] standard.

---

[8] http://www.collibra.com
[9] http://www.omg.org/spec/SBVR/1.0/

*Ontological analysis* seeks further domain abstraction from fact types that represent different perspectives on the same business concepts. Perspective divergence and convergence are principal mechanisms in BSM to reconcile perspectives that are taken by different people and are based on different glossaries, conceptual hierarchies, and code systems. The result is an ontology that represents a higher level of abstraction for common domain concepts that can be applied for *semantic interoperability* [5]. BSM is currently limited to one specific type, i.e., *knowledge-intensive communities* that have explicitly set *semantic interoperability requirements* (ibid.). In this respect, we cannot claim that we account for decentralized governance yet. Summarising, BSM has to be repurposed for compliance goals of service networks, and its community model has to be dynamic.

Important activities in BSM are context-driven lexical disambiguation of terms for concepts and their linking in upper-level conceptual hierarchies [6] and other types of relationships. Other important considerations in formal ontological analysis are *essence* and *rigidity* [12]. An entity's property is essential if it necessarily holds throughout its lifecycle. A property (e.g., being human) is rigid if it is essential to all its instances. Rigid properties are required for *identity* (to distinguish entities from each other), and *unity* (to distinguish parts from wholes). In this paper, we will touch upon these notions when exploiting SBVR's modal logic capabilities to impose the possibility or necessity of certain facts about service systems.

**Ontology of Dynamic Entities.** In order to accommodate for $OR_3$, we rely on previous work [15] on a conceptual apparatus of an ontology that was designed to handle the conceptualisation of dynamic entities and the notion of a transient property. We illustrated the design of a *property possession algebra* for conceptualizing the behaviour of transient properties across the lifecycle of corresponding entities. In other words, we can define for every fact type (that actually expresses a predicate for an entity), a possession formula. For example, a dispossession formula may use an SBVR "impossibility" statement[10] :

 — **It is impossible that a** Service *has* **a** Price **if the** Service *has* **not** *been approved* **or the** Service *is* **not** *provided by* **at least one** Service System.

Either of the two facts that (i) the Service has not been approved or (ii) is not yet provided by at least one Service System is a sufficient Circumstance that excludes the validity of a Service having a Price.

## 6    A Proposal for Business Service Semantics

Based on our requirements analysis in Sect. 3 and 4, we propose a framework for the ontological representation and governance of business service semantics in compliant service networks. The baseline for our approach is the BSM method and the SBVR KR grammar both discussed in Sect. 5 .

---

[10] We are using caps for NOUNS (SBVR NOUN CONCEPTS), showing *relationships* (SBVR *verb concepts* or fact types) using italics, and using bold face for **keywords** such as **if**.

## 6.1  SDL-Compliant Upper-Level Model

To meet $OR_1$, our upper-level model comprises key SDL concepts ACTION, RE-SOURCE, SERVICE SYSTEM and SERVICE. To accommodate $OR_3$ partially, we provide an extension point to model CIRCUMSTANCES that allows for temporal causal reasoning about resource possession formula. To meet $GR_1$ and $GR_2$, we extend this upper-level model with IG concepts such as ACTOR and COM-PETENCE. We follow a fact-oriented analysis approach by which we abstract elementary fact types based on service science literature discussed in Sect. 2.

**Action.** We first introduce a general notion of ACTION adopted from the Formal Framework for Information System Concepts (FRISCO) [10]. We replace a FRISCO action's theme/patients called *actands* with the SDL-compliant concept of (operant and operand) RESOURCE.

– ACTION *part of* COMPOSITE ACTION / COMPOSITE ACTION *has part* ACTION
– ACTION *acted upon by* OPERANT RESOURCE/OPERANT RESOURCE *acts in* ACTION
– ACTION *acts on* OPERAND RESOURCE/OPERAND RESOURCE *acted upon in* ACTION

To illustrate modal logic capacities of SBVR, we require an ACTION to act on at least one OPERAND RESOURCE; hence necessitating a certain fact, e.g., we could state:

– **It is necessary that an** ACTION *acts on* **at least one** OPERAND RESOURCE

**Circumstance.** We could also link an ACTION to a triggering external CIR-CUMSTANCE, that could be either a STATE, EVENT, or PROCESS.

– ACTION *guarded by* CIRCUMSTANCE / CIRCUMSTANCE *guards* ACTION

Circumstances provide extensions points for the definition of operational service semantics. E.g., distinguishing between event types is important in the context of temporal causal reasoning, as shown by [32], and control flows.

**Resource.** We distinguish between two types of RESOURCE that, in ACTIONS, play the role of either theme/patient (OPERAND) or agent (OPERANT). Note, in the rest of this paper we only verbalize one reading direction for fact types:

– OPERANT RESOURCE *is a* RESOURCE
– OPERAND RESOURCE *is a* RESOURCE

Next, we define *service systems* as specialisations of *operant resources*. We discuss specialisations of operand resources in the treatment of applications in next subsection.

**Service System.** Maglio [16] defines a SERVICE SYSTEM as an open system that is capable of improving the state of another system through sharing or applying its own RESOURCES; and improving its own state by acquiring external RE-SOURCES. Its pivotal role also highlights the importance of working systems for realizing value creation proposed by Alter [2]. We contribute to the latter when introducing the notion of COMPETENCE that will be important for compliance of service-related ACTIONS. Accordingly, a SERVICE SYSTEM is an OPERANT RESOURCE and can be either a (working) INDIVIDUAL or ORGANIZATION, the latter being a composite of INDIVIDUALS [26].

- SERVICE SYSTEM *is a* OPERANT RESOURCE;
- SERVICE SYSTEM *controls* RESOURCE;
- INDIVIDUAL *is a* SERVICE SYSTEM (e.g., "John Doe");
- ORGANISATION *is a* SERVICE SYSTEM (e.g., "IG Council");
- ORGANISATION *owns* SERVICE SYSTEM.

The above definition requires that SERVICE SYSTEMS see value in having interactions with each other, which brings us to the definition of a SERVICE.

**Service.** A SERVICE is a value co-creating COMPOSITE ACTION constituted by a number of INTERACTION EVENTS in which OPERANT RESOURCES of one SERVICE SYSTEM act upon OPERAND RESOURCES for the benefit of another SERVICE SYSTEM. When delivered, a SERVICE is an EVENT (perdurant in DOLCE), and therefore bound to time and space. We adopt the SDL-compliant *Resource-Service-System* model, recently introduced by Poels [26] and is inspired by the well-known Resource-Event-Agent (REA) model [18]. To indicate the flow of value, Poels distinguishes between service *provider* and a service *integrator* roles. The economic notion of reciprocity entails a duality in the conception of SERVICE, resulting in a reflexive "requiting" service in which the integrator and provider swap their roles. Moreover, economic agent in REA is replaced by the SDL concept *Service System*. We devise the following fact types to state a *Service* as a special type of *Composite Action*.

- SERVICE *is a* COMPOSITE ACTION;
- SERVICE *is requited by* SERVICE;
- SERVICE *provided by* SERVICE SYSTEM;
- SERVICE *is integrated by* SERVICE SYSTEM.

Note, in order to reason about value creation, we have to further distinguish between value-creating interactions and non-value-creating interactions. E.g., Poels (ibid.) applied ISPAR conditions in this context. This would open a window to adopt the benefits from speech act theory as well.

**Actor.** In order to account for our $GR_1$ and $GR_2$, we must introduce additional concepts that have not been considered before in this context. Until now, the semantics of the role of a RESOURCE in a SERVICE was limited to the –economic – label of provider or integrator. However, for a compliant orchestration every ACTION a SERVICE constitutes, we want to know the detailed ACTOR roles and responsibilities, as well as the required COMPETENCIES. To this end, an OPERANT RESOURCE acting in a SERVICE plays the role of a designated ACTOR role that comes along with a permission to perform certain ACTIONS. We adopt an SVBR-featured deontic rule to define a permission.

- ACTOR *is a* OPERANT RESOURCE;
- **It is permitted that** ACTOR *acts in* ACTION.

We can adopt the widely-used RACI roles to define specific responsibility assignment and devise four relationships accordingly:

- ACTOR *responsible for* ACTION; ACTOR *accountable for* ACTION;
- ACTOR *is consulted about* ACTION ; ACTOR *informed of* ACTION.

These relationships may imply certain combinations of the earlier introduced permissions. We could further exclude combinations of role and actor can play in the context of a specific action using the following SBVR syntax.

- **No** ACTOR *is responsible for* **and** *is consulted about* **the same** ACTION.

Or we could state implications of roles for the sake of inferencing:

- **It is always true that an** ACTOR *is informed of* ACTION **if the** ACTOR *is responsible for* that ACTION.

**Competency.** A COMPETENCY is modeled as a special type of OPERAND RESOURCE controlled by an INDIVIDUAL. The HR-XML consortium proposed to model a REUSABLE COMPETENCY DEFINITION (RCD) as: *"a specific, identifiable, definable, and measurable knowledge, skill, ability and/or other deployment-related characteristic (e.g. attitude, behavior, physical ability) which a human resource may possess and which is necessary for, or material to, the performance of an activity within a specific business context"*[11]. Hence, we devise following concept types:

- COMPETENCY *is a* OPERAND RESOURCE
- ATTITUDE ; KNOWLEDGE ; SKILL ; LEARNING OBJECTIVE *is a* COMPETENCY

There are many open RCD repositories that could be adopted for this purposes. E.g., HR-BA-XML (official German extension of Human Resource XML), SOC (Standard Occupational Classification System), BKZ (Occupation Code) which is a German version of SOC, NAICS (North American Industry Classification System); and finally, WZ2003 (Classification of Industry Sector) which is the German classification for economic activities.

## 6.2   Application of the Ontology

We demonstrate the the modeling of business semantics in the context of service-oriented Information Governance. We have implemented these applications in Collibra's Business Semantics Glossary product.

---

[11] http://ns.hr-xml.org/

**Modelling Service System Perspectives.** SBVR and BSM acknowledges the existence of multiple perspectives on how to represent concepts (by means of *vocabularies*), and includes the modelling of a governance model to reconcile these perspectives (insofar practically necessary) in order to come to an ontology that is agreed and shared (by means of communities and speech communities) [5].

- A *semantic community* (itself an ORGANISATION) groups ORGANISATIONS and controls a shared body of business service semantics. Domain concepts are identified by a URI.
- A *speech community* is a subset of ORGANISATIONS from a semantic community that control a set of vocabulary RESOURCES to refer to this body of shared meanings.
- A *vocabulary* is a meaningful grouping of lexical RESOURCES (e.g., noun types, fact types and rules primarily drawn from a single natural language or jargon) to represent conceptions within a body of shared semantics.

The participation of INDIVIDUALS in the governance of the vocabulary controlled by their ORGANISATION is contrained by specific governance services. The latter are defined – as domain specialisations of our upper-level mode – by assigning ACTOR roles to INDIVIDUALS for certain ACTIONS on these LEXICAL RESOURCES.

**Dynamic Actor Type Management.** Types of ACTOR can be dynamically defined as a noun concept with a gloss in a designated ACTOR VOCABULARY. For example, consider:

- BUSINESS STEWARD *is a* ACTOR

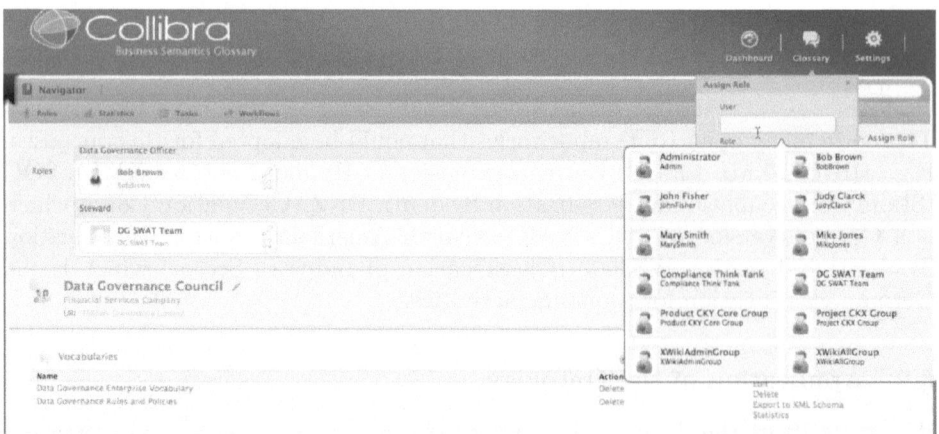

**Fig. 1.** Assigning INDIVIDUAL "Bob Brown" to play ACTOR in a specific VOCABULARY for a "DG Council" service. This implies a number of permittable ACTIONS on the vocabulary's constituents.

where the term is mapped on the following gloss articulating the term for this role: "expert in a certain business unit or line of business". Responsibility can be assigned to ACTOR type definitions as follows:

– **It is permitted that** BUSINESS STEWARD *acts in* ADDNOUNCONCEPT;

where ADDNOUNCONCEPT *is a* ACTION; one of the many that can be performed on vocabulary RESOURCES.

**Assigning Individuals to Actor Types.** Based on their COMPETENCY, INDIVIDUALS are assigned to an ACTOR type; permitting or obligating them to play a role in a certain ACTION. The following screenshot shows an assignment of a role is done for the business semantics management of a service called "Data Governance Council" in a a financial service company.

## 7 Discussion and Conclusion

We proposed a method for ontological representation and governance of business service semantics. Currently, no commercial tool, aside from the prototype in Collibra's Business Semantics Glossary used to demonstrate the feasibility of our solution, exists. Hence, we find our effort in this work as paving the road towards the development of improved service-integration tools that are better equipped to facilitate inter-silos communication. The next step is to investigate the automatic configuration of roles and responsibilities along peers in modelling quality and compliance of their services by, i.a., matching competency and reputation profiles, based on earlier work [7].

We will validate our approach in the Flanders research Information Space (FRIS) case study [15]. FRIS is a knowledge-intensive community of interest for two main reasons. First, it exhibits participatory characteristics that are typical to open networks. The actors are inter-dependent yet highly autonomous, heterogeneous, and distributed; including research institutes, funding agencies, patent offices and industrial adopters. The FRIS community has a minimum level of governance. The Flemish Public Administration has limited means to enforce information quality and compliance requirements on its FRIS peers; hence a high level of trust is assumed. Yet they inter-dependency on value creation is a main incentive. Secondly, the FRIS information space[12] itself is a true product of open value cocreation. FRIS publishes information about innovation-related entities such as researchers, projects, proposals, publications, and patents that is provided and consumed by all actors. FRIS will also benefit from external (Open Data) sources as we demonstrated earlier in [8]. This will make the discussion of quality and compliance even more complicated.

---

[12] The FRIS portal currently consists of 22636 projects, 3596 publications, 1981 organizations and 17096 researchers: `http://researchportal.be/`

# References

1. Akkermans, H., Gordijn, J.: Ontology Engineering, Scientific Method and the Research Agenda. In: Staab, S., Svátek, V. (eds.) EKAW 2006. LNCS (LNAI), vol. 4248, pp. 112–125. Springer, Heidelberg (2006)
2. Alter, S.: Service system fundamentals: Work system, value chain, and life cycle. IBM Systems Journal 47(1), 71–85 (2008)
3. Cardoso, J., Pedrinaci, C., Leidig, T., Rupino, P., De Leenheer, P.: Open semantic service networks. In: Proc. of ISSS, pp. 1–15. Institute for Applied Informatics Leipzig (2012)
4. Cardoso, J., Winkler, M., Voigt, K., Berthold, H.: IoS-based services, platform services, SLA and models for the internet of services. Communications in Computer and Information Science 50, 3–17 (2011)
5. De Leenheer, P., Christiaens, S., Meersman, R.: Business semantics management: a case study for competency-centric HRM. Computers in Industry 61(8), 760–775 (2010)
6. De Leenheer, P., de Moor, A.: Context-driven disambiguation in ontology elicitation. In: Shvaiko, P., Euzenat, J. (eds.) Proc. of the 1st Context and Ontologies Workshop, AAAI/IAAI 2005, pp. 17–24 (2005)
7. De Leenheer, P., Debruyne, C., Peeters, J.: Towards social performance indicators for community-based ontology evolution. In: Tudorache, T., Correndo, G., Noy, N., Alani, H., Greaves, M. (eds.) Proceedings of ISWC Workshops. CEUR (2009)
8. Debruyne, C., De Leenheer, P.: Insights in Business Semantics Management: Case Studies drawn from the Flemish Public Administration. In: Handbook for the Second European Business Intelligence Summer School. Springer (2012)
9. Erl, T.: Service-Oriented Architecture: A Field Guide to Integrating XML and Web Services. Prentice Hall (2004)
10. Falkenberg, E.: FRISCO: A framework of information system concepts. Technical report, IFIP WG 8.1 Task Group (1998)
11. Ferrario, R., Guarino, N., Janiesch, C., Kiemes, T., Oberle, D., Probst, F.: Towards an ontological foundation of services science: The general service model. In: Wirtschaftsinformatik, p. 47 (2011)
12. Guarino, N., Welty, C.A.: Identity, unity, and individuality: Towards a formal toolkit for ontological analysis. In: ECAI, pp. 219–223. IOS Press (2000)
13. Halpin, T., Morgan, T.: Information Modeling and Relational Databases, 2nd edn. Morgan Kaufmann (2008)
14. Khatri, V., Brown, C.V.: Designing data governance. Commun. ACM 53(1), 148–152 (2010)
15. Limonad, L., De Leenheer, P., Linehan, M., Hull, R., Vaculín, R.: Ontology of Dynamic Entities. In: Atzeni, P., Cheung, D., Ram, S. (eds.) ER 2012 Main Conference 2012. LNCS, vol. 7532, pp. 345–358. Springer, Heidelberg (2012)
16. Maglio, P., Srinivasan, S., Kreulen, J., Spohrer, J.: Service systems, service scientists, SSME, and innovation. Commun. ACM 49(7), 81–85 (2006)
17. Martin, D., Domingue, J., Sheth, A.P., Battle, S., Sycara, K.P., Fensel, D.: Semantic web services, part 2. IEEE Intelligent Systems 22(6), 8–15 (2007)
18. McCarthy, W.E.: The REA Accounting Model: A Generalized Framework for Accounting Systems in a Shared Data Environment. Accounting Review 57(3), 554 (1982)
19. Meersman, R.: The use of lexicons and other computer-linguistic tools in semantics, design and cooperation of database systems. In: Proc. of the Conf. on Cooperative Database Systems (CODAS 1999), pp. 1–14. Springer (1999)

20. Nonaka, I., Takeuchi, H.: The Knowledge-Creating Company: How Japanese Companies Create the Dynamics of Innovation. Oxford University Press (1995)
21. Normann, R., Ramirez, R.: From value chain to value constellation: Designing interactive strategy. Harvard Business Review 71, 65–77 (1993)
22. Osterwalder, A.: The Business Model Ontology - a proposition in a design science approach. PhD thesis, University of Lausanne, HEC (2004)
23. Papazoglou, M.P., Traverso, P., Dustdar, S., Leymann, F.: Service-oriented computing: a research roadmap. Int. J. Cooperative Inf. Syst. 17(2), 223–255 (2008)
24. Parasuraman, A., Zeithaml, V.A., Berry, L.L.: A conceptual model of service quality and its implications for future research. Journal of Marketing 49(4), 41–50 (1985)
25. Pedrinaci, C., Domingue, J.: Toward the next wave of services: Linked services for the web of data. Journal of Universal Computer Science (2010)
26. Poels, G.: The Resource-Service-System Model for Service Science. In: Trujillo, J., Dobbie, G., Kangassalo, H., Hartmann, S., Kirchberg, M., Rossi, M., Reinhartz-Berger, I., Zimányi, E., Frasincar, F. (eds.) ER 2010. LNCS, vol. 6413, pp. 117–126. Springer, Heidelberg (2010)
27. Polanyi, M.: The Tacit Dimension. Anchor Books (1966)
28. Razo-Zapata, I.S., De Leenheer, P., Gordijn, J., Akkermans, H.: Fuzzy Verification of Service Value Networks. In: Ralyté, J., Franch, X., Brinkkemper, S., Wrycza, S. (eds.) CAiSE 2012. LNCS, vol. 7328, pp. 95–110. Springer, Heidelberg (2012)
29. Razo-Zapata, I.S., De Leenheer, P., Gordijn, J., Akkermans, H.: Service Network Approaches. In: Handbook of Service Description: USDL and its Methods, pp. 45–74. Springer (2011)
30. Ryan, H., Spyns, P., De Leenheer, P., Leary, R.: Ontology-Based Platform for Trusted Regulatory Compliance Services. In: Meersman, R. (ed.) OTM-WS 2003. LNCS, vol. 2889, pp. 675–689. Springer, Heidelberg (2003)
31. Sampson, S.E., Froehle, C.M.: Foundations and implications of a proposed unified services theory. Production and Operations Management 15(2), 329–343 (2006)
32. Terenziani, P., Torasso, P.: Time, action-types, and causation: An integrated analysis. Computational Intelligence 11(3), 529–552 (1995)
33. Thomas, O., Fellmann, M.: Semantic epc: Enhancing process modeling using ontology languages. In: Hepp, M., et al. (eds.) SBPM. CEUR Workshop Proceedings, vol. 251. CEUR-WS.org (2007)
34. Vargo, S., Lusch, R.: Evolving to a new dominant logic for marketing. Journal of Marketing 68(1), 1–17 (2004)
35. Weber, K., Otto, B., Österle, B.: One size does not fit all—a contingency approach to data governance. ACM Journal of Data and Information Quality 1(1) (2009)
36. Zittrain, J.: The Future of the Internet and How to Stop it. Yale University Press (2009)

# Simulation-Based Quantification of Business Impacts Caused by Service Incidents

Axel Kieninger, Florian Berghoff, Hansjörg Fromm, and Gerhard Satzger

Karlsruhe Institute of Technology, Karlsruhe Service Research Institute,
Englerstrasse 11, 76131 Karlsruhe, Germany
{Axel.Kieninger,Florian.Berghoff,
Hansjoerg.Fromm,Gerhard.Satzger}@kit.edu

**Abstract.** Today, business processes heavily depend on IT, so that business results are affected by the quality of supporting IT services. To gauge the quality of service from a business point of view, we need to consider the service incidents that occur over a reference period and evaluate the effect of each service incident individually. In this work, we address this problem by developing a procedure to monetarily quantify the negative impact of single service incidents on the service customer business.

We first review related literature to identify approaches to quantifying the negative consequences associated with a service incident. Based on our findings, we propose a simulation-based procedure for estimating the monetary impact. Contrary to existing approaches, we first apply business process simulation as a formal analysis technique to determine the effects of *single* service incidents on process performance. Then, the impact on process performance is translated into its monetary equivalent.

**Keywords:** IT Service Management, Business Impact Analysis, Discrete-event Business Process Simulation.

## 1 Introduction

Today, IT services represent an integral part of business processes (BPs). Due to the dependence of business processes on IT, business results may be impacted by the quality of supporting IT services. Therefore, the quality of an IT service should be defined in a way that it matches business requirements.

In practice, the target quality of a service – i.e., the quality level aimed to be achieved – is often defined using technical metrics[1], such as availability, throughput, or response time [1]. The actual value of these indicators, which is realized over a reference period, is usually determined by a sequence of service incidents[2] that occur,

---

[1] As opposed to "business impact metrics"

[2] i.e., of "unplanned interruptions" to a service or "reductions in the quality" of a service, which are observable from a business point of view (adapted from the definition of an "incident" in [2, p. 254])

J.F. e Cunha, M. Snene, and H. Nóvoa (Eds.): IESS 2013, LNBIP 143, pp. 170–185, 2013.

but may not reflect the associated business impact. Since different service incidents may adversely affect business operations to different degrees, "aggregate" technical metrics may not necessarily indicate the impact that specific service quality levels have on business operations [3]. For instance, few long service disruptions (a specific type of service incidents) might cause more severe consequences for the business than many short interruptions [4], even though they result in the same level of service availability (aggregate service indicator) over the reference period [3].

In order to gauge the quality of service from the business point of view, we have to consider the different service incidents that occur over a reference period and evaluate the effect of each service incident individually. The sum across all service incidents' effects will then denote the overall business impact. A thorough understanding of the relationship between a single service incident and its financial implications may then be leveraged, for example, to compare IT service offers and to identify the one providing the best trade-off between business impact and service price (cf. [5]).

In this work, we develop a procedure to *monetarily* quantify the negative impact of single service incidents on the customer business, which we denote as "business costs". In Section 2, we review related literature describing approaches that may be used to assess the costs that a business incurs due to single service incidents. The generic scenario defined in Section 3 summarizes basic assumptions and highlights requirements that a procedure for quantifying the impact of a service incident should satisfy. In Section 4, we describe our simulation-based procedure for quantifying the impact of a service incident. We shortly present the application of our procedure to an order-picking process in Section 5. Finally, Section 6 summarizes and discusses our approach, as well as outlines future work.

## 2    Related Work

This paper is part of a larger research project, in which we address an IT service customer's challenge of selecting the cost-optimal service[3] among different options offered by external providers. In previous works, we defined concepts that customers and providers should consider when describing service performance aspects as well as service requirements (e.g. [3]) and we developed a mechanism to formalize the negotiation between a customer and different providers (e.g. [5]). The procedure introduced in the upcoming sections supports the customer in determining its input for the cost-optimal mechanism.

In the following, we discuss existing approaches related to the topic at hand. The relevant literature was identified in a thorough forward and backward search without temporal restrictions, following the review approach by Webster and Watson [6, p. xv-xvi]. Google scholar was used as primary source, and the keywords searched were "business impact", "service incident", "downtime loss", "cost of downtime", "interruption cost", "service level", "operational risk", "business process simulation" and "discrete-event simulation", as well as combinations thereof.

---

[3] i.e. the one minimizing the sum of service price and monetarily quantified business impact induced through service performance issues (service incidents)

In [7], Wiedemann provides a structured approach to analyze the business impact of IT service outages in practice and to estimate the resulting business costs in a quantitative way. The procedure, however, does not contain an explicit model to evaluate the impact of IT service outages on business operations (i.e., to derive the impact on BPs and their performance). Also, Wiedemann discusses the subject of business impact analysis in the context of IT risk management and focuses on rare events having a severe impact on the business (cf. [7, p. 40]). In contrast, we address IT service incidents which may occur on a more frequent basis and may usually be associated with much shorter durations.

Suh and Han [8] propose a model-based procedure to link IT system unavailability to business costs through application of the Analytical Hierarchy Process. They suggest decomposing the business model into functions and sub-functions and identifying the organization's assets supporting them. However, the business cost estimate is solely based on the company's average income stream. There is no further analysis of business costs associated with the interruption of business operations.

Moura et al. specify performance objectives for the BPs supported and capture the negative impact of IT service incidents as deviation from these objectives in [9]. To translate missed performance objectives into business costs, a cost rate is estimated for each BP (based on historic data), while the importance of BPs is described through relative weights. The authors explicitly aim to provide a rather "simple quantitative loss analysis" and to keep the cost of modeling low, at the same time noting that simulation, for example, would allow for a more detailed analysis.

The works referred to so far describe "comprehensive" approaches to link service outages or degradations to business costs. Following Sauvé et al. [1], an evaluation of business costs should be composed of two steps: (1) map service incidents with distinct features to changes in the value of BP-related metrics[4], which measure BP behavior (to capture the negative impact on the BP level), and (2) map changes in the value of BP-related metrics to business costs (to express the impact in business terms). Subsequently, we discuss approaches that specifically relate to either of these two steps:

Jin et al. [10], for instance, apply discrete-event simulation to investigate the effect of different service (quality) levels on business performance. The authors do not particularly consider service incidents. But, similar to the goals of our approach, they observe business performance as a function of various service-related attributes.

Jakoubi et al. [11] simulate the aggregate impact of different service availability levels on the BPs supported. They also consider how degradations in business performance may translate into financial consequences in terms of revenue loss and penalty payments. Yet, the authors do not offer a more general procedure to translate changes in BP-related metrics into comprehensive business cost estimates. In contrast to our work, they do not focus on single service incidents and their effect on the business.

Patterson [12] and Dübendorfer et al. [13] offer specific models to estimate the costs of service downtime. While Patterson suggests an "easy-to-calculate estimate" accounting for lost revenue and for the costs of employees unable to perform their tasks during service downtime, Dübendorfer et al. develop a more elaborate

---

[4] Such as transaction throughput and number of delayed shipments

calculation formula. However, these authors do not provide approaches to linking service incidents to degradations in BP performance.

We summarize the review of related approaches restating the most important findings: Existing "comprehensive" approaches to analyzing and quantifying the negative impact of service incidents provide valuable insights on how to structure an impact analysis in practice and on how to approach an evaluation of business costs. However, the approaches discussed are primarily based on document analysis and interviews and, thus, rely on the stakeholder's ability to accurately assess and anticipate the negative impact resulting from service incidents.

At the same time, simulation has proven to be a very flexible and powerful tool to quantitatively analyze the impact of service quality on BP performance. When the BP model reaches a certain degree of complexity (in terms of structure or behavior), a simulation-based approach may in fact be the only "feasible means" of quantitative analysis (cf. [14, p. 145]). To the best of our knowledge, simulation has so far not been integrated into an overall procedure to derive comprehensive business cost estimates for single service incidents.

## 3    Scenario Description and Assumptions

In this work, we assume a company (henceforth denoted as "the customer") to purchase an IT service from an internal or external IT service provider. The service is directly relevant and observable from the customer point of view as certain activities in the customer's BPs directly depend on the provided service. Hence, if the service is temporarily malfunctioning or unavailable, this will impact the execution of supported activities and translate into a degradation of the customer's regular business operations. These consequences are to be expressed through business costs.

In order to be able to determine the business costs of different service incidents in isolation of each other, we must assume that service incidents can be treated as separate events and that their adverse consequences can be analyzed individually, without having to consider previous or subsequent events. This requires that the negative impacts of different incidents on business operations are independent of each other (i.e. that when a service incident disrupts operations, supported BPs are running under normal conditions).

Finally, the business cost estimates need to be based on the current structure and functionality of the customer's BPs. Thus, we ensure that the BPs considered will not be modified once a business cost analysis has been conducted. If this was the case (e.g. because the analysis reveals weaknesses in the current BP setup that need to be eliminated), the customer should re-evaluate the business costs that result from different service incidents.

## 4    A Simulation-Based Procedure for the Estimation of Business Costs

We adopt the basic structure from Wiedemann [7] as foundation for our approach to derive business cost estimates. While Wiedemann assumes that the parameters in the evaluation model reflecting the expected impact of a service incident can be determined through interviews or document analysis *alone* [7, p. 123], we will detect a service incident's impact through BP simulation, linking incident features (e.g. the duration and time of occurrence of a service incident) to changes in the value of BP-related metrics. Thus, we adopt and make use of an existing formal BP analysis technique to determine the effects of service incidents on supported BPs. We specifically propose the use of discrete-event simulation as it allows us to model the stochastic and dynamic aspects of a process, resulting in a more accurate evaluation of a service incident's impact[5].

We subdivide our approach into four steps (see Fig. 1): (1) identify the different types of business costs (business cost components) relevant to the specific scenario, (2) link these business cost components to associated BP-related metrics, (3) simulate the impact of single service incidents on business operations, and (4) estimate the business costs associated with the single service incidents.

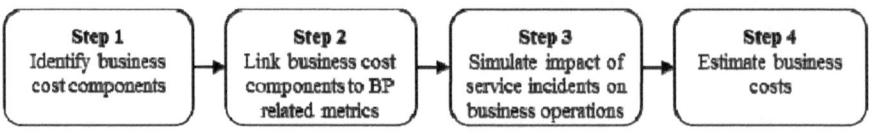

**Fig. 1.** Four steps towards the determination of business costs

In the following sections, we explain each of the four steps in greater detail.

## 4.1     Step 1: Identify Relevant Business Cost Components

The identification of relevant effects requires the business to anticipate the way it will react and operate in case of a service incident, and to evaluate whether or not (and under which conditions) certain consequences could actually be incurred (cf. [7, p. 129]). To structure and facilitate the analysis of potential business cost components, we apply a comprehensive classification scheme, which subdivides the adverse consequences of a service incident into multiple business cost categories.[6]

At the highest level (and adapted from [7]), we classify the negative impact of a service incident into (1) losses in revenue, (2) additional expenses, and (3) intangible costs (i.e. costs, which are not easily quantifiable). The first two categories cover the effects of a service incident that can easily be expressed in monetary terms, either causing an immediate decline in revenue or an increase in the expenses incurred. Intangible costs, on the other hand, refer to consequences of a service incident that are difficult to quantify (cf. [16, p. 254f]), such as the dissatisfaction of employees or customers. We refine losses in revenue and additional expenses through categories from profit loss statements[7], while at the same time incorporating the different effects associated with service incidents in related literature.

---

[5] According to Tumay [15, p. 59], discrete-event simulation represents the most "capable and powerful" tool for the simulation of business processes.

[6] We will present the details of our "business cost framework" in separate works.

[7] The elements of which we assume to be cash-effective

As a whole, the classification scheme serves as a guide to identifying the classes of damage that may be relevant to a specific scenario. For example, it may be used to structure interviews with experts and relevant stakeholders. Finally, it will help us to organize (and calculate) business costs in a systematic way. The result of this step is a list of business cost components (representing types of monetary consequences to be expected in the specific scenario) classified into the categories of the business cost framework.

## 4.2    Step 2: Link Business Cost Components to Business Process-Related Metrics

Once the different business cost components relevant to the specific scenario are identified, we need to link them to corresponding BP-related metrics. That is, for each effect which will translate into business costs for the service customer, we need to determine a driver or metric on the BP level which may be impacted by the occurrence of a service incident, and based on which the respective business cost estimate can be computed. The choice and definition of BP-related metrics depends on the business cost components identified and the specifics of the business process under consideration.

For example, certain steps in a manufacturing process could be disrupted when a supporting IT service becomes unavailable. This might delay the completion of urgent orders and result in additional expenses in terms of penalties to be paid to the respective customers (business cost component). The driver on the BP level is simply the number of penalty payments made (BP-related metric). Accordingly, the additional expenses could finally be computed by multiplying the number of additional penalty payments with the (average) payment amount. In this example, the condition under which a penalty payment occurs would need to be specified and checked during the execution of the simulation model in Step 3.

On the whole, Step 2 requires that we prepare a formula for each business cost component (i.e. a mapping to a BP-related metric), which allows us to calculate the monetary impact resulting from potential changes in the value of a BP-related metric. Also, we may have to specify conditions for the measurement of each metric, which will later be implemented in the simulation model. This information could, for example, be obtained through interviews with process stakeholders.

## 4.3    Step 3: Simulate the Impact of Service Incidents on Business Operations

We use simulation to evaluate how different service incidents cause changes in the value of BP-related metrics (depending on the severity of the incident and its time of occurrence). In order to determine differences in the value of BP-related metrics, we have to compare business operations in the absence of a service incident (i.e. under regular circumstances) to those in the presence of one. Any change in the value of the BP-related metrics can then be attributed to the occurrence of the incident. Simulation experiments will be set up accordingly.

In general, the simulation of BPs can be divided into the following steps (cf. [17, p. 1365f]): (1) define modeling objectives, (2) decide on model boundaries, (3) collect

176     A. Kieninger et al.

and analyze data on the BPs, (4) develop a BP simulation model, (5) test the model through verification and validation techniques, (6) conduct simulation experiments, (7) analyze simulation results, and (8) recommend BP changes. These steps may be executed in an iterative manner and need not necessarily represent a fixed sequence (cf. [17]; [18]).

Since the modeling objective is fixed in the context of this work (we aim to evaluate the impact of single service incidents on process performance) and the model boundaries have been set as well (we assume that BPs to be included in the analysis have already been identified), we will not further elaborate on the first two steps (1 and 2) of the BP simulation procedure. Also, we will not focus on the last step of the simulation approach (8) because we do not intend to recommend BP changes based on our simulation results. Hence, to simulate the impact of different service incidents on the customer business, we only adopt the steps from (3) to (7), re-labeling them as steps 3.A, 3.B, and so forth (see Fig. 2).

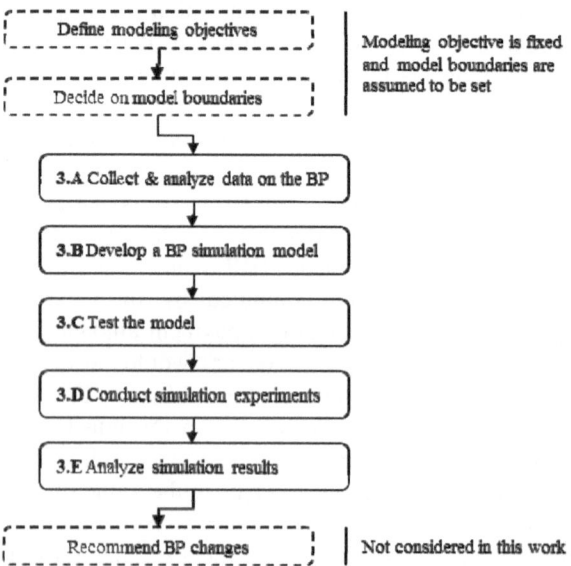

**Fig. 2.** Steps involved in business process simulation (based on [17])

While the steps from collecting and analyzing the data to testing the model (3.A to 3.C) help us to construct a simulation model that captures the relevant elements of the real system, the steps of conducting experiments and analyzing output (3.D and 3.E) are used to finally simulate and evaluate the effect of different service incidents. In the following, we will elaborate on each of these steps individually.

**Step 3.A – Collect and Analyze Data on the Business Process.** Prior to building a simulation model of the BPs to be considered, we need to collect the data required to formally describe and implement them (cf. [17, p. 1365]). This may include (cf. [19]; [20]):

- Information about the process structure (such as the logical arrangement of activities),
- Data for the characterization of activities and resources (such as activity processing times, resource allocations and capacities),
- Information on events (such as inter-arrival times for the different transaction types) and
- Information on routings (such as logical conditions or probabilities for branchings in the process).

Since our goal is to simulate the impact of service incidents on process performance, we should not only gather information on the processes' structure and behavior under regular circumstances, but also on the way in which the business is affected in case of a service incident and on the way it operates while the service is malfunctioning. For instance, the following two considerations may be relevant in creating an accurate BP simulation model: First, it appears reasonable to specify for each service incident whether the execution of tasks supported by the IT service is completely stopped while the service is malfunctioning or whether it can (to some extent) be maintained, e.g. by processing transactions in an alternative way. Second, we may have to determine whether activities whose execution is disrupted by the occurrence of a service incident can be resumed "from the point at which interruption took place" or whether they must be repeated (i.e. whether the respective transaction must be reprocessed from scratch) (cf. [21, p. 73f]). Again, expert interviews and document analyses support this step.

**Step 3.B – Develop a Business Process Simulation Model.** The process of building a BP simulation model (using simulation software) may be depicted as an iterative process [17, p. 1365]. Starting with an initial (high-level) representation of the system, more and more refinements should be made to the simulation model until the BPs are captured at the required level of detail.

In general, there may be multiple ways to model a system or certain parts of a system (cf. [18, p. 288]). Similarly, the occurrence of a service incident may be captured in various manners. This holds especially true since the way in which we model a service incident will depend on the type of service incident and on the way it affects supported activities. For example, the impact of a service outage might have to be modeled in a different way than a throughput reduction of an IT service. To model service outages, for instance, we may define the IT service as a resource which is utilized by certain activities and becomes unavailable when an incident occurs (cf. [18, p. 122]). In contrast, a reduced throughput incident may be best described by a decline in the processing rate of related activities.

Besides the development of a simulation model which mimics the behavior of the real system, we also have to ensure that the performance metrics of interest (i.e. the BP-related metrics required for the computation of business costs) are recorded when the model is executed.

**Step 3.C – Test the Model.** Before we can leverage the simulation model, we should carefully test the model by applying "as many model verification and validation techniques as feasible" [17, p. 1366]. This may include setting up test scenarios in which the model logic may "fail" [18, p. 540], and showing the model to people familiar with the business process in order to seek feedback (cf. [20]; [18]).

**Step 3.D – Conduct Simulation Experiments.** In the context of this work, the purpose of experimenting with the simulation model is to gauge the impact of different service incidents on BP performance, measured through changes in the value of BP-related metrics. In order to analyze the effects of different service incidents (which may, e.g., differ in their duration as well as in their time of occurrence), we need to create multiple configurations of the "general" simulation model which we constructed and tested in the previous steps (cf. [18, p. 40]). On the one hand, we require a configuration of the BP model devoid of a service incident, which will be used as base case. On the other hand, we must set up one configuration for each service incident to be analyzed. The results produced by these configurations will then be compared to the base case in order to identify changes in the value of BP-related metrics induced by the different service incidents.

In the following, we will first introduce experimental design issues related to the simulation of single simulation scenarios (such as setting the time frame of a simulation and the number of replications to be made). Then, we will elaborate on the setup of different model configurations that will be used in order to evaluate the impact of different service incidents.

*Set the Simulation Time Frame.* In most cases, simulations can be categorized as terminating or steady state [18, p. 258]. In case of a terminating simulation, the initial conditions as well as the stopping conditions are well defined. On the other hand, a steady state (or non-terminating) simulation refers to systems that are continuously operating [22, p. 28], i.e. the initial conditions are not of interest and there is no well-defined stopping point [18, p. 258].

Since our aim is to simulate the impact of service incidents on business operations, the length of a simulation run should (ideally) be chosen in a way that the negative consequences resulting from a service incident are completely captured. With respect to a *terminating system*, the terminating condition should be set in a way that the simulated period covers all changes in the value of BP-related metrics that were specifically caused by the incident. When analyzing processes operating in *steady state*, we may take the following approach: (1) we start a simulation run and wait for the system to reach its steady state, (2) we simulate the occurrence of a service incident, which may cause the system to leave its stationary state, and (3) we terminate the run when the system has recovered and re-approached steady state again (cf. [23]).

In order to make the base case comparable to the different service incident scenarios, we should ensure that the simulated period is the same in all experiments.

*Set the Number of Replications.* Aiming to create a valid model of a real system, we often have to account for uncertainty [18, p. 38]. Activity processing times, for example, may follow a specific probability distribution, which should be included in the simulation model. However, stochastic input causes randomness in the output, too ([22]; [18]). That is, if we run a stochastic system multiple times, the results produced by the model will usually vary from replication to replication.

In order to deal with the randomness in a simulation model, we need to make several simulation runs and analyze the output from these replications statistically [22, p. 25]. In the context of this work, we focus on estimating the expected value of the different BP-related metrics and on estimating the expected change in the value of these metrics due to a service incident.

The expected value of a specific measure is estimated by the sample mean, which represents an unbiased point estimator (cf. [18, p. 611]). To quantify the "imprecision" involved in the estimate, we form a confidence interval which covers the true mean with a specified probability of (approximately) $(1-\alpha)$ [18, p. 40 & 612].

The more replications we produce, the higher the accuracy of the point estimator is, reflected in the width of the confidence interval. We may leverage this relationship to estimate the number of replications required to achieve a desired precision in the estimates (cf. [18, p. 261f]). Thus, we can avoid creating too many replications, while at the same time reaching an acceptable accuracy.

***Set up Model Configurations for the Analysis of Scenarios.*** As indicated above, the basic configuration of the BP model represents the scenario devoid of a service incident (base case). All other configurations correspond to simulation scenarios, in which we model the occurrence of one specific service incident each. A "service incident scenario" can be characterized by two dimensions, each of which may influence the resulting impact on business operations: (1) the simulated service incident characterized by its type (such as service outage) and properties (such as service incident duration), and (2) the point in time during the simulation period at which the service incident occurs, i.e. its time of occurrence (TOC).

For example, if we were interested in analyzing the impact of outage incidents (service incident type) within the time frame of a single day, we could create multiple scenarios differing by the duration of the simulated service incident (service incident properties) and by the time of the day at which the incident takes place (TOC).

While there may be a great number of possible service incident scenarios, we have to decide on a limited set of scenarios to be included in the analysis. The more scenarios we simulate, the more insights we can gain, but the greater is the time and effort involved. Therefore, we might focus on the set of service incident scenarios considered most relevant. As a first step, we could narrow down the range of possible scenarios by deciding on intervals of service incident properties to be considered for each service incident type, and by specifying certain time windows (within the simulated time period) during which the occurrence of a service incident might be most critical. Within the defined range, the goal is to understand how the impact on BP performance differs by service incident type, service incident properties, and by the time of occurrence. Lastly, we have to select the set of scenarios to be simulated. The selection process may generally be supported by design of experiment techniques [22, p. 173ff].

***Simulate.*** Having decided on the simulation time frame to be used and the number of replications to be made to achieve the desired accuracy, we simulate the service incident scenarios (model configurations) considered.

**Step 3.E – Analyze Simulation Results.** At this point, we assume that the simulation of different service incident scenarios as well as of the base case scenario has been completed. Also, we assume that in each simulation experiment (scenario) a sample of "observations" for the different BP-related metrics to be considered has been generated.

This data is utilized for further statistical analysis. In particular, we compare the values of the BP-related metrics from the single service incident scenarios to those from the base case, deriving point estimates and confidence intervals for the expected changes in these values (induced by the different service incidents).

To estimate the mean difference in the value of a specific BP-related metric, we first collate the output data from the base case and from a service incident scenario simulation, and compute the difference in the results of each replication (cf. [22, p. 279])[8]. Then, if we consider the differences in the values of a BP-related metric as a "sample" on its own, we can compute the sample mean to estimate the expected change between the base case and the service incident scenario and may determine the respective confidence interval (cf. [22, p. 279f]).

This analysis is applied to any pairwise comparison between a service incident scenario and the base case, and to any BP-related metric recorded.

## 4.4    Step 4: Estimate Business Costs

In this last step, we compute the business costs associated with each of the service incidents considered. The business costs associated with a particular service incident (occurring at a specific point in time) are determined by summing up the costs across all business cost components. The value of each business cost component is calculated from the expected change in the value of the associated BP-related metric, which we estimated in the previous step.

# 5    Application of the Procedure to an Order-Picking Process

We tested our simulation-based procedure for the estimation of business costs using the example of an order-picking process at a warehouse. Order-picking is part of the outbound processes, initiated by the receipt of customer orders and followed by checking, packing, and shipping activities [24, p. 23ff]. Processes at a warehouse are generally facilitated by a warehouse management system (WMS), that is, a complex software system coordinating the "flow of people, machines, and product" [24, p. 33]. In our example, we consider the features of the WMS in support of the order-picking process as an IT service.

## 5.1    Description of the Order-Picking Process

The order-picking process in our example is organized into four separate picking stations linked by a conveyor belt. At the beginning of the process, boxes for the

---

[8] This approach requires that the different scenarios are simulated with so-called "common random numbers" (cf. [19, p. 279])

different customer orders are manually placed on the conveyor. Depending on the items on a customer order, a box will visit one or several of the picking locations. At each station, a single operator collects the items required for the specific order (from the items stored at this station) and places them in the box. Once an order is completed, the container is transferred to the shipping area.

Each picking station has a capacity of (at most) three boxes: one order being in process, the other two orders waiting in a buffer. If a box cannot access a station because it is (temporarily) crowded, it will continue to circulate on the conveyor belt. We assume that there is neither a pre-defined sequence that a box will follow to visit the different stations, nor are the boxes dynamically routed to specific locations. Instead, whenever a box passes a picking station (which holds required items and has not been visited yet), it tries to gain immediate access. Throughout the process, information is exchanged with the WMS, which holds information about the customer orders and the locations to be visited by each box.

We assume that the WMS, which supports the order-picking process, may temporarily be unavailable, putting the picking process to an abrupt halt. That is, we consider outage incidents (incident type) whose level will be specified by the outage duration (incident property). Further, we assume that the conveyor is stopped in such cases, since the flow of boxes as well as picking at the stations is dependent on information provided by the WMS. Except for outage incidents, no other service incident types are considered.

The picking process as a whole starts at 9 o'clock in the morning. At the beginning of each hour, a batch of orders is released to the process. That is, customer orders arriving before 9 a.m. are handed on to the order-picking process at 9 a.m., those arriving between 9 and 10 a.m. are released at 10 a.m., and so forth. The last batch of orders is released for picking at 4 o'clock in the afternoon. Usually, the hour after the release of a batch will suffice to pick all orders on the batch. The time between the completion of an order batch and the release of the next order batch is idle time. Finally, we assume that only orders picked before 4.30 p.m. can be shipped the same day; orders completed after 4.30 p.m. will be shipped the next day. This distinction will be important as we additionally assume that customers who order before 3 o'clock in the afternoon are promised same-day shipping.

## 5.2    Determination of Business Costs

In the following, we shortly elaborate on the single steps of our procedure.

**Step 1: Identify Relevant Business Cost Components.** Two business cost components are identified to be relevant in the context of our example: additional personnel expenses and losses in operating revenue. Additional personnel expenses are incurred if the time that is lost due to a service incident must be made up at the end of the shift, requiring operators at the picking stations to work longer than under normal circumstances. Losses in operating revenue, on the other hand, are driven by shipping fee waivers granted to customers. This will occur if orders eligible for same-day shipping, which would have been picked on time under normal conditions, are not completed early enough to be shipped the same day.

**Step 2: Link Business Cost Components to Business Process-related Metrics.** Additional labor expenses are driven by the number of additional labor minutes paid by the business (BP-related metric), while the losses in operating revenue are related to the number of shipping fee waivers granted to customers (BP-related metric). These metrics represent the output that will be recorded in the simulation experiments. We assume that the cost per additional labor minute of a picking operator equals $ 0.50 and that the shipping fee amounts to $10.00 (on average).

**Step 3: Simulate the Impact of Service Incidents on Business Operations.** First, we need to further specify the order-picking process (3.A). The number of orders in a batch, for example, is each modeled as a Poisson distribution, where the expected batch size differs by the time of the day (Table 1).

**Table 1.** Mean size of the order batches released for picking in the course of a single day

| Time of day | 9:00 | 10:00 | 11:00 | 12:00 | 1:00 | 2:00 | 3:00 | 4:00 |
|---|---|---|---|---|---|---|---|---|
| Mean batch size | 30 | 45 | 60 | 50 | 45 | 60 | 50 | 40 |

The number of picking stations to be visited by each customer order is described through the probability distribution given in Table 2.

**Table 2.** Probability distribution of the number of picking stations to be visited by an order

| Number of picking stations to be visited | 1 | 2 | 3 | 4 |
|---|---|---|---|---|
| Probability | 0.2 | 0.2 | 0.5 | 0.1 |

Further, the time it takes an operator at a picking station to complete an order is assumed to be Triangular-distributed with a minimum value of 45, a mode of 65, and a maximum value of 75 seconds. The dimensions of the conveyor belt and the conveyor speed are specified as well.

Second, we build and test (3.B and 3.C) the business process model as a discrete-event simulation model in Arena. We particularly ensure that the BP-related metrics defined (i.e. the number of labor minutes paid and the number of shipping fee waivers granted) are recorded by the simulation model. To track the number of shipping fee waivers, we check for each customer order in the simulation model whether it qualifies for same-day shipping and whether it is completed early enough to be shipped the same day.

Finally, we simulate the service incident scenarios of interest (as well as the base case scenario) and analyze the output (3.D and 3.E). In particular, we consider service outages occurring between 10.30 a.m. and 03:50 p.m., with durations ranging between 10 and 80 minutes.

**Step 4: Estimate Business Costs.** Based on the changes in the number of labor minutes paid and shipping fee waivers granted (obtained in Step 3) we finally estimate the business costs associated with the different service incidents.

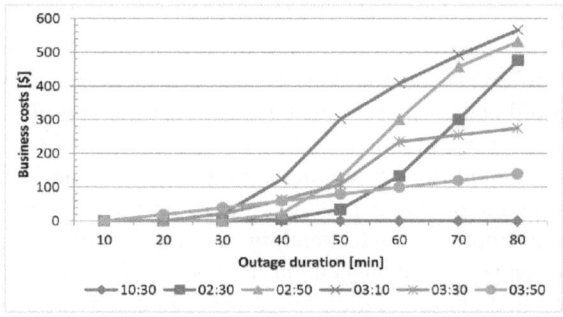

**Fig. 3.** Estimates for the expected business costs

The results of our case study (see Fig. 3) show that the business costs associated with outage incidents may increase non-linearly with the outage duration, and that the impact on the business may also differ by the time of occurrence.

# 6    Conclusion and Outlook

In this work, we developed a procedure to determine the impact of single service incidents on the customer's business processes.

First, we reviewed related literature to identify approaches that could be used in quantifying the negative consequences associated with a service incident. Based on our findings, we proposed a simulation-based procedure for the estimation of business costs. Second, we described a structured procedure for estimating the business costs associated with service incidents of different types and properties. Contrary to existing approaches, we incorporate BP simulation as a formal analysis technique in order to determine the effects of different service incidents on business operations. Thus, the dynamic and stochastic aspects of BPs can be explicitly captured, resulting in a more accurate evaluation of a service incident's impact on the business.

Having put forward our simulation-based procedure, we are fully aware of a number of limitations and challenges: First, even though simulation is a powerful method, it might not always be applicable. For example, a lack of data or unpredictable behavior of agents or entities could impede the development of an accurate BP model. In these cases, an alternative approach, such as the business impact analysis approach by Wiedemann [7], might be preferable. Second, the process of building and executing an appropriate simulation model may be a costly procedure. Therefore, it may be worthwhile to conduct a preliminary evaluation in order to decide whether the gain in accuracy that may be achieved through the use of simulation (compared to alternative analysis techniques) justifies the additional effort. Third, we implicitly assumed the service customer to be risk-neutral focusing our analysis on the expected business costs associated with different service incidents. However, the data samples generated through simulation could as well be used to estimate the variance in business costs. Fourth, we evaluated the impact of single service incidents, assuming that their consequences could be analyzed in isolation of each other. If this assumption is not valid, we could alternatively simulate a variety of characteristic service incident patterns and determine the business costs that would result from the different combinations of service incidents. Lastly, due to space limitations, we could neither present the business cost framework which we refer to in the context of our procedure, nor could we demonstrate the applicability of our approach in greater detail. In future works, we will present an in-depth evaluation of our approach, applied to the order-picking process outlined above.

Our results contribute to understanding the impact of service quality on the business and thus support the management of IT services from a business perspective. We are convinced that our simulation-based procedure can enhance the estimation of business costs. A thorough understanding of the relationship between single service incidents and their financial implications may, for example, be leveraged to compare IT service offers, and to identify the one providing the best trade-off between business impact and service price (e.g., [5]).

# References

1. Sauvé, J., Moura, A., Sampaio, M., Jornada, J., Radziuk, E.: An introductory overview and survey of business-driven IT management. In: 1st IEEE/IFIP International Workshop on Business-Driven IT Management, Vancouver, pp. 1–10 (2006)
2. OGC: IT infrastructure library (ITIL): Service operation. The Stationary Office (TSO), London (2007)
3. Kieninger, A., Satzger, G., Straeten, D., Schmitz, B., Baltadzhiev, D.: Business Cost Budgets: A Methodology to Incorporate Business Impact into Service Level Agreements. International Journal of Service Science, Management, Engineering, and Technology 3(3), 49–64 (2012)
4. Franke, U.: Optimal IT service availability: Shorter outages, or fewer? IEEE Transactions on Network and Service Management 9(1), 22–33 (2012)
5. Kieninger, A., Straeten, D., Kimbrough, S., Schmitz, B., Satzger, G.: Leveraging Service Incident Analytics to Determine Cost-Optimal Service Offers. In: 11th International Conference on Wirtschaftsinformatik. AIS, Leipzig (forthcoming, 2013)
6. Webster, J., Watson, T.: Analyzing the past to prepare for the future: Writing a literature review. MIS Quarterly 26(2), xiii–xxiii (2002)
7. Wiedemann, J.: IT-Notfallvorsorge im betrieblichen Risikomanagement: Entwicklung eines Gestaltungsmodells unter Berücksichtigung ökonomischer Aspekte am Beispiel einer TK-Unternehmung. Ph. D. thesis, Bochum (2008)
8. Suh, B., Han, I.: The IS risk analysis based on a business model. Information and Management 41(2), 149–158 (2003)
9. Moura, A., Sauvé, J., Jornada, J., Radziuk, E.: A quantitative approach to IT investment allocation to improve business results. In: 7th IEEE International Workshop on Policies for Distributed Systems and Networks, pp. 87–95. IEEE Computer Society, London (2006)
10. Jin, L.-J., Machiraju, V., Sahai, A.: Analysis on service level agreement of web services. Technical report, HP Laboratories (2002)
11. Jakoubi, S., Tjoa, S., Goluch, S., Kitzler, G.: A formal approach towards risk-aware service level analysis and planning. In: International Conference on Availability, Reliability, and Security, pp. 180–187. IEEE Computer Society, Krakow (2010)

12. Patterson, D.: A simple way to estimate the cost of downtime. In: 16th USENIX Conference on System Administration, pp. 185–188. ACM, Berkeley (2002)
13. Dübendorfer, T., Wagner, A., Plattner, B.: An economic damage model for large-scale internet attacks. In: 13th IEEE International Workshop on Enabling Technologies: Infrastructures for Collaborative Enterprises, pp. 223–228. IEEE Computer Society, Modena (2004)
14. van Hee, K.M., Reijers, H.A.: Using Formal Analysis Techniques in Business Process Redesign. In: van der Aalst, W.M.P., Desel, J., Oberweis, A. (eds.) BPM 2000. LNCS, vol. 1806, pp. 142–160. Springer, Heidelberg (2000)
15. Tumay, K.: Business process simulation. In: 28th Winter simulation conference, pp. 55–60. IEEE Computer Society Press, Crystal City (1995)
16. Schwalbe, K.: Information technology project management. Thomson Course Technology, Cambridge (2006)
17. Hlupic, V., Robinson, S.: Business process modelling and analysis using discrete-event simulation. In: 30th Winter Simulation Conference, pp. 1363–1370. IEEE Computer Society Press, Los Alamitos (1998)
18. Kelton, W., Sadowski, R., Sturrock, D.: Simulation with Arena. McGraw-Hill Higher Education, Boston (2004)
19. Rosenkranz, F.: Geschäftsprozesse: Modell- und computergestützte Planung. Springer, Berlin (2006)
20. Greasley, A.: Using business process simulation within a business process reengineering approach. Business Process Management Journal 9(4), 408–420 (2003)
21. Gaver Jr., D.P.: A waiting line with interrupted service, including priorities. Journal of the Royal Statistical Society 24(1), 73–90 (1962)
22. Banks, J.: Handbook of Simulation: Principles, Methodology, Advances, Applications, and Practice. Wiley, New York (1998)
23. Pang, G., Whitt, W.: Service interruptions in large-scale service systems. Management Science 55(9), 1499–1512 (2009)
24. Bartholdi, J., Hackman, S.: Warehouse & distribution science: Release 0.95, http://www.warehouse-science.com

# IT Governance Mechanisms: A Literature Review

Rafael Almeida, Rúben Pereira, and Miguel Mira da Silva

Department of Computer Science, Instituto Superior Técnico, Lisbon, Portugal
{rafael.d.almeida,rubenfspereira,mms}@ist.utl.pt

**Abstract.** Nowadays information technology (IT) is present in all organizations. This pervasive use of technology has created a critical dependency on IT that calls for a specific focus on IT Governance (ITG). Organizations with effective governance have actively adopted a set of ITG mechanisms. However, ITG mechanisms are not well defined among the literature and in some cases there are incongruities in their definition. In this paper we intend to perform a literature review (LR) in order to elicit which are the main ITG mechanisms as well as to describe them and state what they are useful for. We finish our work with conclusion, contributions, limitations and future work.

**Keywords:** IT Governance, IT Governance Mechanisms, Literature Review.

## 1 Introduction

Since IT (IT) has become crucial to the support, sustainability and growth of the business [35][36], this pervasive use of technology has created a critical dependency on IT that calls for a specific focus on IT Governance (ITG) [1][28].

ITG has been a concern in the last 20 years [50]. However, good ITG is no longer a "nice to have", but a "must have" [29] and can contribute to higher returns on assets at a time when businesses are increasing their technology investment [5]. Indeed, Gartner states that ITG has been recognized as a CIO top-10 issue for more than five years and has risen in priority between 2007 and 2009 [34].

Enterprises with effective ITG have actively implemented a set of ITG mechanisms that encourage behaviors consistent with the organization's mission, strategy, values, norms, and culture [7]. ITG can be deployed using a mixture of various structures, processes and relational mechanisms [16]. When designing ITG, it is important to recognize that it is contingent upon a variety of sometimes conflicting internal and external factors. Determining the right mechanisms is therefore a complex endeavor [1].

Among the literature several authors argued that organizations should use ITG mechanisms [1][3][12], but few researches attempt to describe and provide a complete explanation on ITG mechanisms. Plus, there is not a consensus about all the existent ITG mechanisms. The majority of the authors point a set of ITG mechanisms without justifying why those and not others, were selected. What's more, in some cases they overlap each other.

J.F. e Cunha, M. Snene, and H. Nóvoa (Eds.): IESS 2013, LNBIP 143, pp. 186–199, 2013.
© Springer-Verlag Berlin Heidelberg 2013

In this work we propose to perform an extensive Literature Review (LR) in order to elicit all the relevant ITG mechanisms describing them and pointing out the main references. This work aims to solve the incongruities and inconsistencies about ITG mechanisms, to thereby increase the consensus about this subject. To do this, it is necessary show the incongruities and inconsistencies and how to solve this problem.

In the next section we introduce the research methodology where we elicit the main steps to perform a LR. Afterwards we describe the problem this research intends to help solve. We follow with a LR regarding ITG mechanisms and identify and describe the main ITG mechanisms. Then, we describe how we evaluate our work. We finish with conclusion about the research as well as contributions, limitations, and future work.

## 2    Research Methodology

A review of prior, relevant literature is an essential feature of any academic project. An effective review creates a firm foundation for advancing knowledge. It makes theory development easier, closes areas where there is a plethora of research, and uncovers areas where research is needed [32]. A LR is *"the use of ideas in the literature to justify the particular approach to the topic, the selection of methods, and demonstration that this research contributes something new."* [37].

Constructing a review is a challenging process because we often need to draw on theories from a variety of fields. Conducting an effective LR that will yield a solid theoretical foundation should also provide a firm foundation to the selection of the methodology for the study [39]. Nevertheless, the LR represents the foundation for research in IS. As such, to review articles is critical to strengthen IS as a field of study [32].

To have a quality IS research we should conduct a LR that will enable researchers to find out what is already known. When proposing a new study or a new theory, researchers should ensure the validity of the study and reliability of the results by making use of quality literature to serve as the foundation of their research.

In a review of literature researchers should use sources that substantiate the presence of the problem under investigation [38].We analyzed the current literature about LR and identified the most important steps and tips to be followed in order to provide an effective LR. These steps can be seen in Table 1.

## 3    Problem

The dependency on IT becomes even more imperative in our knowledge-based economy, where organizations are using technology in managing, developing and communicating intangible assets such as information and knowledge [40].

Corporate success can, of course, only be attained when information and knowledge, very often provided and sustained by technology, is secure, accurate, reliable, and provided to the right person, at the right time, and at the right place [41][45].

**Table 1.** Literature Review Main Steps

| Nº | STEP | Description | This Paper |
|---|---|---|---|
| 1 | Identifying relevant literature | A high-quality review is complete and focuses on concepts. A complete review covers relevant literature on the topic and is not confined to one research methodology, one set of journals, or geography. The quality of the literature used plays a significant role in advancing the knowledge of the researcher and the overall Body of Knowledge (BoK) [31][32]. | All document |
| 1.1 | Validating the quality of the IS literature | In order to select the source material for the review, the following steps must be performed [31][32][33]:<br>a) The major contributions are likely to be in leading journals. You should also examine selected conference proceedings, especially those with a reputation for quality.<br>b) Go backward by reviewing the quotations for the articles identified in step 1 to determine prior articles you should consider.<br>c) Go forward to identify articles citing the key articles identified in the previous steps. | Several journal articles, the main digital libraries (IEEE, ACM,etc) |
| 1.2 | Testing for applicability to your study | While searching for quality literature is essential, it is also important to identify articles that are applicable to the proposed study.<br>This issue has two critical facets. The first deals with the inclusion or exclusion of articles from the LR, and the second deals with ethical and unethical use of references [31][33]. | Only papers with focus on ITG and ITG mechanisms were considered |
| 2 | Structuring the review | Concept-Centric against Author-Centric. Thus, concepts determine the organizing framework of a review [32]. | Table 2, Table 3, Table 4 |
| 2.1 | Writing arguments and argumentation theory | Describe the problem and support it with good references [31]. | Section 1, Section3 |
| 2.2 | Apply the literature | Application is demonstrated by activities such as demonstrating, illustrating, solving, relating, and classifying. In the context of the LR, application is most directly revealed by the two-step process of [31]:<br>a) Identifying the major concepts germane to the study;<br>b) Placing the citation in the correct category. | Spread over the article |
| 2.3 | Theoretical development in your article | Add knowledge and advice for possible future work [32]. | Section 6.2 |
| 2.4 | Creating discussion and conclusions | Discussion and conclusions [32]. | Section 6.1 |
| 3 | Tips for LR | Tips for doing a good LR [31]. | All Document |
| 3.1 | Know the literature | Describes what the work is about [31]. | All Document |
| 3.2 | Comprehend the literature | Demonstrates that you understand the work and if possible provides some examples [31]. | All Document |
| 3.3 | Analyze the literature | Demonstrates the work relevance [31]. | All Document |
| 3.4 | Synthesize the literature | Several references for one phrase instead of a reference for each phrase [31]. | When Possible |
| 3.5 | Evaluate the literature | Demonstrate if the work is already validated or not [31]. | All Document |
| 3.6 | Tone | A successful LR constructively informs the reader about what has been learned. In contrast to specific and critical reviews of individual papers, it tells the reader what patterns you are seeing in the literature. Do not fall into the trap of being overly critical [32]. | All Document |
| 3.7 | Tense | Present or past tense? We think that we should use the present, because it gives to the reader a great sense of immediacy. There is an exception: an author's opinion can change with time, so we should use the past tense when quoting someone [32]. | All Document |
| 4 | Evaluating the theory | With each revision, the paper ripens. Expose your paper to the fresh air and sunshine of collegial feedback. With each discussion, new ideas emerge. The ripening process is facilitated with hard work and frequent revisions [32][47]. | Section 5 |

This major IT dependency also implies a huge vulnerability that is inherently present in certain complex IT environments [42][43][46]. The question of the 'productivity paradox' - why IT have not provided a measurable value to the business world - has puzzled many practitioners and researchers [41][42][43].

All the issues described above point out that the critical dependency on IT calls for a specific focus on ITG [1][28]. ITG is a concept that has suddenly emerged and become an important issue in the IT field [44]. Precisely when this new challenge began surfacing is unknown, but it is now a discussion issue within most organizations. Some corporations and government agencies began with the implementation of ITG to achieve a fusion between business and IT and to obtain needed IT involvement of senior management. In surveys, CIOs also indicate ITG as an important management priority [16].

To implement ITG, organizations use a mixture of various structures, processes and relational mechanisms. When designing ITG, it is important to recognize that it is contingent upon a variety of sometimes conflicting internal and external factors. Determining the right ITG mechanisms is therefore a complex endeavor and it should be recognized that what strategically works for one company does not necessarily work for another [30], even if they work in the same industry sector [1].

However, ITG mechanisms are not well defined among the literature and this paper intends to identify, describe and clarify the most relevant ITG mechanisms.

# 4    Literature Review

Throughout this research we tried to follow the main steps (Table 1) we have identified in order to provide an effective LR. We started looking into journals articles. Moreover, we also looked into some of the most known communities, as IEEE and ACM. After the identification of the most relevant articles in those communities' digital libraries, we then follow the articles referenced in each identified article. We also identified the main authors and looked for their future and prior work.

We read 58 articles about ITG mechanisms from which 27 articles were identified as relevant to this study.

The selection criteria for the ITG mechanism articles were based on:

- Articles must explicitly be about ITG
- Articles must explicitly mention ITG mechanisms
- Articles must contain a clear and not ambiguous definition of the mentioned ITG mechanisms

We have adopted a concept-centric approach instead an author-centric approach as advised in step 2 of the Table1. A concept-centric approach guarantees a good synthesis of the literature [32]. In Table 2, we can see an example of the application of the concept-centric approach.

In section 3 we emphasize the problem under which this paper is grounded as advised in step 2.1 of the Table 1.

Possible future work (step 2.3 of Table 1) is proposed in section 6 where we explain how future researchers can improve this work and add knowledge to ITG BoK.

In section 6, we will draw conclusions about this research and argue about the limitations that we found in the course of our research. We will also provide the contributions that this paper adds to the current ITG Bok (step 2.4 of Table 1).

Throughout this LR we worked hard to follow as much as we could the tips presented in step 3 of Table 1.

As recommended in step 4 of the Table 1, in section 5 we explain how we have evaluated our theory in order to have the best theory. In Table 2 we summarize the Structure mechanism found in the LR, in Table 3 we summarize the Processes mechanisms found in LR and in Table 4 we summarize the Relational mechanisms found in LR. We also provide the respective references of each mechanism.

**Table 2.** ITG Structure Mechanisms

| Structure | |
|---|---|
| Integration of governance /alignment tasks in roles & responsibilities | [1][2] [3][ 10][ 16][ 18] |
| IT strategy committee | [1][2][3][8][10][12][15][16][18] |
| IT steering Committee | [1][2][8][9][10][11][12][13][15][16][18] |
| CIO on Board | [1][10][12][18][19] |
| IT councils | [25][27] |
| IT leadership councils | [7][22][25] |
| E-business advisory board | [1][10][19] |
| E-business task force | [1][10][19] |
| IT project steering committee | [1][3][10][13] |
| IT organization structure | [1][10][12][16][18] |
| • Centralized | [1][2][4][9][11][12][15][19][21][22] |
| • Federal | [1][2][4][7][9][11][12][15][19][21] |
| • Decentralized | [1][2][4][9][11][12][15][19][21][22] |
| IT expertise at level of   board of directors | [3][12] |
| IT audit committee at level of board of directors | [3][12][14] |
| CIO on executive committee/CIO reporting to CEO and/or COO | [3][4][12][13][17][28] |
| ITG function/officer | [3][4] |
| Architecture steering committee | [3][4][8][12][15][25][28] |
| IT investment committee or capital improvement | [4][12][15][22] |
| Business/IT relationship managers | [12][15][17][19][25] |

In Table2, Table 3 and Table 4 we have tried to standardize the ITG mechanisms since we believe this standardization may help to fulfill this paper problem. For example, the IT BSC that in the article [4] appears as a Relational Mechanism that is placed here as a Process Mechanism, once that choice is the most used among the literature [2][3][10][19].

Likewise we have grouped some ITG mechanisms, taking into account the definitions proposed by the authors. One example is: Working with non-conformist, provided by [12] that was joined with ITG campaigns provided by [3]. The same occur with the merge of Web-Based Portals [12] and IT portal [4]. The reasons that led to this merge were based on the similarity of both definitions.

**Table 3.** ITG Processes Mechanisms

| Processes | |
|---|---|
| IT BSC | [1][2][6][10][16][18][19] |
| Strategic Information System Planning | [1][2][3][16] |
| • Business System Planning | [1][2][3][16] |
| • Critical Success Factors | [1][6][16][19] |
| • Competitive forces model of Porter | [1][16] |
| • Business Process Reengineering approach | [1][16] |
| • Value chain models of Porter | [1][16] |
| Frameworks ITG | [1][2][10][16][18] |
| • COBIT | [1][2][3][10][14][16][18] |
| • COSO/ERM | [3][28] |
| • ITIL | [1][2][10][14][16][18] |
| Service Level Agreement | [1][2][3][4][5][10][11][12][15][18][19] |
| Business/IT alignment model | [1][10][14] |
| • Strategic Alignment Model (SAM) | [1][2][10][19] |
| ITG Maturity Models | [1][10][16] |
| Portfolio management | [3][ 4][26] |
| • Information Economics | [1][2][3][4][6][10][16][18][19][26] |
| • Business Cases | [3][13][19] |
| • ROI | [1][3][12][16][18] |
| • VALIT | [2][3][14] |
| Chargeback | [3][4][7][12][15][25] |
| ITG assurance and self-assessment | [3][15] |
| Project governance/management methodologies | [3][10][13] |
| IT budget control and reporting | [3][7][11][13] |
| Demand management | [4][26] |
| Architectural exception process | [12][27] |

**Table 4.** ITG Relational Mechanisms

| Relational | |
|---|---|
| Active participation by principle stakeholders | [1][10][19] |
| Collaboration between principle stakeholders | [1][10][19] |
| Partnership rewards and incentives | [1][2][10][18][19][20] |
| Business/IT collocation | [1][2][3][10][19] |
| Shared understanding of business/IT objectives | [1][2][10][11][18][19] |
| Cross-functional business/IT training | [1][2][3][10][18][19] |
| Cross-functional business/IT job rotation | [1][2][3][10][16][18][19] |
| ITG awareness campaigns | [3][12] |
| Corporate internal communication addressing on a regular basis | [3][11] |
| IT leadership | [3][13][15][28] |
| Informal meeting between business and IT executive/senior management | [3][23][25] |
| Executive/Senior management give the good example | [3][23][28] |
| Business/IT account management | [3][28] |
| Knowledge management (on ITG) | [3][12] |
| • Web-based (IT) portals | [3][4][12][15][18] |
| Senior management announcements | [12][22] |
| Office of CIO or ITG | [12][17][27] |

Moreover, we have eliminated all the ITG mechanisms with only one reference, to maintain the consistence of this research and ensuring in this way that the ITG mechanisms that appear in this table are the mechanisms that actually drive to a better agreement of the experts and scientific community.

## 4.1    Types of Mechanisms

As previously stated in this paper, enterprises must design and implement three types of ITG mechanisms [16] in order to promote desirable IT behaviors.

All these types of ITG mechanisms are important and they must be combined in order to create a holistic approach that promotes effective and efficient ITG throughout the organization.

The description of the three types of ITG mechanisms are detailed below:

- **Structure Mechanisms:** The most visible ITG mechanisms are the organizational units and roles responsible for making IT decisions, such as committees, executive teams, and business/IT relationship managers [2][12][24][27].
- **Processes Mechanisms:** Formal processes for ensuring that daily behaviors are consistent with IT policies and provide input back to decisions. These include IT investment proposal, architecture exception processes, Strategic Information System Planning, chargebacks, among others [2][12][24].
- **Relational Mechanisms** – The relational mechanisms complete the ITG framework and are paramount for attaining and sustaining business-IT alignment, even when the appropriate structures and processes are in place. For attaining and sustaining business-IT alignment, mechanisms like announcements, advocates, channels and education efforts are used [6][24][27][28].

Not all researchers give the same name to the different types of ITG mechanisms however the meaning is equivalent. For example, Weill and Ross [12] call communication mechanisms while Grembergen and De Haes [2] use the term relational mechanisms to the same type of ITG mechanisms. In this paper we have chosen to call these mechanisms relational mechanisms. This decision is due to the fact that relational mechanism is the term most used among ITG literature [10][13][19].

## 4.2    Structure Mechanisms

In this section we will describe the structure mechanisms. Unfortunately, due to space limitations we only provide the description of some mechanisms.

**IT Steering Committee:** The IT steering committee is situated at executive level. It is responsible for determining business priorities in IT investment [3]. It assists the Executive in the delivery of the IT strategy, overseeing the day-to-day management of IT service delivery and IT projects. IT steering committee focuses particularly on implementation [1], tracking IT investments, setting priorities and allocating scarce resources [8]. Firms using steering committees have been found to exhibit greater business executive attention to IT-related activities, a greater commitment to IT planning practices and a forward-looking IT project portfolio [9].

**IT Strategy Committee:** The IT Strategy Committee operates at the board level. The IT Strategy Committee – composed of board and non-board members – should assist the board in governing and overseeing the enterprise's IT-related matters. This committee should ensure that IT is a regular item on the board's agenda and should work in close relationship with the other board committees and with management in order to provide input, and to review and amend the aligned enterprise and IT strategies [1][3][16].

**CIO on Board:** ITG effectiveness is only partially dependent on the CIO and should be viewed as shared responsibility and enterprise wide commitment towards sustaining and maximizing IT business value. The presence of the CIO on Board will ensure that IT will be a regular item on the board's agenda and that it will be addressed in a structured manner. That presence will also enhance the ability of the board to understand the role of IT in business strategy and to map the ITG role of the executive team. The CIO should report on a regular basis to the board [12][16][19].

**CIO on Executive Committee/ CIO Reporting to CEO and/or COO (Chief Operation Officer):** CIO has a direct reporting line to the CEO and/or COO. This ensures that IT is part of the executive team where most strategy discussions begin and end. With that interaction IT can be an enabler of the organization [3][4].

**Architecture Steering Committee:** Committee composed of business and IT people providing architecture guidelines and advises on their applications. The main goal of this committee is identify strategic technologies [3][12][15][25].

**Business/ IT Relationship Managers:** Business/IT relationship managers Business/IT relationship managers act as the intermediary between the business and IS, playing a critical daily two-way role by helping IS understand how business operates and giving the business units an entry point to IS. They play an important role in communicating mandates and their implications and supporting the needs of business units managers while help them see benefits rather than inconveniences [12][15].

**IT Expertise at Level of Board of Directors:** Members of the board of directors have expertise and experience regarding the value and risk of IT. A lack of board oversight for IT activities is dangerous; it will put the firm at risk in the same way that failing to audit its books would [3][51].

### 4.3    Process Mechanisms

In this section we will describe the process mechanisms. Unfortunately, due to space limitations we only provide the description of some mechanisms.

**IT Balanced Scorecard (IT BSC):** An important part in the implementation process of strategic alignment is the performance measurement of IT and of IT related to the business. BSC has been applied in the IT function and its processes. Recognizing that IT is an internal service provider, the proposed perspectives of BSC should be changed accordingly, with corporate contribution, user orientation, operational excellence, and future orientation. Linking the business BSC and the IT BSC is a supportive mechanism for ITG [1][2][16].

**Chargeback:** Chargeback is an accounting mechanism for allocating central IT costs to business units. The purpose of chargeback is to allocate costs so that business units IT costs reflect the use of shared services while the shared services unit matches its costs with the business it supports. When IT understands its costs and charges out accordingly, chargeback processes demonstrate the cost saving resulting from shared services. Enterprises with effective costing mechanism find that chargeback can foster useful discussions between IT and business units about IT charges, leading to better-informed ITG decisions [3][12][15].

**Service Level Agreements:** A Service Level Agreements (SLA) is defined as "a written contract between a service provider of a service and the customer of the ser-vice". The functions of SLAs are: Define what levels of service are acceptable by users and are attainable by the service provider; define the mutually acceptable and agreed upon set of indicators of the quality of service. Three basic types of SLAs can be defined: in-house, external and internal SLAs. The differences between those types refer to the parties involved in the definition of the SLA.

The negotiation of SLAs should be completed by an experienced and multi-disciplinary team that equally represents the user group and the service provider.

The major governance challenges are that the service levels are to be expressed in business terms and that the right SLM/SLA process has to be put in place [1][2][16].

**Architectural Exception Process:** Technology standards are critical to IT and busi-ness efficiency. But occasionally exceptions are not only appropriate, they are neces-sary. Enterprises use the exception process to meet unique business needs and to gauge when existing standards are becoming obsolete.

Without a viable exception process, business units ignore the enterprise wide stan-dards and implement exceptions with no approval.

The effectiveness of the architecture exception process depends on the ability of the IT unit to research and define standards and on the enterprise's commitment to technology standards [12][27].

**Demand Management:** Demands for IT resources come from all directions and in all forms. Some demand is routine, other demand is strategic and complex.

Demand management forces all IT demand through a single point, where the de-mands can be consolidated, prioritized and fulfilled [4][26].

## 4.4     Relational Mechanisms

In this section we will describe the relational mechanisms. Unfortunately, due to space limitations we only provide the description of some mechanisms.

**ITG Awareness Campaigns:** Campaign to explain to business and IT people the need for ITG. Working with managers who stray from desirable behaviors is a neces-sary part of generating the potential value of governance processes. Therefore, it is necessary to communicate with those managers in order to educate them for IT issues [3][12].

**IT Leadership:** The ability of the CIO or similar role to articulate a vision for IT's role in the company and ensure that this vision is clearly understood by managers throughout the organization. Hence, we can say that the goal of IT leadership is to have coordination across the enterprise [3][15][23].

**Informal Meetings between Business and IT Executive/Senior Management:** Informal meetings, with no agenda, where business and IT senior management talk about general activities, directions, etc. (e.g. during informal lunches) [3][25].

**Corporate Internal Communication Addressing on a Regular Basis:** Internal corporate communication regularly addresses general IT issues [3][23].

**Executive/Senior Management Giving the Good Example:** Senior business and IT management acting as "partners" [3][23].

Summarizing, we can argue that our theory consist in an analysis of the literature in order to elicit the most common ITG mechanisms. In our theory we have tried to eliminate some gaps that, as were aforementioned, may difficult the implementation of ITG.

We also have defined some of the ITG mechanisms presented in Table 2. These definitions are important since it is important to have a deep knowledge about the meaning of the ITG mechanisms before choosing the most suitable to the organizations.

## 5    Evaluation

An evaluation of a theory in a LR is a difficult and nebulous task [32]. In this section we describe how we evaluated our research so far in order to validate our theory. Our theory, as it was aforementioned state that there are some gaps about ITG mechanisms that need to be solved. Our theory provides a contribution to solve these problems. As we can see in Section 4, some similar definitions were merged into the same mechanism. This standardization will be useful to all the ITG practitioners and to the scientific community.

As Weick [47] argued, a theory must be explanatory. The resulting theory of this research consists in the identification of the most relevant ITG mechanisms. In this theory, we gathered information from several articles and books, and then, we not only summarized the most important ITG mechanisms but also described them.

We argue that our theory is explanatory once it explains the most important ITG mechanisms and also provides their definition. Unfortunately, due to space limitations, we couldn't provide the definition of all the identified ITG mechanisms. Some authors as Davis and Lewis [48][49] argued that a theory must be interesting and relevant. In our viewpoint, this theory is relevant and interesting since, as stated in section 3, ITG is one of the CIO top issues and ITG mechanisms have been pointed as the best way to implement ITG in organizations. However, the ITG literature lacks a formal and consensual definition of ITG mechanisms. Therefore, we argue that this theory help ITG community to understand the ITG mechanisms as well as their purpose.

An important step in evaluation of LR researches is peer-review. Therefore we submitted our work to other researchers (as advised in step 4 of Table 1) so they can advise us of possible improvements. After that, we review our research taking into consideration their comments. The most relevant advice was that we should remove all the ITG mechanisms with less than two references in order to consolidate our theory.

# 6    Discussion and Conclusions

In our opinion, one of the main contributions of this paper is the clarification of some relevant ITG concerns. Several researchers use and propose ITG mechanisms but do not describe them or tell what they are about. We argue that such fact is a lack of knowledge in ITG literature that must be solved. It is urgent to understand what kind of ITG mechanisms exist and what their purpose is. Thus, in this paper we try to clearly explain the most important ITG mechanisms.

Some important authors in ITG literature (for example Weill, De Haes, Grembergen, etc.) use ITG mechanisms in their research. However, even these researchers have some incongruities among them since they use different names to the same ITG mechanism. In this paper we tried to solve this problem by formalizing the ITG mechanisms and mitigating ambiguities.

To sum up, this paper presents and describes all the most important ITG mechanisms. Plus, we have eliminated some incongruities about ITG mechanisms' names and definitions.

## 6.1    Contributions and Limitations

Quality research must provide justifications for the potential contributions provided by the proposed study. Such justifications should demonstrate how the proposed research contributes something new to the overall BoK or advances the research field's knowledge [32].

In this section we describe the contributions of this paper to ITG field BoK. We believe that having a set of formalized ITG mechanisms will help researchers and practitioners to understand and select which are the most appropriate ITG mechanisms and their importance to achieve effective and efficient ITG.

Furthermore, we believe that the presented set of ITG mechanisms as well as their description will increase the knowledge about the meaning and importance of the mechanisms, facilitating their correct adoption by organizations.

Finally, we believe that this research mitigates ambiguities among the ITG mechanisms and their respective meanings.

Of course our research has some limitations as well. So far we took into consideration 58 articles, which can be viewed as a small set of ITG articles for a LR paper. However, ITG is a recent discipline [24][28] and we argue that 58 articles are a considerable amount of researches to analyze.

Plus, as previously stated, from 58 we excluded 31 articles because they did not follow our criteria. It is more than 50% of the initial articles. This is evidence that many researchers use and propose ITG mechanisms but few attempt to describe them and explain what they are useful for.

Therefore, we argue that the main contribution of this research is the identification and description of the main ITG mechanisms.

## 6.2    Future Work

According to step 2.3 (Table 1), in this section we must provide some work that can and must be done in the future in order to go further in the ITG field.

We believe that in the future some researchers must analyze ITG case studies in order to understand how organizations are adopting ITG mechanisms. Then, researchers should study which ITG mechanisms are more appropriated to each kind of organization always taking into consideration the context of each organization. Possibly the ITG contingency factors already proposed in ITG literature [29] could be well applied for this purpose.

As previously stated, we should have a holistic approach in ITG. So, we argue that another future work should be concerned with the identification of which mechanisms can or must work together and which ones are not combinable at all.

Last but not least, the identification of new ITG mechanisms must be a continuous work and we argue that future researchers should complement and improve the presented ITG mechanisms (Table 2) with new and innovative ITG mechanisms.

# References

1. Van Grembergen, W., De Haes, S., Guldentops, E.: Structures, Processes and Relational Mechanisms for IT Governance. In: Van Grembergen, W. (ed.) Strategies for Information Technology Governance. Idea Group Publishing, Pennsylvania (2003)
2. Van Grembergen, W., De Haes, S.: Information Technology Governance: Models, Practices, and Cases. IGI Publishing (2008)
3. Van Grembergen, W., De Haes, S.: Information Technology Governance: Achieving Strategic Alignment and Value. Springer Science, LLC (2009)
4. Symons, C.: IT Governance Framework: Structures, Processes, and Communication (2005)
5. Webb, P., Pollard, C., Ridley, G.: Attempting to Define IT Governance: Wisdom or Folly? In: 39th Annual Hawaii International Conference on System Sciences, p. 194a. IEEE, Hawaii (2006)
6. Ribbers, P., Peterson, R., Parker, M.: Designing Information Technology Governance Processes: Diagnosing Contemporary Practices and Competing Theories. In: 35th Hawaii International Conference on System Sciences, pp. 3143–3154. IEEE, Hawaii (2002)
7. Weill, P.: Don't Just Lead, Govern: How Top-Performing Firms Govern IT. MIS Quarterly Executive 3(1), 1–17 (2004)
8. ITGI. Board briefing on IT. IT Governance Institute, 2nd edn (2003)
9. Huang, R., Zmud, R.W., Price, R.L.: Influencing the effectiveness of IT governance practices through steering committees and communication policies. EJIS 19(3), 288–302 (2010)

10. Lunardi, G.L., Becker, J.L., Maçada, A.C.G.: The Financial Impact of IT Governance Mechanisms' Adoption: An Empirical Analysis with Brazilian Firms. In: 42nd Hawaii International Conference on System Sciences, pp. 1–10. IEEE, Hawaii (2009)

11. Luftman, J.: Assessing Business-IT alignment Maturity. Communications of AIS 4(14) (2000)

12. Weill, P., Ross, J.: IT Governance: How Top Performers Manage IT Decision Rights for Superior Results. Harvard Business School Press, Boston (2004)

13. Thomas, H., Hamel, F., Uebernickel, F., Brenner, W.: IT Governance Mechanisms in Multisourcing – A Business Groups Perspective. In: 45th Hawaii International Conference on System Sciences, pp. 5033–5042. IEEE, Hawaii (2012)

14. Spremić, M.: IT Governance Mechanisms in Managing IT Business Value. WSEA Transactions on Information Science and Applications 6(6), 906–915 (2009)

15. Broadbent, M., Weill, P.: Effective IT Governance. By design. Exp. Premier, Gartner (2003)

16. De Haes, S., Van Grembergen, W.: IT Governance and Its Mechanisms. Information Systems Control Journal 1 (2004)

17. Making Time: The office of the CIO. Exp. premier, Gartner (2004)

18. Lunardi, G.L., Dolci, P.C., Becker, J.L., Maçada, A.C.G.: Governança de TI no Brasil: uma análise dos mecanismos mais difundidos entre as empresas nacionais. SEGeT – Simpósio de Excelência em Gestão e Tecnologia

19. Peterson, R.: Information Strategies and Tactics for Information Technology Governance. In: Van Grembergen (ed.) Strategies for Information Technology Governance. Idea Group Publ. (2004)

20. Montazemi, A.R., Pittaway, J.J.: Getting them to think outside the circle: IT Governance, CIOs' external advice networks, and firm performance. Brunel University, University Kingdom (2012)

21. Sambamurthy, V., Zmud, R.W.: Arrangements for Information Technology Governance: a theory of multiple contingencies. MIS Quarterly 23(2), 261–290 (1999)

22. Weill, P., Ross, J.: IT Governance on One Page. MIT Sloan Working Paper no.4517-04 (2004)

23. De Haes, S., Van Grembergen, W.: An exploratory study into the design of an IT Governance minimum baseline through Delphi research. Communications of the Association for Information Systems 22(24) (2008)

24. De Haes, S., Van Grembergen, W.: IT Governance structures, processes and relational mechanisms: Achieving IT/Business alignment in a major Belgian financial group. In: 38th Hawaii International Conference on System Sciences, p. 237b. IEEE, Hawaii (2005)

25. Broadbent, M.: CIO Future – Lead With Effective Governance. In: ICA 36th Conference, Singapore (2002)

26. Heier, H., Borgman, P.B., Maistry, M.G.: Examining the relationship between IT Governance software and business value of IT: Evidence from four case studies. In: 40th Hawaii International Conference on System Sciences, p. 234c. IEEE, Hawaii (2007)

27. Weill, P., Ross, J.: A matrix approach to designing IT Governance. Sloan Management Review 46(2) (2005)

28. De Haes, S., Van Grembergen, W.: Analysing the Relationship Between IT Governance and Bussiness/IT Alignment Maturity. In: 41st Hawaii International Conference on System Sciences, p. 428. IEEE, Hawaii (2008)

29. Pereira, R., Mira da Silva, M.: Designing a new Integrated IT Governance and IT Management Framework Based on Both Scientific and Practitioner Viewpoint. International Journal of Enterprise Information Systems, IJEIS 8(4) (2012)

30. Reich, B.H., Benbasat, I.: Factors that influence the social dimension of alignment between business and Information Technology objectives. MIS Quarterly 23(1), 81–113 (2000)
31. Levy, Y., Ellis, T.J.: A Systems Approach to Conduct an Effective Literature Review in Support of Information Systems Research. Informing Science Journal 9 (2006)
32. Jane, W., Watson, R.T.: Analyzing the past to prepare for the future: Writing a Literature Review. MIS Quarterly 26(2), xiii–xxiii (2002)
33. Creswell, J.W.: Research Design: Qualitative, Quantitative, and mixed methods approaches, 2nd edn. Sage Publications, Inc. (2002)
34. Gerrard, M.: IT Governance, a Flawed Concept: It's Time for Business Change Governance. Gartner Research (2009)
35. Law, C.C., Ngai, E.W.: IT Business Value Research: A Critical Review and Research Agenda. International Journal of Enterprise Information Systems, IJEIS 1(3), 35–55 (2005)
36. Quershil, S., Kamal, M., Wolcott, P.: Information Technology Interventions for Growth and Competitiveness in Micro-Enterprises. International Journal of E-Business Research, IJEBR 5(1), 117–140 (2009)
37. Hart, C.: Doing a literature review: Releasing the social science research imagination. Sage Publications, United Kingdom (1998)
38. Barnes, S.J.: Assessing the value of IS journals. Communications of the ACM 48(1), 110–112 (2005)
39. Ngai, E.W.T., Wat, F.K.T.: A literature review and classification of electronic commerce research. Information & Management 39(5), 415–429 (2002)
40. Patel, N.V.: An emerging strategy for e-business IT Governance. In: Van Grembergen, W. (ed.) Strategies for Information Technology Governance. Idea Group Publishing, Hershey (2003)
41. Kakabadse, N.K., Kakabadse, A.: IS/IT Governance: Need for an integrated model. Corporate Governance 1(9), 9–11 (2001)
42. Duffy, J.: IT/Business alignment: Is it an option or is it mandatory? IDC document # 26831 (2002)
43. Duffy, J. (2002). IT Governance and business value part 1: IT Governance – An issue of critical importance. IDC document # 27291 (2002)
44. Pereira, R., Mira da Silva, M.: Towards an Integrated IT Governance and IT Management Framework. In: 16th International Conference on Enterprise Distributed Object Computing, EDOC. IEEE, Beijing (2012)
45. ITGI. CobiT: Governance, Control and Audit for Information and Related Tecnhology, http://www.iti.org
46. ITGI, Board briefing on IT Governance (2001), http://www.itgi.org
47. Weick, K.: Definition of Theory. In: Nicholson, N. (ed.) Blackwell Dictionary of Organizational Behaviour. Blackweel, Oxford (1995)
48. Davis, M.S.: That's Interesting! Philosophy of Social Science (1), 309–344 (1971)
49. Lewis, M.W., Grimes, A.J.: Metatriangulations: Building Theory from Multiple. Academy of Management Review 24(4), 672–690 (1999)
50. Pereira, R., Mira da Silva, M.: A Literature Review: Guidelines and Contingency Factors for IT Governance. In: 9th European, Mediterranean and Middle Eastern Conference on Information Systems, EMCIS. ISEing, Munich (2012)
51. Nolan, R., McFarlan, F.W.: Information Technology and the Board of Directors. Harvard Business Review (2005)

# A Model-Driven Environment for Service Design, Simulation and Prototyping

Biljana Bajić-Bizumić[1], Claude Petitpierre[1],
Hieu Chi Huynh[2], and Alain Wegmann[1]

[1] École Polytechnique Fédérale Lausanne (EPFL),
CH-1015 Lausanne, Switzerland
[2] Faculty of Computer Science and Engineering,
Ho Chi Minh City University of Technology (HCMUT), Vietnam
{biljana.bajic,claude.petitpierre,hieu.huynh,alain.wegmann}@epfl.ch

**Abstract.** In this paper, we present an environment that contains tools for service design, simulation and prototyping. The main goal of this research is to provide the designer with a method for flexible service modeling. The models generated from this method are then simulated using the Alloy Analyzer tool, or prototyped in the given target language, like Java. In this way, the designer can analyze the behavior of the modeled services and verify if they satisfy business needs and requirements. At the heart of the environment is a flexible, semi-automatic, model-driven tool for designing business services and transforming them through multiple model layers to IT services by capturing the design decisions. The modeling language is based on predefined parametrized functional units. The applicability of this approach is demonstrated by a running example based on the consulting project we undertook at the General Ressort company.

**Keywords:** Service Design, Service Science, Business-Driven Development, Model Transformation.

## 1 Introduction

Services have been defined through different perspectives in the service science literature. In this paper, we adopt the definition in [3, p. 1], "Business service is a business-related work activity or duty performed for others to produce a business outcome. It is the expectation of the business person that the service will accomplish this outcome. The person generally does not care how it is accomplished, as long as it is done in an effective manner from a business perspective."

A business service may be supported by one or more IT service(s), and may consist almost entirely of IT services, especially where these services are directly used by customer. Examples include online banking and online shopping.

ITIL v.3 defines a IT service as "a service provided to one or more customers, by an IT service provider. An IT Service is based on the use of information technology and supports the customer's business process. An IT Service is made up from a combination of people, processes and technology." [4]

J.F. e Cunha, M. Snene, and H. Nóvoa (Eds.): IESS 2013, LNBIP 143, pp. 200–214, 2013.

Based on these definitions, we will explain our approach for transforming business services to IT services, as well as for simulating and prototyping them.

The main goals of any service-oriented design include flexible support and adaptability of business services and improved business-IT alignment, i.e. orchestration of the lower level IT infrastructure services to deliver the desired business-level customer services. The existing approaches, however, have failed to fully meet these goals. One of the major reasons for this deficiency is the gap that exists between the perceptions of computer science and management science of term "service". In practice, the business and technology perspectives of services have to be considered separately. Even simple changes to one perspective (e.g. due to new regulations or organizational change) require error-prone, manual re-editing of the other one [5]. Over time, this leads to the degeneration and divergence of the respective models and specifications; this thereby aggravates maintenance and makes expensive refactoring inevitable.

Our approach for aligning business services with IT services is model-driven, semi-automatic, and flexible, enabling the implementation design of business services. It proposes the set of models corresponding to the model-driven architecture (MDA) defined levels. A central aspect of our method is that, in the service design process design decisions are captured in each step. This way, they are clearly separated from the automatic part of the transformation. Thus, the design process is done semi-automatically. In these steps, the designer can independently make the decisions about different service components, features and all aspects relevant to the service design. In this way, he can flexibly change the design.

In the design process, the designer begins by identifying the services required by the customers, then follows by capturing the design decisions. Based on these decisions, intermediate model layers and finally IT services are generated. These services are necessary for the implementation of the application supporting the customer's requirements. This process allows business analysts to represent services from a business point of view, while facilitating the design and development of IT services.

The details embedded in an IT service design model-layer enable the execution of the model on the given target platform, such as JEE (Java Enterprise Edition), creating a prototype. All the model layers can be translated and simulated with the Alloy Analyzer tool [6], so that the designer can see how each of the model layers behave, by viewing a few instances of the model.

We illustrate our approach by the running example based on a consulting project we undertook at a company that sells parts for watches in Switzerland, General Ressort (GR).

We organize the paper as follows. In Section 2, we explain our modeling environment. In Section 3, we discuss service design. In Section 4, we discuss service simulation and prototyping of the model layers. We present related work in Section 5. The final section concludes the study and discusses the future work.

## 2     Modeling Environment

Our modeling environment uses a spiral process for service design and prototyping, because it allows incremental refinement through each time around the
spiral. At each iteration around the cycle, the service prototypes are extensions
of an earlier prototypes. In this way, the designer can analyse and validate how
the design decisions can influence the design and implementation of the services.

There are four model layers in our service design process and three in-between
steps that capture the design decisions in predefined matrix formats. The designer captures the decisions in **predefined matrix formats** by using 'define
and distribute' pattern. This means, in each step, the designer defines new
elements in the system, which become the columns of the matrix. Also, the designer distributes some existing elements shown in rows of the matrix to the new
elements. After service design process, the last layer of the IT service design can
be transformed to the intermediate project containing data needed by BUD tool
[7] to generate the prototype. In addition, each of service design layers can be
simulated in Alloy.

In order to understand all parts of the environment and the example, we will
explain the main principles of the proposed modeling approach, mostly based on
Catalysis approach [8].

### 2.1     Modeling Approach

The central aspect of our approach is a system and its two main aspects: the
organizational and functional [9]. For both aspects, we define the black-box and
the white-box view of the system (Figure 1a). The organizational black-box
view of the system is called 'system as a whole', and it hides the organizational
aspects of the system; unlike the organizational white-box view of the system,
called 'system as a composite', which reveals a system's construction. Similarly,
the functional white-box view of the system is called 'action as composite' and it
provides insight into system's functionality, unlike the functional black-box view
('action as a whole') that hides them. As we can see in Figure 1a, when moving
down the organizational axis, we refine a system into its components. When we
moving from left to right on the functional axis, we refine system's behavior into
its component behavior.

There is also a special view of a system and a type of the action, called 'action
as n-ary relationship', where one action is distributed among many systems
connected with one action binding in between (Figure 1b). In this way, it is
specified what part of action is in which system. However, the action parts are
still dependent on each other and cannot be treated separately; only together
can they be seen as one action.

Another important characteristic of our approach is that it places the action
on an equal footing with the object, because good decoupled design requires
careful thought about what actions occur and what they achieve. Therefore,
behaviour and data are equally important in the proposed method and **each
model layer contains both the behaviour and data part of the services.**

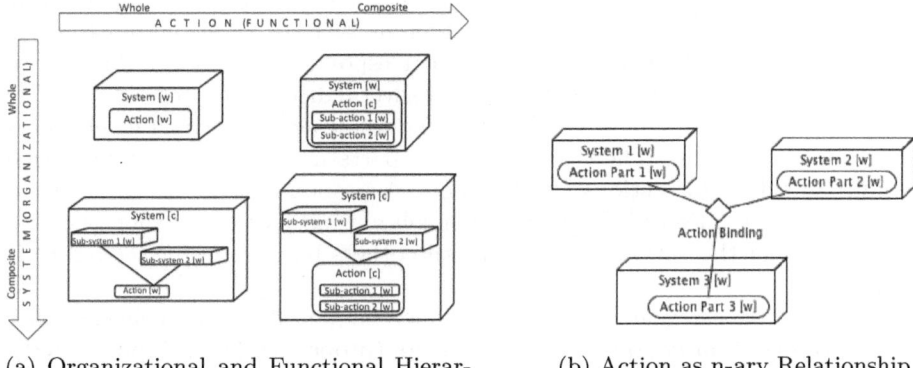

(a) Organizational and Functional Hierarchy

(b) Action as n-ary Relationship

**Fig. 1.** System and Action Representation

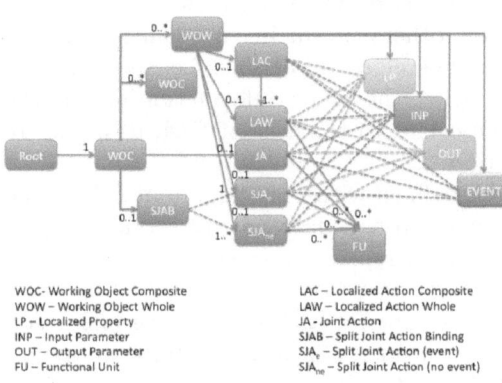

WOC- Working Object Composite
WOW – Working Object Whole
LP – Localized Property
INP – Input Parameter
OUT – Output Parameter
FU – Functional Unit

LAC – Localized Action Composite
LAW – Localized Action Whole
JA - Joint Action
SJAB – Split Joint Action Binding
SJA$_e$ – Split Joint Action (event)
SJA$_{ne}$ – Split Joint Action (no event)

(a) Meta Model

| Catalysis Term | Business Term for This Example |
|---|---|
| WOC (Working Object Composite) | Market Segment/Company with internal structure (stakeholders/roles) |
| WOW (Working Object Whole) | Company/Roles without internal structure |
| Root | Market Segment |
| Action | Service |
| JA (Joint Action) | Joint Business Service |
| SJA (Split Joint Action) | Joint IT Service |
| LA (Localized Action) | Localized Business/IT Service |

(b) Catalysis and Business Corresponding Terms

**Fig. 2.** Meta Model and Corresponding Business Terms

## 2.2   Meta-model

In order to understand the models given in this paper, we show the meta-model with relevant elements in Figure 2a. The full lines in the meta-model correspond to the 'contain' relationship, where one element is inside the other. The dashed lines correspond to the 'is linked to' relationship, where one element is related to the other with a line. The concepts used in the meta-model are based on Catalysis terms. The table with the corresponding business terms can be seen in Figure 2b.

The root element of any model is working object as composite (*WOC*), representing the system of interest, in this case the market segment. It is composite, because it contains the main stakeholders, such as the service provider (company providing the service) and service client (customer company). *WOC* reveals the system structure, therefore it can contain other $WO$s (whole and composite). It can also contain actions shared among different systems (joint action ($JA$) or split joint action binding ($SJAB$)). $SJAB$ corresponds to the action binding in 'action as n-ary relationship', i.e. it connects several distributed actions in different systems, thus making one action. $JA$ is the whole action with all its elements between many systems. There are no action parts in the other system. $SJAB$ has links to split joint actions ($SJA$s). They correspond to the action parts in 'action as n-ary relationship'. One of them contains a link to the event, showing who is initiating the action $SJA_e$, while the others have no event related to it $SJA_{ne}$.

$WOW$ does not reveal its structure. Therefore, it does not contain other $WO$s. It can contain actions or data elements (properties ($LP$), inputs ($INP$), outputs ($OUT$) and $EVENT$s). These actions can be joint actions ($SJA$ and $JA$) or localized ($LA$), meaning they are inside just one $WO$, and are not split between many $WO$s. As with all other whole-composite relations, localized action composite ($LAC$) can have many localized action whole ($LAW$s).

As a service is a duty performed for others producing outcome, it always has some input and output parameters. Therefore, all actions, i.e. services ($LA$, $JA$, $SJA$) contain inputs and outputs. Also, they have information about who is initiating the service captured in the event. In the case of $SJA$, it applies to only one action part related to the action.

In addition, in our approach service is defined with functional units ($FU$) and properties ($LP$), representing the behavioural and data part of service, respectively. This does not apply to $LAC$, because it represents the grouping of objects for many $LAW$s (services).

There are four different types of services, one for each model layer of our service design process. The top-level layer is business service, as defined in Section 1. Thus, it represents the service that the customer needs. This service is transformed to the joint business service, joint IT service and finally independent localized IT services for each system of interest.

## 2.3 Predefined Parametrized Functional Units

One of the specificities of our approach is to have a single language to describe all different viewpoints of service systems, from business to IT. To this end, we have introduced the concept of predefined, parametrized functional units. They represent atomic logic elements with given parameters, so that they are flexible for modification. For each of them, we need to define general structure and parameters (Figure 3).

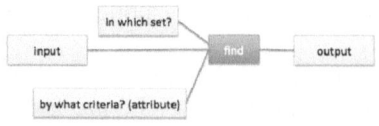

**Fig. 3.** General Parameters of find Functional Unit

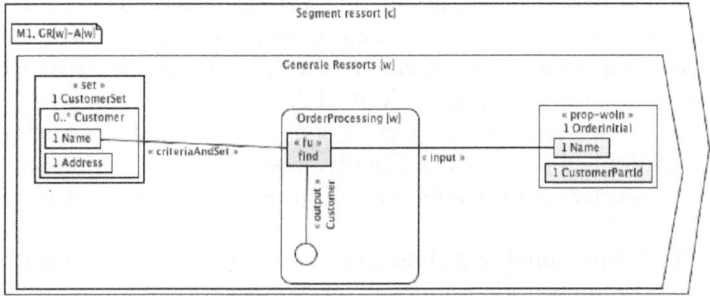

(a) Service Design - Modeling Environment

```
module predefined_find [element,attribute]

fun find ( criteria : element -> attribute, input : one attribute, whichSet : set element) : one element {
   { output : one element | (a.criteria = input and a in whichSet)}
}
```

(b) Service Simulation - Alloy

```
public {Element} find{Element}(String input) {
    EntityManager em = Manager.open();
    {Element} output = null;
    try {
        EntityTransaction tx = em.getTransaction();
        tx.begin();

        String q = "SELECT {element} FROM {WhichSet} {element} WHERE
        {.repeated section attributes}
            {.section stringAttribute}
                {.section finder}{criteria}
                {.end}
            {.end}
        {.end} = '" + input +"'";

        Query result = em.createQuery(q);
        Collection<{Element}> {element}s = (Collection<{Element}>) result.getResultList();
        if ({element}s.size() == 1)
            output = ((ArrayList<{element}>) {element}s).get(0);
        tx.commit();
    } finally {
        Manager.close();
    }
    return output;
}
```

(c) Service Prototyping - Java Using JSON Templates

**Fig. 4.** find Functional Unit in Different Parts of Environment

As we can see, for 'find' functional unit, there are four parameters:

- the set in which we want to find the element
- the criteria we apply to search an element (attribute)
- the concrete value with which we want to compare attribute (input value)
- the element found in the set by given criteria (output value).

Based on this general description, 'find' functional unit is shown in different parts of the environment, see Figure 4. In service design part, we can see all the parameters in diagram in Figure 4a. Notice that in this case, 'criteria' and 'whichSet' parameters are shown in one line 'criteriaAndWhichSet'. The reason for this is that we wanted to have design as clear as possible without having redundant lines. From this line connected to the criteria element, we can conclude the 'whichSet' as a parent element of 'criteria'.

Similarly, in service simulation part (Figure 4b) we have predefined Alloy function with all defined parameters. Finally, in service prototyping part (Figure 4c) we can also see the parameters used in Java environment based on JSON templates.

Similar to 'find' functional unit, based on general parameters defined for other functional units, the description and semantic of functional units are defined in other parts of the environment.

## 3   Service Design at General Ressort

For a better understanding of the design process, we illustrate each design step by applying it to the example of company GR. For the purpose of this paper, we focus only on a simplified business service of order processing. We illustrate the design steps in our approach based on this example. By convention, information in italics are the corresponding names of the elements in the model.

The simplified business service is executed as follows: "GR gets order (*OrderInitial*) from the customer that contains a unique customer name and unique customer part id. The person dealing with orders (*OrderEntryPerson*) receives the information about the order (*OrderInitial*) and finds the customer and the part by unique information in the enterprise resource planning system (*ERP*). Finally, he creates the confirmed order (*OrderConfirmed*) in the *ERP*."

Finally, here is the description of the model layers and steps of the proposed design process. Due to the lack of space, we will show just the first transformation in the details. For the other steps, please refer to [10].

**Business Service Design.** In the first layer, the designer specifies the business services, see Figure 5. As it can be seen, we show a segment composed of company *GeneralRessort* and *CustomerCompany*. There is one main business service that is modeled: *OrderProcessing*. We do not show either the organization of the company or the sub-services (sub-actions). Therefore, this model layer represents the system as a whole (*GeneralRessort[w]*), action as a whole (*OrderProcessing[w]*).

As already mentioned in Section 2, both the behavioural and data part of the services are shown. The behavioural part is shown by predefined functional units (*fu*). They represent atomic operations, such as *find, create*, etc. They can be parametrized as explained before (by links *criteriaAndWhichSet, input, output*). *Set* properties represent the set of elements of one kind, e.g. *Customer*. The relation between these elements is shown by *relationship*. For each property we show cardinality and name.

The inputs and outputs are marked by *prop-woIn* and *prop-woOut*. The business service order processing has input parameter *OrderInitial* with *Name* and

*CustomerPartId* and one output parameter, *OrderConfirmed. woIn* and *woOut* mean that they come into and go out from the system *GeneralRessort* from and to outside (*CustomerCompany*), respectively.

Also, each service has one event (in this case *event-woIn*) associated to it, showing the entity that initiates the service. In this step, there are no roles, therefore the event is shown inside the whole system *GeneralRessort*.

Functional units can be connected with lines containing circle that can be annotated by the name of the data they share, such as *Customer*, meaning that *fu find* and *create* share one data of the type *Customer*.

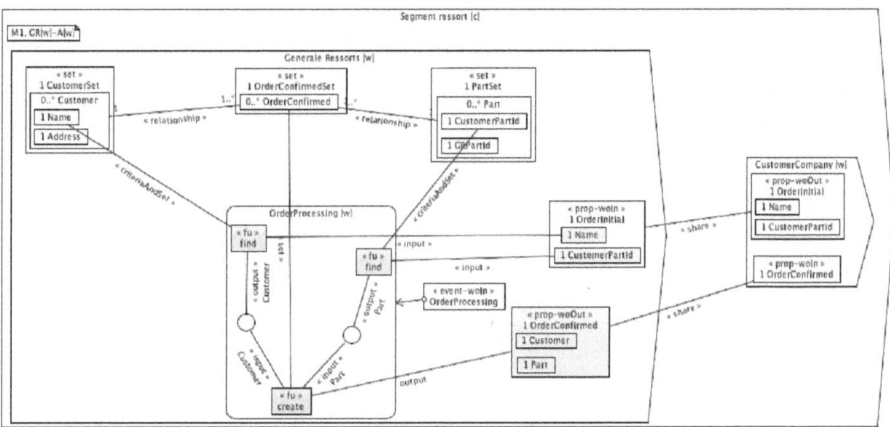

**Fig. 5.** Business Service Design

**Joint Business Service Design.** In the next model layer, the company construction is revealed and joint business services are defined by providing details about the business service-related data responsibilities within the company's roles. Therefore, the layer corresponds to the system as a composite, action as a whole.

The designer defines the roles (organizational units) in the system and distributes the service-related data to these roles, according to their responsibilities. This can be seen in matrices in Figure 6.

The designer defines roles: *OrderEntryPerson* and *ERP*, marked in the matrices and in the next model layer.

Then all data from the model layer in Figure 5, shown in the rows of the matrix, are distributed to the newly defined roles (Figure 7).

As we can see, joint business service design contains defined business services without changes of the functional units. However, the properties related to service, as well as the inputs and outputs are distributed to the newly defined roles. Notice that there is only one service defined between many roles, it is still unknown which role is responsible for which part of the service performance.

**Joint IT Service Design.** In this step, new services are defined, and existing functional units are distributed to these services. This way we define which role

| | OrderEntryPerson | ERP |
|---|---|---|
| (<<prop-woIn>> OrderInitial) Name | | |
| (<<prop-woIn>> OrderInitial) CustomerPartId | X | |
| <<prop-woOut>> OrderConfirmed | X | |
| <<set>> CustomerSet | | X |
| <<set>> PartSet | | X |
| <<set>> OrderSet | | X |
| <<event-woIn>> OrderProcessing | X | |

| | Roles |
|---|---|
| 1 | OrderEntryPerson |
| 2 | ERP |

(a) Role Definition                                        (b) Data Responsibility

**Fig. 6.** Step 1 - Design Decisions from Figure 5 to Figure 7

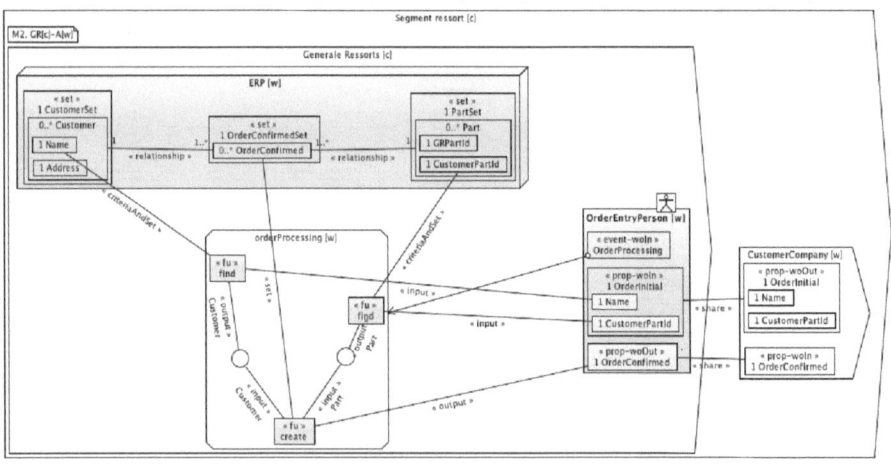

**Fig. 7.** Joint Business Service Design

performs which part of the service. This provides insight into the functional decomposition of the system, without a complete split of services. Therefore, this layer corresponds to system as a composite, action as a n-ary relationship.

**Localized IT Service Design.** In this step, new sub-services (and implicitly their events) are defined, and functional units are distributed to these services. In this layer, services are completely split and systems are independent. Therefore, this layer represents system as a composite, action as a composite. This model contains IT services that are platform independent and ready to be executed in any target language. In addition, it also contains the human services and human-human interactions, which are very often important to show in a consulting project.

## 4    Service Simulation and Prototyping at General Ressort

One of the main challenges in service design is addressing the question on how to prototype services (to generate, develop, test and evaluate ideas) throughout the design process [11]. In this section, we will briefly explain how the simulation and prototyping is done in the proposed approach.

In order to check whether the model corresponds to the customer's needs and requirements, we simulate model layers, thus enabling the designer to simulate the behaviour of the model layer and to find the design mistakes in the early phase. In addition, the last model can be executed in the given target platform, which also provides one way of validation.

### 4.1 Service Simulation

To simulate services, we use Alloy[12], a simple, but expressive declarative language. We first formalize the models in Alloy and then we run and simulate them using the Alloy Analyzer tool [6]. We use Alloy, because it can be also used to check the refinement between different model layers, as it is explained in [13].

We have developed a tool that semi-automatically transforms models to the Alloy code. The tool takes the meta-model of our modeling method, Alloy meta-model and predefined functional units as input. Based on the inputs, it generates the Alloy code, which can be run and analyzed in our tool, because the Alloy Analyzer tool is integrated in our tool via Alloy Analyzer API (Application Programming Interface). The exact mapping of our meta-model to Alloy meta-model will be explained in a separate paper. The underlying idea is that static elements of the model are mapped to Alloy signatures, and dynamic elements (services) are mapped to Alloy predicates and functions.

As this approach de-couples the tasks of service composition from particular service logic. The logic of the service is contained in a special Alloy library containing all Alloy functions based on predefined parametrized functional units. One example of such function is given in Figure 4. Services are then combined in the main function, based on the description in the model. Our goal is to use special declarative process language based on states and data for service composition. So far, we have used a simple combination of services, where inputs and outputs of given services should be directly mapped onto one another. Currently, we are working on developing the whole declarative process language, that could be used to show different constraints and combinations of services.

The result of one of the simulations of the GR case is shown in Figure 8. As illustrated, the customer and part are created in case they do not already exist in the set. *Company_pre* and *Company_post* are the states of the company General Ressort, before and after the order is processed, respectively. As we can see, they both have the same *OrderInitial* that is the input to the service and *OrderConfirmed* that is output of the service. Before the order processing, there was no customer with the name *Name* given in *OrderInitial*, so the new customer *Customer* with this name is created in *customerSet* that is in *Company_post*. In addition, the *OrderConfirmed* contains information about that customer and becomes member of *OrderSet*. We do not provide the Alloy code here, due to the constraints with paper length.

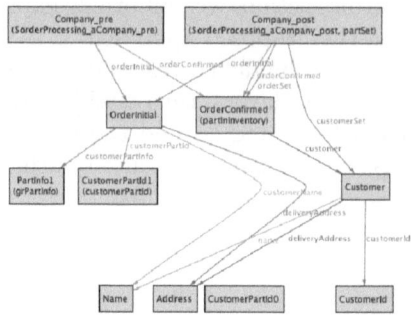

**Fig. 8.** Result of Alloy model simulation

The goal in the future is to provide simulation results in a more user-friendly form. For example, by transforming errors back to the models and marking them there.

### 4.2   Service Prototyping

Our prototyping tool is based on BUD tool [7]. It takes the last model as an input and transforms it to an executable prototype. It works in 2 steps:

- Generates an intermediate language independent file (JSON)
- Generates an executable application for the target programming language.

The BUD tool is based on JSON templates, a minimal but powerful templating language [14]. JSON templates enable us to define program logic using templates for any language and data dictionary. The data dictionary determines which part of the template should be replaced with what information, as explained in [14].

In the first step, our prototyping tool transforms the last model into the data dictionary written using JSON (Java Script Object Notation). In the second step, the templates and the data dictionary (JS file) are combined and parsed using JavaCC [15], and the corresponding files are created. In Figure 9, we can see how we can generate file 'CustomerJPA' using the data dictionary and the template. Note that this is a shorter version of the template, made for the purpose of this paper.

The example given shows just the static part of the service system. Similar to Alloy, the dynamic part contains service logic and service composition separately. The example of service logic is given in Figure 4. Service composition is shown in a separate part of template file. Currently, there are no special conditions for service compositions, therefore this part is missing. However, in our future work as already stated, we plan to develop new declarative process language, and to show example of its usage.

Discussing the platform implementation constraints and other details of this step fall out of the scope of this paper. For more information, please refer to [7].

**Fig. 9.** BUD tool

## 5   Related Work

The proposed environment for service design, prototyping and simulation is MDA (model driven architecture)-based [16]: it proposes a set of models extending from the CIM (computation-independent model) level, the highest level of abstraction of the MDA, to the PIM (platform-independent model) and PSM (platform-specific model) levels. Business service and joint business service design correspond to the CIM level, because they represent the context and purpose of the model without any computational complexities. Joint IT service design and localized IT service design correspond to PIM level. It describes which part is done by software application and gives its behaviour and structure regardless of the implementation platform. In the service prototyping part of the process, the intermediate project containing the templates and specification objects corresponds to the PSM level, because they are strictly related to the specific application platform.

We take the basic principles of our service design technique from the Catalysis [8] approach. Therefore, unlike some object-oriented methods, our approach does not always begin by assigning responsibilities for services to specific roles. We believe in not taking decisions all at once. We first state what happens, then we state which role is responsible for doing it and which one is responsible for initiating it; and finally we state how it is done. Another specific aspect of Catalysis adopted in our approach is that it places the behaviour on an equal footing with the data. Therefore, unlike many other approaches for business-IT alignment of services, like [5,17,18], that are process oriented, in our approach each layer contains both the behaviour and the data.

The central aspect of our approach is to capture the design decisions. In this way, the designer creates the business service design and enters the design decisions that need to be made, and the rest is done automatically. Unlike other service design methods that provide multi-perspective view of the service system, e.g. [19], our method clearly separates the design decisions of the automatic part of transformation, thus enabling the designers to have a multi-perspective view of the system and to zoom in and out the models in order to see the system with as much detail as they need. This way, they can quickly prototype business requirements and evaluate several architectures. This is something that, to the best of our knowledge, is not undertaken by the other techniques.

Also, the language used for different layers is the same in our approach. The declarative approach and the predefined functional units employed by us in developing the models have made this possible.

In addition, we believe that using declarative business process provides more flexibility in service design. From our experience, very often in the projects the sequence of services is not known. Also, in this way, the process is more configurable, and the designer can decide in a separate step from many possible execution paths; or it can be concluded from the data dependency in the model. This way, the designer's decisions are supported and not restricted like in imperative business processes. One of the main references for the declarative business processes is the work described in [20]. Also, many different approaches are nicely categorized and described in [21]. We are planning to conduct further research work on this topic. Our goal is to provide a declarative process language that will be based on data and states, not just the process. This way, by providing completely declarative environment by applying Poka-yoke principle [22], we believe we can prevent the designer from restricting the decisions and imperative operations.

Also, one of the challenges of the service design, which is not covered very well by the other techniques, is the prototyping of the models [11]. We also provide a prototyping in a given target language and simulation of the models using the Alloy Analyzer tool.

Finally, the modeling methodology presented in this paper, is a part of the systemic enterprise architecture methodology (SEAM) [23]. SEAM has been applied in designing viable service systems [24] and aligning customer value and service implementation in service system [9]. Also, it has been applied in value modeling in service systems from an appreciative system perspective [25].

## 6   Conclusions and Future Work

In this paper, we presented a model-driven, flexible, semi-automatic environment for aligning business services with IT services, thus enabling the implementation design of business services. We briefly presented the whole environment, containing the service design and service simulation and prototyping. Then, we explained each of the parts in more details. We illustrated the design process by the example based on the consulting project we undertook in the company General Ressort based in Switzerland, which sells parts for watches.

The proposed service design process includes four model layers containing service design and three in-between steps, in which the design decisions are captured. Capturing the design decisions is the central aspect of our approach. It enables clear separation of the decisions that need to be made by the designer and the automatic part of transformation. Each model layer can be transformed with our tool to Alloy code and simulated using the integration of Alloy Analyzer API in our tool. The last layer has enough technical details so that it can be executed on the given target language, such as Java. We provide the tools for all parts of the process.

So far, we have tested the approach iteratively on the laboratory examples based on the consulting projects, specifically designed to investigate the ideas of the proposed service design process. In the future, we will validate the approach by conducting real case studies, i.e. designing in real situations. Also, we will provide more user-friendly representations of the results of simulation.

As another important conclusion, we have realized that it is very difficult for people not to think imperatively in terms of sequences, etc., as we use this mode of thinking in everyday life. However, it can be very useful to use declarative specification, as it is more flexible, and as it supports the human decisions, and does not restrict them. Our goal is to have a simple, but powerful declarative environment, that could support designer decisions. So far, we have used this idea to use the same language in all different viewpoints. However, what we still miss is a declarative process language based on states and data. Developing this language is one of the main goals in our future. This way, by providing completely declarative environment by applying Poka-yoke principle, we believe we can prevent the designer from restricting the decisions and imperative operations.

**Acknowledgments.** The authors would like to thank Arash Golnam to very useful discussions and valuables comments and suggestions, and to Patrick Fleury from the company General Ressorts who provided us the case study on which our research was based.

# References

1. Chen, H.M.: Towards Service Engineering: Service Orientation and Business-IT Alignment. In: Proceedings of the 41st Hawaii International Conference on System Sciences (2008)
2. Crawford, C., Bate, P., Cherbakov, L., Holley, K., Tsocanos, C.: Toward an on demand service-oriented architecture. IBM Systems Journal 44(1), 81–107 (2005)
3. Blecher, M., Sholler, D.: Defining Business and SOA Services (2009), http://www.gartner.com/id=1002314
4. OGC: ITIL v3, Glossary of Terms, Definitions and Acronyms (2007), http://www.itilfoundations.com
5. Buchwald, S., Bauer, T., Reichert, M.: Bridging the Gap Between Business Process Models and Service Composition Specifications. In: Service Life Cycle Tools and Technologies: Methods, Trends and Advances, pp. 124–153. Idea Group Reference (2011)
6. Jackson, D.: Alloy Analyzer tool (2011), http://alloy.mit.edu/alloy/

7. Petitpierre, C.: Bottom Up Creation of a DSL Using Templates and JSON. In: SPLASH 2011 (2011)
8. D'Souza, D., Wills, A.: Objects, components, and frameworks with UML - The Catalysis approach, 4th edn. Addison-Wesley (2001)
9. Golnam, A., Regev, G., Ramboz, J., Laprade, P., Wegmann, A.: Systemic Service Design: Aligning Value and Implementation. In: Morin, J.-H., Ralyté, J., Snene, M. (eds.) IESS 2010. LNBIP, vol. 53, pp. 150–164. Springer, Heidelberg (2010)
10. Bajic, B., Petitpierre, C., Quang Tri, D., Wegmann, A.: From Business Services to IT Services by Capturing Design Decisions. In: BMSD, Geneva, pp. 94–104 (2012)
11. Vaajakallio, K., Mattelmaki, T., Lehtinen, V., Kantola, V., Kuikkaniemi, K.: Literature Review on Service Design, extreme-design project. Technical report, University of Art and Design Helsinki Helsinki University of Technology (2009)
12. Jackson, D., Schechter, I., Shlyakhter, I.: ALCOA: The Alloy constraint analyzer. In: Proceedings of the 22nd International Conference on Software Engineering (ICSE), Limerick, Ireland (June 2000)
13. Rychkova, I.: Formal Semantics for Refinement Verification of Enterprise Models. PhD thesis, EPFL (2008)
14. JSON (2009),http://json-template.googlecode.com/svn/trunk/doc/Introducing-JSON-Template.html
15. JavaCC (2012), http://java.net/projects/javacc/
16. O.M.G.: Model driven architecture. Document number ormsc/2001-07-01 (2001), http://www.omg.org/mda/
17. Koehler, J., Hauser, R., Sendall, S., Wahler, M.: Declarative techniques for model-driven business process integration. IBM Systems Journal 44(1) (2005)
18. Zhao, Y., Li, J., Li, Z., Ma, D.: Towards Hierarchical Modeling and Analysis of Web Services Choreography. In: Snene, M., Ralyté, J., Morin, J.-H. (eds.) IESS 2011. LNBIP, vol. 82, pp. 1–15. Springer, Heidelberg (2011)
19. Zignale, D., Kubicki, S., Ramel, S., Halin, G.: A Model-Based Method for the Design of Services in Collaborative Business Environments. In: Snene, M., Ralyté, J., Morin, J.-H. (eds.) IESS 2011. LNBIP, vol. 82, pp. 68–82. Springer, Heidelberg (2011)
20. Pesic, M., van der Aalst, W.M.P.: A Declarative Approach for Flexible Business Processes Management. In: Eder, J., Dustdar, S. (eds.) BPM Workshops 2006. LNCS, vol. 4103, pp. 169–180. Springer, Heidelberg (2006)
21. Hachani, S., Gzara, L., Verjus, H.: Business Process Flexibility in Service Composition: Experiment Using a PLM-Based Scenario. In: Snene, M., Ralyté, J., Morin, J.-H. (eds.) IESS 2011. LNBIP, vol. 82, pp. 158–172. Springer, Heidelberg (2011)
22. Poka-Yoke (2012), http://en.wikipedia.org/wiki/Poka-yoke
23. Wegmann, A.: On the Systemic Enterprise Architecture Methodology (SEAM). In: ICEIS (2003)
24. Golnam, A., Regev, G., Wegmann, A.: A Modeling Framework for Analyzing the Viability of Service Systems. International Journal of Service Science, Management, Engineering, and Technology (IJSSMET) 2, 51–64 (2005)
25. Regev, G., Hayard, O., Wegmann, A.: Service Systems and Value Modeling from an Appreciative System Perspective. In: Snene, M., Ralyté, J., Morin, J.-H. (eds.) IESS 2011. LNBIP, vol. 82, pp. 146–157. Springer, Heidelberg (2011)
26. Castro, V., Marcos, E., Wieringa, R.: Towards a service-oriented MDA-based approach to the alignment of business processes with IT systems: from the business model to a web service composition model. International Journal of Cooperative Information Systems 18(2), 225–260 (2008)

# Towards a Taxonomy of Service Design
# Methods and Tools

Rui Alves[1] and Nuno Jardim Nunes[1,2]

[1] Madeira Interactive Technologies Institute,
Polo Científico e Tecnológico da Madeira, 2nd floor, Caminho da Penteada
9020-105 Funchal, Madeira, Portugal
[2] Universidade da Madeira, Campus Universitário da Penteada,
9020-105 Funchal, Madeira, Portugal
rui.alves@m-iti.org, njn@uma.pt

**Abstract.** Service Design multidisciplinary heritage provides a wide array of methods and tools to practitioners. This can be overwhelming for inexperienced service designers or may present a threat to the coherence of consultancy organizations creating services for third parties. We present a reflection on the use of tools and methods in Service Design and propose a taxonomy, both to provide guidance to newcomers and enforce team coherence. By surveying ten distinct sources, both from industry and academia, we collected more than 160 methods and tools. Each method's relevance for the community was inferred from its frequency on the survey and the most relevant were clustered according to six dimensions: why, who, what, how, when and where. The resulting clusters were visualized in four quadrants charts for each dimension. Based on this proposal, practitioners can then address each problem from several perspectives, using the most appropriate tool.

**Keywords:** Service Design, Design Methods, Design Tools.

## 1 Introduction

Services are increasingly important in modern economies [16]. This greater relevance demands deeper understanding and study, specially bearing in mind that services involve complex experiences, include multiple stakeholders and therefore require a multidisciplinary approach [20]. Thus, Service Science, Management, Engineering and Design (SSMED) is emerging as a discipline aimed at understanding innovating service systems [25]. SSMED brings together many different disciplines supporting service management, marketing, engineering, delivery, design and innovation.

Within this context, Service Design (SD) is described as the outside-in perspective on service development [19], more specifically it is defined as applying design methods and techniques to the design of services [17]. Coming from the tradition of human-computer interaction (HCI) methods, SD builds on a user/customer-centric perspective to specify a service from the systematic application of ethnographic research, human-centered models and iterative design based on continuous evaluation with end users/customers.

J.F. e Cunha, M. Snene, and H. Nóvoa (Eds.): IESS 2013, LNBIP 143, pp. 215–229, 2013.
© Springer-Verlag Berlin Heidelberg 2013

SD's multidisciplinary populated this field with a myriad of methods and tools. This richness provides a wide range of options to SD practitioners, but such diversity presents some risks, namely: new practitioners' learning curve, and coherence maintenance in consultancy organizations creating services for third parties.

As today service domains and interactions become vastly more complex, designers are required to communicate their ideas more effectively, depending on different organizations, channels, contexts, platforms and devices. Here, we argue that for an effective communication of design ideas to service development and engineering a common modeling framework, needs to emerge, capturing the important common elements required to model and convey the design details.

Here we provide a first attempt to create a taxonomy of SD methods and tools. Based in a study of ten distinct sources, both from industry and academia, this paper presents a guide to the most relevant SD methods and tools. We reviewed 164 methods and tools and categorized them into different clusters.

In order to ground and clarify the scope of SD, we present a brief explanation of the basic concepts as well as the service, SSMED, SD, experience economy and then the experience cycle. We then derive a discussion of design process from the concepts related to service and service design. Finally we present the definitions for most relevant SD tools and methods and propose the classification as taxonomy.

## 2    Foundation

According to Edvardsson, a service is "a chain of (sequential, parallel, overlapping and/or recurrent) value creating activities or events, which form a process. In this process, the customer often takes part by performing different elements in interaction with the employees (other customers or equipment) for the purpose of achieving a particular result" [12]. Therefore, services are activities or events that form a process to achieve a particular added value. This process is fundamentally different from what underlies products. Services deal largely with intangibles and the provision is hard to separate from consumption [20]. It is said to happen at the point of delivery, it cannot be stored or owned [20]. Besides the fact that services are intangible, it encompasses complex experiences and their quality is difficult to measure [20]. Services comprise different components, products and space [20], which customers interact with. Customers' total experience is made up from their perception across these different service touchpoints [20]. Thus, organizations providing services need to address research, innovation and development in a new way. This is where SD and SSMED come in [20]. Here we present a definition of this paper ground concepts.

### 2.1    Service Science, Management, Engineering and Design

Arguing for a designers' view of SSMED Evenson illustrates the role that design plays in support of service science, management and engineering [14]. Collaboration between SD and service science lies in the social understanding of expectations and expectation setting, how these vary across cultures and impact how people perceive and understand dynamic information at the point of need. The overlap between design and management lays in the area of value creation and brand management, in particular the effect of co-creation in the perception of value and the challenge of managing emergent behavior as people participate in the design process [14]. At the intersection with engineering is the development of service platforms and architectures that designers employ to fuel adoption and use, requiring a design level understanding of how these elements can be reflected and updated seamlessly [14].

Since the lack of a common set of references, language and tools is the main challenge in supporting cooperation between these disciplines, models play a critical role to overcome it. As services account four times more jobs than manufacturing, is key to provide an effective communication between design and engineering in order to answer to the rising demand for design in service development.

## 2.2    Service Design

Because services are often associated with immaterial, living and complex objects manufactures at the point of delivery, they are seldom considered an "object of design". Still, since early 80s Shostack [27] proposed service blueprinting as an approach to design services, many started looking at SD as a systematic process, similar to product and interaction design. Since then many schools (KISD and Ivrea) focus on SD (introduced as an academic field in the 1990s [11], p. 354]), in a more conscious and systematic practice, based on a deep understanding of the person's context, the delivering organization and their market strategies.

Although there is no common definition of SD, existing ones fall in the academic or industry [26] category. The Design Dictionary states that SD addresses the functionality and form of services from customers' perspective. It aims at ensuring that service interfaces are useful, usable, and desirable from their point of view and effective, efficient, and distinctive from the supplier's perspective [11], p. 355.

SD as a discipline is complementary to service development and engineering and is mostly concerned with visualizing and expressing complex human to human, human to machine and machine to machine interactions that define a customer journey that simultaneously builds value, utility and delight [14], [29], [33]. Customers' perceive their experience across the multiple service touchpoints, which is analyzed next.

## 2.3    Experience Cycle

There is a growing emphasis in business practice on creating meaningful and memorable customer experiences [22]. This trend denotes a paradigm shift known as the experience economy: a transition from selling services to selling experiences [22]. This involves allowing the designer to think of the design problem in terms of designing an integrated experience, perceived holistically by people [2], as opposed to designing one or more specific artifacts.

Dubberly and Evenson decomposed and visualized the experience cycle in five stages [11]: i) connect and attract, ii) orient, iii) interact, iv) extend and retain, and v) advocate. This model describes the steps people go through in building a relationship with a service. According to it, a good product or service experience is: compelling (it captures the user's imagination), orienting (it helps users navigate the product and the world), embedded (it becomes a part of users' lives), generative (it unfolds, growing as users' skills increase) and it should be reverberating (it delights so much that users tell other people about it, they advocate) [11].

## 2.4    Design Process

A design process, in the context of SD, is a collection of activities that takes one or more types of input and creates an output that is of value to the customer [16]. Back in 2004, Dubberly surveyed over 100 descriptions of design and development processes from several fields [10]. In this paper, the taxonomy presented is rooted in the four stages model (discover, reframe, envision and create) [19], which is analogous to the Analysis-Synthesis Bridge Model [9]. In Mendel's model, discover is about understanding the current situation. Reframe understands the current *"as is"* in non-obvious ways. Envision is to explore potential solutions and create is about designing the future [19]. The next section aims at providing guidance to newcomers and to enhance team coherence, from the SD process perspective.

# 3    Analysis of SD Tools and Methods

We have analyzed different sources [1], [26], [29], [31], [32], [33], [34], [35], [36], [37] for tools and methods related to SD (for further detail, please refer to the appendix). From these sources we have extracted a list of 164 tools and methods used in SD, which in turn were classified by frequency. The relative relevance to the SD community is visualized in Fig. 2, where the bigger the relevance, the bigger the font size. A methodology is a set or system of methods, principles, and rules for regulating a given discipline. A Method is an established, habitual, logical, or prescribed practice or systematic process of achieving certain ends with accuracy and efficiency, usually in an ordered sequence of fixed steps. A tool is anything used as a means of accomplishing a task or purpose whereas a technique is a systematic procedure, formula, or routine by which a task is accomplished.

Upon analyzing the data gathered, and in line with Segelstrom's findings [25], it seems to exist evidence that there is a set of basic techniques, which are almost universally used, as well as a long tail of techniques only used by a few companies. The numbers are self-explanatory: 71% of surveyed methods and tools were upheld by one single source.

In our analysis, aiming at providing guidance to newcomers and enhancing team coherence, we decided to focus on methods and tools that gathered at least three or more references. This accounts for 25 methods or tools, 15% of this study sample.

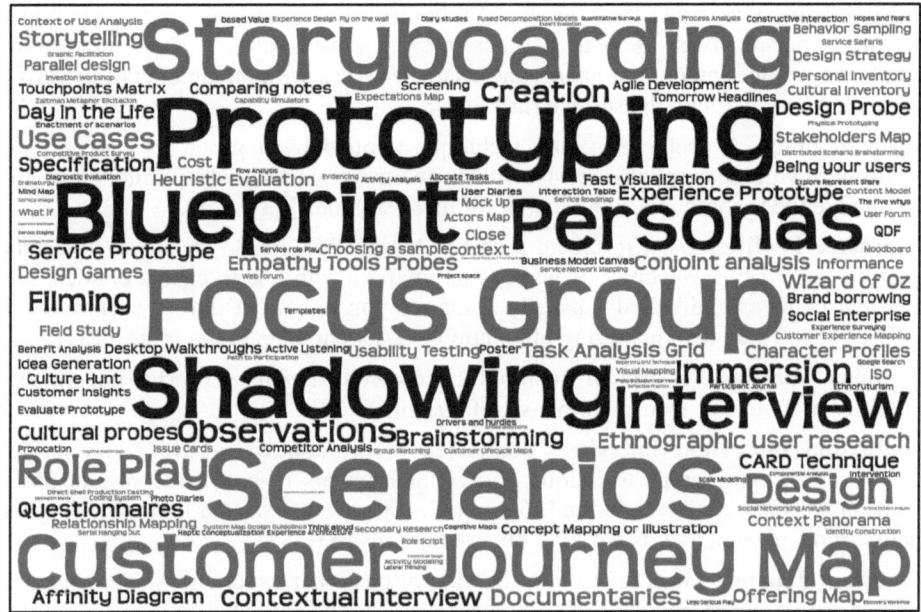

**Fig. 1.** Word cloud of all 164 methods and tools analyzed

## 3.1 Selected Methods and Tools

In this section we present the selected methods and tools (Fig. 3), and provide a short description of each one.

**Fig. 2.** Word cloud of selected methods and tools

**Affinity Diagram.** A creative process to gather and organize large amounts of data, ideas or insights [37], evidencing data's natural correlations [29]. Can be used to analyze findings from field studies or usability evaluation [37].

**Blueprint (Service Blueprint).** A visual schematic incorporating users' and service providers' perspectives, as well as other relevant parties [26], p. 204. This model details the service interaction nature and characteristics, with enough detail to verify, implement and maintain the service [29].

**Brainstorming.** A problem-solving technique applied by a group of people, who contributes with ideas spontaneously. This is an uncensored activity. Whiteboards and post-its are the favored recording media for these sessions [13], p. 49.

**Character Profiles.** Used to create a shared knowledge, inside the team, about the service users [29]. Succinct ways of summarizing the key characteristics and experiences of an individual - usually someone you have met during user research [34]. They can also help justifying innovations to stakeholders in the project [31].

**Conjoint Analysis.** A form of quantitative research offering powerful insight into customer preferences, from a simple set of questions [33].

**Contextual Interview.** Interviews conducted in the context in which the service occurs. This ethnographic technique allows interviewers to both observe and probe the behavior they are interested in [26], p. 162. It paves the way for understanding the reality of people and avoids working on assumptions [33].

**Customer Journey Map.** It is a visualization of customer experiences over time and space required to accomplish a certain goal [17]. The touchpoints where users interact with the service are used to construct a "journey" [26], p. 158. This model allows designers to see what parts of the service work for the user (magic moments) and what parts might need improving (pain points) [31].

**Cultural Probes.** Used to gather insights about the daily life of communities [36]. The probes are usually given to participants for a prolonged period of time, during which they can produce richly engaging material for design inspiration [26], p. 168.

**Documentaries.** Is a visual method to discover what matters to people, what they value. This tool informs and inspires the design processes at early stages [34]. It is believed that film captures human expressivity and emotion in ways that other purely observational studies cannot [36].

**Empathy Tools/Probes.** Enables designers to break out of the trap of designing for themselves and to see the challenge from the end user stand point [33]. These tools can help finding out not just what people are saying and doing, but also what they are thinking and feeling (people do not always do, think or feel what they tell you) [33].

**Ethnographic User Research.** The purpose of user research is to gain a thorough understanding of users, to unlock the reasons why users do the things they do (drivers) and the reasons why they do not do things (hurdles). This unveils patterns of behavior in a real context [33].

**Experience Prototype.** A simulation of the service experience that foresees some of its performances through the usage of the specific physical touchpoints involved [29]. The experiential aspect of whatever representations are needed to successfully (re)live or convey an experience with a product, space or system [4].

**Focus Group.** A forum of selected people controlled by an impartial moderator to give feedback to design ideas [36]. Helps service designers get a broad overview of users' reactions to, and ideas about, a topic [31].

**Immersion (workshop).** Also known as empathic research or role-playing, provides deep information, not obtainable by observational research. It allows the designer to understand not just the physical use of products and spaces, but how the individual feels emotionally and socially in situations and tasks [1].

**Observations.** Used to identify problems about an existing situation or a prototype design, which can arise when people interact with services [31].

**Personas.** Archetypes built after a preceding exhaustive observation of the potential users [29]. They represent a "character" with which client and design teams can engage [26], p. 178. There should be a correct balance between contextual and holistic insight, concerning emotional, qualitative and lifestyle issues [8]. The narrative can become complicated by potentially distracting details [23], p. 505.

**Prototyping.** The service prototype is a tool for testing the service by observing the interaction of the user with a prototype of the service put in the place, situation and condition where the service will actually exist [29]. Intended to test the function and performance of a new design before it goes into production [13], p. 317.

**Questionnaire/Survey.** Used to provide statistics to inform the project direction [31].

**Role Play.** Also referred as service enacting, is a method for designing services that amounts to a new form of rapid prototyping: acting out service situations very quickly clarifies the direction the SD process should take [13], p. 356. Role-playing means physically acting out what happens where users interact with products or services [31]. The implied condition is thinking that the service really exists and then building a potential journey through some of its functionalities [29].

**Scenarios.** Design scenarios are essentially hypothetical stories, created with sufficient detail to meaningfully explore a particular aspect of a service [26], p. 184. Either written or drawn, scenarios are useful to design, or communicate, services and experiences, where multiple interactions will happen over a period of time [34]. User's needs could be anticipated and demonstrated trough this [13], p. 226.

**Service Prototype.** Simulates a service experience. These simulations can range from being informal "role-play" style conversations, to more detailed full-scale recreations involving active user participation, props, and physical touchpoints [26], p. 192. They can generate deeper understanding than written descriptions or visual depictions, which do not deal as well with the time-related and intangible aspects of services [33].

**Shadowing.** Researchers immerse themselves in customers' lives, front-line staff, or people behind the scenes in order to observe their behavior and experiences [26], p. 156. It offers a vital advantage over traditional forms of research like surveys or focus groups: they let you spot the real moments when problems occur as well as situations where people say one thing but actually do something quite different [33].

**Stakeholders Map.** A model with a visual representation of staff, customers, partner organizations and other stakeholders involved in a particular service. Allows the interplay between these various groups to be charted and analyzed [26], p. 150.

**Storyboarding.** A representation of use cases, put together in a narrative sequence [29]. It is a series of drawings, or pictures, used to visualize a sequence of events, either for a situation where a service is used, or the hypothetical implementation of a new service prototype [26], p. 186. Includes information about the location where the interaction takes place, present the people as personalities, and provide details about actions and things people are doing as they interact [15].

**Task Analysis Grid.** The task analysis grid is an interesting alternative to the standard requirements documents [29].

# 4     Classification and Visualization of Methods and Tools

In the past, several authors gave their contribution in order to visualize SD tools and methods [1], [9], [20], [28], p. 50. In this section we propose a new set of visualizations. This approach is inspired on the six ways we see [24]: who/what, how many, where, when, how, and why. Selected methods and tools are displayed in these six dimensions, using four quadrants charts. Each quadrant contains a word cloud in which each method or tool font size is relative to its frequency on our survey. The proposed taxonomy builds on Aldersey-Williams et al [1], Campos and Nunes [5], Mendel [20] and Tassi [29] contributions to define the axis for each chart.

## 4.1     Why – The Motivation to Use the Tool or Method

Building on Campos and Nunes [5] and Mendel [20] the proposed axis present a clear distinction to guide the designer on what to use, grounding the designers motivation either on the domain (solution or problem) or the main purpose (to know/learn or to make/create). The quadrants cluster four major groups where we can find tools to brainstorm/learn about users (in the Know/Problem quadrant), models to communicate (in the Know/Solution quadrant), and tools to create, and prototype the service (in the Solution/Make quadrant).

   It is noticeable that the majority of the methods are used to understand the problem (Fig. 4). Moreover, the second most important chunk is related to models, mainly used to communicate existing and proposed solutions. Finally, covering the make-solution quadrant we can find prototyping related methods and tools.

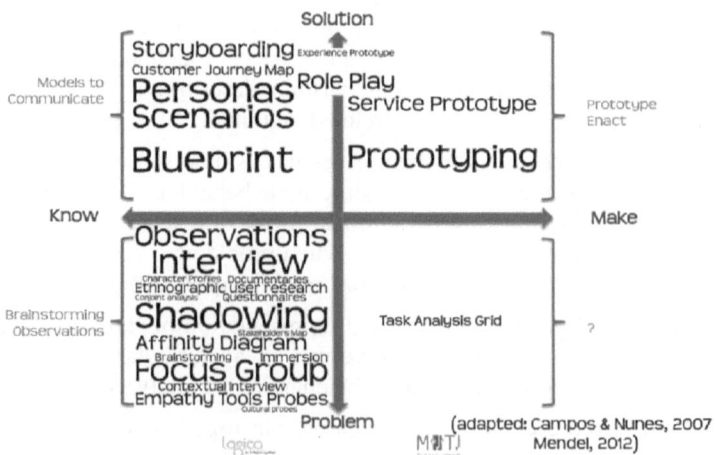

**Fig. 3.** Why: The motivations

## 4.2    Who – The Recipients

Based on Tassi's categorization [29], our proposal can help designers to select the method or tool that fits their audience best. There is a set of tools that can be used virtually with any stakeholders (central square in Fig. 5). The Specialist/Designer quadrant encompasses tools and methods used internally by the design team. Is it clear that there is an aggregation targeting designers and specialists.

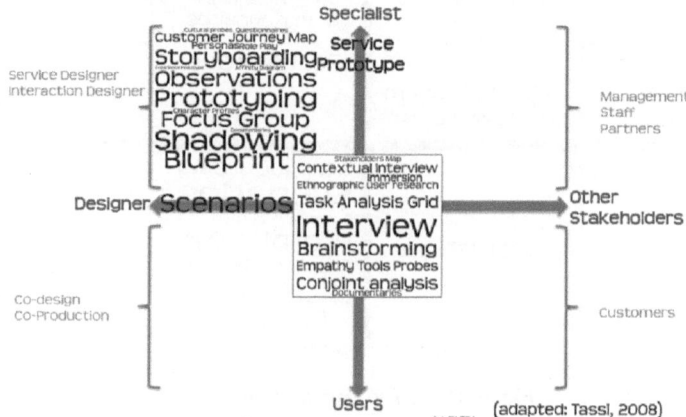

**Fig. 4.** Who: The recipients

## 4.3    What – The Content Targeted in Each Method or Tool

In this dimension we build again on Tassi's work [29] and the proposed axis are meant to evaluate the content. Either targeted to users versus a system approach or the context versus the service offering. It is noticeable that existing methods and tools cover mostly the users, the context and the offering than systems (Fig. 6).

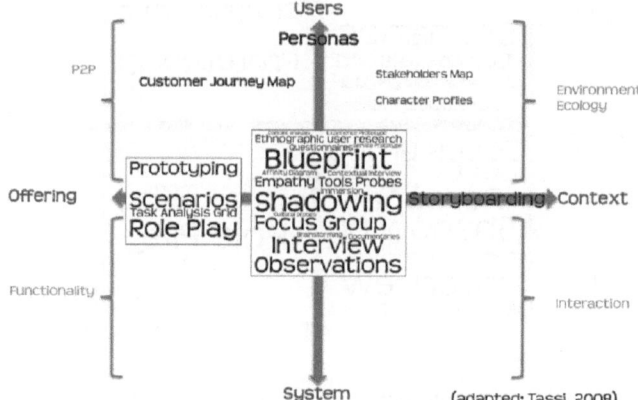

**Fig. 5.** What: The targeted content

## 4.4     How – The Representations Used

We found a balance on participatory versus non-participatory tools. Yet, we found participatory tools bend to be informal while non-participatory tend to be more formal (Fig. 7).

**Fig. 6.** How: The representations used

## 4.5     When – The Activities in the Design Process

This section is especially interesting because it mirrors the design process. In the presented chart, adapted from Mendel [20], we realize how know versus make is clearly unbalanced, in favor of knowing (Fig. 8).

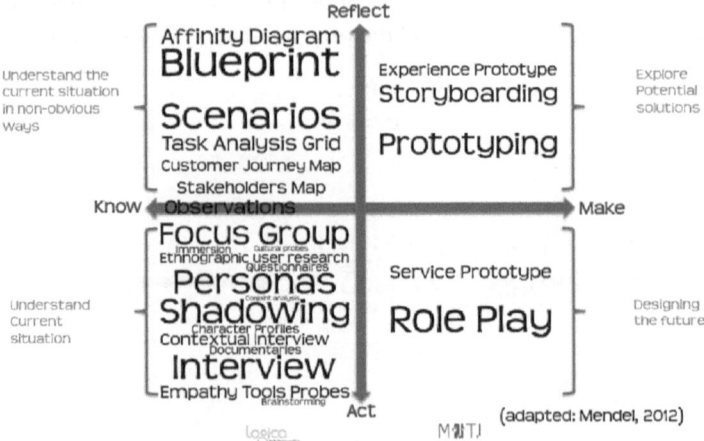

**Fig. 7.** When: The design process activities

### 4.6    Where – The Location Where the Method or Tool Usually Takes Place

Our proposal is inspired in Aldersey-Williams et al [1] and the axis are divided in private indoor spaces, such as the design office and other methods and tools that can take place anywhere. Specifically for public spaces or outdoors no tools were found.

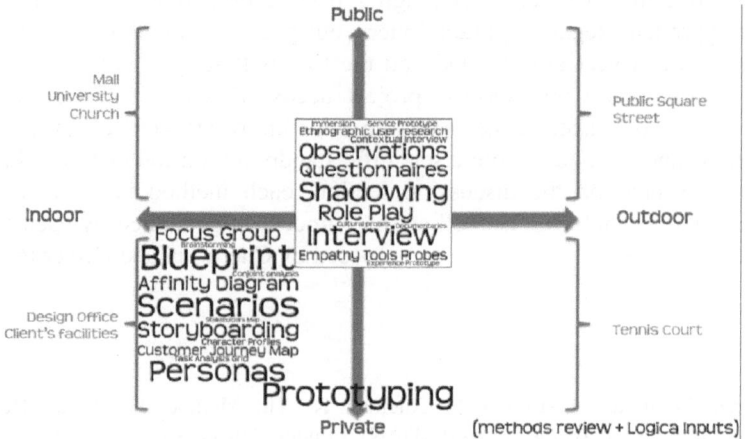

**Fig. 8.** Where: The location where the method or tool usually takes place

## 5    Discussion

So far, proposed taxonomies tend to be bound to a specific stakeholder view and lack a holistic approach. We propose a taxonomy covering six dimensions, attempting to overcome this limitation. On top of contributing to provide guidance to newcomers and increase coherence on SD teams, this paper identified some trends regarding SD methods and tools, which could open new discussion to improve the community practice. We found that the majority of the methods are used to understand the problem (Fig. 4), and evidence pointing towards an aggregation targeting designers and specialists (Fig. 5) seems to emerge. Existing methods and tools cover mostly the users; the context and the offering (Fig. 6) while the systems are somehow disregarded. Further investigation should be conducted to address these apparent trends. Participatory tools are more likely to be informal while non-participatory tend to be more formal (Fig. 7), raising the question if there are empty gaps on the existing toolkit for SD practitioners. On Fig. 8 we realized how unbalanced know versus make is, in favor of knowing. We could not find tools to be specifically used in public spaces or outdoor. Again, new doubts may rise, wondering when this apparent evidence is bound to SD nature or is it due to a lack on existing methods and tools.

## 6    Conclusion and Future Work

SD practitioners are exposed to complex problems and being able to use the appropriate tools and methods. Hence, the proposed taxonomy is a way to help SD practitioners to address each problem from several perspectives, using the most appropriate tool or method(s) for a specific case. The proposed taxonomy includes six dimensions that cover distinct facets: 1) the motivation to use the tool, 2) the audience, 3) the targeted content, 4) the representations used, 5) the activities in the design process, and 6) the location where the method or tool likely takes place.

Future work includes activities ranging from a practitioner point of view to a scientific approach. Regarding practitioners, our goal is to build a tool where several parameters of a project are inputted and the tool will suggest which set of tools is more likely to fit best that specific project needs. This tool could be used to log methods and tools usage, further extending our knowledge on real world usage of existing tools and methods. From a scientific standpoint, on top of researching on the questions presented on the discussion section, each method internal and external validity should be analyzed, as well as the output data generated by each method or tool (either subjective or objective), as proposed by Cherubini and Oliver [6].

# References

1. Aldersey-Williams, H., Bound, J., Coleman, R.: The Methods Lab | User Research for Design. Design for Ageing Network (DAN), London, UK (1999)
2. Bitner, M.J.: Servicescapes: The Impact of Physical Surroundings on Customers and Employees. The Journal of Marketing 56, 57–71 (1992)
3. Brown, T., et al.: Design thinking. Harvard Business Review 86, 84 (2008)
4. Buchenau, M., Suri, J.F.: Experience prototyping. In: Proceedings of the 3rd Conference on Designing Interactive Systems, pp. 424–433 (2000)
5. Campos, P., Nunes, N.J.: Practitioner tools and workstyles for user-interface design. IEEE Software 24, 73–80 (2007)
6. Cherubini, M., Oliver, N.: A refined experience sampling method to capture mobile user experience (2009)
7. Davenport, T.H.: Process innovation: reengineering work through information technology. Harvard Business School Press (1993)
8. Dubberly, H.: ON MODELING Design in the age of biology: shifting from a mechanical-object ethos to an organic-systems ethos. Interactions 15, 35–41 (2008)
9. Dubberly, H., Evenson, S.: On modeling The analysis-systhesis bridge model. Interactions 15, 57–61 (2008)
10. Dubberly, H.: How do you design? Dubberly Design Office, San Francisco, USA (2004)
11. Dubberly, H., Evenson, S.: The experience cycle. Interactions 15, 11–15 (2008)
12. Edvardsson, B., Gustafsson, A., Johnson, M.D., Sandén, B.: New Service Development and Innovation in the New Economy. Studentlitteratur (2000)
13. Erlhoff, M., Marshall, T. (eds.): Design Dictionary. Birkhäuser Architecture (2003)
14. Evenson, S.: Designing for Service. In: Proceedings of DPPI, Eindhoven (2005)
15. Greenberg, S., Carpendale, S., Marquardt, N., Buxton, B.: The narrative storyboard: telling a story about use and context over time. Interactions 19, 64–69 (2012)
16. Hammer, M., Champy, J.: Reengineering the corporation: a manifesto for business revolution. Harper Business (1993)
17. Hegeman, J.: Mapping the Journey. UX Lisbon, Lisbon (2012)

18. Holmlid, S., Evenson, S.: Bringing service design to service sciences, management and engineering. In: Service Science, Management and Engineering Education for the 21st Century, pp. 341–345 (2008)
19. Mager, B.: Service Design – A Review. Köln International School of Design, Köln (2004)
20. Mendel, J.: A taxonomy of models used in the design process. Interactions, 81–85 (2012)
21. Moritz, S.: Service Design. Practical access to an evolving field (2005)
22. Pine II, B.J., Gilmore, J.H.: Welcome to the Experience Economy. HBR (1998)
23. Pruitt, J., Adlin, T.: The Persona Lifecycle: Keeping People in Mind Throughout Product Design. Elsevier (2006)
24. Roam, D.: The Back of the Napkin: Solving Problems and Selling Ideas with Pictures. Marshall Cavendish (2009)
25. Segelström, F.: Communicating through Visualizations: Service Designers on Visualizing User Research. In: DeThinking Design, ReThinking Services–First Nordic Conference on Service Design and Service Innovation (2009)
26. Stickdorn, M., Schneider, J.: This is Service Design Thinking: Basics - Tools - Cases. BIS Publishers (2011)
27. Shostack, L.: Designing Services that Deliver. Harvard Business Review (1984)
28. Tassi, R.: Design Della Comunicazione e Design Dei Servizi (2008)
29. Tassi, R.: Service Design Tools, http://www.servicedesigntools.org/
30. Zeithaml, V.A., Bitner, M.J.: Service Marketing. The McGraw-Hill Companies (1996)
31. Design Council - Design methods, http://www.designcouncil.org.uk/about-design/how-designers-work/design-methods/
32. Designing With People, http://designingwithpeople.rca.ac.uk/methods
33. Engine Service Design | Service Design, http://enginegroup.co.uk/service_design/methods/
34. Methodbank, http://www.methodbank.com/
35. Services - Adaptive Path, http://adaptivepath.com/work/services
36. The Design Exchange, http://www.thedesignexchange.org/methods
37. UsabilityNet: Methods list, http://www.usabilitynet.org/tools/list.htm

# Appendix: Methods and Tools Grid

| Tool/Method | URL | URL | URL | URL | URL | URL | URL | URL | URL | URL | URL |
|---|---|---|---|---|---|---|---|---|---|---|---|
| 1. Actors Map | ● | | | | | | | | | | |
| 2. Active Listening | | | | | ● | | | | | | |
| 3. Activity Analysis | | | | | ● | | | | | | |
| 4. Activity Modeling | | | | | ● | | | | | | |
| 5. Agile Development | | | | | | | | | | ● | |
| 6. Affinity Diagram (Cluster and vote) | ● | | ● | ● | | | ● | | | | |
| 7. Allocate Tasks | | | | | | | ● | | | | |
| 8. Behavior Sampling | | | | | ● | | | | | | |
| 9. Being your users | | | ● | | | | | | | | |
| 10. Blueprint (Service Blueprint) | ● | ● | ● | ● | | | | | ● | ● | |
| 11. Brainstorming (Scribble-Say-Slap) | | | ● | ● | | | ● | | | | |
| 12. Brand borrowing | | | ● | | | | | | | | |
| 13. Business Model Canvas | | | | | | | | | | ● | |
| 14. Canonical Abstract Prototyping | | | | | ● | | | | | | |
| 15. CARD Technique | | | | | ● | | ● | | | | |
| 16. Capability Simulators | | | ● | | | | | | | | |
| 17. Character Profiles | ● | | ● | ● | | | | | | | |
| 18. Choosing a sample | | | ● | ● | | | | | | | |
| 19. Close-ended questions | | | | | ● | | | | | | |
| 20. Co-Creation | | ● | | | | | | | | ● | |
| 21. Co-Design (Service User Workshops) | | | ● | | | | | | | | ● |
| 22. Coding System | | | | | ● | | | | | | |
| 23. Cognitive Maps | | | | | ● | | | | | | |
| 24. Cognitive Walkthrough | ● | | | | | | | | | | |
| 25. Collaborative authoring in Wikis | | | | | ● | | | | | | |
| 26. Comparing notes | | | ● | ● | | | | | | | |
| 27. Competitive Product Survey | | | | | ● | | | | | | |
| 28. Competitor Analysis | | | | | | | ● | | | | |
| 29. Componential Analysis | | | | | ● | | | | | | |
| 30. Concept Mapping/Illustration | | | | | ● | | | ● | | | |
| 31. Conjoint analysis (Techniques) | | ● | | | ● | | | | | | ● |
| 32. Constructive Interaction | ● | | | | | | | | | | |
| 33. Content Model | | | | | ● | | | | | | |
| 34. Context Panorama | ● | | | | | | | | | | |
| 35. Contextual Interview (Inquiry) | | ● | ● | | | | ● | | | | |
| 36. Context of Use Analysis | | | | | | | ● | | | | |
| 37. Contextual Design | | | | | ● | | | | | | |
| 38. Cost-Benefit Analysis | | | | | | | ● | | | | |
| 39. Critical incident Analysis | | | | | | | ● | | | | |
| 40. Customer Experience Mapping | | | | | | | | ● | | | |
| 41. Customer Insights | | | | | | | ● | | | | |
| 42. Customer Journey Map | ● | ● | ● | ● | | | | ● | ● | | |
| 43. Customer Lifecycle Maps | | | | | | | | ● | | | |
| 44. Culture Hunt | ● | | | | | | | | | | |
| 45. Cultural Inventory | | | | | ● | | | | | | |
| 46. Cultural probes | | | ● | | ● | | | | | ● | |
| 47. Day in the Life | | | | | | ● | | | | ● | |
| 48. Documentaries (pseudo/design) | | | ● | | ● | ● | | | | | |
| 49. Design-in-context | | | | | ● | | | | | | |
| 50. Design Games | ● | | | | | ● | | | | | |
| 51. Design Guidelines | | | | | | | ● | | | | |
| 52. Design Probe | | | | | | ● | | | | | ● |
| 53. Design Strategy | | | | | | | | ● | | | |
| 54. Desktop Walkthroughs | | ● | | | | | | | ● | | |
| 55. Diary studies | | | | | ● | | | | | | |
| 56. Diagnostic Evaluation | | | | | | | ● | | | | |
| 57. Direct Shell Production Casting | | | | | ● | | | | | | |
| 58. Discovery Workshop | | ● | | | | | | | | | |
| 59. Distributed Scenario Brainstorming | | ● | | | | | | | | | |
| 60. Dramaturgy | | | | | ● | | | | | | |
| 61. Drivers and hurdles | | | | ● | | | | | | | |
| 62. Empathy Tools/Probes (Emphatic Design) | | ● | | | ● | ● | | | | | ● |
| 63. Enactment (of scenarios) | | | | | ● | | | | | | |
| 64. Ethnofuturism | | | | | ● | | | | | | |
| 65. Ethnographic user research (auto/classic/Quick&Dirty/Rapid/Video/Mobile) | | ● | | | ● | ● | | | ● | | ● |
| 66. Evidencing | ● | | | | | | | | | | |
| 67. Evaluate Prototype | | | | | | | ● | | | | |
| 68. Expectations Map | | | | | | | | | ● | | |
| 69. Experience Architecture | | | | | | | | ● | | | |
| 70. Experience Design | | | | | | | | ● | | | |
| 71. Experience Prototype | ● | | | ● | ● | | | | | | |
| 72. Experience Roadmaps | | | | | | | | ● | | | |
| 73. Experience Surveying | | ● | | | | | | | | | |
| 74. Expert Evaluation | | | | | | | ● | | | | |
| 75. Explore, Represent, Share | | | | | ● | | | | | | |
| 76. Fast visualization | | | | ● | | | | | | | |
| 77. Field Study | | | | | | | ● | | | | |
| 78. Filming | | ● | ● | | | | | | | | |
| 79. Flow Analysis | | | | | ● | | | | | | |
| 80. Fly on the wall | | | | | ● | | | | | | |

| Method / Tool | 1 | 2 | 3 | 4 | 5 | 6 | 7 | 8 | 9 | 10 |
|---|---|---|---|---|---|---|---|---|---|---|
| 81. Focus Group | | | • | • | • | • | | | | • |
| 82. Focus Group (Quantify Data) | | | | | • | | • | | | |
| 83. Fused Decomposition Models | | | | | • | | | | | |
| 84. Google Search | | | | | • | | | | | |
| 85. Graphic Facilitation | | • | | | | | | | | |
| 86. Group Sketching | • | | | | | | | | | |
| 87. Haptic Conceptualization | | | • | | | | | | | |
| 88. Heuristic Evaluation | • | | | | | | • | | | |
| 89. Hopes and fears | | | | • | | | | | | |
| 90. Idea Generation | | | | | | | | | • | |
| 91. Identity Construction | | | | | • | | | | | |
| 92. Immersion (workshop) | | | • | | | • | | | | • |
| 93. Informance | • | | | | | | | | | |
| 94. Interaction Table | • | | | | | | | | | |
| 95. Intervention/Provocation | | | | | | • | | | | |
| 96. Interview (Extreme users/Re/Contextual) | | | | | • | • | • | | • | • |
| 97. Invention workshop | | | • | | | | | | | |
| 98. ISO 13407 | | | | | | | • | | | |
| 99. Issue Cards | • | | | | | | | | | |
| 100. Lateral Thinking | | | | | | • | | | | |
| 101. Lego Serious Play | • | | | | | | | | | |
| 102. Mind Map | • | | | | | | | | | |
| 103. Mock Up | • | | | | | | | | | |
| 104. Moodboard | • | | | | | | | | | |
| 105. Motivation Matrix | • | | | | | | | | | |
| 106. Observations | | | • | • | • | • | | | | • |
| 107. Offering Map | • | | • | | | | | | | |
| 108. Parallel design | | | | | | | • | | | |
| 109. Participant Journal | | • | | | | | | | | |
| 110. Path to Participation | | • | | | | | | | | |
| 111. Personal Inventory | | | | | • | | | | | |
| 112. Personas | • | • | | | | • | | • | • | |
| 113. Photo Diaries | | | | | • | | | | | |
| 114. Photo Elicitation Interview | | | | | • | | | | | |
| 115. Physical Prototyping | | | | • | | | | | | |
| 116. Poster | • | | | | | | | | | |
| 117. Process Analysis | | | | | | • | | | | |
| 118. Project space | | | • | | | | | | | |
| 119. Prototyping (Evolutionary/Rough/Low-Fi/Rapid) | • | • | | | | • | • | • | • | • |
| 120. QDF-based Value | | | | | • | | | | | |
| 121. Quantitative Surveys | | | | | • | | | | | |
| 122. Questionnaires (attitude) /Survey | | | | | • | • | • | | | • |
| 123. Relationship Mapping | | • | • | | | | | | | |
| 124. Reflective Practice | | | | | • | | | | | |
| 125. Repertory Grid Technique | | | | | • | | | | | |
| 126. Role Play | • | | | • | • | | | | | • |
| 127. Role Script | • | | | | | | | | | |
| 128. Scale Modeling | | | | | • | | | | | |
| 129. Scenarios (based Design) | | | • | • | • | • | • | | • | • |
| 130. Screening | | | | | • | | | | | |
| 131. Secondary Research | | | | | • | | | | | |
| 132. Serial Hanging Out | | | | | • | | | | | |
| 133. Service Image | • | | | | | | | | | |
| 134. Service Network Mapping | | | • | | | | | | | |
| 135. Service Prototype | • | • | | | | | | • | | |
| 136. Service Roadmap | | | | | | | • | | | |
| 137. Service role Play | | | | | | | | • | | |
| 138. Service Safaris | | | | | | | | • | | |
| 139. Service Staging | | | | | | | | • | | |
| 140. Shadowing | | | • | • | | • | | • | | • |
| 141. Social Enterprise | | | | | | • | | | | |
| 142. Social Networking Analysis | | | | | • | | | | | |
| 143. Specification (Service Specification) | • | • | | | | | | | | |
| 144. Subjective Assessment | | | | | | | • | | | |
| 145. Stakeholders Map | | | • | | | | | | | |
| 146. Storytelling | • | | | | | | | • | | |
| 147. Storyboarding | • | • | • | | | • | • | • | | |
| 148. System Map | • | | | | | | | | | |
| 149. Task Analysis Grid | • | | | | | | • | | | • |
| 150. Technology Probe | | | | | • | | | | | |
| 151. Templates | • | | | | | | | | | |
| 152. The five whys | | | | | | | | • | | |
| 153. Think aloud | | | | | | | | | | • |
| 154. Tomorrow Headlines | • | | | | | | | | | |
| 155. Touchpoints Matrix | • | | • | | | | | | | |
| 156. Usability Testing | • | | | | | | • | | | |
| 157. Use Cases | • | | | | | | • | | | |
| 158. User Forum | | | | | | • | | | | |
| 159. User Diaries | | | | • | | | | | | |
| 160. Visual Mapping | | | • | | | | | | | |
| 161. Web Forum | | | | | | • | | | | |
| 162. What if... | | | | | | | | • | | |
| 163. Wizard of Oz | • | | | | | | • | | | |
| 164. Zaltman Metaphor Elicitacion | | | | | • | | | | | |

# A Survey of Tool Support for the Animation of IT Services Process Models Execution

Marco Roque[1] and Fernando Brito e Abreu[1,2]

[1] DCTI, ISCTE-IUL, Avª das Forças Armadas,
1649-026 Lisboa, Portugal
[2] CITI, FCT/UNL, Campus da Caparica, Quinta da Torre,
2829-516 Caparica, Portugal
marco_roque@iscte.pt, fba@iscte-iul.pt

**Abstract.** Process modeling notations are frequently used to model IT service management processes, namely in the realm of ITIL. The nature of IT services, such as in checking SLAs fulfillment, calls for tool provision of model-based animation features for process execution to be used for monitoring, simulation, replay or scenario identification purposes. This paper reports the results of a structured review on those animation features, as provided by state-of-the-art process simulation, modeling and mining tools. A process animation assessment framework is proposed. Conclusions drawn point out to several shortcomings of the current state of the art.

**Keywords:** IT services, ITIL, process models, model-based animation, process execution, tool survey.

## 1    Introduction

Many tools support IT Service Management (ITSM) activities nowadays, such as incident management tools, configuration management databases (CMDB), change and release management tools. Process modeling tools also became widespread in the ITSM community, since the emergence of the IT Infrastructure Library (ITIL) [1], a reference framework that has a process-model based view of designing, deploying, controlling and managing IT operations.

Last version of ITIL (V3, 2011 update) includes 26 processes, which are grouped in 5 sets: *Service Strategy*, *Service Design*, *Service Transition*, *Service Operation* and *Continual Service Improvement*. We are particularly interested in Service Level Management (SLM), one of the 8 *Service Design* processes, that concerns continual identification, monitoring and review of the quality of provided IT services, as specified in Service Level Agreements (SLAs) [2, 3]. SLM ensures that arrangements are in place with internal IT support-providers and external suppliers in the form of Operational Level Agreements (OLAs) and Underpinning Contracts (UCs), respectively. The SLM process is in close relation with the *Service Operation*

J.F. e Cunha, M. Snene, and H. Nóvoa (Eds.): IESS 2013, LNBIP 143, pp. 230–245, 2013.

processes[1] to control their activities. As such, it involves assessing the impact of change upon agreed service quality, expressed in SLAs, what makes it the natural place for metrics to be established and monitored against a benchmark. We have proposed a metamodel-based approach to express those kind of metrics [4]. We are currently working on a process model-based approach for checking SLA fulfillment or violation diachronically during service operation, thus requiring a model-based view of process execution. That kind of observation is required in several situations, which basically differ in the origin of events that are fed to the process model and make it progress through its execution:

- *process monitoring*: events are captured and reproduced in real-time;
- *simulation*: events are artificially generated from a stochastic model;
- *process replay*: pre-recorded events (captured during monitoring or simulation) are reproduced;
- *process scenario*: a single process instance flows through the model from creation to extinction, to illustrate one of a set of possible process paths.

Model-based observation of process execution is operationalized by superimposing animation features upon the static model. These process animation features can be used for planning, design, optimization and reengineering of real production, manufacturing, logistic or service provision systems which are likely to be found in most medium to large size companies.

To progress in the aforesaid research thread on model-based SLA checking, we called for a survey on tool support for the animation of IT service process models. Tool surveys are a frequent exercise in technical literature, since both researchers and practitioners require in-depth and up-to-date views of their pros and cons [5, 6]. In our case, since ITSM process models are mostly expressed using Business Process Modeling (BPM) techniques [7], we searched on *IEEE Xplore, SpringerLink, ScienceDirect, ACM Digital Library* and *Wiley Online Library*, with the following search string:

| *"business process model" AND (simulation OR animation OR monitoring) AND "tool survey"* |
|---|

Very few works were found. Only two of them are close enough the problem being tackled, to deserve being mentioned. In the first, seven criteria categories, each with a score, that should be used to evaluate and choose a simulation tool, are proposed [8]. Those criteria cover simulation, modeling, execution, testing and process animation aspects. However animation features are not discussed in detail in this research work. The second paper surveys business process simulation visualization aspects [9]. Although this work does not present classification criteria or tool evaluation, it categorizes the existent simulation animation features in three types: static graphic, dynamic animation and virtual reality.

---

[1] Event Management, Incident Management, Request Fulfillment, Problem Management and Access Management.

The aforementioned lack of surveys on process modeling techniques for visualizing process execution was the main driver for producing this paper. Its main contributions are (i) proposing (in section 2) a set of evaluation criteria (taxonomy) that grants objectivity in the assessment exercise of process animation features provided by BPM tools and, (ii) providing evidence on its feasibility to survey a set of those tools (in section 3). This paper concludes by presenting the summary of collected data and by drawing some conclusions (in section 4).

# 2     A Taxonomy on Tool Support for Process Animation

ITSM managers use existing BPM tools to design and tailor their ITSM processes. In *Service Design,* static BPM constructs are used, while in *Service Operation* we want to trace the process models produced at design time to their execution. The constructs of a static BPM model include stakeholders (aka actors or roles), events, activities, decision points (aka gateways) and flows connecting all of the previous. However, to observe process execution upon a BPM model, we need to overload it with animation constructs such as *process instances, queues, resources, global variables* and *attributes* [10-12].

A *process instance* is like a token that travels in the process workflow. The same process instance can change its "nature" throughout the workflow, for instance representing a client in one activity and a document like an invoice of that same client in another activity. A *queue* is associated with each activity, to hold the process instances while required resources are not available. A *resource* is an asset required to perform an activity upon process instances, such as a person, a computer or a factory machine. *Attributes* and *global variables* represent additional information on the process being executed. An attribute represents data from a single component (e.g. # instances that wait in a given queue), while a global variable represents data from the model as a whole (e.g. # instances that were processed during an execution).

To grant objectivity in our survey and allow replication, we developed the following taxonomy with several criteria organized in groups: *model component animation, animation customization* and *interaction controls* to be described hereafter. Each criterion within a group is expressed on an ordinal scale, where the score 0 is assigned if the evaluated feature is unavailable and the highest score (3) corresponds to the best known state of the art.

## 2.1     Model Component Animation

This group of criteria (*queue, resource and activity animation, process instance animation, sequence flow animation, attributes and global variables animation*) evaluates tool capabilities to animate each modeling component. This animation is usually shown along the component to represent changes of an attribute. The following tables describe the corresponding grading scales.

| Queue, Resource and Activity animation | |
|---|---|
| 0 | **No support** |
| 1 | **Numeric values only:** Numbers are placed near the corresponding activity. |
| 2 | **Bar with shape and color changes:** A bar is shown near the activity and its size and/or color changes over time. |
| 3 | **Animated figure:** An animated figure changes its appearance. |

| Process instance animation | |
|---|---|
| 0 | **No support** |
| 1 | **Indicative default figure animation:** Represents a false type of animation, since it does not show the passage of a process instance through the sequence flow. Instead, the animation only appears if a sequence flow arrow is selected to merely indicate its path in the model. |
| 2 | **Default figure animation:** The process instances are animated throughout process execution, but are all presented with an equal figure. |
| 3 | **Fully animated figure:** Process instances change their representation during process execution in order to express different natures, like a client or a document. |

| Sequence flow animation | |
|---|---|
| 0 | **No support** |
| 1 | **Color change only at process instance passage:** The sequence flow changes its color to show the passage of a process instance. |
| 2 | **Color change:** The sequence flow can be animated with several colors, each with a specific meaning. This can be used to represent if a sequence flow path has more process instances trips than other paths of the model (e.g. with a brighter color). |
| 3 | **Color and form change:** The sequence flow arrows can become wider or thinner and change its color. The sequence flow arrows can become wider with the passage of process instances and its color can also become brighter. This can be useful to distinguish paths in the process that have more traffic than others. |

| Attributes and global variables animation | |
|---|---|
| 0 | **No support** |
| 1 | **Numeric values only:** Attribute or global variables values are shown during process execution. |
| 2 | **Temporal evolution graphics:** Graphics displaying the evolution of attribute or global variables value over time may be shown. |
| 3 | **Multi variable/attribute graphics:** Graphics combining the values of various attributes or/and global variables may be shown. |

## 2.2    Animation Customization

The animation customization group of criteria (*queue and activity customization, resource customization, process instance customization, sequence flow customization, attributes and global variables customization*) refers to the capability of choosing how model components are animated. The grading scales for these criteria are described in the following tables.

**Queue and Activity customization**

| | |
|---|---|
| 0 | No support |
| 1 | **Customization of presented numeric values / bars:** We may choose which component attribute is shown as numeric value and/or animated bar. |
| 2 | **Customization of animated figure:** We may customize an animated figure next to the component. |
| 3 | **Cumulative customization:** Both the customization of presented numeric values/bars (grade 1) and animated figures (grade 2) are supported. |

**Resource customization**

| | |
|---|---|
| 0 | No support |
| 1 | **Customization of presented numeric values / bars and representative figure:** We may choose the representative static figure for the resource and also which resource attribute is shown as numeric value and/or animated bar. |
| 2 | **Customization of animated figure:** We may choose the representative figure for each resource state (e.g.: busy, fail or idle). |
| 3 | **Cumulative customization:** We may customize the presented numeric values / bars and representative figure (grade 1), as well as the animated figure (grade 2). |

**Process instance customization**

| | |
|---|---|
| 0 | No support |
| 1 | **Customization of representative figure:** We may choose the representative figure for process instances. |
| 2 | **Customization of figure by sequence flow:** We may choose the representative figure of process instances for each sequence flow. |
| 3 | **Customization of figure changing logic:** We may specify a logic that defines which figure should be shown for each process instance. For instance, the figure may change depending on the value or range of an attribute. |

**Sequence flow customization**

| | |
|---|---|
| 0 | No support |
| 1 | **Customization of color:** We may choose the color that is presented when a process instance passes in the sequence flow. |
| 2 | **Customization of color changes:** We may choose how the sequence flow changes color. It is possible to choose the colors, the attribute and attribute value that make the sequence flow present each color. |
| 3 | **Customization of color and shape changes:** It is possible to customize the change in sequence flow thickness and color. |

**Attributes and global variables customization**

| | |
|---|---|
| 0 | No support |
| 1 | **Customization of numeric values:** We may choose attributes and global variables to be presented in a chosen position of the model as a numeric value. |
| 2 | **Customization of graphics:** We may customize graphics that represent attributes and global variables. |
| 3 | **Cumulative customization:** We may customize the numeric values (grade 1), as well as the graphics (grade 2). |

## 2.3    Interactivity Controls

The interactivity controls group of criteria (*animation speed control, animation interaction control, animation visualization control*) includes the type of controls that enable the user to interact with process execution.

| Animation speed controls | |
| --- | --- |
| 0 | **No support** |
| 1 | **Play controls:** We may play, pause, resume and stop the process execution. |
| 2 | **Speed controls:** We may execute the process faster or slower and go directly to a chosen date/time. |
| 3 | **Cumulative control:** We may use both the play (grade 1) and speed (grade 2) controls. |

| Animation interaction controls | |
| --- | --- |
| 0 | **No support** |
| 1 | **Path choice control:** We may flow through the model, following a process instance and deciding where the instance should go in the gateways. |
| 2 | **Visual interactive animation control:** We may control model components by manipulating their attributes, as well as global variables. This type of animation helps understanding model behavior and validate it [13, 14]. |
| 3 | **Cumulative control:** We may use the path choice control (grade 1), as well as the visual interactive animation control (grade 2). |

| Animation visualization controls | |
| --- | --- |
| 0 | **No support** |
| 1 | **Zoom and viewport:** We may zoom and change the viewport. |
| 2 | **Animation filter:** We may choose which components to be animated. |
| 3 | **Cumulative control:** We may use the zoom and viewport features (grade 1), as well as the animation filter (grade 2). |

# 3    Tools Survey

Relevance, diversity and availability were the three basic criteria used in the tool sample selection. *Relevance*, in this context, stands for the availability of rich model animation features. We discarded tools that missed the description of those features in their online documentation. Regarding *diversity*, we tried to look at diverse origins, instead of limiting the survey to a limited target (e.g. just simulation tools) or modeling notation (e.g. just BPMN [15] tools). Last, but not least, *availability* had a considerable influence on our tool sampling process, since the only way to effectively evaluate a tool is by being able to obtain a fully functional version of it for a sufficient period of time. Several tools had only limited functionality trials or could not be obtained easily for evaluation and therefore could not be considered in this survey.

Although moderate in size, the chosen sample of six tools (see Table 1) meets the previous criteria.

**Table 1.** Tool survey sample

| TOOL (VERSION) / PRODUCER | NOTATIONS | SCOPE |
|---|---|---|
| Arena (14) / Rockwell Automation | Proprietary | Simulation |
| SIMUL8 (2012) / SIMUL8 Corporation | Propriet., BPMN | Simulation |
| WebSphere Business Modeler Advanced  (7.0) / IBM | BPMN | Modeling |
| Savvion Process Modeler (8.0) / Progress | BPMN | Modeling |
| TIBCO Business Studio (Community Edition, 2012) / TIBCO Soft. | BPMN | Modeling |
| ProM UITopia (6) / Eindhoven Technical University | Petri nets, EPC, BPMN | Mining |

Each tool will now be reviewed, in a separate subsection, regarding the aforementioned animation features. To facilitate the assessment exercise, an illustration of an animation example is presented. That illustration has a set of numbers placed on top of it to identify the model components' animations. The corresponding scores, for each of the 15 evaluation criteria in the proposed taxonomy, are presented jointly in section 3.7.

### 3.1    Arena

Arena is a general-purpose simulation tool that can be used in diverse systems such as assembling lines and call centers. It has rich animation capabilities and is well-established in the marketplace, with several books dedicated to its usage [10, 12, 16]. It uses a straightforward proprietary notation where modeling constructs map easily to those described in section 2.

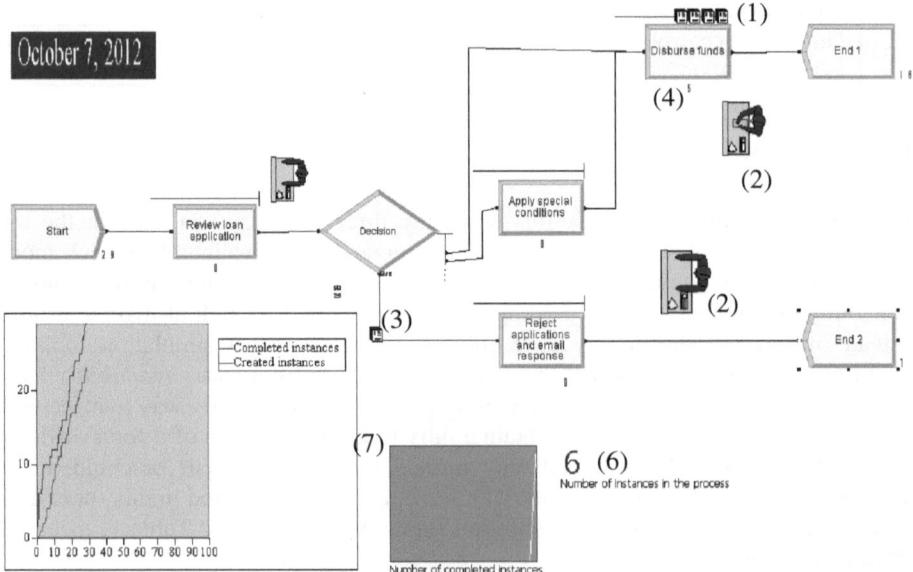

**Fig. 1.** Arena animation example

In Fig. 1 is possible to identify the queues (1) filled with several process instances on top of an activity, as well as the process instances (3) that travel the sequence flow. It is also possible to see a global variable (6) exposed as a numeric value, a graphic representation (7) of a global variable and the combination of two variables in the same graphic. The resources (2) change the appearance according to its state, as seen in Fig. 1, where two idle resources and a busy one are presented. On the other hand, activities (4) show only the number of process instances being processed.

Customization is also provided in Arena, by allowing choosing the animated figure for all components, except for activities and sequence flows. It is also possible to customize graphics for attribute/global variable presentation. For the activities it is only possible to customize the numeric values presented by choosing which activity attributes should be shown.

## 3.2    Simul8

This is also a general purpose simulation tool. The evaluated version supports modeling with BPMN, but the animation capabilities were not as good as the ones that the tool provides for its proprietary modeling language, what lead us to choose the latter.

In Fig. 2 the queues (1) are represented as a tank together with a numeric value that shows the number of process instances waiting in the queue. The resources (2) do not change according to their state, instead, are the activities (4) that have an associated

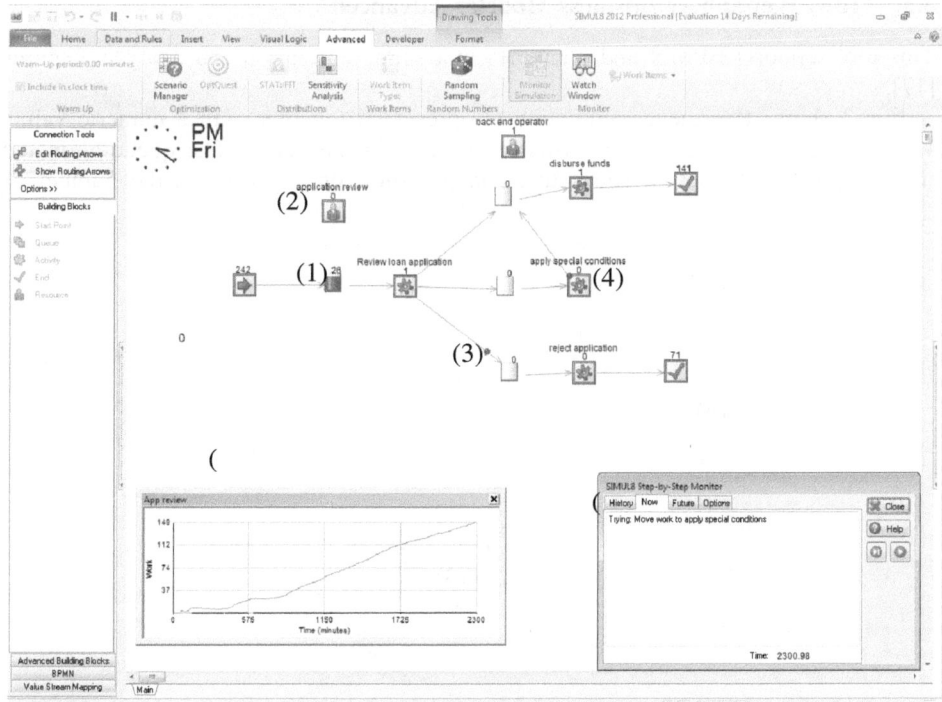

**Fig. 2.** Simul8 animation example

state (e.g.: idle, busy or fail) and change its presentation according to it. It is possible to show the movements of resources from one activity to another when a resource is allocated to more than one activity. There is also a numeric value next to the resource figure that indicates the number of resources from that group that are not being used by an activity. Process instances can be programmed to change their appearance. In Fig. 2 instances (3) appear as red dots. Simul8 supports the presentation of attributes as numeric values and also supports graphics (6) that can combine several attributes/global variables.

Simul8 provides animation customization capabilities, namely in the "visual logic" feature that allows the user to configure changes to activity, process instance and resource appearance. It is possible to choose from some available animations for the queue presentation. Regarding the resources, it is only possible to choose the representative static figure for each resource group, while process instances can have their figure changed over time. Simul8 allows customizing the activity figure for each state, as well as constructing graphics that can be composed by attributes and/or global variables. Concerning the interactivity controls, Simul8 provides a feature called "monitor simulation" (7) that enables the user to see the log of events, the event being processed and the future events that will be performed. This feature enables also the user to play an event at a time. Regarding the speed controls, Simul8 allows to play, pause and stop, choose the animation speed and jump the animation to a certain point in the simulation.

### 3.3     IBM WebSphere Business Modeler Advanced 7.0

This tool supports BPMN and combines modeling, simulation and analysis features [17].

Fig. 3 shows the queues animation (1) presented together with a numeric value, which indicates the number of instances waiting in the queue. The queue animated figure consists in a set of sticks that change color, one by one, as the number of

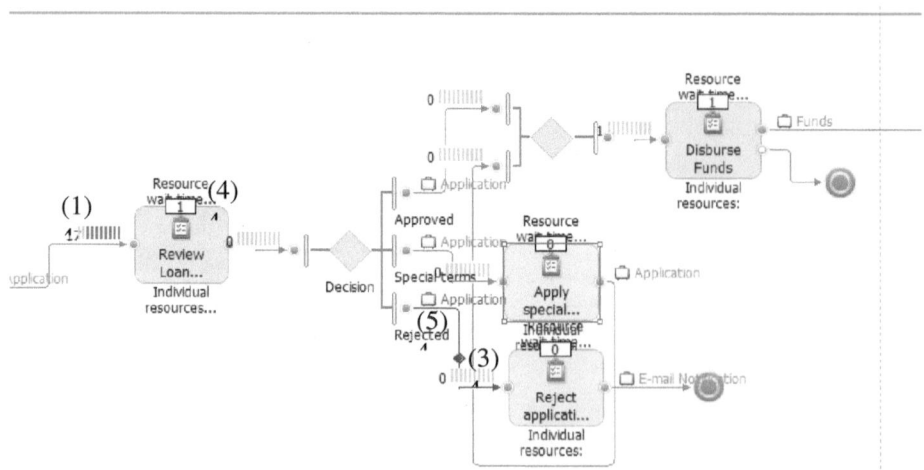

**Fig. 3.** Websphere animation example

process instances increases. When the queue becomes full, all sticks change to red. Process instances (3) are presented with the same figure (red marker). In Fig. 3 we can also see the activities animation (4) with the number of instances being processed and also the color change from green to grey indicating that the activity is being executed. Sequence flow (5) turns red when an instance travels through it.

Websphere does not support any type of customization for the animation, and regarding the interaction controls it features only start, pause and stop.

### 3.4     Progress Savvion Process Modeler 8.0

This business process modeling tool supports BPMN and has some simulation animation features [18]. Its market relevance is corroborated by Gartner [19].

Although its animation features are not impressive, since it only covers activities and sequence flows, it has some aspects that deserve some attention, like its ability to identify high throughput activities, as well as possible bottlenecks [18]. As represented in Fig. 4, an activity (4) turns red if the total of its processed instances is greater than the average of all activities processed instances. It turns blue if that total is less than the average and white if the total is equal to the average. Besides, the total number of processed instances for an activity is also shown. The sequence flow (5) follows the same color changing logic as the activities, but based on the number of process instances that travelled through the sequence flow.

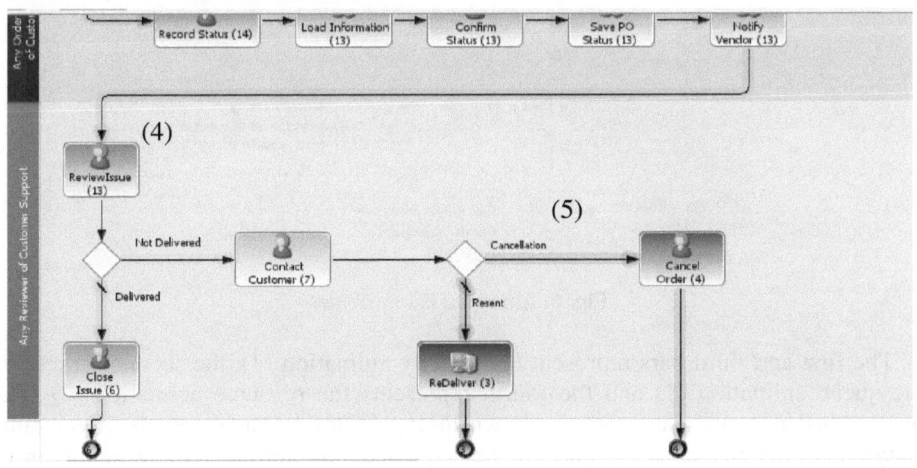

**Fig. 4.** Savvion animation example

Animation customization is not supported for any component and the only provided interactivity controls are the speed control, start, pause and stop.

### 3.5     Tibco Business Studio Community Edition

Tibco Business Studio is another example of a tool that provides business process modeling with BPMN and has simulation capabilities. Tibco is also a major player in this area, as identified by Gartner [19].

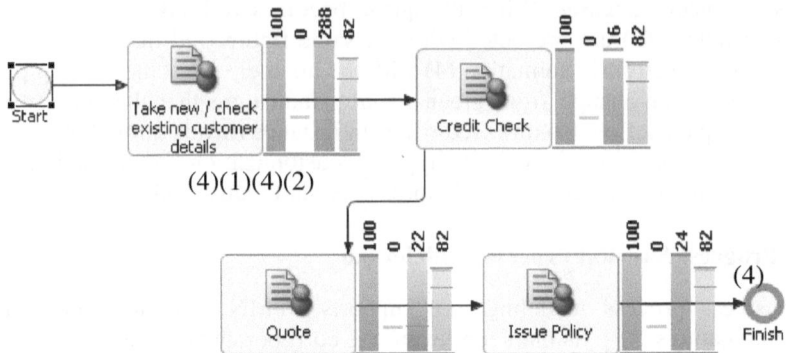

**Fig. 5.** Tibco animation example

Business Studio animation features include four bars placed at the right side of the corresponding activity. Those bars change colors from green to blue and finally to red. Each bar represents a different attribute and has a numeric value on top. The bar attributes are presented in Fig. 6.

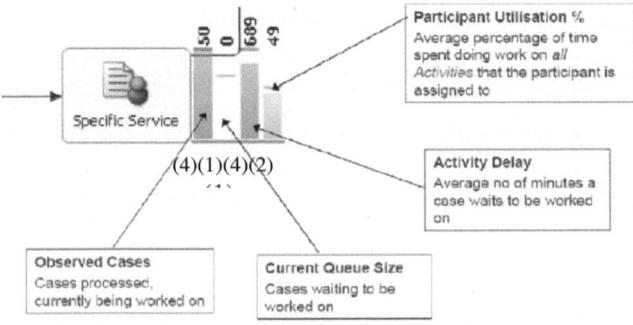

**Fig. 6.** Animated bar attributes

The first and third bars represent the activity animation (4), the second represents the queue animation (1) and the fourth represents the resource animation (2). The process instances animation is not shown in any figure, but as the evaluation results suggest, it only indicates the path of the sequence flow through the presentation of several colored circles that pass through the sequence flow continuously.

The tool does not support any kind of animation customization and the interactivity controls provided are just the animation speed controls that allow controlling the animation speed, as well as to play, pause and stop the animation.

### 3.6 ProM UITopia

ProM UITopia is the only process mining tool in our sample. Its creators claim that business process models can be seen as roadmaps and several cartography ideas (e.g. difference between highways and local roads representation in a map) can be used to increase models' understandability [20]. The roadmap metaphor contributes with animation innovations that are not present in the other analyzed tools.

ProM UITopia animation is compared with a movie that shows process execution traces. In ProM the latter were captured through process mining techniques, instead of being generated by a simulation. The implementation of the cartography metaphor is as follows: color brightness and thickness of sequence flows change during animation (5), depending on the number of instances that traversed them. Process instances (3) are presented with a white circle that leaves a trail as a comet. Activities (4) also change its color going from a darker red to a brighter one as its number of execution increases.

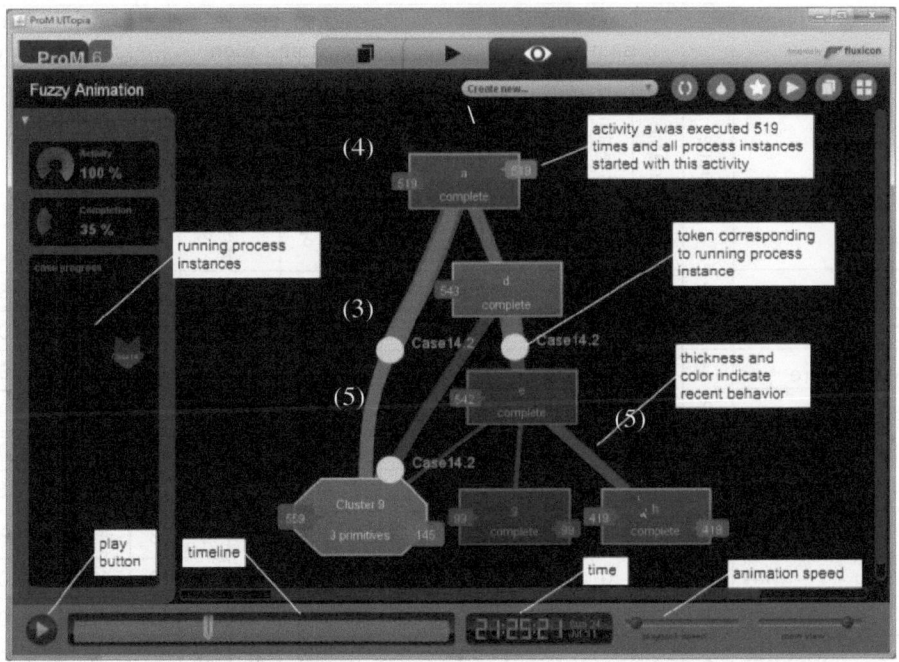

**Fig. 7.** ProM UITopia animation example (source: [20])

Animation customization is not supported for all model components and animation interactivity only includes speed, pause and play controls.

### 3.7   Results Summary

The summary of the assessment exercise performed with the support of the proposed taxonomy for process model animation features is presented in Table 2. Its last five rows present some statistics on the observed scores for each of the 15 criteria: the maximum score observed, the minimum score, the most frequent score observed (mode), the median score and finally the sum of the scores across the whole sample. The latter can be considered as a measure of the relative importance that tool makers in the sample assign to the animation characteristics underlying each criteria of the proposed taxonomy.

Results show a wide dispersion on the availability of the underlying animation features, since the full classification range (0 to 3) was observed for the vast majority of the criteria. The evident exception is the ability to customize the animation of *sequence flows,* the only modeling element where we could not find support for that feature. Regarding the central tendency of the scores, we can observe that both the median and the mode vary a lot across the 15 evaluation criteria. Also the sum of the scores presents a wide variability.

**Table 2.** Sample scores and statistics

| | Component animation | | | | | | Animation customization | | | | | | Animation interactivity | | |
|---|---|---|---|---|---|---|---|---|---|---|---|---|---|---|---|
| | Queue | Resource | Process instance | Activity | Sequence Flow | Attribs / global vars | Queue | Resource | Process Instance | Activity | Sequence Flow | Attribs / global vars | Speed controls | Interaction controls | Visualization controls |
| Arena | 3 | 3 | 2 | 1 | 0 | 3 | 3 | 3 | 2 | 1 | 0 | 3 | 3 | 3 | 3 |
| Simul8 | 3 | 1 | 3 | 3 | 0 | 3 | 3 | 1 | 3 | 3 | 0 | 3 | 3 | 2 | 0 |
| Websphere | 2 | 0 | 2 | 1 | 1 | 0 | 0 | 0 | 0 | 0 | 0 | 0 | 1 | 0 | 0 |
| Savvion | 0 | 0 | 0 | 3 | 2 | 0 | 0 | 0 | 0 | 0 | 0 | 0 | 3 | 0 | 0 |
| Tibco | 2 | 2 | 1 | 2 | 0 | 0 | 0 | 0 | 0 | 0 | 0 | 0 | 3 | 0 | 0 |
| ProM UITopia | 0 | 0 | 2 | 3 | 3 | 0 | 0 | 0 | 0 | 0 | 0 | 0 | 3 | 0 | 1 |
| MAX | 3 | 3 | 3 | 3 | 3 | 3 | 3 | 3 | 3 | 3 | 0 | 3 | 3 | 3 | 3 |
| MIN | 0 | 0 | 0 | 1 | 0 | 0 | 0 | 0 | 0 | 0 | 0 | 0 | 1 | 0 | 0 |
| MODE | 3 | 0 | 2 | 1 | 0 | 0 | 0 | 0 | 0 | 0 | 0 | 0 | 3 | 0 | 0 |
| MEDIAN | 2 | 1 | 2 | 2 | 1 | 0 | 0 | 0 | 0 | 0 | 0 | 0 | 3 | 0 | 0 |
| TOTAL | 10 | 6 | 10 | 13 | 6 | 6 | 6 | 4 | 5 | 4 | 0 | 6 | 16 | 5 | 4 |

We have produced an ordering of the sampled tools regarding their achieved values on the 15 evaluation criteria proposed in our taxonomy. On Table 3 we have calculated a final score for each tool that allowed us to rank them. That aggregated score is a weighted sum of the frequencies of each of the animation features. The weight in that sum is the value of each score. For instance, the final score of Arena was calculated as follows:

$$Score_{Arena} = 9 * 3 + 2 * 2 + 2 * 1 + 2 * 0 = 33$$

**Table 3.** Final rank of surveyed tools regarding animation features

| Tool | Score 3 | Score 2 | Score 1 | Score 0 | FINAL SCORE |
|------|---------|---------|---------|---------|-------------|
| Arena | 9 | 2 | 2 | 2 | 33 |
| Simul8 | 9 | 1 | 2 | 3 | 31 |
| ProM UITopia | 3 | 1 | 1 | 10 | 12 |
| Tibco | 1 | 3 | 1 | 10 | 10 |
| Savvion | 2 | 1 | 0 | 12 | 8 |
| Websphere | 0 | 2 | 3 | 10 | 7 |

# 4    Conclusions and Future Work

We have found roughly two groups of tools when it comes to the support of process execution animation features. On one side we have the process simulation tools (*Arena* and *Simul8*) that have overall very sophisticated animation features. On the other side we have the process mining (*ProM*) and process modeling tools (*Tibco, Savvion* and *Websphere*). The latter lag behind considerably on animation and customization features for attributes and global variables, as well as on interaction and visualization controls.

A more interesting conclusion of our survey was that the provided support for process model animation features underlying each criteria of the proposed taxonomy is very diverse, although a few of those animation features (queue, process instance and activity animation and speed controls) have a much stronger support and wider coverage. On the low end we have activity, resource and sequence flow customization, as well as the availability of visualization controls. Producing a sound explanation for the fact that process modeling tool producers put such a diverse emphasis on the support of the process model animation features would require a larger sample. Some candidate explanatory variables for this variability are the targeted application domain and the process observation objective (e.g. monitoring, mining, simulation, replay or scenario construction).

This survey was particularly useful in providing us an updated view on the current state-of-the-art of process animation features, since we have provisions for deploying our metamodel-based approach to SLA dynamic checking for ITSM process models in a tool with such features. However, we should be aware of two important threats to the external validity of this survey. First, due to the small sample size, we cannot generalize our results. Second, those results will be outdated in a few years' time, due to likely improvements in new versions of the tools.

As a consequence, we believe the more lasting and valuable contribution of this paper lies on our proposal for the classification of model animation features in process execution. We expect other researchers will take it as a basis for more comprehensive assessments in terms of tools' coverage.

**Acknowledgment.** This work is partly supported by grant PEst-OE/EEI/UI0527/2011 of Centro de Informática e Tecnologias da Informação (CITI/FCT/UNL).

# References

[1] Schaaf, T.: The IT Infrastructure Library (ITIL) – An Introduction for Practitioners and Researchers. In: Bandara, A.K., Burgess, M. (eds.) AIMS 2007. LNCS, vol. 4543, pp. 235–235. Springer, Heidelberg (2007)

[2] Correia, A., Brito e Abreu, F., Amaral, V.: SLALOM: a Language for SLA Specification and Monitoring. Presented at the INFORUM 2011 (session: Engenharia Conduzida por Modelos), Coimbra, Portugal (2011)

[3] Correia, A., Brito e Abreu, F., Amaral, V.: SLAME: A Service Level Agreements Method for Elicitation. Presented at the $11^a$ Conferência da Associação Portuguesa de Sistemas de Informação (CAPSI 2011), Lisbon, Portugal (2011)

[4] Brito e Abreu, F., de Braganca, R., da Porciuncula, V., Freitas, J.M., Costa, J.C.: Definition and Validation of Metrics for ITSM Process Models. In: 2010 Seventh International Conference on the Quality of Information and Communications Technology (QUATIC), pp. 79–88 (2010)

[5] Grepl, R.: Real-Time Control Prototyping in MATLAB/Simulink: Review of tools for research and education in mechatronics. Presented at the International Conference on Mechatronics (ICM 2011) (2011)

[6] Martignoni, R.: Global Sourcing of Software Development - A Review of Tools and Services. Presented at the Fourth International Conference on Global Software Engineering (ICGSE 2009) (2009)

[7] Dockal, L.: Tool for supporting IT Infrastructure Library based on integration of Business Process Management system and MS SharePoint. Diploma thesis, Faculty of Informatics, Masarik University, Brno, Czech Republic (2012)

[8] Tewoldeberhan, T.W., Verbraeck, A., Valentin, E., Bardonnet, G.: An evaluation and selection methodology for discrete-event simulation software. Presented at the 34th Winter Simulation Conference (2002)

[9] Du, X., Gu, C., Zhu, N.: A survey of business process simulation visualization. Presented at the International Conference on Quality, Reliability, Risk, Maintenance, and Safety Engineering (ICQR2MSE) (2012)

[10] Chung, C.A.: Simulation Modeling Handbook: A Practical Approach. CRC Press, Inc. (2003)

[11] Tumay, K.: Business process simulation. Presented at the 27th Conference on Winter Simulation, Arlington, Virginia, United States (1995)

[12] Kelton, W.D., Sadowski, R.P., Sadowski, D.A.: Simulation with Arena. McGraw-Hill (2002)

[13] Rekapalli, P.V., Martinez, J.C.: A message-based architechture to enable runtime user interaction on concurrent simulation-animations of construction operations. Presented at the 39th Conference on Winter Simulation, Washington, D.C. (2007)

[14] Rohrer, M.W.: Seeing is believing: the importance of visualization in manufacturing simulation. Presented at the 32nd Conference on Winter Simulation, Orlando, Florida (2000)

[15] OMG, Business Process Model and Notation (BPMN) - Version 2.0, vol. formal/2011-01-03, ed: Object Management Group, p. 538 (2011)

[16] Altiok, T., Melamed, B.: Simulation Modeling and Analysis With Arena. Academic Press (2007)

[17]  IBM. WebSphere Business Modeler Advanced (October 28, 2012),
      `http://www-01.ibm.com/software/integration/`
      `wbimodeler/advanced/`
[18]  P. Software, Progress Savion Business Manager 8.0: Process Modeler User's Guide:
      Progress (2012)
[19]  Sinur, J., Hill, J.B.: Magic Quadrant for Business Process Management Suites, Gartner
      (2010)
[20]  van. de Aalst, W.M.P., de Leoni, M., ter Hofstede, A.H.M.: Process Mining And Visual
      Analytics: Breathing life into business process models. In: Floares, A. (ed.)
      Computational Intelligence. Nova Science Publishers, Hauppauge (2012)

# Factors Influencing the Internationalization of Services Firms: The Case of Design, Engineering and Architecture Consulting Firms

Maria R.A. Moreira[1], Miguel A.S. Maia[1], Paulo S.A. Sousa[1,2], and Raquel F.Ch. Meneses[1]

[1] Faculty of Economics, Universidade do Porto,
R.Dr. Roberto Frias, s/n, 4200-464 Porto, Portugal
[2] LIAAD-INESC Porto LA, Portugal
mrosario@fep.up.pt, miguelmaia_esmz@hotmail.com,
{paulus,raquelm}@fep.up.pt

**Abstract.** Globalization has created countless opportunities for the internationalization of a wide range of services. Recent technological innovations associated with the reduction or elimination of trade barriers, resulted in an exponential expansion of service firms. This paper analyzes the internal and external factors that influence the decision to operate internationally. The hypotheses are empirically examined through a survey sent to 322 firms from the design, architecture and engineering sector. Multivariate analysis is used to ascertain the main determinants of internationalization in these firms.

The findings indicate that the main reasons underlying the internationalization of these service firms are the size of the firm, the competitive environment and the staff's degree of international experience. These factors, which influence the management's attitudes toward operating internationally, determine the firm's degree of internationalization. Moreover, firms that have a high number of senior managers with a graduate course and higher skills in foreign languages are more prone to internationalize. Some practical implications are presented for service firms that are in the process of internationalizing.

**Keywords:** Internationalization, service firms, exportation, influencing factors.

## 1 Introduction

The globalization of businesses and recent technological innovations as well as the reduction or even elimination of trade barriers and the celebration of international service trade agreements (General Agreement on Trade in Services and the European Union Service Directive), have created numerous opportunities for the service industry in the world economy.

The service sector represents about 67% of the GDP worldwide and about 55% of the GDP of developed countries [1]. In the OECD countries, the service sector has been strongly converted to generate employment, being responsible for more than

J.F. e Cunha, M. Snene, and H. Nóvoa (Eds.): IESS 2013, LNBIP 143, pp. 246–262, 2013.
© Springer-Verlag Berlin Heidelberg 2013

70% of total employment. However, in the majority of these countries, the increase in productivity is much slower, a fact that led the OECD to stress the need for further research in order to detect how services can be more competitive and go international. This is also the reason why we decided to study the factors that influence the internationalization of services. The literature has generally only provided models and theories focusing specifically on the internationalization process of industrial organizations, and some of the models and approaches to services still lack empirical validation [2-3]. In addition there are conflicting views in the literature on the applicability of the existing theories to services [4-5]. Indeed, several studies (e.g. [6]) highlight that future research on the internationalization of management consultancy should aim to build on the existing exploratory effort, using a quantitative research design approach.

The main aim of this study was to analyze the factors that influence design, architecture and engineering consulting firms to operate internationally, and to quantify the impact of these factors. Although a number of studies have explored this matter, they are mostly based on a single case study approach (e.g. [7]), and not a quantitative one. To accomplish this objective, we analyzed the companies' internal and external features, their structure, perceived barriers to internationalization and the determinants behind the choice of a certain country. The research methodology used, in line with studies in the area, was the quantitative analysis of surveys sent to 322 firms from the design, architecture and engineering consulting sector. An exploratory analysis of different hypotheses was also conducted based on the literature review.

Moreover, multivariate analysis was employed to ascertain the main determinants of internationalization and the results were compared with those from studies on other countries in order to determine similarities and differences among distinct economic, geographic and social realities.

This paper begins with a brief review of the relevant literature on the aspects involved in the research (services' features, internationalization strategies and theories). Subsequently, the methodology used is described, the results of statistical analysis are presented and the analysis and quantification of the impact of the factors that influence design, architecture and engineering consulting firms to operate internationally is made (aim 2). The paper ends with the conclusion, describing the study's limitations and paths for future research.

## 2    Theoretical Background

Several studies (e.g. [5], [8]) identify the features that distinguish services from manufactured goods: (1) intangibility (services are not transportable or storable), (2) inseparability (production and consumption occur simultaneously), (3) perishability (services cannot be saved and must be consumed as they are produced), and (4) heterogeneity (services are unique and difficult to standardize). Intangibility is, according to Bateson and Hoffman [9], the mother of all the differences between services and goods. This feature constitutes a challenge to all firms that want to enter new markets, especially international ones, due to linguistic and cultural barriers. Moreover, services have different degrees of these characteristics: there is a continuum between pure goods and pure services.

## 2.1     Internationalization Strategies in Services

When studying the different forms of internationalization, it appears that export activities tend to be more risky when made by service organizations than those conducted in industrial organizations [10]. This occurs due to the fact that the products / goods of services have, as we have seen, distinct features [8]. Most of the literature on internationalization and its strategies are guided by the needs of the industrial sector [10]. There is therefore a lack of literature on the strategies used by service providers.

According to Grönroos [10] and [11], the literature is divided into three streams. In the first stream, some authors (e.g., [12-13]) argue that the internationalization of service companies and manufacturing industries go through a similar process and that there is no need to adapt existing models of internationalization. A second group of authors (e.g., [14-15]) argues that there are significant differences between the internationalization of a product (material) and a service (immaterial/intangible). A third group of authors (e.g., [16-17]) is of the opinion that the internationalization of service firms cannot be considered in general, since there should be a distinction between different types of services. Erramilli [16] divides the services into *hard services* (e.g., architectural design, insurance) and *soft services* (e.g., catering, healthcare).

Five key strategies for the internationalization of services can be identified regardless of the characteristics and type of service: 1) Direct export, 2) Export in partnership; 3) Direct entry, 4) Indirect entry (joint venture with local company); 5) Electronic commerce [10]. The strategies are not mutually exclusive and, in some cases, are similar to the strategies of the companies that produce goods [10].

The literature shows ambiguities ([2], [10]) and different perspectives regarding the internationalization strategies of service firms ([12], [15], [18-19]), mostly as a consequence of the features of services. Concerning the entry modes, it is unanimous that, in service companies, they are similar to those used by manufacturing companies [10]. The literature also stresses the use of new technologies, such as the internet, as a strategy and entry mode for service firms [10], [20].

## 2.2     The Applicability of Internationalization Theories to Service Providers

Several theories have been presented as approaches that explain the internationalization of firms which may be applied to the service sector. These can be divided into two major groups [3]: economic approaches (Internalization, Eclectic Paradigm) and behavioral approaches (Uppsala School, Networks, Business Strategy and Resource-Based View). The description of each theory is summarized in Table 1.

## 2.3     Theories of Internationalization and Service Providers

The theories listed above describe the different aspects of the complex phenomenon of the internationalization of firms. However, according to Coviello and McAuley [41], those theories do not compete nor are they mutually exclusive, but rather, they complement each other. Each theory has its own specific advantages and disadvantages [14].

**Table 1.** Summary of the theories of internationalization

| Internatio-nalization theories | Definition/description | Authors |
|---|---|---|
| Internaliza-tion Theory | The theory is based on the analysis of transaction costs. The axiom of the general internalization theory is that firms choose the location of internationalization, as well as the maintenance mode in the market, whereby the overall transaction costs are minimized. | [3], [21] |
| Eclectic Paradigm | The theory is based on transaction costs and analyzes the transfers and rewards of the firms' ownership. It points to several reasons for companies to start operations abroad: market demand, increasing efficiency, seeking strategic assets and capabilities outside their country. According to Andersen (27), the eclectic paradigm is a synthesis of the internalization theory and the transaction costs. | [15], [21-24] |
| Uppsala School | The Uppsala model examines the expansion to foreign markets, trying to identify the various stages at which such expansion occurs. It describes the internationalization as a behavioural process through which a company moulds itself to the internationalization process in incremental and sequential stages, as a result of the development of knowledge and learning. The model advocates internationalization in stages due to the lack of knowledge and due to uncertainty. | [21], [25-27] |
| Theory of Networks | The theory argues that the development in the international market does not only depend on the combination of the company's competitive advantages. The success of internationalization depends on the networks and on the strategic alliances developed. These networks involve both external and internal networks. | [28-34] |
| Business Strategy | According to this, companies take into account a wide range of variables when looking at the benefits and costs of internationalization. Two groups of variables are identified as relevant: external factors (e.g., workforce, market's accessibility and attractiveness, cultural distance, ease of transportation) and internal factors (e.g., size, industry, capital resources, and experience in international trade). | [3], [35] |
| Resource-Based View | This view argues that firms with scarce, valuable and inimitable resources generate competitive advantages, and thus enable higher than normal rates of return. The attributes of the companies are the fundamental drivers of performance and the sustainable advantage necessary for internationalization. | [36-40] |

Over the last decade, there has been a lively debate on the applicability of stage models of internationalization to service firms [42]. The criticism is centred on a series of studies that found that the conventional theory of stages of internationalization (Uppsala Model) does not adequately explain the process of internationalization of certain businesses, especially small [30].

Regarding the theory of networks, the literature emphasizes the collaborative nature of the internationalization of services based on knowledge and contact networks ([14], [30]). However, due to the nature of the services, they require greater customer-producer interaction than goods, which hinders the standardization of the product, since each customer wants a custom service. Moreover, this theory focuses only on the interdependencies between the actors [3]. Thus, the theory of networks provides only a partial explanation for the internationalization of services and needs to be complemented with broader aspects of company strategy [3].

The approach to business strategy, compared with the approaches mentioned above, is more comprehensive and seems to be flexible enough to deal with the development, characteristics and objectives of service companies [3]. Additionally, it is able to capture the influence of the environment [14]. One criticism, though, notes that this approach places excessive focus on the value of business characteristics, rather than on value creation.

# 3    Methodology

Based on the conceptual model presented by Patterson [4], we studied the relationships between the different determinants and the tendency of service firms to globalize.

## 3.1    Key Elements in the Decision to Internationalize and Hypotheses

To identify the key elements, it is necessary to determine, in accordance with the theories of internationalization, which features to include in the study and which theories best explain the internationalization of services.

The model proposed by Patterson [4] uses more than one underlying theory for the construction of its analysis scheme. The conceptual model adopted is based on the following theoretical views: the Resource-Based View, the Business Strategy and the Uppsala Model. The theories suggest several categories of factors that need to be incorporated in the model. In this context and in line with Patterson [4], the following five factors should be used as key elements: 1) Capacities and characteristics of firms, 2) Barriers to internationalization, 3) Perceptions of the risks and benefits of internationalization; 4) Competitiveness; and 5) Management features. (Figure 1).

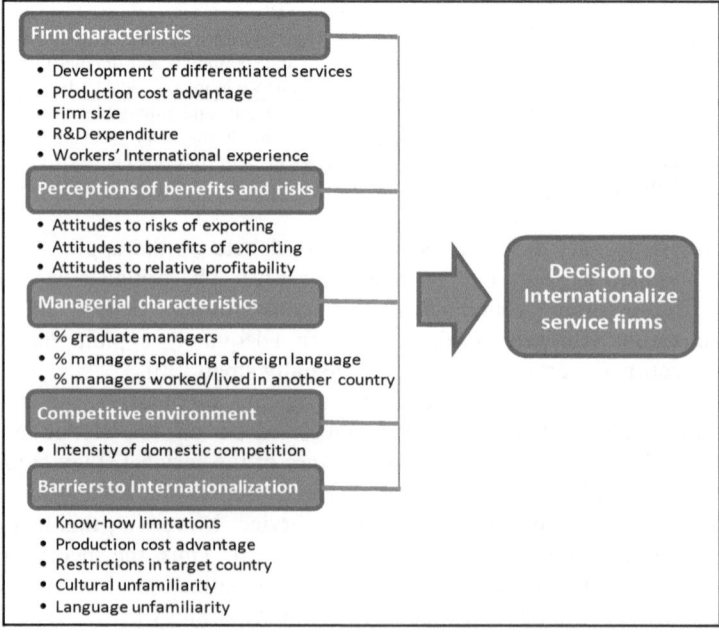

**Fig. 1.** Determinants of the service companies' decision to internationalize (Adapted from Patterson [4])

Based on each key element, a set of hypotheses were formulated, as discussed by several authors, which are summarized in the Table 2.

**Table 2.** Research hypotheses

| Key elements | Research hypothesis | Authors |
|---|---|---|
| Capacities and characteristics of companies | H1- Firm size is positively related with the decision to operate internationally. | [4], [44] |
| | H1a: Companies that have a higher number of employees with international experience are the most active internationally. | [45-46] |
| | H1b: Companies that have advantages in production costs or differentiated products are the most active internationally. | [4], [47-48] |
| | H1c: Firms that have higher investments in R&D maintain more regular contacts with international markets. | [4] |
| Barriers to internationalization | H2 – Existing restrictions in the destination country (customs costs and initial investment costs) are perceived as the main obstacle to internationalization. | [4], [49] |
| | H2a: Unawareness of linguistic and cultural differences of the foreign markets are perceived as a major barrier to internationalization. | [49-51] |
| | H2b: Limitations in know-how are perceived as the most significant obstacle to internationalization | [4] |
| | H2c: Protectionism of local technicians and companies is a barrier to the internationalization of service firms. | Explora-tory |
| Perception s risks and benefits of internat. | H3 - The attitudes and perceptions regarding the risk of internationalization differ between companies operating and not operating internationally. | [4], [52-54] |
| | H3a: Companies that do not operate internationally regard internationalization as being more expensive, with higher risks and less profitable than firms that already have contacts with the international market. | [52], [54-55] |
| Competi-tiveness | H4 - Companies that experience (and understand) the high competitive intensity of domestic markets, have greater contact with international markets than those who do not face such domestic pressures. | [4], [53] |
| Management features | H5 - Companies with a higher number of graduate managers maintain more regular contacts with international markets. | [4-5] |
| | H5a: Companies with a higher number of employees with skills in foreign languages maintain more regular contacts with international markets. | [4-5] |
| | H5b: Companies that have a large number of workers who have worked abroad are the most active internationally. | [4-5], [56] |

## 3.2    'Theoretical' Model Specification

According to the theoretical approaches examined in the previous sections and from the key elements and hypotheses described above, we present the determinants that may explain the decision to internationalize in the service sector. They are grouped according to their characteristics and following the Patterson (2004) model:

1) *Capacities and characteristics of companies*, including firm size (Size), the number of services provided by the company (Num_Serv), and the level of investment in R&D (Inv_RD);
2) *Barriers to internationalization*, which includes the number of perceived barriers (Num_Barr), the importance attributed to the initial investment costs (Imp_InvCosts), the importance given to cultural differences (Imp_DifCult) and language (Imp_DifLang), the importance attributed to know-how limitations (Imp_LimKH), perceptions of protectionism for local technicians (Imp_ProtTecn), and the degree of unfamiliarity with the foreign market (Unfam_Mkt);
3) *Perceptions of the risk and benefits of internationalization*, which encompasses the perceived risk of operating internationally (Perc_Risk), the perception of the cost (Perc_Cost), and the perception of its profitability (Perc_Profit);

4) *Competitiveness*, which includes the intensity of national competitiveness (Int_Competitive);

5) *Management features*, which covers the number of graduate managers (Num_GManager), the foreign language skills of managers (Num_Lang), and the employees' international work experience (Int_Exp).

In this study, we used multivariable estimation techniques to assess the extent to which variables such as firm size, degree of skilled personnel or the importance of market diversification affects the decision to internationalize. The following equation represents the 'theoretical' model adopted:

$$Dec\_Internat = \begin{pmatrix} Size; \ Num\_Serv; Inv\_RD \\ Num\_Barr; \ Imp\_InvCosts; Imp\_DifCult; Imp\_DifLang; Imp\_LimKH; Imp\_ProtTecn; Unfam\_Mkt \\ Perc\_Risk; \ Perc\_Cost; \ Perc\_Profit \\ Int\_Competitive \\ Num\_GManager; \ Num\_Lang; \ Int\_Exp \end{pmatrix}$$

The following table (Table 3) summarizes the determinants considered in the 'theoretical' model as well as information on the sources and the expected effect on the decision to internationalize.

**Table 3.** Determinants of the 'theoretical' model

| Group | Determinant | Variable measurement | Source | Expected signal |
|---|---|---|---|---|
| Decision to Internationalize | | Yes/No question regarding operate/have contact internationally | Question-naire | |
| Characteristics of companies | Firm Size | Turnover (2009) | SABI | + |
| | | Employees (2009) | SABI | + |
| | | Turnover/employees | Calculus | + |
| | Number of services provided by the company | Number of services | | + |
| | Level of investment in R&D | Amount (in Euros) | | + |
| Barriers of internationalization | Number of perceived barriers | Number of obstacles | | − |
| | Importance attributed to initial invest costs | | | − |
| | Importance given to cultural differences | | | − |
| | Importance given to language difference | | | − |
| | Importance attributed to know-how limitations | | | − |
| | Perceptions of protectionism for local | Likert scale (5 points) | Question-naire | − |
| | Degree of unfamiliarity with the foreign | | | − |
| Perceptions risks, benefits | Perceived risk of operating internationally | | | − |
| | Perception of the cost | | | − |
| | Perception of its profitability | | | + |
| Intensity of national competitiveness | | | | + |
| Management features | Number of graduate managers | | | + |
| | Foreign language skills of managers | Value provided | | + |
| | Nº employees with international work | | | + |

## 3.3    Description of the Population and Sampling Criteria

Based on the literature review, the questionnaire focused on the five key elements just described. The questionnaire in its final form consisted of nineteen questions and was sent electronically (e-mail) directly to the head of the selected companies.

According to Yin [57], the sample should consist of a group of companies that belong to the population and there should be a correspondence between the structure of the samples and the structure of the population. Thus, the survey was administered to the 375 biggest firms (turnover volume) from the design, architecture and engineering consulting sector (in the SABI - System Analysis of Iberian Balance – database). Further information was requested from the sector's association - the APPC (Portuguese Association of Engineering and Management Consultants) - having also sent questionnaires to 183 members of the APPC. 74 members of the APPC were already among the 375 largest companies in the sector (obtained via SABI). During the contact process, it was found that some companies were insolvent or had been dissolved, were unreachable or not eligible for the questionnaire. Therefore, the final number of companies that received the questionnaire was 322. From these 322 companies, only 54 companies responded. All the questionnaires were valid for statistical analysis, representing a response rate of 16.8%, which puts this study in parity with other studies.

# 4    Empirical Results

First, a descriptive analysis of the questionnaire answers is conducted, followed by the empirical validation of the research hypotheses, and finally, the key findings are presented and discussed in light of the existing literature.

## 4.1    Descriptive Analysis and Validation of Research Hypotheses

The companies that responded to the questionnaire had a turnover (for 2009) of 261.055 thousand euros and employed 2584 workers. On average, each company had an annual turnover of about 4.834 thousand euros and 48 employees. Moreover, 70% of them are involved in engineering projects and 66% are dedicated to project management.

The respondent companies regard international markets as riskier and more expensive to operate, but more profitable than domestic markets. These results are fully in line with those reported by Winsted and Patterson [53]. With regard to competitiveness, we found that the firms surveyed assume that the domestic market is saturated or exhausted.

The barriers/obstacles to internationalization can create structural and operational constraints that often result in failures in the internationalization process. According to Patterson [4], the obstacles are one of the most important key elements in the decision to globalize.

Most companies consider that protectionism of local technicians and companies (in the country where the company can internationalize) is the main obstacle to their internationalization, followed by the costs associated with the initial investment. We can also add the obstacle associated to unfamiliarity with the foreign market.

In order to test the research hypotheses, the IBM SPSS Statistics software (version 19.0) package was used. Table 4 shows the tests employed to validate each hypothesis as well as the p-value obtained and the decision concerning the hypothesis.

**Table 4.** Statistical test results

| Key elements | Research hypothesis | Statistical Test | p-value | Decision |
|---|---|---|---|---|
| Capacities and characteristics of companies | H1 | Mann-Whitney | 0.004 | Reject H0 |
| | H1a | | 0.000 | Reject H0 |
| | H1b | | 0.335 | Retain H0 |
| | H1c | | 0.051 | Retain H0 |
| Barriers to internationalization | H2 | McNemar | 0.556 | Retain H0 |
| | H2a | | 0.000 | Reject H0 |
| | H2b | | 0.000 | Reject H0 |
| | H2c | Friedman | 0.042 | Reject H0 |
| Perceptions of the risk and benefits of internationalization | H3 | Mann-Whitney | 0.764 | Retain H0 |
| | H3a | | 1.00 | Retain H0 |
| Competitiveness | H4 | Mann-Whitney | 0.261 | Retain H0 |
| Management features | H5 | Mann-Whitney | 0.039 | Reject H0 |
| | H5a | | 0.023 | Reject H0 |
| | H5b | | 0.54 | Retain H0 |

According to the results of the hypothesis tests performed concerning H1, firms that have a higher turnover are more prone to internationalization. This finding is in line with Patterson [4] and Castellacci [44]'s results. Moreover, in the case of Portuguese firms, and in line with the findings presented by Hassel et al. [45] for Germany, the number of employees with international experience is higher in firms that operate internationally (H1a).

The hypothesis that firms that have a broader variety of services (differentiated "products") (H1b) are the most active internationally stems from the conclusions drawn by Coviello and Martin [47], Zou et al. [48] and Patterson [4]. However, no conclusions can be drawn about the impact of this variable on the decision to internationalize or not. For companies in the service sector in analysis, the diversity of services does not seem to influence their level of internationalization. The same can be concluded for H1c.

With respect to the barriers to the internationalization, Samiee [49] and Patterson [4] suggest that costs are the major obstacle, whereas Guenzi and Pelloni [50] and Sichtmann [51] indicate unawareness of linguistic and cultural differences as the main barrier. Patterson [4] also considers that a major barrier to internationalization is limitations in know-how. In our study, the three obstacles to which companies attributed the most importance as barriers to internationalization are protectionism to local technicians and businesses, unfamiliarity with the foreign market and the costs of initial investment.

Regarding the other factors, it should be noted that Portuguese companies whose management structures include graduate managers with foreign language skills are more prone to internationalize (H5 and H5a).

As for the companies' perception of the risk of operating internationally, of profitability and costs, it seems that these do not influence the company's level of internationalization, in contrast with the findings of Aaby and Slater [52], Leonidou et al. [54] and Patterson [4]. The diversity of services offered, more competitive factor prices, the level of investment in R&D and the pressure of the internal market show no statistically significant influence on the company's level of internationalization.

## 4.2    Differences on Averages, Correlations between Variables and Implications for the Model

In this section, an exploratory analysis of data is conducted and the relationships between the 'theoretical' model's variables are explored, so as to complement the validation of the research hypotheses. To accomplish this analysis, the Mann-Whitney test was employed, to assess whether there is evidence of significant statistically differences between the averages of each group (firms that operate internationally and firms that do not act in the international market), in the various dimensions of the variables not included in the previous section. Table 5 summarizes the information on the average differences of all variables.

**Table 5.** Differences in averages - Mann-Whitney test

| Group | Determinant | Variable measurement | All companies | Firms not in the international market | Firms that operate intern. | p-value (M-W) |
|---|---|---|---|---|---|---|
| Characteristics of companies | Firm Size | Turnover (2009) | 4.834,35 | 1.749,23 | 5.812,56 | 0.004[a] |
| | | Employees (2009) | 48 | 16 | 58 | 0.002[a] |
| | | Turnover/employees | 114.6 | 117.61 | 113.64 | 0.326 |
| | N° services provided by company | N° services selected | 3.85 | 4.46 | 3.66 | 0.335 |
| | Level of investment in R&D | Amount (in Euros) | 72.05 | 12.86 | 92.85 | 0.051[b] |
| Barriers to internationalization | Number of perceived barriers | N° obstacles selected | 2.15 | 2.0 | 2.2 | 0.657 |
| | Imp. attributed to init. invest costs | Likert scale (5 points) | 3.36 | 3.85 | 3.19 | 0.133 |
| | Imp. given to cultural differences | | 2.45 | 2.33 | 2.49 | 0.78 |
| | Imp. given to language differences | | 2.67 | 2.58 | 2.69 | 0.819 |
| | Imp. attributed to know-how lim. | | 2.62 | 3.0 | 2.5 | 0.193 |
| | Perceptions of protectionism for local technicians | | 3.14 | 3.36 | 3.08 | 0.558 |
| | Degree of unfamiliarity of the foreign market | | 3.10 | 3.83 | 2.88 | 0.009[a] |
| Perceptions of the risk /benefits | Perceived risk of operating internationally | | 3.5 | 3.62 | 3.46 | 0.764 |
| | Perception of the cost | | 4 | 4 | 4 | 1.00 |
| | Perception of its profitability | | 3.43 | 3.23 | 3.49 | 0.155 |
| Intensity of national competitiveness | | | 4.22 | 4.0 | 4.29 | 0.261 |
| Management features | Number of graduate managers | Value provided | 6.38 | 4.23 | 7.07 | 0.039[a] |
| | Foreign language skills of managers | | 6.3 | 4 | 7.02 | 0.023[a] |
| | N° employees with international work experience | | 12.7 | 1.23 | 16.34 | 0.000[a] |

[a] significance level of 5%    [b] significance level of 10%

Based on the Mann-Whitney test for differences in means between firms operating abroad and firms that operate only in the domestic market, significant differences were found in only three of the five groups of determinants into which the variables were classified. In the group concerning *Characteristics of Firms*, we found significant differences in the determinants 'Company size' and 'Level of Investment in R&D'; in the group *Barriers to internationalization*, only in the determinant 'Importance attributed to unfamiliarity with the external market' presented significant differences. In the last group, *Management features*, the determinants 'Number of graduate managers', 'Number of managers with foreign language skills' and 'Number of employees with international experience' revealed significant differences between the two groups, with a significance level of 5%. The analysis suggests the potentially relevant role of firm size, the amount invested in R&D, the importance attributed to unfamiliarity with the external market, the managers' educational level, and the international experience of the workers, with quite different averages between the two groups of companies.

After testing the differences between the two groups of firms for all variables, the multivariate analysis should be preceded by an analysis of the correlation matrix among the relevant variables in order to assess the degree of explanation of the variables and avoid including (explanatory) variables which could be highly correlated.

Based on the analysis of the Pearson coefficients, we can conclude that there is a significant correlation of the dependent variable (internationalization decision) with six variables: firm size (with a Pearson correlation value of 0.412), the number of employees (Pearson correlation 0.487), unfamiliarity with the external market (-0.429), the number of employees with international experience (0.526), the level of investment in R&D (0.324), the perception of the initial investment costs (Pearson coefficient -0.35), and the number of managers with international experience (0.5). This analysis suggests that, on average, larger companies, companies that invest more in R&D, have more employees with international experience, and more graduate managers, tend to internationalize, which confirms the results obtained with the Mann-Whitney test. Moreover, we found that the greater the perception of the initial investment costs and the importance attributed to unfamiliarity with the market, the lower the propensity to internationalize. This finding is also in line with the results obtained using the Mann-Whitney test, with only a slight difference in relation to the initial investment cost.

Analyzing the independent variables, we found that several items are strongly correlated, which could lead to problems of multicollinearity in the estimation. This question can have two meanings: that the variables are measuring the same factor, or that they have a common dependency on another unmeasured variable in the model Maroco, [58]. The variable 'turnover' is strongly related to the number of workers (Pearson correlation coefficient of 0.818). We decided to keep only one of them (turnover), because we believe it is more representative of firm size than the number of workers. The variable 'number of graduate managers' reveals a strong correlation with the variable 'number of managers who speak one or more foreign languages' (Pearson correlation coefficient of 0.976). Therefore, we opted to keep only one variable, the level of graduate managers. A similar situation occurs between the variables 'importance of cultural differences' and 'importance of language differences' (0.694). We decided to eliminate the variable 'importance of language differences' because it has the greatest number of correlations with other variables with a significance level of 5%.

## 4.3    Results from the Multivariate Analysis and Discussion of the Results

In this section, an analysis of causality is performed using multivariate techniques, to analyze the degree of explanation of each variable.

When the dependent variable type is nominal (assuming the value 0 for firms that operate only in the domestic market and 1 for those operating internationally), the appropriate method to estimate the theoretical model is the binary logistic regression. This is the procedure described to model, in probabilistic terms, the occurrence of one of the two achievements of the classes of the variable. The independent variables may be qualitative and/or quantitative. The logistic model can thus assess the significance of each of the model's independent variables.

The following table (Table 6) shows the results of the logistic estimation, using various methods to select the independent variables. The empirical results of the decision to internationalize, based on the logistic regression, has the dummy variable Int_Dec as the dependent variable, which assumes the value 1 if the company operates abroad and 0 otherwise.

Table 6. Empirical results based on logistic regression

| Group | Determinant | Method A | Method B |
|---|---|---|---|
| | Constant | -7.511 | 6.481 |
| Characteristics of companies | Firm Size | 2.194[a] | --- |
| | Number of services provided by the company | --- | --- |
| | Level of investment in R&D | --- | 5.66[b] |
| Barriers to international- lization | Number of perceived barriers | --- | --- |
| | Importance attributed to the initial investment costs | --- | --- |
| | Importance given to cultural differences | --- | --- |
| | Importance attributed to know-how limitations | --- | --- |
| | Perceptions of protectionism for local technicians | --- | --- |
| | Degree of unfamiliarity with the foreign market | -1.374[a] | -2.470[b] |
| Perceptions of the risk and benefits | Perceived risk of operating internationally | --- | --- |
| | Perception of the cost | --- | --- |
| | Perception of its profitability | --- | --- |
| Intensity of national competitiveness | | 1.552[a] | --- |
| Management features | Number of graduate managers | --- | --- |
| | Number of employees with international work experience | --- | 7.964[b] |
| | N | 54 | 54 |
| Goodness of fit | Hosmer and Lemeshow | 4.059 | 3.489 |
| | (p-value) | 0.852 | 0.9 |
| | % correct | 81.8% | 93.1% |

[a] significance level of 5%    [b] significance level of 10%

The tests of goodness of fit (Hosmer-Lemeshow test and estimated percentage of correct observations) allow us to conclude that the model using the Forward Stepwise LR method has a good quality adjustment. In fact, concerning the Hosmer-Lemeshow test, a p-value above 0.10 means that it does not reject the null hypothesis, namely that the models represent reality well (and the 2 models have p-values of 0.852 and 0.9). Furthermore, over 80% of the estimated values of the dependent variable are correctly predicted by the models.

The results indicate that, on average, firm size is the key determinant in the choice to internationalize (corresponding to a p-value of 0.045 <5%). The positive sign and statistically significant estimated coefficient for the firm size, indicates that firms with higher sales volumes tend, on average, to operate more abroad. This relationship confirms the study of Winsted and Patterson (1998). In addition, there are four factors that strongly explain the decision to internationalize. They are the number of workers with international experience (p-value of 0.058), the domestic competitive pressure (p-value of 0.039), the level of investment in research and development (p-value of 0.041), and the importance attributed to unfamiliarity with the market (p-value of 0.049).

The positive sign on the number of employees with international experience shows that the more open the company to employees with international experience, the greater the propensity to internationalize. In fact, a company that employs workers with international experience has added impetus to internationalize, not only because of the experience factor (lower risk associated with the uncertainty of the market) but also because the employees can be drivers of change within the company, encouraging the desire to grow across the organization to other more distant markets.

The variable 'domestic competitive pressure' reveals a similar pattern: the positive and statistically significant sign associated with this variable (1.552) means that the more saturated the market, the greater the propensity to internationalize. This result corroborates the study of Winsted and Patterson [53] and Patterson [4], which show that the companies that claim they experience and understand high competitive intensity domestically, maintain greater contact with international markets than those that do not face such domestic pressures.

The variable 'investment in R&D' also has a positive impact on the decision to internationalize, with a coefficient of 5.66. The companies that have higher investments in R&D maintain regular contacts with international markets, as Patterson [4] argued in his study.

Conversely, the negative and statistically significant degree of unawareness of the foreign market indicates that companies where the risk perception (i.e., unfamiliarity with the market) is higher, have less propensity to internationalize. This relationship had already been determined by several authors ([4], [52-54]) and is now confirmed for the service companies in study.

Finally, it is important to note that some of the elements the literature considered as determinants of the decision to internationalize were not significant for the firms under analysis. This is the case of the expected impact of the perceived cost of operating internationally and the expected return on the decision to operate abroad. We expected that, like Burton and Schlegelmilch [55], Aaby and Slater [52] and

Leonidou et al. [54], the perception of additional costs in the process of opening to foreign markets would lower the company's willingness to do so and/or the (higher) expected profitability of internationalization would act as an incentive.

## 5    Conclusion

One of the characteristics of economic development is seen in the increasing trend to outsource economies and the ability they have to internationalize services. The remarkable advancements of information and communication technologies have enabled many services to be 'exportable'.

The competitive pressures in domestic markets as well as the globalization of economic activities have encouraged many service companies to seek new business opportunities across borders. Despite the growing importance of trade and intensive investment in services, there are few studies on the internationalization of services, as well as the construction and validation of theories. In fact, the literature on the internationalization of firms tends to focus more on the industrial sector and multinational companies, implying thus the need for additional research in the service sector.

In order to analyze the factors influencing the internationalization of service firms based on a quantitative analysis, we surveyed service companies from the design, architecture and engineering consulting sector. We also conducted an exploratory analysis of different hypotheses based on the literature review. Moreover, a multivariate analysis was employed to ascertain the main determinants of internationalization and the results were compared with studies on other countries, in order to determine similarities and differences among economic, geographic and social distinct realities.

In line with the conclusions of previous studies, firm size is a distinguishing factor between companies that operate internationally and those that do not, both in terms of number of employees and in terms of turnover. Also, the number of employees with international experience is higher in companies operating abroad. We also noted that companies that have managers with more technical and foreign language skills are more open and more prone to internationalize.

The study also allowed us to conclude that companies perceive international markets as riskier, more expensive to operate, but also more profitable than domestic markets. It is also important to note that the main obstacles reported by firms were protectionism of local technicians and businesses, the costs associated with the initial investment and unfamiliarity with external markets, which contradicts some recent studies.

We also noted that competitive pressure is a booster to internationalization.

It is clear that more research on the development of theory and research on the sector are recommended. We believe there is a need to develop new theories that explain and predict the behaviour of a service-oriented company, integrating the various theoretical constructs, including the unique characteristics of services, the country characteristics and the market characteristics.

**Acknowledgement.** This work is funded by the ERDF through the Programme COMPETE and by the Portuguese Government through FCT - Foundation for Science and Technology, project PTDC/EGE-GES/099741/2008 and PTDC/EGE-GES/117692/2010.

# References

1. OCDE: Annual Report. Paris: The Organisation for Economic Cooperation and Development (2005)
2. Gerbrands, G.: Internationalization of service organizations: a study of the factors that influence the internationalization of service organizations. PhD Thesis, University of Twente, Nederlands (2008)
3. Lejpras, A.: Determinants of internationalization: differences between service and manufacturing SMEs. Deutsches Institut für Wirtschaftsforschung, Paper N. 886 (2009)
4. Patterson, P.G.: A Study of Perceptions Regarding Service Firms' Attitudes Towards Exporting. Australasian Mark. J. 12(2), 19–38 (2004)
5. Javalgi, R.G., Martin, C.L.: Internationalization of services: identifying the building block for future research. J. Services Mark. 21(6), 391–397 (2007)
6. Depreya, B., Lloyd-Reasona, L., Ibehb, K.I.N.: The internationalisation of small-and medium-sized management consultancies: an exploratory study of key facilitating factors. Service Industries J. 32(10), 1–13 (2011)
7. Krull, E., Smith, P., Ge, G.L.: The internationalization of engineering consulting from a strategy tripod perspective. Service Industries J. 32(7), 1097–1119 (2012)
8. Lovelock, C.H., Yip, G.S.: Developing Global Strategies for Service Businesses. California Manage. Rev. 38(2), 64–86 (1996)
9. Bateson, J.E.G., Hoffman, D.K.: Marketing de serviços, 4th edn. Porto Alegre, Bookman (2001)
10. Grönroos, C.: Internationalization strategies for services. J. Service Mark. 13(4/5), 290–297 (1999)
11. Brouthers, K.D., Brouthers, L.E.: Why service and manufacturing entry mode choices differ: the influence of transaction cost factors, risk and trust. J. Manage. Stud. 40, 1179–1204 (2003)
12. Agarwal, S., Ramaswami, S.N.: Choice of foreign market entry mode: impact of ownership, location and internationalization factors. J. Int. Bus. Stud. 23(1), 1–27 (1992)
13. Elango, B., Abel, I.: A comparative analysis of the influence of country characteristics on service investments versus manufacturing investments. Americ. Bus. Rev. 22(2), 29 (2004)
14. O'Farrell, P.N., Wood, P.A., Zheng, J.: Regional influences on foreign market development by business service companies: elements of a strategic context explanation. Regional Stud. 32(1), 31–48 (1998)
15. Javalgi, R.G., Griffith, D.A., White, D.S.: An empirical examination of factors influencing the internationalization of service firms. J. Services Mark. 17(2), 185–201 (2003)
16. Erramilli, M.K.: Entry mode choice in service industries. Int. Mark. Rev. 5(7), 50–62 (1990)
17. Blomstermo, A., Sharma, D.: Choice of foreign market entry mode in service firms. Int. Mark. Rev. 23(2), 211–229 (2006)
18. Erramilli, M.K., Rao, C.P.: Service Firms' International Entry-Mode Choice: A Modified Transaction-Cost Approach. J. Marketing 57(7), 19–38 (1993)

19. Rosenbaum, S.M., Madsen, T.K.: Modes of foreign entry for professional service firms in multi-partner projects. Service Industries J. 32(10), 1653–1666 (2012)
20. Philippe, J., Léo, P.Y.: Influence of entry modes and relationship modes on business services internationalisation. Service Industries J. 31(4) (2011)
21. Carneiro, J., Dib, L.A.: Avaliação comparativa do escopo descritivo e explanatório dos principais modelos de internacionalização de empresas. INTERNEXT - Revista Electrónica de Negócios Internacionais da ESPM 2(1), 1–25 (2007)
22. Dunning, J.H.: Toward an eclectic theory of international production: Some empirical tests. J. Int. Bus. Stud. 11(1), 9–31 (1980)
23. Dunning, J.H.: The eclectic paradigm of international production: A restatement and some possible extensions. J. Int. Bus. Stud. 19(1), 1–31 (1988)
24. Dunning, J.H.: Reappraising the eclectic paradigm in an age of alliance capitalism. J. Int. Bus. Stud. 26(3), 91–461 (1995)
25. Johanson, J., Vahlne, J.-E.: The internationalization process of the firm - A model of knowledge development and increasing foreign market commitments. J. Int. Bus. Stud. 8, 23–32 (1977)
26. Johanson, J., Vahlne, J.E.: The Uppsala internationalization process model revisited: From liability of foreignness to liability of outsidership. J. Int. Bus. Stud. 40(9), 1411–1431 (2009)
27. Andersen, O.: On the internationalization process of firms: A critical analysis. J. Int. Bus. Stud. 24(3), 209–231 (1993)
28. Cunningham, M.T., Culligan, K.: Competitiveness through networks of relationships in information technology product markets. In: Paliwoda, S.J. (ed.) New Perspectives on International Marketing. Routledge, London (1991)
29. Johanson, J., Mattsson, L.-G.: Network positions and strategic action - an analytical framework. In: Axelsson, B., Easton, G. (eds.) Industrial Networks. A New View of Reality, pp. 206–217. Routledge, London (1992)
30. Bell, J.: The internationalization of small computer software firms: A further challenge to stage' theories. European J. Mark. 8, 60–75 (1995)
31. Bjorkman, I., Forsgren, M.: Nordic international business research: a review of its development. Int. Stud. Manage. Organization 30(1), 6–25 (2000)
32. Andersson, U., Forsgren, M., Holm, U.: The strategic impact of external networks: subsidiary performance and competence development in multinational corporation. Strategic Manage. J. 23(11), 979–996 (2002)
33. Lee, M., Stanley, Y.W.S., Lam, H.: Event and rule services for achieving a Web-based knowledge network. Knowledge-Based Systems 17, 179–188 (2004)
34. Balbinot, Z., Graeml, A.R., Macada, A.A.: A internet e a estratégia de internacionalização das empresas Brasileira. BASE – Revista de Administração e Contabilidade da Unisinos 5(3), 188–197 (2008)
35. Kim, W.C., Hwang, P.: Global strategy and multinationals entry mode choice. J. Int. Bus. Stud. 23(1), 29–53 (1992)
36. Wernerfelt, B.A.: Resource-Based View of the Firm. Strategic Manage. J. 5(2), 171–180 (1994)
37. Barney, J.: Firm resources and sustained competitive advantage. J. Manage. 17(1), 99–120 (1991)
38. Barney, J.: Gaining and sustaining competitive advantage, 2nd edn. Prentice Hall, Upper Saddle River (2002)
39. Ruzzier, M., Hisrich, R.D., Antoncic, B.: SME internationalization research: past, present, and future. J. Small Bus. Enterprise Development 13(4), 476–497 (2006)

40. Barney, J.B., Hesterly, W.S.: Administração Estratégica e Vantagem Competitiva Casos brasileiros. Pearson Education, São Paulo (2007)
41. Coviello, N.E., McAuley, A.: Internationalisation and the smaller firm: A review of contemporary empirical research. Manage. Int. Rev. 39(3), 223–256 (1999)
42. Wickramasekera, R.G., Oczkowski, E.: Stage models re-visited: a measure of the stage of internationalisation of a firm. Manage. Int. Rev. 46(1), 39–55 (2006)
43. Ghoshal, S.C.A., Barlett, M.P.: A new manifesto for management. Sloan Manage. Rev. 40(3), 41–54 (1999)
44. Castellacci, F.: The internationalization of firms in the service industries: Channels, determinants and sectoral patterns. Technological Forecasting & Social Change 77(3), 500–513 (2010)
45. Hassel, A., Höpner, M., Kurdelbusch, A., Rehder, B., Zugehör, R.: Two Dimensions of the Internationalization of Firms. J. Manage. Stud. 40(3), 705–723 (2003)
46. Lommelen, T., Matthyssens, P.: The internationalization process of service providers: a literature review. Research on Int. Service Mark.: A State of the Art 15, 95–117 (2005)
47. Coviello, N.E., Martin, K.: Internationalization of service SMEs: an integrated perspective from the engineering consulting sector. J. Int. Mark. 7(4), 42–66 (1999)
48. Zou, S., Fang, E., Zhao, S.: The effects of export marketing capabilities on export performance: An investigation of Chinese exporters. J. Int. Mark. 11(4), 32–55 (2003)
49. Samiee, S.: The internationalization of services: trends, obstacles and issues. J. Services Mark. 13(4/5), 319–336 (1999)
50. Guenzi, P., Pelloni, O.: The Impact of Interpersonal Relationships on Customer Satisfaction and Loyalty to the Service Provider. Int. J. Service Industry Manage. 15(4), 365–384 (2004)
51. Sichtmann, C., Selasinsky, V.M.: Exporting Services Successfully: Antecedents and Performance Implications of Customer Relationships. J. Int. Mark. 18(1), 86–108 (2010)
52. Aaby, N.E., Slater, S.: Management Influences on Export Performance: A Review of the Empirical Literature 1978-1988. Int. Mark. Rev. 6(4), 6–25 (1988)
53. Winsted, K.F., Patterson, P.G.: Internationalization of services: the service exporting decision. J. Services Mark. 12(4), 294–311 (1998)
54. Leonidou, L., Katsikeas, C.S., Piercy, N.F.: Identifying Managerial Influences on Exporting: Past Research and Future Directions. J. Int. Mark. 6(2), 74–102 (1998)
55. Burton, F.N., Schlegelmilch, B.B.: Profile analyses of non-exporters versus exporters grouped by export involvement. Int. Mark. Rev. 1(27), 38–49 (1987)
56. Sacramento, I., Almeida, V.M.C., Silva, M.S.M.: The Internationalization Process of Services Firms: A Two-Case Study in Brazil. Latin American Bus. Rev. 3(2), 43–64 (2002)
57. Yin, R.K.: Case study research–Design and methods, 2nd edn. SAGE Publications (1994)
58. Maroco, J.: Análise Estatística com o PASW Statistics. Editora Report Number (2010)

# A Proposal for a Mobile Ticketing Solution for Metropolitan Area of Oporto Public Transport

Marta Campos Ferreira, Maria Henriqueta Nóvoa, and Teresa Galvão Dias

FEUP – Faculdade de Engenharia, Universidade do Porto
Rua Dr. Roberto Frias, 4200-465 Porto, Portugal
{mferreira,hnovoa,tgalvao}@fe.up.pt

**Abstract.** The use of mobile phones to make payments is already a wide-spreading reality. While some mobile payment solutions achieved a considerable success and are already in use, others failed in the pilot phase. Nevertheless, there is an area where mobile payments have been quite successful: mobile ticketing in public transport. In fact, there are several advantages of mobile ticketing over traditional ticketing systems, such as queue avoidance, ubiquitous and remote access to payment, and the lack of need to carry coins and cash. This paper intends to propose a mobile payment system to be implemented in the Public Transport of Metropolitan Area of Oporto. After defining the payment ticketing model, a prototype was developed and tested by a sample of users. These tests allowed gathering some feedback about the feasibility of the system as well as useful insights about the concept, new in public transport in Portugal. The findings attained so far suggest that users considered the system extremely useful, since it is more convenient than traditional systems, improving the travelling process and experience. It was also clear that users valued the integration of additional and complementary services with mobile payments, such as real-time traffic information, maps and schedules. There are also several barriers to the adoption of such a system elicited by users, such as premium price, complex interfaces and perceived risks, such as security and privacy concerns.

**Keywords:** mobile payment systems, public transport, mobile ticketing, mobile payment adoption.

## 1 Introduction

The evolution of mobile devices and their increasing functionality is changing the way people use mobile phones. Currently, it is already possible to make payments with mobile phones in several countries. Hence, mobile payment can be defined as the use of a mobile device (mobile phone, PDA, wireless tablet) "to initiate, authorize and confirm an exchange of financial value in return for goods and services." [1]

Mobile payments may be very useful in several areas such as retail, transport and entertainment, and they are often integrated with other complementary services, such as information services, loyalty programs, smart advertisement, physical and logical access, and check-in services.

J.F. e Cunha, M. Snene, and H. Nóvoa (Eds.): IESS 2013, LNBIP 143, pp. 263–278, 2013.

In Portugal the introduction of mobile payments has been very slow, being the first mobile payment system implemented in August 2012, in the Azores islands. This system [2] allows customers to pay the car park using a mobile phone and is based on a pre-charge account. In October 2012 another similar system emerged in Sintra [3], offering three methods of alternative payments: Short Message Service (SMS), pre-charged account or MB Phone (a bank account associated to a mobile phone number).

This paper intends to propose a mobile payment system to be implemented in the Public Transport Network of the Metropolitan Area of Oporto (AMP) based on Wi-Fi and Global Positioning System (GPS) technologies. The existing payment system is based on contactless cards that proved to be an interesting solution, since they are more secure, flexible and with larger memory capacity than paper tickets. However several advantages of mobile payments over traditional ticketing systems can be outlined: time and place independence, availability, remote and ubiquitous access to payment services, and queue avoidance [4]. These advantages are particularly important when there are no other payment methods available or in cases of urgency.

Additionally, using mobile phones to pay for a journey may enhance travellers' overall experience. In fact, in public transport services, contactless ticketing and payment solutions showed an increase in traveller satisfaction due to its easy and convenient characteristics [5].

The definition of the mobile payment system for AMP Public Transport was based on literature review about theories and determinants of mobile payments adoption, available technologies and installed infra-structure, as well as an analysis of the current ticketing scheme of AMP Public Transport Network. After this research, the mobile payment system was defined and a prototype developed, which was tested by a sample of users.

One of the main contributions of this article was the validation of the proposed concept. Since the concept of making payments with mobile phones is relatively new in Portugal, this first test with a group of consumers was important to assess the usefulness of such a system and the intention of use by customers. Participants provided useful inputs to improve the mobile payment system and their answers to the questionnaires corroborated some determinants of mobile payment adoption reviewed in the literature.

The outline of the current article is as follows: first the mobile payment systems and traditional ticketing systems in public transport sector are characterized. Then the factors that influence the consumer adoption of mobile payments are explored. After the contextualization of the problem, the research approach is presented as well as the proposed system. Finally the results are discussed and the conclusions are presented.

## 2    Mobile Payments and Traditional Ticketing Models in Public Transport Sector

Ticketing systems have been developed over the years, and today various types may coexist even in the same city. Paper tickets were the first to appear and are still widely used worldwide. Despite of being less expensive and easy to combine with other payment technologies, they are susceptible to fraud and have limited data collection capabilities. Magnetic stripe cards are also a ticketing media and although they support a high number of uses, they are susceptible to accident erasure and have a large variance in reliability.

Contactless cards, which appeared in the 90s, are rapidly replacing these two types of tickets. They use Radio Frequency Identification (RFID) or Near Field Communication (NFC) to establish a communication between the card and the validation device. This system has many advantages over traditional payment methods such as secure data transfer, large memory capacity and resistance to fraud.

Mobile ticketing systems are more recent and are based on the use of the travellers' mobile phone to pay for the trip. The use of mobile phones in public transport allows not only to make payments but also to process and exchange a large amount of information between the customer and the service provider. The traveller may access real-time information about maps, timetables, nearby stops and points-of-interest, making the actual payment transaction the final step of a series of data exchange.

Public Transport Operators (PTOs) started to use the most basic mobile phone features, like making phone calls and sending text messages, to make travel tickets purchase. For instance, Paybox in Austria allows the Austrian railway OBB customers to purchase travel tickets via SMS or through the Vodafone live! Portal [6], allowing the customers to pay for the tickets through their monthly phone bills. Proximus SMS-Pay in Belgium, Mobipay in Spain and AvantixMetro in UK are also examples of mobile ticketing systems based on SMS already implemented.

While SMS can be considered a simple and easy to use technology, it has limitations when used to make payments. SMS uses store and forward technology, does not use any encryption method and there is no proof of delivery within the SMS protocol [7]. Most SMS-based mobile payment models do provide a proof of delivery, requiring a second separate message to be sent, which increases the costs of a transaction. This problem is particularly pertinent when small payments are at stake. Additionally, in the study conducted by Nina Mallat [4], interviewees reported a number of problems, such as: the message formats are often complicated and slow to key in, the existence of various payment codes and premium service numbers make them difficult to remember and difficulty in finding instructions to make payments.

The evolution of mobile phones to smart phones has broadened the range of payment possibilities [8]. And when contactless technologies like NFC were added to smart phones, more functionality became possible. Tickets can be purchased, downloaded, and accessed on the phone, and when in contact with NFC-enabled readers, the tickets are redeemed and a receipt is sent [5]. Several pilots of NFC-enabled phones have been launched in the public transport area. For instance, the Touch&Travel service in Germany allows passengers to make payments with their mobile phones. Travellers have to tap their NFC-enabled mobile phone to the Touchpoint device at the departing station and at the destination. The length of the journey and the ticket price are calculated at the end of the journey, and the customer receives, each month, a statement with all travel data and an attached invoice [9]. However, there are some authors [7] that don´t consider this a real mobile payment, because customers don't use their mobile phones to pay the bill.

A NFC pilot was also launched in London, where 500 customers were given Nokia handsets with Oyster functionality. Passengers could top up their Oyster by touching their handset on Oyster ticket machines in tube stations or at Oyster tickets shops. Key findings of the research were that customers maintained high levels of interest and satisfaction throughout the trial and that the main customer benefits were convenience, ease of use, and status [5].

Other authors [10], [11] propose further mobile ticketing models for public transport based on Global Positioning Technologies (GPS). According to these models, apart from having a smartphone with Wi-Fi and GPS technologies, the user only needs to check-in when starting a trip and check-out at the end. The customer is also located by the service provider during his trip at defined intervals. At the end of the journey, the system determines the route within the public transport network and calculates the price, which is then debited from the customers' account. This kind of system may be the future of mobile ticketing since it is really convenient and easy to use for customers, as they are not required to have any particular knowledge about tariffs or ticketing machines [11]. Nevertheless it requires a well-established location-services infra-structure from the PTOs side, also raising privacy concerns from the customers' side.

Moreover, other mobile phone features like the screen, web browser, camera and sound allow PTOs to offer more services to passengers, enhancing customers' travel experience. According to Philippe Vappereau [12] customers want to be informed about the services they use and everything related to them. This means that PTOs must integrate different services with ticketing, such as real-time information, guidance and event information. These services attract potential clients, enhance PTOs image and increase long-term public transport usage. Service-Oriented Architecture (SOA) and Service-Oriented Infrastructure (SOI) models may be a good solution to provide these highly-customized services with very low costs [13]. This shift is a move away from the smart ticketing concept to a smart urban mobility context [14].

Besides all perceived advantages, there are also disadvantages and problems related to the use of mobile phones to make payments, such as low battery life, security and risk concerns, and low adoption by senior people. Hence, it is important to understand the critical factors behind the usage of this technology. The factors that determine the consumer adoption of mobile payments will be briefly discussed in the next section.

## 3     Factors Influencing Mobile Payments Adoption

A variety of research models have been introduced to explain innovation usage. The Technology Acceptance Model (TAM) is one of the first and the most influential research model to explain users' IT adoption behaviour [15]. TAM originates from Theory of Reasoned Action (TRA), which depicts user behaviour from a social psychology's point of view [16]. According to TAM, the intention to use a particular system is determined by two major variables: perceived usefulness and perceived ease of use of the system. Perceived usefulness is defined as the degree to which a person perceives that adopting the system will boost his job performance. Perceived ease of use is defined as the degree to which a person believes that adopting the system will be free of effort. These two beliefs determine the attitude toward using the system and that attitude, together with perceived usefulness, determines the use intention. Use intention then predicts the actual system use.

Although TAM was originally intended to predict IT systems usage in the workplace, this model was also applied to predict consumer acceptance in a variety of settings, including, wireless LAN usage [17], acceptance of handheld Internet devices [18], adoption of internet banking [19], and attitudes towards self-service solutions [20]. TAM was also used as a baseline of several studies about factors influencing mobile payment adoption [21], [22], [23].

Another multidisciplinary theory frequently applied in IS adoption research is the diffusion of innovations theory developed by Rogers [24]. According to this theory, users are only willing to accept innovations if those innovations provide a unique advantage compared to existing solutions. The theory determines five innovation characteristics that affect the adoption of the innovation: relative advantage, complexity, compatibility, trialability, and observability. According to Tornatzky & Klein [25], especially the relative advantage, complexity and compatibility, appear as constant determinants of technology adoption decision, and are therefore deemed as valid predictors for mobile payments adoption as well [4].

The relative advantages in the context of mobile payment systems are related to time and location independent purchase possibilities [4]. Compatibility captures the consistency between an innovation and the values, experiences, and needs of potential adopters [24]. Thus mobile payment systems must be compatible with consumers' purchase transactions, habits, and preferences. Complexity and usability problems have contributed to the low adoption of a variety of payment systems, such as smart cards and mobile banking [26], [27]. Hence, mobile payment systems must be well designed in order to overcome mobile phone limitations, such as small displays and keypads, limited transmission speed and short battery life, and therefore deliver convenient and user-friendly solutions to customers.

Other constructs such as costs have also a direct effect on consumer adoption if the cost is passed on to customers [4]. Wu and Wang [28], found in their research that the costs are relevant in predicting the adoption of mobile commerce. Additionally, Dahlberg et al. [29] advises researchers to find out what will be an acceptable cost to consumers, in various payment scenarios and for various products and services.

The concepts of perceived risk and trust have emerged as important determinants of mobile commerce adoption [30]. In the context of electronic services, security risk, conceptualized as the likelihood of privacy invasion, has been found to be a particularly critical concern among customers [31]. Making a mobile payment is often associated with potential loss of privacy and personal data [32], further increasing the perceived risk of mobile payment services. Potential risk also occurs from software failures, loss and theft of the mobile device and loss of privacy due to security system failures [33]. Still, trust in mobile payment service providers and merchants reduces perceived risk of mobile payments [4].

Mallat et al. [21] studied the factors that influenced the adoption of mobile ticketing service in public transport. The proposed research model was based on TAM, diffusion of innovations theory and trust theories, and resulted on eleven determinants of technology adoption model, presented in Fig. 1. Their findings corroborate the TAM model, where ease of use and usefulness have a significant effect on the adoption decision. But they also found that compatibility of the mobile ticketing service with consumer behaviour is a major determinant of adoption.

Moreover, mobility and contextual factors, including budget constraints, availability of other alternatives, and time pressure in the service use situation also have a strong effect on the adoption decision.

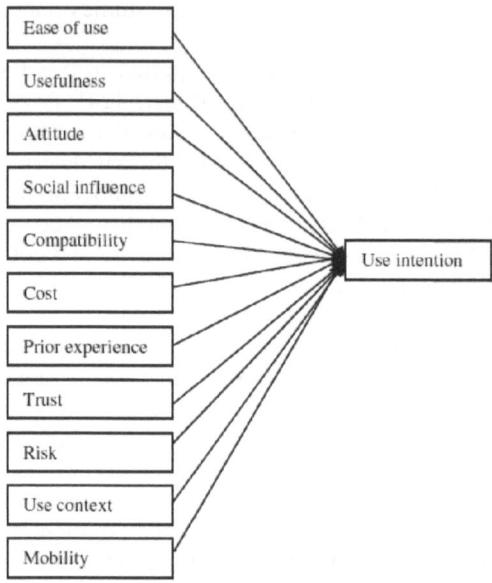

**Fig. 1.** Research model of mobile ticketing service adoption in public transport [21]

In Portugal there are no mobile payment's systems in Public Transport, and as demonstrated in literature review there are numerous advantages of such a system in relation to traditional ones. Thus, this paper intends to propose a mobile payment system to be implemented in Metropolitan Oporto Area Public Transport Network.

Firstly the problem will be contextualized and the ticketing system used by PTOs in AMP will be presented. Then the research methodology will be presented, followed by a description of the proposed mobile payment system. To conclude, the results of the analyses will be reported.

## 4    Case Public Transport of Metropolitan Area of Oporto

The Metropolitan Area of Oporto is served by an extensive public transport network which includes buses (STCP), light rail (Metro do Porto) and trains (CP – Portuguese railways). Together, they created TIP (Transportes Indermodais do Porto), an entity that is responsible for managing the intermodal tickets (Andante) in the AMP. In September 2012 the public transport operators STCP (buses) and Metro do Porto (light rail) were merged into a single administration.

The electronic ticketing system in AMP is an open (ungated) system that required a significant technological investment, such as card readers along the platforms at each metro station and at each bus vehicle, and handheld devices for conductors.

The pricing policy implemented in the AMP is based on two types of price discrimination: journey-based and passenger-based. The price for the journey-based perspective was settled based on a zone concept. The AMP network was divided into zones, with a flat rate within each zone, and the price is determined according to the number of zones crossed by the passenger. Once the ticket is validated, the passenger can travel, within a certain period of time, in the zone he chose. After that period of time, the traveller must validate the ticket again. The price of the tickets also depends on the characteristics of the passenger – passenger-based price discrimination. Thus, the price varies depending on whether the passenger is a child, student or senior.

Tickets are available in several types: zonal single ticket, season ticket and multi-journey ticket. The ticketing system adopted in AMP is the contactless card – Andante – based on RFID technology. Travellers can buy the contactless cards or recharge them at ticket vending machines, Service Provider Stores and spots, Third Party Agents and inside the vehicle (bus). Each Andante card can only contain one type of ticket at the same time (e.g., it cannot have a Zone2 ticket and also a Zone3 ticket), but it can contain several tickets of the same type (e.g., 10 Zone2 tickets).

In order to travel along the AMP network, passengers must buy the Andante contactless card and charge it with zone tickets. Then, they must validate the travel card in the reader at the beginning of the journey, and the ticket is redeemed. There is no need to validate the Andante at the end of the journey, but travellers must validate the travel card every time they change vehicle.

## 5    Research Approach

The definition of the mobile payment model for AMP Public Transport was based on literature review about related subjects such as Human Computer Interaction (HCI), mobile payment adoption theories and available technologies. It was also necessary to understand the context-of-use of the mobile payment system: installed infra-structure, ticketing scheme, financial constraints, and customers' needs. These subjects are detailed in Fig. 2, and were divided into general and context-of-use subjects.

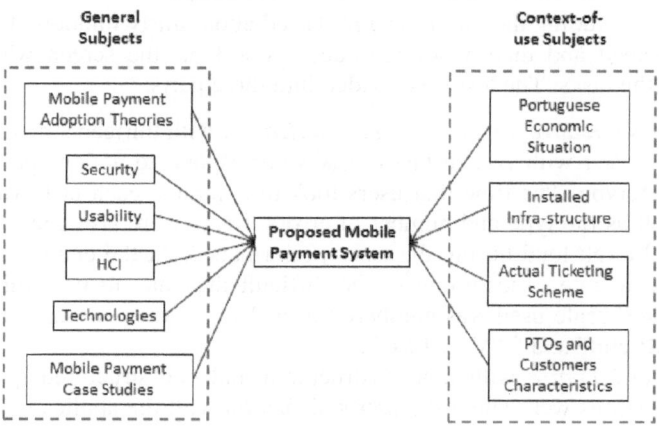

**Fig. 2.** Baseline subjects of the definition of the mobile payment system

After this research, the needs were identified, the use cases defined and the requirements elicited. This process resulted on a web prototype of the mobile payment application, developed with Proto.io tool. After the definition of the mobile payment system, it has been necessary to validate the concept and to evaluate the proposed prototype. Evaluation represents a very important step in product/service design, since it provides users and experts' feedback about the system [34], and allows the identification of usability issues in the prototype before presenting it to end-users.

In this case, the evaluation of the system comprised two different and complementary approaches. The first one consisted on the inspection technique called Heuristic Evaluation. This technique developed by Jakob Nielsen [35], [36] consists on the evaluation of an interface design by experts. Evaluators are guided by a set of usability principles (heuristics) and evaluate whether user-interface elements are conform to those principles. This evaluation was done by three experts (Nielsen [37] recommends between three and five) and allowed to identify some usability problems, such as lack of feedback and undo buttons in some screens, words inconsistency and complex information presented to the users. The usability problems identified by the experts were solved, allowing the preparation of the next evaluation phase.

The second evaluation procedure that was used was the usability testing. This can be seen as an irreplaceable usability practice, since it gives direct input on how real users use the system [38]. This technique was combined with the administration of a questionnaire, which allowed gathering some qualitative data. The main goals of the usability testing were to check how users navigate around the application to perform a number of pre-specified tasks, and how the topics categorization was understood by the users. These tests and the questionnaires were also valuable to receive initial comments about the application usefulness and the acceptance of the concept.

The tests were conducted in a test environment, so that users could concentrate on the pre-assigned tasks. Users were randomly sampled in the campus of the University of Porto in both strata among 17-60-year-old citizens. This usability testing was divided in two phases, and each phase comprised 7 different participants (Dumas and Redish [39] consider that 5-12 users is acceptable). After the first phase of tests the prototype was improved, taking into account users' feedback, and the order of the tasks was changed. Then a new set of tests was conducted.

Each test, including the questionnaire, lasted about thirty minutes. The participants were videotaped and their voice recorded, as well as the screen where they were performing the tasks. The test was divided into three parts:

1. *Questionnaire for sample characterization* with thirteen structured questions.
2. *User test* with twelve tasks. Tasks correspond to actions performed on the prototype. The time that users took to complete each task was recorded, as well as the type and number of errors. Users were also encouraged to speak and think loud during the tasks performance. At the end of each task, users had to rate it according to the difficult they had to perform the task. The Likert scale used was numbered from 1 to 5, where 1 was considered "Very Difficult" and 5 "Very Easy".
3. *Questionnaire* with nine unstructured and one structured questions. These questions were about the user satisfaction with the application and about the concept of the mobile payment itself.

The application of this methodology led to the development of a prototype for mobile payment system presented in the next section.

# 6    Proposed Mobile Payment System

The proposed system must require the minimum investment cost from the PTOs and travellers' point-of-view, achieving at the same time the maximum consumer acceptance possible. Hence, to achieve this goal decisions had to be made considering the most suitable technologies for the AMP network, which led to Wi-Fi and GPS technologies.

SMS and NFC technologies were not considered a viable option, due to different reasons. SMS technology was not chosen because of the premium price associated. PTOs in Portugal cannot support a steadily increase in their costs and past experiences in AMP public transport network states that reflecting the premium price in consumers is not a good option as well. When, in 2005, STCP launched a new service, called SMS Bus, which provided real-time traffic information, passengers used it massively while the SMS was free. When travellers had to pay for the SMS, the demand for this service dropped dramatically. NFC technology was also excluded because the penetration of NFC-enabled smartphones in Portugal is still very low, and it would require huge investments to convert the existing readers into NFC readers.

Therefore, in the proposed system, the purchase and validation of tickets will be made over-the-air, and the GPS technology will be used to locate the traveller and reduce the number of options when it comes to purchase or validate a ticket, making the system easier to use. The user can buy the travel ticket in two ways: he chooses the departure and the arrival station and the system automatically converts this information into zones (Fig. 3 – Part a), or, alternatively, he chooses the zone ticket he wants to buy and selects the number of tickets for each zone (Fig. 3 – Part b).

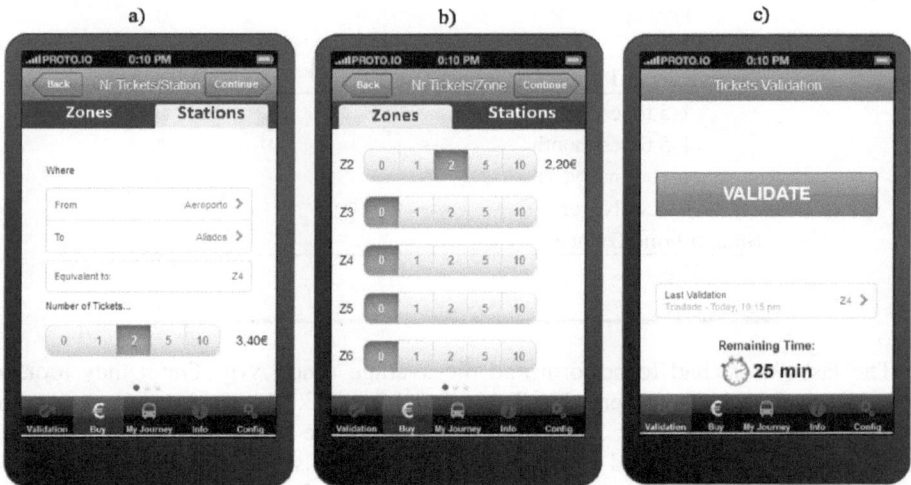

**Fig. 3.** Mobile payment system prototype screens: a) buy tickets by choosing the departure and ending station; b) buy tickets by choosing the type (zone); c) validation and remaining time

The system can hold more than one type of ticket at the same time and several tickets of the same type. To validate the ticket, the user has to choose which ticket, of those stored in his virtual wallet, he wants to use. Once the ticket is validated, the user can travel in the zone he chose for a certain time, and he can check the remaining time on the display (Fig. 3 – Part c).

Furthermore, and in order to attract potential consumers, it is important to offer additional services beyond payment. Hence the proposed mobile payment system also comprises several additional services such as find near stations, provide past travelling information, check tickets balance, check prices and maps, as well as access real-time traffic information.

# 7     Results

The sample was about 14 users (7 in the first test group and other 7 in the second), among 17-60-year-old citizens, and they all have different backgrounds (lawyers, engineers, students, professors, psychologists). Most of them (9 in 14) use the public transport at least monthly and 10 in 14 have a smartphone. The characterization of the sample is detailed in Table 1.

**Table 1.** Sample Characterization

| Characteristics | Nr Participants |
|---|---|
| **Age** | |
| Under 20 year old | 2 |
| Between 20-35 year old | 9 |
| Between 36-50 year old | 2 |
| Between 51-65 year old | 1 |
| **Gender** | |
| Female | 3 |
| Male | 11 |
| **Frequency of Public Transport Use** | |
| 1-5 times/week | 5 |
| 1-5 times/month | 4 |
| 1-10 times/year | 3 |
| Rarely/Never | 2 |
| **Smartphone Owner** | |
| Yes | 10 |
| No | 4 |

The tasks users had to perform and the average time (Avg. Time) they took to complete each task are presented in Table 2 and Table 3. The results were divided in these two tables, were Table 2 presents the results of the first test group, and Table 3 of the second. The standard deviation (STD Time) was also computed in order to measure the variability around the mean. Finally, Table 2 and Table 3 also present the average rate (Avg. Rate), which derives from the assessment of users on the ease of completing each task, according to the Likert Scale introduced in Section 5.

According to the usability testing results, all users completed all tasks successfully. Older people and non-technological professionals (e.g. lawyers) took more time to perform the tasks than the others, but they all found "easy" or "very easy" to perform the majority of the tasks. Users found equally easy to buy tickets choosing the stations (Task 6) or choosing the zones (Task 5). The information in the remaining time screen (Task 9) was simplified between one test group and the other, explaining the fact that users of the first group considered "relatively easy" to interpret the information, while users of the second group found "very easy" to interpret it. Furthermore, almost all average rates are over 4, which means that users considered "easy" and "very easy" to perform the tasks, hence these usability tests are a good indicator of the ease-of-use of the proposed system.

During the tests users contributed with considerable amount of qualitative inputs to improve the prototype. Additionally, the results of the performance of the tasks, such as the number and type of error per task and the number of users making a particular error, also provided important insights that helped to improve the system.

**Table 2.** Performance and Rate per Task – First Test Group

| Task | Avg. Time (s) | STD Time | Avg. Rate |
|---|---|---|---|
| 1 - Register on the Application | 101 | 47 | 4,9 |
| 2 - Plan a Journey | 41 | 15 | 4,1 |
| 3 - Browse Maps | 21 | 8 | 4,6 |
| 4 - Check Prices | 18 | 11 | 4,7 |
| 5 - Purchase Tickets by Zone | 47 | 11 | 4,3 |
| 6 - Purchase Tickets by Station | 46 | 17 | 4,3 |
| 7 - Check Tickets Balance | 19 | 7 | 4,3 |
| 8 - See Past Journeys | 17 | 15 | 4,4 |
| 9 - Interpret Remaining Time Information | 15 | 17 | 3,7 |
| 10 - Add a Bank Account | 56 | 13 | 4,7 |
| 11 - Disable Automatic Renewal | 25 | 28 | 4,1 |
| 12 - Turn Off Sound and Vibration Options | 13 | 8 | 4,7 |

**Table 3.** Performance and Rate per Task – Second Test Group

| Task | Avg. Time (s) | STD Time | Avg. Rate |
|---|---|---|---|
| 1 - Register on the Application | 100 | 28 | 4,6 |
| 2 - Plan a Journey | 45 | 9 | 4,4 |
| 3 - Browse Maps | 25 | 10 | 4,3 |
| 4 - Check Prices | 22 | 14 | 4,3 |
| 5 - Purchase Tickets by Zone | 26 | 7 | 4,6 |
| 6 - Purchase Tickets by Station | 38 | 13 | 4,6 |
| 7 - Check Tickets Balance | 21 | 14 | 3,9 |
| 8 - See Past Journeys | 15 | 9 | 4,4 |
| 9 - Interpret Remaining Time Information | 9 | 4 | 4,9 |
| 10 - Add a Bank Account | 81 | 69 | 4,1 |
| 11 - Disable Automatic Renewal | 26 | 19 | 4,3 |
| 12 - Turn Off Sound and Vibration Options | 8 | 4 | 4,7 |

After the usability testing procedure, users had to answer to a questionnaire. Despite being administered in a small sample, the answers provided important feedback about the mobile application and about the concept of buying public transport tickets with a mobile phone. The usefulness of such a system was clear among all participants.

Participants found this payment method more convenient compared with traditional ticketing systems, because of the possibility to avoid queuing and access payment services anywhere and anytime, independent of the stores opening hours. Users also valued the fact they don't need to carry cash around and considered the process of buying easier and faster, as demonstrated in the following transcription:

*"Very useful, it avoids queues, and I don't need to carry coins and notes with me."*

Since the actual system implemented in AMP Public Transport Network doesn't allow carrying more than one type of ticket in the same Andante card, users appreciated the fact they don't need to carry as many cards as types of tickets, being possible to have all types in the same device. They also liked the possibility of automatic renewal of the monthly travel card.

*"I like the option of renew automatically the monthly travel card. Nowadays, at the end of each month I have to go to a physical store to renew the monthly travel card. You can imagine how huge the queues are!"*

Users usually have problems to identify the number of zones they are going to cross, in order to buy the correct ticket. Thus, the option of purchasing a ticket choosing the departure and the ending station was considered very convenient. Users also attributed great importance to the fact that the application offered additional services beyond the payment. They valued having the information about public transport schedules and maps, and also personalized information.

*"Very useful, because it joins information about public transport with the possibility of buying and validating tickets."*

When asked about mobile payments security and risks concerns, some of the interviewees felt safe about using such an application. Others were apprehensive about some risks, such as the unauthorized use of the mobile phone and payment features, in the case of lost or stolen device. Users would feel safer if they could set up a Passcode or PIN for payments above a certain value. They also suggested the possibility to define a limit per transaction or a monthly limit. In the case of the payment system being associated to a bank account, users would need more information about the process.

Participants also suggested that the possibility to set up PINs to access some menus that are more susceptible (payments, bank accounts ...) should be possible. Users' privacy was also mentioned and perceived as a risk. They were concerned about what type of information will be stored on the mobile phone.

*"What type of data will be kept on the mobile phone? And if someone hack my phone and access my personal data?"*

When asked about the price they were willing to pay for such a service, all interviewees answered they would only pay the price of the application. They were not willing to pay an additional price per ticket purchased: if this was the solution provided by AMP, they would prefer instead to use the traditional ticketing systems. Few users would be able to pay recursively an additional price, only considered feasible under certain circumstances, such as being late, or in a hurry.

Finally, all interviewees stated that they would use a mobile payment system to buy and validate travel tickets. They considered the system useful, with several advantages over traditional ticketing systems, potentiating their intention of use.

The theories and determinants of mobile payment adoption presented in section 3 are evident in users' answers. These were interpreted and grouped into factors that influence the adoption of mobile payments, and these findings are summarized in Table 4.

**Table 4.** Factors Influencing Mobile Payment Adoption

| Factors Influencing Mobile Payment Adoption | Sub-factors | Potential Effect on Adoption |
|---|---|---|
| Ease of use | • The average rating of the tasks was "easy" or "very easy". | • Positive |
| Usefulness | • Very useful. Many advantages over traditional ticketing systems. | • Positive |
| Relative Advantages | • Remote and ubiquitous access to payment. | • Positive |
| | • Avoid queues. | • Positive |
| | • Not necessary to carry cash. | • Positive |
| | • Easier and faster to purchase tickets. | • Positive |
| | • Several types of tickets in the same device. | • Positive |
| | • Centralization of several services in the same device. | • Positive |
| Additional Services | • Information about public transport (maps, schedules, …) | • Positive |
| | • Personalized information (past journeys, tickets balance, …) | • Positive |
| Compatibility | • Users' needs: information about public transport, monthly travel card automatic renewal, respecting purchase and validation habits. | • Positive |
| Complexity | • Some options weren't in the right menu. | • Negative |
| | • Some options/menus didn't have the right name. | • Negative |
| Risks and Security | • Unauthorized use. | • Negative |
| | • Where and what type of information is stored. | • Negative |
| | • Set PINs and Passcodes. | • Positive |
| | • Privacy concerns. | • Negative |
| Cost | • Premium price | • Negative |

The final column indicates the potential effect that each sub-factor may have in the consumer adoption of mobile payments. Ease of use, usefulness, relative advantages, additional services and compatibility have a positive effect on mobile payment adoption, while complexity, perceived risks and premium price have a negative effect.

# 8     Conclusions

The purpose of this paper was to propose a mobile payment system to be implemented in Public Transport of the Metropolitan Area of Oporto and to test the concept among real users. After defining the payment ticketing model, a prototype was developed and tested with users. The findings suggest that users considered the system easy-to-use, intuitive and functional. The usefulness of such a system was also consensual among participants. Remote and ubiquitous access to payment, queue avoidance, and the possibility to have several types of tickets in the same device were the major advantages reported by users. The integration of additional services with payment and validation features in the same device was really valued by the customers. The proposed solution centralizes information in a single channel, which is currently scattered across several channels. The introduction of additional services appears to be an important factor in the decision of adopting a mobile payment system; however this factor is not much explored by current adoption models. This may be an important factor to be explored in future research.

Users also valued the fact that the new ticketing system was consistent with their habits and needs, enhancing their experience at the same time. They considered really useful the renewal of the monthly travel ticket over-the-air, the automatic conversion into zone tickets, and the real-time traffic information provided by the system. Additionally, users criticize some options and menus that were confusing and not easy to understand.

The mobile environment brings some concerns about security and perceived risks, such as unauthorized use of the personal device and personal information, information storage and privacy concerns. Finally users stated that they were willing to pay the value of the application, but they wouldn't pay any extra cost for each ticket purchased. These findings are different from Mallat et al. [21] study where they stated that the cost was not a significant determinant of mobile ticketing adoption. This evidence was explained by the fare structure of Helsinki city public transport, where mobile ticketing is cheaper than using cash to buy a single ticket inside the vehicle.

From a managerial perspective the findings suggest that more attention should be paid to the ease-of-use and usefulness of the system, as well as to the compatibility with the habits and needs of the customers, where developers should try to improve the actual processes. It can also be concluded that a mobile payment system must be integrated with additional and complementary services, in order to achieve consumer acceptance and therefore critical mass.

Due to the explorative nature and small sample of this study, the findings cannot be generalized. They offer a first insight of the potential adoption of such a system in AMP Public Transport, as well as guidelines for the specification of the mobile payment system. Further work must be done, in order to improve the system and test it in real environment.

**Acknowledgments.** This work is being supported by TICE - MOBIPAG project 13847, Mobile Payments National Initiative ("Iniciativa Nacional para Pagamentos Móveis – Serviços Diferenciadores com base em Pagamentos Móveis", www.tice.pt). This project also involves Universidade do Minho, CEDT, Cardmobili, Creative Systems, and Wintouch. Funding is provided under the COMPETE, QREN programme, managed by AdI, in the context of European Union FEDER. IBM CAS Portugal, INEGI and IDMEC Pólo FEUP are also supporting the project at FEUP (www.fe.up.pt/IBM-CAS-Portugal).

# References

1. Au, Y.A., Kauffman, R.J.: The economics of mobile payments: Understanding stakeholder issues for an emerging financial technology application. Electronic Commerce Research and Applications 7(2), 141–164 (2008)
2. iParque, http://www.iparque.pt/
3. Pagamento Móvel de Estacionamento, https://estacionamento.pagamentomovel.pt/sintra/
4. Mallat, N.: Exploring Consumer Adoption of Mobile Payments – A Qualitative Study. The Journal of Strategic Information Systems 16(4), 413–432 (2007)
5. NFC Forum: NFC in Public Transport. Technical report, NFC Forum (2011)
6. Paybox, http://www.paybox.at/
7. Boer, R., Boer, T.: Mobile Payments 2010: Market Analysis and Overview. Technical report, Chiel Liezenber (Innopay) and Ed Achterberg, Telecompaper (2009)
8. Becker, A., Mladenow, A., Kryvinska, N., Strauss, C.: Aggregated survey of sustainable business models for agile mobile service delivery platforms. Journal of Service Science Research 4(1), 97–121 (2012)
9. Touch&Travel, http://www.touchandtravel.de/
10. Bohm, A., Murtz, B., Sommer, C., Wermuth, M.: Location-based ticketing in public transport. In: Proceedings of the 8th International IEEE Conference on Intelligent Transportation Systems, Austria (2005)
11. Ferreira, M.C., Cunha, A., Cunha, J.F., Nóvoa, M.H., Dias, T.G., Cunha, M.M.: A Survey of current trends in smartphone based payment and validation services for public transport users. In: The Art & Science of Service Conference, Maastricht (2012)
12. Vappereau, P.: Calypso developments: benefits, technology and implementations. Eurotransport Magazine 10(3), 24–43 (2012)
13. Auer, L., Kryvinska, N., Strauss, C.: Service-oriented Mobility Architecture Provides Highly-configurable Wireless Services. In: The IEEE Wireless Telecommunications Symposium, Prague (2009)
14. Global Platform: Global Platform's Value Proposition for the Public Transport Industry: Seamless, Secure Travel throughout Multiple Transport Networks. White Paper, Global Platform (2009)
15. Davis, F.D., Bagozzi, R.P., Warshaw, P.R.: User acceptance of computer technology: a comparison of two theoretical models. Management Science 35(8), 982–1003 (1989)
16. Fishbein, M., Ajzen, I.: Belief, attitude, intention and behaviour: an introduction to theory and research. Addison-Wesley, Reading (1975)
17. Yoon, C., Kim, S.: Convenience and TAM in a ubiquitous computing environement: the case of wirelee LAN. Electronic Commerce Research and Applications 6(1), 102–112 (2007)

18. Bruner II, G.C., Kumar, A.: Explaining consumer acceptance of handheld internet devices. Journal of Business Research 58(8), 553–558 (2005)
19. Lee, M.C.: Factors influencing the adoption of internet banking: an integration of TAM and TPB with perceived risk and perceived benefit. Electronic Commerce Research Applications 3(3), 130–141 (2009)
20. Dabholkar, P.A., Bagozzi, R.P.: An attitude model of technology-based self-service: moderating effects of consumer traits and situational factors. Journal of the Academy of Marketing Science 30(3), 184–201 (2002)
21. Mallat, N., Rossi, M., Tuunainen, V.K., Öörni, A.: An empirical investigation of mobile ticketing service adoption in public transportation. Personal and Ubiquitous Computing 12(1), 57–65 (2008)
22. Schierz, P.G., Schilke, O., Wirtz, B.W.: Understanding Consumer Acceptance of Mobile Payment Services: An Empirical Analysis. Electronic Commerce Research and Applications 9(3), 209–216 (2010)
23. Kim, C., Mirusmonov, M., Lee, I.: An empirical examination of factors influencing the intention to use mobile payment. Computers in Human Behaviour 26(3), 310–322 (2010)
24. Rogers, E.M.: Diffusion of innovations. Free Press, New York (1995)
25. Tornatzky, L.G., Klein, K.J.: Innovation Characteristics and innovation adoption implementation: a meta-analysis of findings. IEEE Transactions on Engineering Management 29(1), 28–44 (1982)
26. Laukkanen, T., Lauronen, J.: Consumer value creation in mobile banking services. International Journal of Mobile Communications 3(4), 325–338 (2005)
27. Szmigin, I., Bourne, H.: Electronic cash: a qualitative assessment of its adoption. International Journal of Bank Marketing 17(4), 192–202 (1999)
28. Wu, J.-H., Wang, S.-C.: What drives mobile commerce?: An empirical evaluation of the revised technology acceptance model. Information & Management 42(5), 719–729 (2005)
29. Dahlberg, T., Mallat, N., Ondrus, J., Zmijewska, A.: Past, present and future of mobile payments research: A literature review. Electronic Commerce Research and Applications 7(2), 165–181 (2008)
30. Siau, K., Sheng, H., Nah, F., Davis, S.: A qualitative investigation on consumer trust is mobile commerce. International Journal of Electronic Business 2(3), 283–300 (2004)
31. Lwin, M., Wirtz, J., Williams, J.D.: Consumer online privacy concerns and responses: a power responsibility equilibrium perspective. Journal of the Academy of Marketing Science 35(4), 572–585 (2007)
32. Bauer, H.H., Reichardt, T., Schule, A.: User requirements for location based services. In: IADIS International Conference e-Commerce (2005)
33. Ghosh, K., Swaminatha, T.M.: Software security and privacy risks in mobile e-commerce. Communications of the ACM 44(2), 51–57 (2001)
34. Sharp, H., Rogers, Y., Preece, J.: Interaction Design: beyond human-computer interaction, 2nd edn. John Wiley & Sons, Ltd., West Sussex (2007)
35. Nielsen, J., Mohlich, R.: Heuristic evaluation of user interfaces. In: Proceedings of ACM CHI 1990 Conference (1990)
36. Nielsen, J., Mack, R.L.: Usability Inspection Methods. John Wiley & Sons, New York (1994)
37. Nielsen, J.: Finding usability problems through heuristic evaluation. In: Proceedings of CHI 1992, pp. 373–800 (1992)
38. Nielsen, J.: Usability Engineering. Academic Press Inc., California (1994)
39. Dumas, J.S., Redish, J.C.: A Practical Guide to Usability Testing: Revised Edition. Intellect Books, Exeter (1999)

# Benchmarking as a Development Tool in Healthcare

Paulus Torkki and Paul Lillrank

Department of Industrial Engineering and Management, Aalto University
Otaniementie 17, P.O. Box 15500, 00076 AALTO, Espoo, Finland
paulus.torkki@aalto.fi

**Keywords:** benchmarking, healthcare operations management, key performance indicators.

## 1 Introduction

Benchmarking (BM) has become one of the most popular management techniques. Since its development at Xerox Corporation in 1979 thousands of articles have been written about it [1,2]. Benchmarking has been used widely in all type of industries and countries [3]. Nandi and Banwet (2000) found 49 different definitions to benchmarking [4]. Many writers [5,6] have found Camp's (1995) formulation "Benchmarking is the search for industry best practices that will lead to superior performance " [7] the most cited and indicative definition. The most commonly cited typology is from the same source: the distinction between internal, competitive, functional and generic benchmarking [7,8].

The purpose of this paper is to define benchmarking more precisely, and to discuss its applications in healthcare.

## 2 Definition of BM

Management is not an exact science that could deliver predictions; such as if you do A, then B will happen. Rather it is a heuristics that should allow researchers and practitioners to deal with complex issues using clear and sharp conceptual language. Therefore definitions are important.

Any management concept needs first a definition of its ontology, i.e. the core phenomenon under study, what it is and what it is not. Second, a concept needs an associated epistemology to describe what can be known, measured, and analysed. Third, especially in engineering and clinical medicine a praxeology is needed describing its supposed use, costs and benefits.

The conceptual confusion in management studies often arises from unclear ontologies. For example, customer value is the difference between what you get and what you give; quality is the difference between specifications and realized outputs. These relations are the ontological cores. Both sides of the relations can be elaborated on endlessly, such as customer value being realized at the point of sales or over the life cycle. Such elaborations may add detail, but may also obscure the core.

J.F. e Cunha, M. Snene, and H. Nóvoa (Eds.): IESS 2013, LNBIP 143, pp. 279–284, 2013.
© Springer-Verlag Berlin Heidelberg 2013

In this paper we claim that the core of BM is a real-to-real comparison production systems: my system in relation to the best comparable system. BM is a way to identify performance (performance BM) and the ways to achieve it (process BM). However, ontology also needs to be clear on what a concept is not. BM is different from alternative ways to do comparisons. Such are, for example, to compare a current state to goals and means that are theoretically derived (six sigma quality), normative (zero defect), innovative (a car for every purse and purpose), ideal types (excellence models), or visionary (insanely great). BM compares real with real.

In this paper we claim that the core of BM is a real-to-real comparison production systems: my system in relation to the best comparable system. BM is a way to identify performance (performance BM) and the ways to achieve it (process BM). However, ontology also needs to be clear on what a concept is not. BM is different from alternative ways to do comparisons. Such are, for example, goals and means that are theoretically derived (six sigma quality), normative (zero defect), innovative (a car for every purse and purpose), ideal types (excellence models), or visionary (insanely great). BM compares real with real.

The real-to-real ontology of BM has epistemological implications. First, performance is captured through empirical, demonstrated and documented key performance indicators (KPI). They can be:

- Results; outputs or outcomes
- Technologies and processes that achieve those results
- Resources staffing those processes
- Governance, incentives, and organizational arrangements to keep those resources productive.

KPIs can be defined and comparisons can be made on different levels of abstraction. That calls for the selection of appropriate variables. Apples can be compared with apples in obvious terms such as size, colour, or sweetness. Apples can be compared with oranges with variables measuring comparable issues, such as vitamin C content. In Healthcare, we can compare hernia and knee arthroscopy surgery using operating room (OR) utilization rates, since utilization relates more to scheduling methods than to the particular procedures of each clinical subspecialty.

Second, as the object of comparison is a system, it can be assumed to have more than one KPI. The relations between the KPI's need to be explicated. They can be dependent, from which may follow trade-offs; or independent, from which follows that there may be several alternative best practices.

Third, BM variables are typically classified into what and how. What results has an organization achieved in terms of productivity, quality, or financial performance? Such measures can usually be extracted from regular reporting. The how –issues require a model that specifies the operating system and explains how the results are achieved. Models can be formulated in two ways. First, if quantitative data is available, a regression model can be built with What as a dependent variable and How's (sub-measures) as independent variables. Second, if a quantitative model cannot be constructed, the how's can be explained by combining performance and process benchmarking as defined by Spendolini 1992 [9]. The purpose is to describe the processes and methods that explain differences between high and low performance systems.

This definition carries practical implications. First, demonstrated best performance and practice is real, therefore, given comparable circumstances, catching up to it does not imply significant risks. Second, as the observed best performance is real, the "it can't be done" –argument against change looses value. Third, assuming there are several successful KPI combinations and the KPIs are not dependent, a follower can compare both single KPIs and combinations thereof. Fourth, an organization that can demonstrate it is the best needs to adopt a theoretical, innovative, or visionary frame for further improvement, and be prepared for the accompanying risks.

This definition carries practical implications. First, demonstrated best performance and practice is real, therefore, given comparable circumstances, catching up to it does not imply significant risks. Second, as the observed best performance is real, the "it can't be done" –argument against change looses value. Third, assuming there are several successful KPI combinations and the KPIs are not dependent, a follower can compare single KPIs and combinations thereof. Fourth, an organization that can demonstrate it is the best needs to adopt a theoretical, innovative, or visionary frame for further improvement, and be prepared for the accompanying risks.

# 3    BM in Healthcare

The real-with-real constellation is particularly important in services. Services in general and health services in particular are open and complex systems. Emergency departments must accept all kinds of patients at any time. All the potential inputs and influences on a patient case can't possibly be controlled. Similar results can be achieved by different means. Therefore BM needs to compare systems and normalize several key variables, such as resource consumption and case mix. The apparent complexity of health services can be reduced by segmentation. Healthcare is not an industry with a single production concept or business model, rather a cluster of operating logics or modes. Following [10] the modes are prevention, emergency, one-visit, electives, emergent cure processes, continuous care, and patient projects. Each mode has different KPIs and requires different ways to manage resources and processes. In this paper we focus on electives. They are procedures where demand is pre-selected and sorted through a referral system, diagnostics and corresponding procedures are reasonably precise, production can be planned and scheduled in advance, and outputs can be counted and evaluated against set quality criteria. Therefore quality-adjusted productivity is a relevant KPI.

The real-with-real constellation is particularly important in services. Services in general and health services in particular are open and complex systems. Emergency departments must accept all kinds of patients at any time. All the potential inputs and influences on a patient case can't possibly be controlled. Similar results can be achieved by different means. Therefore BM needs to compare systems and normalize several key variables, such as resource consumption and case mix.

We compared the productivity differences between 9 Finnish outpatient surgery units. The unit of analysis is a surgery unit, which may contain several operating rooms (OR). The units were located in various hospitals, i.e. one hospital may have several units. The performance data was obtained from hospital information systems and included 28 224 surgeries in total. The resource data was collected from respective HR-systems.

The key output measure was productivity defined as weighted operations per full-time-equivalent (FTE) personnel resources used. The operations were weighted using their historical average throughput time to make the output comparable [110]. Throughput time is defined as the time from patient entering to patient leaving the OR.

It was assumed that differences in productivity are driven by the following sub-measures (Fig.1):

- Adjusted throughput time of the OR, measured procedure-specifically and weighted based on the respective case mix
- Utilization rate  defined as patient-in-OR–time divided by staffed hours
- Resource intensity defined as nurse FTEs per staffed OR.

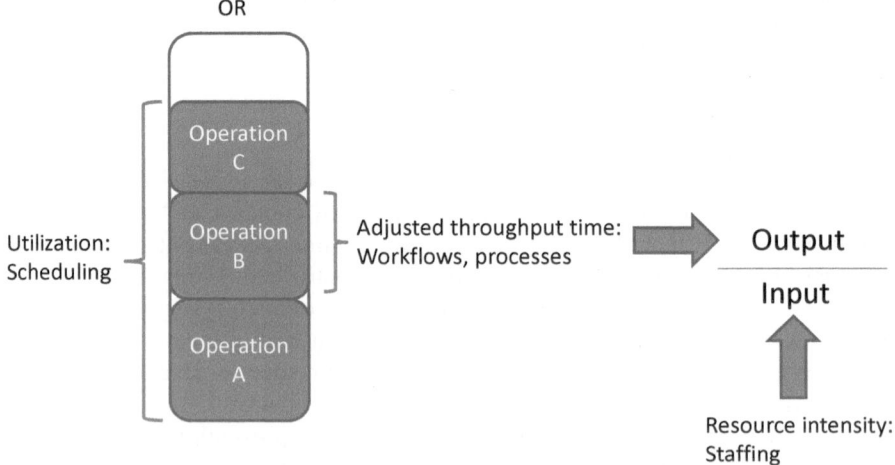

**Fig. 1.** The relationship of sub measures and the related steering mechanisms

The basic information of the compared surgical units A to I is given in Table 1.

**Table 1.** Basic data on the compared surgical units

| Hospital | A | B | C | D | E | F | G | H | I |
|---|---|---|---|---|---|---|---|---|---|
| Number of operations | 2671 | 2050 | 2636 | 2375 | 3955 | 5062 | 2854 | 2311 | 3284 |
| Weighted operations | 3562 | 2598 | 3137 | 3053 | 5761 | 7165 | 4496 | 3323 | 4732 |
| Operating Rooms | 3 | 3 | 3 | 4 | 6 | 8 | 5 | 3 | 4 |
| Nurses (FTE) | 13,7 | 16,5 | 15,3 | 14 | 22,9 | 33,9 | 21,1 | 12,4 | 16 |

The sub-measures are calculated as differences to the averages in Table 2. The data shows that above average productivity can be achieved by different methods: in unit I high productivity derives from low resource intensity combined with high utilization; in units H and A high productivity is mostly due to short throughput time. The correlations between sub-measures were not significant (p>0.05).

**Table 2.** Sub-measures of the compared surgical units as differences (%) to averages

| Hospital | A | B | C | D | E | F | G | H | I |
|---|---|---|---|---|---|---|---|---|---|
| Productivity (weighted operations per FTE) | 12 % | -32 % | -11 % | -6 % | 9 % | -9 % | -8 % | 16 % | 28 % |
| Utilization* | -6 % | -8 % | 1 % | 1 % | 9 % | 5 % | -4 % | -4 % | 7 % |
| Resource intensity** | -5 % | 25 % | 5 % | -8 % | -14 % | 7 % | 13 % | -7 % | -16 % |
| Adjusted throughput time*** | -13 % | 5 % | 4 % | 12 % | 10 % | 5 % | -9 % | -11 % | 0 % |

\* In utilization, + means better value, ** in Resource intensity, - means better value and in ***Adjusted throughput time, - means better value in terms of productivity

We used process BM to understand the best practices explaining the best performances. The units E and I had most developed scheduling systems utilizing procedure-specific historical average duration information. Consequently their utilization rates were high. In unit I the staff management principles were most flexible. The hospital shared resources between surgical units and nurses could be allocated flexibly between units and ORs. Consequently I had the best (lowest) resource intensity. In unit A, concurrent preparation of patients lowered the throughput time. Consequently A had the best (shortest) throughput time.

These methods are not inter-dependent, i.e. a surgical unit can pursue one while ignoring the others. If an unit would apply the best practices on each sub-measure, calculably 38 47 % above average productivity could be achieved: 9 % above average utilization, 16 % below average resource intensity and 13 % below average throughput time.

## 4    Summary and Conclusion

Benchmarking is the real-to-real comparison of production systems aiming at finding best performance and identifying the ways to achieve it. In complex environments care must be taken to define the variables in a comparable way, and, based on Operations management theory, postulate sub-measures that can help explain the different ways to achieve the desirable results. In further studies, the approach will be applied to other segments [10], as data of this study was limited to elective operations.

When using BM as a development tool, combining performance (what) and process (how) data makes it possible to not only identify the best performer, but also to describe how performance is achieved, and what sub-measures can be improved. As a practical example, the units with best utilization rates had more sophisticated scheduling methods which can be applied to other units to improve utilization rates. When KPIs are independent, combining the best achievements on each sub-measure makes it possible to calculate an achievable productivity frontier.

# References

1. Dattakumar, R., Jagadeesh, R.: A review of literature on benchmarking. Benchmark Int. J. 10(3), 176–209 (2003)
2. Yasin, M.M.: Theory and practice of benchmarking: then and now. Benchmark Int. J. 9(3), 217–243 (2002)
3. Adebanjo, D., Abbas, A., Mann, R.: An investigation of the adoption and implementation of benchmarking. Int. J. Oper. Prod. Man 30(11), 1140–1169 (2012)
4. Nandi, S., Banwet, D.: Benchmarking for world class manufacturing – concept, framework and applications. Productivity 41(2), 189–200 (2000)
5. Anand, G., Kodali, R.: Benchmarking the benchmarking models. Benchmark Int. J. 15(3), 257–291 (2008)
6. Anderson, K., McAdam, R.: Reconceptualising benchmarking development in UK organisations: the effects of size and sector. International Journal of Productivity and Performance Management 56(7), 538–558 (2007)
7. Camp, R.C.: Business Process Benchmarking: Finding and Implementing Best Practices, 464 p. ASQC Quality Press, Milwaukee WI (1995)
8. Francis, G., Holloway, J.: What have we learned? Themes from the literature on best practice benchmarking. Int. J. Manag. Rev. 9(3), 171–189 (2007)
9. Spendolini, M.J.: The benchmarking book. Amacom, New York (1992)
10. Lillrank, P., Groop, J., Malmstöm, T.: Demand and Supply–based operating modes—A Framework for Analyzing Health Care Service Production. Milbank Quarterly 88(4), 595–615 (2010)
11. Torkki, P., Alho, A., Peltokorpi, A., Torkki, M., Kallio, P.: Managing urgent surgery as a process: Case study of a trauma center. Int. J. Technol Assess 22(2), 255–260 (2006)

# Towards an Ontology and Modeling Approach for Service Science

Geert Poels, Griet Van Der Vurst, and Elisah Lemey

Center for Service Intelligence
Faculty of Economics and Business Administration
Ghent University
Tweekerkenstraat 2, 9000 Gent, Belgium
{geert.poels,griet.vandervurst,elisah.lemey}@ugent.be

**Abstract.** Service Science is an academic discipline that investigates the organization and operation of service systems and that designs novel solutions for their innovation, engineering and management. As a new interdisciplinary field, Service Science is in need of a solid conceptual foundation that could act as a unifying paradigm for researchers having backgrounds in different disciplines. Apart from common research abstractions and a shared vocabulary, the field would also benefit from modeling artifacts for studying and designing service systems. This paper reports on a research-in-progress that addresses these needs by developing a Service Science ontology, which will be elaborated as the meta-model of a new service system modeling language. The paper summarizes our current research results and contributes to the Service Science literature by presenting a new graphical conceptual model for service systems.

**Keywords:** Service Science, service system, conceptual model, ontology.

## 1 Introduction and Problem Statement

The world's economy manifests itself increasingly as service economy [1, 2]. The evolution in the focus of economy from goods to service [3] and the recognition that service is a research area in its own right [4] has stimulated the development of research fields that study the strategy, design and management of the constituents of the service economy. One of these emerging research fields is Service Science [5-8]. Service Science aims at creating knowledge that informs service system design and innovation through the use of 'smart' (i.e., IT-enabled) services. It is an interdisciplinary field with as main contributing disciplines service management, service engineering and service-oriented computing.

What distinguishes Service Science is the unique lens through which the service economy is studied. The basic unit of analysis is the service system [9], which is a configuration of people, organizations, technology, and shared information set up for the co-creation of value by service providers and clients. The service system is the main abstraction used by Service Science researchers for investigating the architecture, composition, operation and interaction of the entities that are provider and client of services [10].

J.F. e Cunha, M. Snene, and H. Nóvoa (Eds.): IESS 2013, LNBIP 143, pp. 285–291, 2013.

A scientific abstraction becomes an effective instrument for communication, reasoning and action, if it is based on a shared worldview [9]. The need for a common mental model of service system that builds on shared concepts and vocabulary has been expressed by leading Service Science researchers (e.g., [1, 2]). It is also reflected in the call for research on modeling and simulation frameworks for the study and conceptual design of service systems that was made by the Service Science, Management, Engineering and Design (SSMED) community [11]. The formal representation and measurement of work in service systems has been posed as a major research challenge since the start of Service Science [6]. In a recent survey research involving 200 academics and 95 business executives, modeling and simulation were flagged as priority research topics for stimulating service innovation [2].

This paper reports on research-in-progress that was initiated to address two eminent research questions: (i) how to conceptualize service systems such that a broad array of aspects that are relevant to the study and design of service systems is accounted for, and (ii) how to devise a rigorously sound and practically relevant modeling approach for service systems that is based on such a shared conceptualization.

Section 2 presents the research scope, objectives, intended scientific contributions, and research plan. Section 3 presents our preliminary results. Section 4 concludes the paper.

## 2     Research Approach

We will approach the two research questions from the field of Conceptual Modeling, which researches methods and languages for creating representations of real-world domains or situations, the contextual factors that determine modeling effectiveness and efficiency, and the (desirable) characteristics of the resulting representations [12]. An approach centered on the conceptual modeling of service systems responds to the above mentioned research calls for models of service system structure and behavior, but does not address the modeling of the service system image in computer systems – which we acknowledge to be another important research topic, that is, however, outside the intended scope of our research.

A further choice with respect to research approach (and hence impacting research scope) is to start researching the service system conceptualization from the service system worldview of Spohrer and Maglio [13]. This worldview is heavily grounded in Service-Dominant Logic [3, 14], which is a descriptive theory originating in the Marketing discipline that sees all economic activity as service exchanges. Many Service Science researchers have proposed Service-Dominant Logic as the philosophical foundation of Service Science [9, 15, 16], however, the need to introduce systems thinking (based on system/network theories) to cope with the complexity and contextual nature of service systems has also been expressed [17]. The service system worldview of Spohrer and Maglio is influenced by both Service-Dominant Logic (to explain the 'service' in service system) and Systems Sciences (to explain the 'system' in service system). Their worldview crystallizes around a set of ten foundational concepts – service system ecology, service system entities, outcomes, interactions, value proposition based interactions, governance mechanism based interactions, stakeholders, measures, resources, and access rights.

The first research objective is to develop a service system ontology. One of the goals of conceptual modeling is to turn the conceptualizations or worldviews that underlie scientific disciplines and practice areas into explicit descriptions that are called domain ontologies. A service system ontology, represented in a format that facilitates communication and sharing, provides an internally consistent and precise account of service system concepts, their relations, governing axioms, and underlying assumptions about the nature of the real-world and our knowledge of it. As such it offers a language with explicit semantics to researchers and practitioners, on the basis of which they can develop a shared understanding of the phenomena they observe, investigate and construct. The development of such an ontology, based on the foundational concepts of Spohrer and Maglio [13], would present an original and much needed scientific contribution to the field of Service Science [18-19] as well as provide the basis for the accomplishment of the second research objective.

This second research objective entails the transformation of the service system ontology into a meta-model that defines a modeling language for service systems. Meta-models define the constructs and rules that compose modeling languages. By adding graphical modeling symbols (e.g., using a notation like UML), the ontology's concepts and relations can be used as modeling language constructs for creating representations of real-world service systems – to study them – or for conceptually designing new service systems – to build them. The ontology's axioms and assumptions will provide modeling language rules that enforce the construction of service system models that ontologically commit to the underlying domain ontology (which is the outcome of the first research objective). The development of a modeling approach for service systems is a much-desired scientific contribution to Service Science and SSMED [2, 6, 11].

To achieve these objectives, a five-phase research plan was defined: theoretical analysis, ontology development, ontology evaluation, researching the modeling approach, and validation studies.

## 3    Preliminary Results

We are currently in the second research phase. In the first, theoretical analysis phase, we investigated the ten foundational concepts of the proposed service system worldview from the perspective of six theories and conceptual frameworks coming from different disciplines that study service: Service-Dominant Logic [3] (*Marketing*), Unified Services Theory [20] (*Operations Management*), Work System Framework [22] (*Information Systems*), Service Quality Gaps Model [21] (*Service Management, Marketing*), the systems theoretic conceptualization of service systems by Mora et al. [23] (*Service Engineering, Computer Science*), and the service ontology of Ferrario and Guarino [24] (*Applied Ontology*). The goal was to evaluate completeness, clarify the theoretical foundation of the concepts, and identify their relationships and constraints on these relationships.

The main result of the analysis (see [25]) was that all proposed foundational concepts are theoretically supported, though some concepts have more support than others. Also important is that none of the proposed concepts is rejected by the theories. We did identify a couple of issues that need further investigation, sense making and consensus seeking, because of different interpretations or positions taken in the theories used in the analysis: (i) whether service entails value co-production (e.g., Unified Services Theory) or value co-creation (e.g., Service-Dominant Logic); and (ii) whether service is a phenomenon that takes place within the service system (e.g., system theoretic model of Mora et al. [23]) or between service systems (e.g., Work System Framework).

Regarding the completeness of the set of ten foundational concepts, we deduced from the theories and frameworks a missing, eleventh concept, which is service itself. We define service as *mutual value co-creation*, which is the desired outcome of interactions between service system entities. The inclusion of service leads, however, to another issue to be resolved (by future research) and that is whether the 'mutuality' of the value co-creation resides in the service itself (e.g., as in the system theoretic model of Mora et al. [23]) or is realized through the exchange of services (e.g., point of view taken in Service-Dominant Logic).

In related work (see [26]), we investigated the ISPAR (Interact-Serve-Propose-Agree-Realize) model [27], which adds a process dimension to the service system worldview in order to better understand the dynamics of service systems. ISPAR is a normative model of all possible service system interaction outcomes. We investigated in particular whether ISPAR could act as a process model for service (given the position inherent in the service system worldview that service is a process, which is a view endorsed by all theories and models used in the theoretical analysis). We compared ISPAR to two other models (i.e., Alter's service value chain framework [22] and Ferrario and Guarino's layered structure of service activities [24]), which were developed independently from the service system worldview. Whereas neither model is as complete as ISPAR is, our analysis indicated that the representation of ISPAR as a branch model (showing a taxonomy of service system interaction outcomes) has shortcomings with respect to clarity and structure, which may hinder its use as an analysis and design instrument for service processes.

The second, ontology development phase builds upon the results of the theoretical analysis. As a first step in ontology development, we constructed a graphical conceptual model (in UML class diagram notation) of the service system worldview (Fig. 1). The theoretical grounding of the ten foundational concepts, augmented with the eleventh, service concept, allowed identifying relationships between the concepts and constraints on these relationships. Whereas the service system worldview proposed by Spohrer and Maglio [13] is a mere list of concepts, the general structure that we discovered through the theoretical analysis will help in developing a formal ontology out of the worldview. Further, we believe that the graphical model already helps in better understanding the service system worldview as it shows how different concepts (should) relate to each other. Therefore, we will explain the service system conceptualization on which the ontology is based via the graphical conceptual model that we developed.

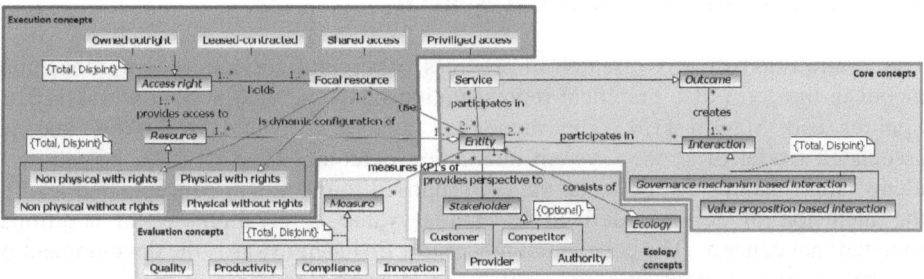

**Fig. 1.** Service system conceptual model

The diagram is overlaid with four coloured areas that further categorize the service system concepts in function of their relationship with the service process. *Core concepts* are those that play a role throughout the entire service process. At least two service system entities participate in interactions that create outcomes. The desired outcome is service, which we define as mutual value co-creation. Co-creation means that resources from all participating entities are needed to create value. Mutual means that an entity is only willing to create value for another entity if it is getting value out of the interactions itself. Value proposition based interactions are purely based on the voluntary reciprocal actions of the participating entities (e.g., free market transactions), whereas governance mechanism based interactions involve the participation of governing bodies (e.g., selling and buying goods through an auction).

*Ecology concepts* play a predominant role in the service process phases preceding the service realisation. The service system ecology is the aggregate of service system entities that are involved in the service system. As such it provides context to the interactions between the entities and to the service itself. The stakeholder concept allows considering the different roles that entities may play. Apart from the customer and provider perspectives, which refer to the main actors, other stakeholders such as authority (for governance mechanism based interactions) and competitor may be relevant, e.g., the value propositions of competitors may impact the service agreement between service provider and customer.

The *execution concepts* are required for service realisation. A service system entity is a dynamic configuration of resources of which there are four types: physical with rights (people), physical without rights (technology, natural resources), non-physical with rights (organizations), and non-physical without rights (shared information). Each entity in the service system needs at least one focal resource that holds the access rights to the other resources in the configuration, so has the discretionary power to utilize resources for the service realization.

Finally, the *evaluation concept* measure, which has four subtypes (quality, productivity, legal compliance, and sustainable innovation), is used in the post-realization phase to evaluate the effect of interaction outcomes on the state of the participating service system entities. As such these measures serve as Key Performance Indicators (KPI's) for service system entities.

# 4 Conclusion and Future Research

The contribution of this research-in-progress paper is a service system conceptual model in the form of a graphical representation of the service system worldview of Spohrer and Maglio [13]. The theoretical analyses of this worldview and its associated model of service system interaction outcomes (ISPAR) [25, 26] allowed identifying relationships between the ten proposed foundational concepts and lead to the inclusion of service, defined as mutual value co-creation, as an additional foundational concept. The conceptual model is a first step towards the development of a formal service system ontology, which can later be turned into a meta-model of a service system modelling language. At the same time, the conceptual model helps in understanding the proposed service system worldview by adding structure to the set of foundational concepts.

Future research will proceed according to the lines set out in the research plan (section 2). Also the remaining definitional issues identified in section 3 need further investigation to resolve them.

# References

1. Baines, T., Lightfoot, H., Peppard, J., Johnson, M., Tiwari, A., Shehab, E.: Towards an operations strategy for product-centric servitization. International Journal of Operations & Production Management 29, 494–519 (2009)
2. Ostrom, A.L., Bitner, M.J., Brown, S.W., Burkhard, K.A., Goul, M., Smith-Daniels, V., Demirkan, H., Rabinovich, E.: Moving Forward and Making a Difference: Research Priorities for the Science of Service. Journal of Service Research 13, 4–36 (2010)
3. Vargo, S.L., Lusch, R.F.: Evolving to a New Dominant Logic for Marketing. Journal of Marketing 68, 1–17 (2004)
4. Edvardsson, B., Gustafsson, A., Roos, I.: Service portraits in service research: a critical review. International Journal of Service Industry Management 16, 107–121 (2005)
5. Chesbrough, H.: Toward a science of services. Harvard Business Review 83, 16–17 (2005)
6. Maglio, P.P., Srinivasan, S., Kreulen, J.T., Spohrer, J.: Service systems, service scientists, SSME, and innovation. Communications of the ACM 49, 81–85 (2006)
7. Spohrer, J., Maglio, P.P., Bailey, J., Gruhl, D.: Steps Toward a Science of Service Systems. IEEE Computer 40, 71–77 (2007)
8. Spohrer, J., Maglio, P.P.: The Emergence of Service Science: Toward Systematic Service Innovations to Accelerate Co-Creation of Value. Production and Operations Management 17, 238–246 (2008)
9. Maglio, P.P., Vargo, S.L., Caswell, N., Spohrer, J.: The service system is the basic abstraction of service science. Information Systems and E-Business Management 7, 395–406 (2009)
10. Maglio, P.P., Spohrer, J.: Fundamentals of service science. Journal of the Academy of Marketing Science 36, 18–20 (2008)
11. IfM, IBM: Succeeding through service innovation: a service perspective for education, research, business and government. University of Cambridge Institute for Manufacturing, Cambridge (2008)
12. Wand, Y., Weber, R.: Research Commentary: Information Systems and Conceptual Modeling – A Research Agenda. Information Systems Research 13, 363–377 (2002)

13. Spohrer, J., Maglio, P.P.: Service science: Toward a smarter planet. In: Karwowski, W., Salvendy, G. (eds.) Introduction to Service Engineering. Wiley, New York (2010)
14. Lusch, R.F., Vargo, S.L.: Service-dominant logic: reactions, reflections and refinements. Marketing Theory 6, 281–288 (2006)
15. Lusch, R.F., Vargo, S.L., Wessels, G.: Toward a conceptual foundation for service science: Contributions from service-dominant logic. IBM Systems Journal 47, 5–14 (2008)
16. Vargo, S.L., Akaka, M.A.: Service-Dominant Logic as a Foundation for Service Science: Clarifications. Service Science 1, 32–41 (2009)
17. Barile, S., Spohrer, J., Polese, F.: System Thinking for Service Research Advances. Service Science 2, i–iii (2010)
18. Ferrario, R., Guarino, N.: Service value chain and value co-creation in an ontological perspective. Paper presented at the 5th International Workshop on Value Modeling and Business Ontology (VMBO), Gent, February 7-8 (2011)
19. Fragidis, G., Tarabanis, K.: Towards an Ontological Foundation of Service Dominant Logic. In: Snene, M., Ralyté, J., Morin, J.-H. (eds.) IESS 2011. LNBIP, vol. 82, pp. 201–215. Springer, Heidelberg (2011)
20. Sampson, S.E., Froehle, C.M.: Foundations and Implications of a Proposed Unified Services Theory. Production and Operations Management 15, 329–343 (2006)
21. Parasuraman, A., Zeithaml, V.A., Berry, L.L.: A conceptual model of service quality and its implications for future research. Journal of Marketing 49, 41–50 (1985)
22. Alter, S.: Service system fundamentals: Work system, value chain, and life cycle. IBM Systems Journal 47, 71–85 (2010)
23. Mora, M., Raisinghani, M.S., O'Connor, R., Gelman, O.: Toward an Integrated Conceptualization of the service and Service system Concepts: A systems approach. International Journal of Information Systems in the Service Sector 1, 36–57 (2009)
24. Ferrario, R., Guarino, N.: Towards an Ontological Foundation for Services Science. In: Domingue, J., Fensel, D., Traverso, P. (eds.) FIS 2008. LNCS, vol. 5468, pp. 152–169. Springer, Heidelberg (2009)
25. Lemey, E., Poels, G.: Towards a Service System Ontology for Service Science. In: Kappel, G., Maamar, Z., Motahari-Nezhad, H.R. (eds.) ICSOC 2011. LNCS, vol. 7084, pp. 250–264. Springer, Heidelberg (2011)
26. Lemey, E., Poels, G.: Towards a Process Model for Service Systems. In: Snene, M. (ed.) IESS 2012. LNBIP, vol. 103, pp. 1–15. Springer, Heidelberg (2012)
27. Spohrer, J., Anderson, L.C., Pass, N.J., Ager, T., Gruhl, D.: Service Science. Journal of Grid Computing 6, 313–324 (2008)

# Extended DEMO-Based SLAs
# to Specify Customers' Expectations

Mário Almeida, Carlos Mendes, and Miguel Mira da Silva

Avenida Rovisco Pais
1000 Lisboa, Portugal
{mario.almeida,carlos.mendes,mms}@ist.utl.pt

**Abstract.** Currently the services sector gained ground to the manufacturing industry to become one of the most profitable sector and with the greater growth curve. However, the organizations who have been leading the market have a lack of strong conceptual foundation which contributes to the gaps that reduce the services quality. Due to this increase of the gaps became more difficult for the service providers and their customers to align their expectations about the services quality. We propose to reduce the gaps by formally specifying the SLAs, using as foundation the Enterprise Ontology theory. This proposal is a new version of the DEMO-based SLAs with a more complex structure of Service Level Agreement (SLA). We evaluated the new proposal's version by gathering the feedback from experts in the area of SLAs specification. The feedbacks were rather positive since the interviewers agreed with the proposed SLA attributes.

**Keywords:** Service Science, Service Quality, Service Level Agreement, Enterprise Ontology, DEMO.

## 1 Introduction

The growth of the service sector has increased the importance of issues such as the quality of services provided to the customers [1]. To this end, various solutions are on the market and solutions based on ITIL or CMMI are among the most used worldwide[2]. The problem is that these solutions have a lack of theoretical foundation which leads to several inconsistencies between their implementations. This lack contributes to increase the gaps present in the gaps models [3] and leads to a reduction in the quality perceived by the customer.

We propose a solution based on Enterprise Ontology [4], and respective methodology DEMO, that intends to reduce the gap between customers' expectations and the perception of them by the service provider [3]. We propose to close this gap by formally specifying the customers' expectations into Services and Service Level Agreements. Several experiments have been performed [5] [6] [7] which allowed us to mature the proposal. In this paper we present the extended version of our proposal that contains a new structure of attributes for the Service Level Agreements (SLAs). Therefore, the research question that our research seeks to answer is: **Can DEMO be used to specify SLAs in order to model customers' expectations?**

J.F. e Cunha, M. Snene, and H. Nóvoa (Eds.): IESS 2013, LNBIP 143, pp. 292–298, 2013.

Design & Engineering Methodology for Organizations (DEMO) is a methodology for modeling, (re)designing and (re)engineering organizations and networks of organizations. This methodology is based on the Enterprise Ontology (EO) theory. DEMO models are independent of their implementation which helps to build generic models that can be applicable to any king of services [4]. At first glance it is not very clear the link between EO and the concept of service but recent studies [8] specified a service definition in accordance with EO and also a framework for specifying services [9] that served as basis for our proposal.

To evaluate our proposal personal interviews were carried out with seven experts in the field of Information Systems. These experts work in recognized organizations in the market.

The research method used in this paper was the Design Science Research Methodology (DSRM) which aims at the creation and subsequent evaluation of IT artifacts used to solve identified organizational problems [10].

This paper is structured as follows. In Section 2, we present a brief overview of the literature on the research problem area. Afterwards, we present our proposal, namely our DEMO-based proposal to specify the services quality (Section 3). In Section 4, we explain and show the evaluation process and finally we conclude the paper by reinforcing the main conclusions of this research (Section 5).

## 2    Related Work

There are some solutions used to specify service quality that are widely used. We now present two of them: Service Level Management and Web Services based Solutions.

Service Level Management is one of the key processes by which organizations manage their services, because it acts as the interface between the customer and the provider. At its most basic level, Service Level Management is involved in the following activities: define, agree, record and manage levels of service. There are a number of key elements required to ensure that services are fit for purpose and use, and remain so throughout their lifetime: service level requirements, targets and agreements [11].

Current Service Level Management solutions have two main flaws. First, they lack a strong conceptual foundation because they were derived from best practices of several years of implementations - not from a well-founded theory. Consequently, the inexistence of a theory may cause incoherencies among those solutions (second flaw). Service Level Management solutions are process-driven and not service-driven. These solutions are designed to work individually as processes but the interactions between these processes (such as Request Fulfillment, Service Level Management and Incident Management) are usually unclear. For instance, the connection between an incident and an SLA is neither clearly explained in ITIL nor in CMMI.

There are some solutions to specify the services quality that originated in the web services community. In [12] the authors show how to use Web Service Description Language (WSDL) and Web Service Flow Language (WSFL) to specify SLAs. However, this work suffers from the web vision tunnel as it is focused on the web services and does not try to specify business services. For instance, the specifications do not include penalties or prices. The researches in [13], [14] and [15] have the same bottleneck. Despite this trend in the web service community, there are some recent researches that try to overcome the mentioned web service tunnel vision. In [16] a novel framework for specifying and monitoring SLAs for Web Services is introduced: the Web Service Level Agreement (WSLA) framework. This framework is applicable to any inter-domain management scenario such as business process and service management or the management of networks, systems and applications in general. In [17] and [18] business criteria is also included in SLAs. These three solutions represent a new movement in the web service community; however, none is based on a strong conceptual foundation.

# 3    Proposal

This section corresponds to the design and development step of DSRM. In order to solve the problem of the difference between customers' expectations and the perception of those by the service provider, we propose **DEMO-based Service Level Agreements to specify customers' expectations**.

Our proposal for a SLA structure consists of three areas of concern in each of these areas has its specific attributes. This structure, as illustrated in Figure 1, consists of three areas: SLA Basic Information, SLA Responsibility Information and SLA Specific Information.

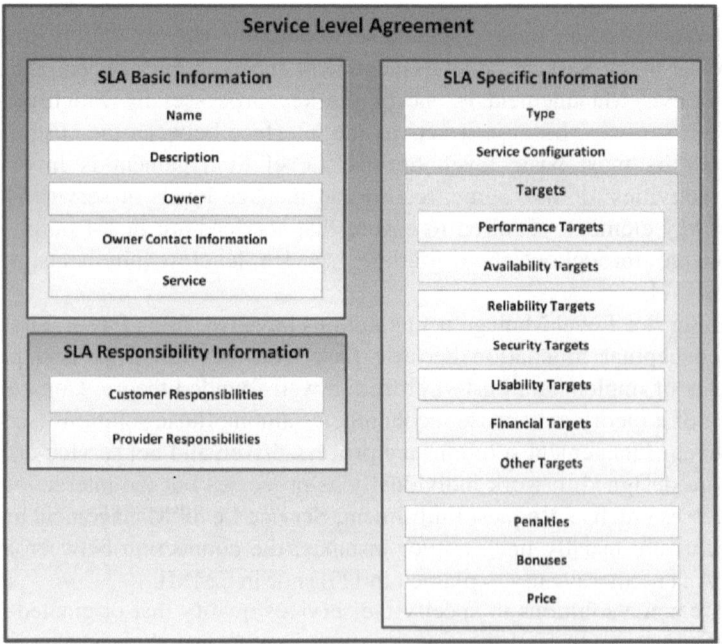

**Fig. 1.** Structure and Attributes of the DEMO-based Service Level Agreement

The **SLA Basic Information** area contains the generic information expected by anyone when listing all SLAs or searching for a particular SLA. In this area the following attributes are specified:

- *Name* – This attribute defines the name of the Service Level Agreement;
- *Description* – This attribute contains a short description of the purpose of the SLA. This description, together with the SLA Name attribute, helps answer the question "What";
- *Owner* and *Owner Contact Information* – These two attributes specify the name of the actor who owns the SLA and possible ways of being contacted by the customer or by another entity related to the SLA: the first attribute can be taken from the Actor Transaction Diagram while the second one is supplied by the Owner. These two attributes answer to the question 'Who is responsible for fulfilling the SLA?';
- *Service* – This attribute defines the service itself (on which this SLA is drawn) and makes the connection between our proposal and the Generic Service Specification Framework [9].

The **SLA Responsibility Information** area contains the information related to the duties and obligation of actors (customer and provider) when implementing the SLA. This area defines what is expected to be performed by each of the entities involved in this contract, in order to avoid misunderstandings or breaches of contract. In this area the following attributes are specified:

- *Customer Responsibilities* – This attribute lists the actions that the customer has to perform in compliance with this SLA. This information can be found in the Process Model and the Information Used Table (IUT) of DEMO;
- *Provider Responsibilities* – This attribute is similar to that mentioned above but with respect to the service provider.

The last area in the SLA, **SLA Specific Information**, contains the unique information for each SLA that defines the metrics and parameters that must be respected by the service provider to match the needs of the customer. This section answers questions such as "What are the targets?" and "What penalties can be applied if the targets are not met?". The area is composed by a set of different combinations of targets and actions for each type of SLA. For each SLA type, the following attributes are specified:

- *Type* – This attribute has the same role as the SLA Name in the SLA Basic Information area but in this case the purpose is to identify a specific combination of targets and actions for the SLA. For each type will be specified the service configuration, the targets and the consequences for fulfillment (or not) of the targets, and assigned a price;
- *Service Configuration* – This attribute relates to the specific features of the service that this type of SLA includes. This information is specified by the Service Provider and it has no direct representation in the DEMO models and diagrams, as it is implementation dependent;

- *Targets* – This attribute is composed by six other attributes that relate to six specific metric of SLA and a seventh attribute that allows some flexibility to add other targets. The six targets types that we propose are: performance, availability, reliability, security, usability and financial. These targets may be partially obtained from the State Model, because this model specifies the state space of the P-world. According to [19], a contract between a provider of service and a consumer of service must set targets to measure compliance;
- *Penalties* and *Bonuses* – these two attributes specify the actions to be taken if the targets are not met (Penalties) or possible bonuses if the targets are met (Bonuses). This information is induced from the Action Model of the EO because this model defines the operational business rules of an enterprise;
- *Price* – This attribute assigns a price to the SLA and has no direct representation in the DEMO models and diagrams, as it is implementation dependent.

With these attributes we intend to capture the customers' expectations, easing the task of service providers on perceiving those expectations and thus contributing to solve one of the gaps in services exchange.

## 4    Evaluation

This section details the evaluation phase of DSRM. Our evaluation strategy can be described using the framework [20] that identifies what is actually evaluated, how it is evaluated, and when the evaluation takes place:

- **What is actually evaluated?** The artifact evaluated is the proposed SLA version (a design product);
- **How is it evaluated?** We used experts' feedback to evaluate the DEMO-based SLA structure and the SLA attributes;
- **When was it evaluated?** It was evaluated ex post, i.e., after the design artifact was developed.

We conducted seven interviews with experts in the service management area in order to collect their feedback about our proposal [21]. These experts hold high positions in international organizations active in providing services and gathering requirements, and have over 10 years of experience in this industry. We interviewed one vice president of sales, three senior operation managers and three services accountable.

For the purpose of the interviews, a few days before we sent them a presentation of our proposal with an explanation of the different attributes and an example of our proposal applied in practice. The interviews were brief, 15 to 20 minutes, and each person was asked to comment the areas that constitute the SLA proposal and respective attributes. They were also asked to suggest new attributes to our proposal, explaining why, and if they agreed that our proposal could be used in a day-to-day business environment.

One of the main conclusions drawn from these interviews was the need to add an attribute that allows some flexibility to the writing of targets that do not fit those six types. We chose to add a seventh attribute to the SLA Targets named, SLA Other Targets, to tackle this gap. Another conclusion was a poor explanation of each attribute and to simplify the name of each attribute. This conclusion forced us to analyze and develop a better description for all attributes of the proposal. Overall, the seven experts all showed interest in putting the proposal into production.

Therefore, the evaluation **indicates** that the answer to the paper research question is YES, **DEMO can be used to specify SLAs in order to model customers' expectations**. We conclude that, as the EO theory describes the interaction between the customer and the provider in a very formal way and since the Service Level Management acts as the interface between customer and provider, the EO provides a solid basis for formalizing the notion of SLA.

## 5    Conclusion

The services are booming in the world. This exponential expansion raises an important question concerning the quality services. This quality is affected by 5 gaps demonstrated in the gaps model [3]. Over the years, various solutions have emerged to align the customers' expectations and the perception of those expectations by the service provider, but none solved the problem completely.

In this paper we summarized proposals based on web services and the Generic Service Specification Framework. Web Services, in addition to being focused on processes rather than services, have a lack of strong conceptual foundation. The GSSF lacks detail, leading to different notions of quality by customers and service providers.

In order to solve the gap between customers' expectations and perception of them by suppliers (gap 1), this paper proposes a definition of Service Level Agreement based on DEMO. Apart from the SLA definition, our proposal specifies a structure for the SLAs with three sections as well as attributes for each of these sections.

The interviews with the seven expert practitioners revealed that our proposal was within the requirements of their organizations. They confirmed that our proposal shows a good degree of maturity and would be a useful contribution to reduce the misalignment between the expectations of their clients and the perception that they have of these expectations.

The last step of DSRM, communication, is being achieved through scientific publications (including this paper) aimed at the practitioners and researchers within the service science area.

## References

[1]  Vandermerwe, S., Rada, J.: Servitization of Business: Adding Value by Adding Services. European Management Journal 6 (1988)
[2]  Hochstein, A., Zarkekow, R., Brenner, W.: ITIL as Common Practice Reference Model for IT Service Management: Formal Assessment and Implications for Practice. In: The 2005 IEEE International Conference, pp. 704–710 (2005)

[3] Parasuraman, A., Zeithaml, V.A., Berry, L.L.: A Conceptual Model of Service Quality and its Implications for Future Research. Journal of Marketing 49, 41–50 (1985)

[4] Dietz, J.: Enterprise Ontology - Theory and Methodology. Springer (2006)

[5] Mendes, C., Almeida, M., Salvador, N., Mira da Silva, M.: Using DEMO-based SLAs for Improving City Council Services. In: International Conference on Knowledge Engineering and Ontology Development (KEOD), Barcelona (2012)

[6] Mendes, C., Mira da Silva, M.: DEMO-based Service Level Agreements. In: 3rd International Conference on Exploring Service Science, Geneva (2012)

[7] Mendes, C., Ferreira, J., Mira da Silva, M.: Identifying Services from a Service Provider and Customer Perspectives. In: Pedrosa, V. (ed.) IC3K 2011. CCIS, vol. 348, pp. 307–322. Springer, Heidelberg (2013)

[8] Albani, A., Terlouw, L., Hardjosumarto, G.: Enterprise Ontology Based Service Definition. In: 4th International Workshop on Value Modelling and Business Ontologies, Amesterdam, The Netherlands (2009)

[9] Terkouw, L., Albani, A.: An Enterprise Ontology-Based Approach to Service Specification. IEEE Transactions on Services Computing (2011)

[10] Hevner, A., March, S., Park, J., Ram, S.: Design Science in Information Systems Research. MIS Quarterly 28, 75–105 (2004)

[11] Office of Government Commerce, ITIL v3 – Service Design: The Stationery Office (2007)

[12] Sahai, A., Durante, A., Machiraju, V.: Towards Automated SLA Management for Web Services. Technical Report, Hewlett-Packard Company (2002)

[13] Tosic, V., Patel, K., Pagurek, B.: WSOL - Web Service Offerings Language. In: Bussler, C.J., McIlraith, S.A., Orlowska, M.E., Pernici, B., Yang, J. (eds.) CAiSE 2002 and WES 2002. LNCS, vol. 2512, pp. 57–67. Springer, Heidelberg (2002)

[14] Dobson, G.: Quality of Service in Service-Oriented Architectures (2004), http://digs.sourceforge.net/papers/qos.html

[15] Frolund, S., Koistinen, J.: QML: A Language for Quality of Service Specification. HP Software Technology Laboratory (1998)

[16] Keller, A., Ludwig, H.: The WSLA Framework: Specifying and Monitoring Service Level Agreements for Web Services. Journal of Network and Systems Management 11(1) (2003)

[17] Andrieux, A., et al.: Web Services Agreement Specification (WS-Agreement). Open Grid Forum (2007)

[18] Liu, Y., Ngu, A.H., Zeng, L.Z.: QoS Computation and Policing in Dynamic Web Service Selection. In: 13th International World Wide Web Conference on Alternate Track Papers & Posters. ACM, New York (2004)

[19] LaBounty, C.: How to Establish & Maintain Service Level Agreements. In: 6th Annual HDI Conference, San Francisco (1995)

[20] Pries-Heje, J., Baskerville, R., Venable, J.: Strategies for Design Science Research Evaluation. In: 16th ECIS, pp. 255-260 (2004)

[21] Kvale, S.: Doing interviews. Sage Publications, London (2007)

# Exploring the Drivers of E-Commerce through the Application of Structural Equation Modeling

Andre F.G. Castro, Raquel F. Ch. Meneses, and Maria R.A. Moreira

Faculty of Economics, Universidade do Porto
R.Dr. Roberto Frias, s/n, 4200-464 Porto, Portugal
andrefilipecastro@gmail.com, {raquelm,mrosario}@fep.up.pt

**Abstract.** E-commerce is a form of trade that has gained increasing attention from consumers and sellers. However, despite high growth rates, e-commerce still has low levels of consumers. This study aims to determine the factors that influence the purchasing decision in e-commerce, in order to better understand acceptance or rejection of e-commerce among consumers. To this end, a first framework was constructed based on previous research on consumer adoption of e-commerce. Then, three categories (derived from interviews) were added. This more complete model was tested using the structural equation model based on partial least squares. The results obtained allow us to conclude that the perceived relative advantage, the ease of use, the drawbacks associated with a non-European Union country of sale and the perceived risk, directly influence the consumer's purchase intent in e-commerce. We also found a set of twelve variables that act as indirect influences.

**Keywords:** e-commerce, influencing factors, drivers/determinants.

## 1  Introduction

With the development and the widespread use of the Internet, the way people shop has changed, as has the way companies offer their products. Given the high growth rates of e-commerce consumerism, it is important to understand the dynamics of e-commerce and the factors that affect the choice of this purchase channel.

The main aim of this study is to determine, through the development and application of an analytical model, which factors can influence (or influence the most) purchasing decisions in e-commerce. This research focuses on building a comprehensive model that portrays the consumer decision to purchase online. We built such a framework based on previous research on consumer adoption of e-commerce ([1], [2], [3], [4], [5], [6], [7]).

A mixed methodology was employed. First, a qualitative study was conducted (adapted from the Grounded Theory) based on exploratory interviews, aimed at determining the specific factors that may influence the purchase decision in e-commerce. The results obtained with the exploratory interviews were integrated into the model resulting from the literature review and the subsequent quantitative test. The model estimation was performed in accordance with the Structural Equation Modeling of Partial Least Squares - PLS.

J.F. e Cunha, M. Snene, and H. Nóvoa (Eds.): IESS 2013, LNBIP 143, pp. 299–305, 2013.

Following the introduction, this paper is divided into four sections. The second presents a literature review. In the third section, the methodology are presented, followed by the results. Finally, the last chapter presents the key findings and the study's limitations.

## 2     Literature Review

This study will use the definition by [8], in that e-commerce corresponds to transactions that take place via the internet, involving the purchase and sale of goods and services that are delivered offline, as well as products that can exist and be delivered in digital form directly to the buyer online.

Three approaches serve as the theoretical basis for the development of our research model - the consumer acceptance model of e-commerce, the understanding and mitigating uncertainty model, and the decision model for electronic commerce. Each of them provides some factors that may affect consumers in different contexts. We selected specific factors from each of the approaches as they fit within the context of e-commerce: buy, intention to buy, ease of use, perceived relative advantage, information security, privacy of information, information quality, seller reputation, social presence, pick up options, convenience, access to information, lower prices and customization.

None of them would provide all the factors required to develop an in-depth model of the factors affecting e-commerce. However, those factors selected allowed us to formulate a number of hypotheses to test:

*H1: The intent of a consumer to purchase via e-commerce positively affects the buying decision through that channel.*

*H2: The ease of use of the internet positively affects the consumer's purchase intention via e-commerce.*

*H3: Perceived Risk by consumers negatively affects Intent to Purchase via e-commerce.*

*H4a: Consumer confidence positively affects the consumer's intention to buy via e-commerce.*

*H4b: Consumer confidence negatively affects the consumer's perceived risk of a transaction via e-commerce.*

*H5: Perceived relative advantage positively affects the intention to buy via e-commerce.*

*H6: Concerns with information security increase the perceived risk in e-commerce.*

*H7: Concerns about the privacy of information increase perceived risk in e-commerce.*

*H8a: The information quality decreases perceived risk in e-commerce.*

*H8b: The information quality increases consumer confidence in e-commerce.*

*H9: A seller's (positive) reputation positively affects consumer confidence in e-commerce.*

*H10: The social presence of a seller positively affects the consumer's confidence in e-commerce.*

*H11: The perception of increased options in e-commerce positively affects the relative advantage perceived in this channel.*

*H12: The perception of convenience in e-commerce positively affects the perceived relative advantage of online shopping.*

*H13: The perception of getting more and better access to information in e-commerce positively affects the perceived relative advantage of using this channel.*

*H14: The perception of getting a low price in e-commerce positively affects the perceived relative advantage of purchasing decisions in this channel.*

*H15: The perception of possible product customization in e-commerce positively affects the perceived relative advantage of using this channel.*

# 3    Methodology

To do this research, a mixed approach was applied. Thus, in a first phase, an exploratory methodology was used, based on an in-depth analysis of interviews, to identify possible new variables that influence consumption in e-commerce, which could be included in the model, following accordingly, *mutatis mutandis*, the methodology of the Grounded Theory [11]. To this end, semi-structured interviews were conducted, between 1st and 11th April at the University of Porto. The data was collected, analyzed, sorted and categorized into concepts that emerged from the data. Later, these concepts gave rise to the properties or subcategories, establishing relationships among them.

In a second phase, a quantitative analysis was performed in order to test the model resulting from the theoretical analysis and the exploratory survey. In order to empirically test the final model resulting from the literature review and the exploratory interviews, a research questionnaire was prepared, involving the collection of a large amount of information related to the target population.

The questionnaire was made up of 35 questions, in both multiple choice and scale evaluation. The application of the questionnaire to potential respondents was conducted via e-mail, where the cooperation of all students of the University of Porto was requested and the purpose of the questionnaire explained. The questionnaire was sent on 20th June 2011, to the entire student population of the University of Porto, and it was available until 31st July. Given the impossibility of studying the entire population of e-consumers, we decided to focus this study on higher education students. As described by [10], several studies have used them as an object of study, since it is recognized that students are a useful *proxy* for characterizing online consumers. Thus, the survey of the available research was performed, and the PLS was set up, as an estimation method for the model, in order to ascertain the results of the research and to draw conclusions.

# 4    Results

## 4.1    Results from the Qualitative Analysis

The interviews identified a set of enhancing variables that influence consumer intention to buy online, which were not part of the theoretical model.

The list of all variables identified is as follows: shipping costs, urgency of purchase, recommendation from friends, product experimentation requirements, disadvantages associated with the extra-EU countries, widespread use of e-commerce as a way to buy and success of previous experiences.

Only the variables which had been referenced more than three times (more than 50% than the maximum value) since the others could constitute circumstantial and non-significant phenomenon, were included in the model.

Thus, the data from the interviews yielded the following variables to be added to the proposed model:

• Product experimentation requirements - within the variable *perceived risk*, it aims to demonstrate that, in products where there is a high need for experimentation thereof, consumers feel they are faced with a transaction of increased risk, if they choose to buy them via e-commerce;

• Disadvantages associated with the extra-EU countries – this variable tends to directly influence consumer intention to buy from non-EU countries, presenting some drawbacks to online shopping, such as the delay in product delivery, possibility that products be retained at customs and thus require the payment of customs fees, the possible need for payment in currencies other than the consumer's, etc..

• Urgency of purchase - within the variable *perceived relative advantage*, given the time difference between the act of purchase and the act of delivery, consumers may not find it advantageous to purchase via this channel. When they have urgent needs, they resort to traditional retail.

Accordingly, the following hypothesis can be presented:

> **H16**: *The product experimentation requirements increase the perceived risk in e-commerce.*
> **H17**: *The disadvantages associated with extra-EU countries negatively affect consumer intention to buy via e-commerce.*
> **H18**: *The urgency of purchase negatively affects consumer buying intention via e-commerce.*

Schematically the new proposed model, taking into consideration the above factors (light), and the factors from literature review (dark) is presented in Figure 1.

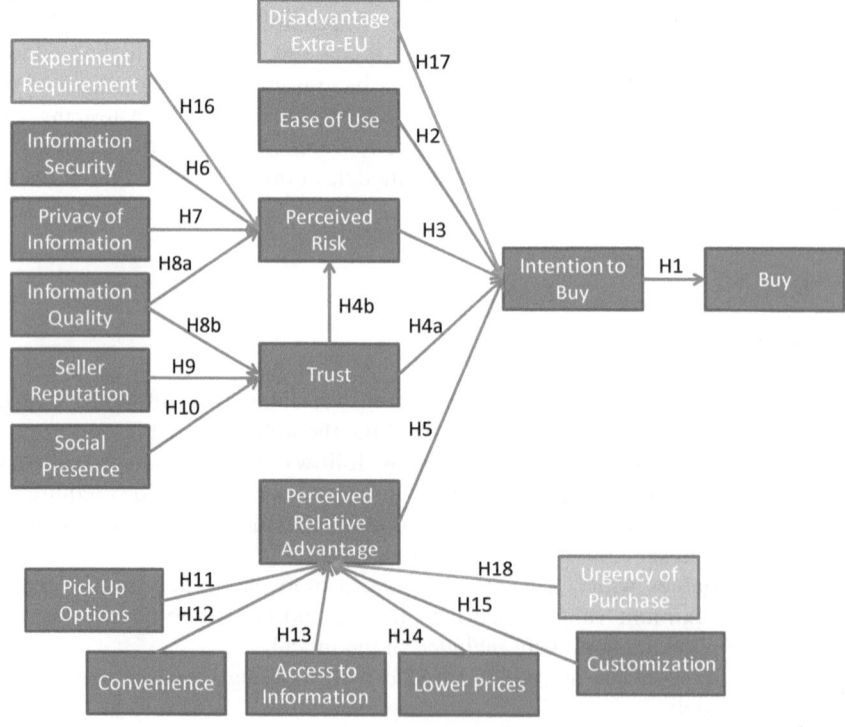

**Fig. 1.** Analysis model

## 4.2    Results from the Quantitative Analysis

The number of valid responses to be statistically analyzed was 1 366 questionnaires with which constituted our database.

We checked the reliability and convergent and discriminant validity of the constructs. To do so, we used some indicators:

- Cronbach's alpha: all variables in our model, the Cronbach alpha have a value greater than 0.6, the minimum acceptable, according to [13] and [14];have urgent needs, they resort to traditional retail.
- Fornell's composite reliability: all model variables have a Fornell confidence value higher than the acceptable one, 0.7 ([10]);
- AVE (average variance extracted): in the model all variables, have a value greater than the minimum value of 0.50 [14];
- The square root of the AVE of each variable must not be less than the correlations of this variable with the other ([15]), which also occurs in the model in question;
- Correlations between all the variables should be less than 0.90, as indicated by [9], which is also confirmed in this model;

Having secured the validity and reliability of measurement models, the structural model estimation was performed via PLS using the SmartPLS software.

In order to decide whether to accept or reject a hypothesis, for a significance level of 5%, the value of 1.96 for the T-Statistic should be obtained as the reference.

At a significance level of 5%, all the assumptions set out in the model, with the exception of hypotheses H4a (T-Statistic=1.7231<1.96) and H10 (T-Statistic= 1.1934<1.96), can be accepted. Regarding hypothesis H4a (consumer confidence positively affects the purchase decision via e-commerce), in the study population, it was not possible to prove the statistical significance of the variable *confidence in consumer purchase intent*. Although this relationship has been validated in previous studies, here, with the data collected, we cannot validate that *trust* has a direct influence on the consumer's intention to buy via e-commerce.

It was also not possible to confirm H10 (the social presence of a seller positively affects consumer confidence in e-commerce) in the population under study; we cannot say that the effort of e-commerce business sellers to equip their sites with systems enabling greater social contact between buyers and sellers, via chat, online customer support, etc.., has a positive impact on consumer trust in the e-commerce universe.

Therefore, taking these two assumptions of the model in question, since they could not be accepted, the final results of estimation model are presented in Figure 2, with the coefficients associated with each hypothesis under consideration, and the R2.

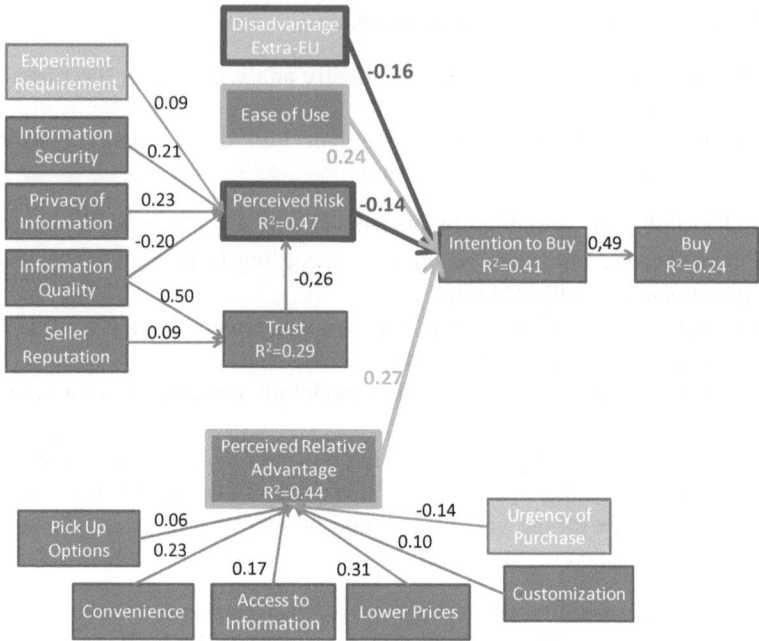

**Fig. 2.** Final results of estimation model

## 5    Conclusion

In this study, we analyzed the factors that influence the decision to purchase *via* e-commerce, thus intending to contribute to a broader understanding of the online shopping phenomenon.

We found that there are a set of four variables that influence directly the consumer's purchase intention through e-commerce: *perceived relative advantage, ease of use, disadvantages associated with the extra-EU countries* and *perceived risk*. The first two factors act as incentives to purchase in e-commerce, where *perceived relative advantage* exerts greater influence. Conversily, the variables *disadvantages associated with the extra-EU countries* and *perceived risk* tend to decrease the intention to use the internet to shop, working as obstacles to online consumption.

This study also found some limitations that should be mentioned. The sample used in the study may not be representative of all consumers. Although students are the group that most often purchases online and are also the target of many research studies on this matter, the conclusions must be relativized to the sphere of study. Hence, it may not be possible to generalize the findings to other groups of consumers.

As avenues for future research, a study could be conducted on different product categories in order to assess if the influence of the factors identified remained the same or vary according to the specifics of the products concerned.

**Acknowledgement.** This work is funded by the ERDF through the Programme COMPETE and by the Portuguese Government through FCT - Foundation for Science and Technology, project PTDC/EGE-GES/099741/2008.

# References

1. Chen, Y.-Y.: Why Do Consumers Go Internet Shopping Again? Understanding the Antecedents of Repurchase Intention. Journal of Organizational Computing and Electronic Commerce 1, 38–63 (2012)
2. Guo, L.: A Research on Influencing Factors of Consumer Purchasing Behaviors in Cyberspace. International Journal of Marketing Studies 3(3), 182–188 (2011)
3. Kamarulzaman, Y.: E-consumer behaviour: Exploring the drivers of e-shopping. European Journal of Social Sciences 23(4), 579–592 (2011)
4. Zhou, L., Dai, L., Zhang, D.: Online shopping acceptance model-A critical survey of consumer factors in online shopping. Journal of Electronic Commerce Research 8, 41–62 (2007)
5. Monsuwé, T., Dellaert, B., Ruyter, K.: What drives consumers to shop online? A literature review. International Journal of Service Industry Management 15(1), 102–121 (2004)
6. Park, C., Jun, J.-K.: A cross-cultural comparison of Internet buying behavior: Effects of Internet usage, perceived risks, and innovativeness. International Marketing Review 20(5), 534–553 (2003)
7. Moore, R., Breazeale, M.: Electronic Commerce Research: The first 15 years in the fields of Marketing, Management, and Information Systems. Marketing Management Journal 20, 105–122 (2010)
8. Coppel, J.: E-commerce: Impacts and Policy Challenge. Economics Department Working Papers 252, 1–10 (2000)
9. Pavlou, P., Liang, H., Xue, Y.: Understanding and Mitigating Uncertainty in Online Exchange Relationships: A Principal-Agent Perspective. MIS Quarterly 31(1), 105–136 (2007)
10. Kim, D., Ferrin, D., Rao, H.: A trust-based consumer decision-making model in electronic commerce: The role of trust, perceived risk, and their antecedents. Decision Support Systems 44, 544–564 (2008)
11. Glaser, B., Strauss, A.: The discovery of grounded theory. Aldine, Chicago (1967)
12. Lu, C.-S., Lai, K.-H., Cheng, T.C.E.: Application of structural equation modeling to evaluate the intention of shippers to use Internet services in liner shipping. European Journal of Operational Research 180(2), 845–867 (2007)
13. Sekaran, U.: Research methods for business – a skill building approach, 4th edn. John Wiley and Sons, New York (2005)
14. Hair, J., Anderson, R., Tatham, R., Black, W.: Multivariate Data Analysis. Prentice Hall, Upper Saddle River (2006)
15. Fornell, C., Larcker, D.: Evaluating structural equation models with unobservable variables and measurement error. Journal of Marketing Research 18, 39–50 (1981)

# A Model for Open, On-Demand, Collaborative Education for Service Science

Theodor Borangiu, Monica Drăgoicea, Ecaterina Oltean, and Iulia Iacob

University Politehnica of Bucharest
Faculty of Automatic Control and Computers
313 Splaiul Independentei, 0600042-Bucharest, Romania
theodor.borangiu@cimr.pub.ro, monica.dragoicea@acse.pub.ro

**Abstract.** This paper presents a proposal concerning the development of a sustainable support for modern education in services. It accounts for the development of a dedicated higher education study program on Service Science Management and Engineering (SSME) on different levels, i.e. master, undergraduate and compact modules dedicated to a lifelong education process (the SSME education model). The proposed approach addresses both research and curricula development on different service sectors, aiming to foster the new Science of Service at national level.

**Keywords:** Service Science, education models, service innovation.

## 1   Introduction

The main scope of the new Science of Service is to classify and explain how different types of service systems interact and evolve in order to co-create value through a continuous chain of interactions between service providers and consumers [1]. A new concept introduced in order to detail concepts related to Service Science is SSME - Service Science, Management and Engineering, describing a whole domain of study that allows engineers, economists and managers to interact and cooperate in order to analyse, develop and exploit complex dynamic systems, i.e. the service systems [2]. In a broader acceptance, SSME is a domain where scientific understanding, engineering practices and managerial tools meet in order to design, create and deliver complex service systems [3], [4]. From an academic point of view, Service Science closely relates to labour market qualifications and necessary competences for different service sectors that educational and research programs in services can provide [5]. There is an acknowledged demand today to develop a large number of higher education programs in SSME, emphasizing the need to create a format by itself, contrary to an implicit tendency to dissipate knowledge related to Service Science among already existing educational programs in specific domains [6]. Considering the multidisciplinary perspective on knowledge related to the new Science of Service, first attempts were made in order to closer relate service science and service innovation [7], to embed the new discipline of service science into a research agenda [8], or to make an initial proposal for a Service Science discipline classification system [9]. Other

J.F. e Cunha, M. Snene, and H. Nóvoa (Eds.): IESS 2013, LNBIP 143, pp. 306–312, 2013.

approaches try to define guiding principles to develop service science disciplines [10] or to develop specific curricula in services [11], [12]. There have been also reported approaches to develop specific reference models [13] and Master programs in specific areas of study related to Service Science [14], [15]. At the same time, dedicated projects approached specific areas related to curricula and competencies development for service innovation. Among these, DELLIISS project [16] developed an European skill card in order to foster cooperation between higher education and enterprises. It is in the framework of the INSEED project [17] that the proposal of a reference model for a complex higher education program in SSME is formulated (section 2). The main artefact is the **SSME model** that proposes a modern vision on a complex educational model on three levels (undergraduate, masters and doctorate) to approach *service innovation* (section 3). It provides professional competencies in different service sectors (section 4) and support for specific lifelong learning education for service innovation (section 5).

## 2    Problem Statement

This proposed approach to develop a higher education program to shape adaptive innovators for modern services in the SSME perspective takes into consideration different requirements and patently statements.

(**R1.**) There is an obvious trend that each of the developed countries is experiencing today showing that most of the labour force goes into different service businesses;

(**R2.**) There is an obvious necessity to increase both volume and quality in services for the economic benefit of society in a whole and for a better quality of life;

(**R3.**) Services in different service sectors can be grouped into three basic system categories, i.e. **Execute, Transform, Innovate** [1]. Inside each category there are common specificities that require both basic knowledge and different supplementary professional competences (see also Fig. 1 in section 3);

(**R4.**) We can apply the service innovation multilevel framework [7] on each of the three levels - *requirements-*, *competencies-* and *service resources* - in order to define curricular areas for the *new higher education in services model* that would provide professional competences in SSME for modern service development;

(**R5.**) In order to define the new higher education in services model we can use the transposition of: a) the service innovation multilevel framework [7], of the methodology and of the technological and organizational directions for innovation to support and provide requirements, competencies and resources for services; b) the partnership context in value co-creation through services [1]; c) the principles and the methodology for configuration, interconnecting, integration, exploitation and innovation of resources in sets of disciplines for the defined curricular areas.

(**R6.**) We can associate disciplines from the defined sets with profession (labour activity) categories in services. The discipline list is contained in the knowledge areas associated to the major dimensions of the service systems;

(**R7.**) There is a necessity for the continuous adaptation and improvement of provided knowledge and competences in the initial education cycles (undergraduate, master, doctorate) in SSME through dedicated lifelong learning programs;

(**R8.**) There is a need to sustain the migration ability of the graduated student of a service sector education program between occupation profiles in three different categories: a) *service performer*; b) *service transformer*; c) *service innovator*.

## 3   Higher Education Model for SSME - A Proposal

According to the above mentioned statements, the development of *a new higher education program* dedicated to train adaptive innovators for modern service systems implementation requires to define *an educational model in SSME* - the **SSME model**. The **SSME model** defines *different levels of higher education*. It takes as a starting point the service innovation multilevel framework [7], over which the curricular areas, professional competencies, sets of disciplines and types of occupations available to students are superimposed (Fig. 1). It has the following characteristics that answer to the above mentioned requirements.

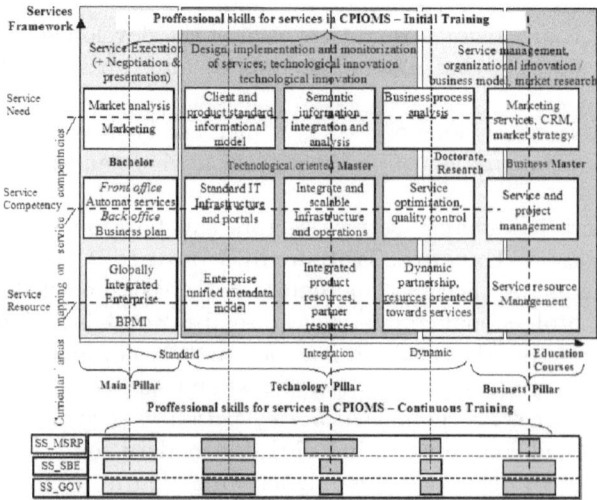

**Fig. 1.** SSME model and service innovation multilevel framework - correlation

(**C1.**) The SSME model addresses to higher education units (in Romania) in certain study profiles: engineering (technology oriented), economics (business oriented) and medical schools.

(**C2.**) The SSME model highlights: A) **LS**. An *undergraduate level* in service systems: (**LS**) - [Main Pillar]; B) **MS**. Two types of *master levels* in service systems: (**MS-T**) - a technology-oriented master program in services (engineering)

[Technology Pillar]; (**MS-E**) - a business-oriented master program in services (economics) [Business Pillar]; C) **DS**. A *doctorate level* for services, with the following aspects: (**DS-T**) - a technology-oriented doctoral program for complex service systems (engineering); (**DS-E**) - a business-oriented doctoral program for complex service systems (economics); D) **CS**. A *lifelong education program* in services, on both directions: technology-oriented and business-oriented. Grouping modules of disciplines that forms professional competencies in service systems requires the following classification [1]: d1) **SS_MSRP** (*major technology-orientation*) - systems that move, store, harvest, process; d2) **SS_SBE** (*moderate orientation towards technology and business*) - systems for health, welfare and wise education; and d3) **SS_GOV** (*major orientation towards business*) - systems that govern.

(**C3.**) In order to foster a major knowledge orientation of the new higher education program in SSME, the **SSME model** enforces the definition of a new fundamental study domain called *Service Science*.

(**C4.**) The SSME model includes the following types of Masters programs in Services: A) General programs [**MS-T** type or **MS-E** type]; B) IT-oriented programs [**MS-T** type]; C) Business-oriented programs [**MS-E** type]; D) Programs oriented towards different service sector in society [**MS-T** or **MS-E** type].

# 4 Professional Competences in the SSME Model

The **SSME model** provides professional competencies for service systems on each of the three education levels.

(**PC1.**) The undergraduate level provides competences for service realization, negotiation and presentation.

(**PC2.**) The Master level (IT oriented) provides competences in service design, implementation and monitoring, and technological innovation for services (resources and competencies for services).

(**PC3.**) The Master level (business oriented) provides competencies in service management, organizational innovation for services, new business and research models, provisioning and market strategy (competencies and requirements).

(**PC4.**) The Master level (service sectors oriented) provides competences in resources management fostering domain related service ecosystem development.

Curricular areas are associated to the mentioned levels as follows (Fig. 1):

(**CA1.**) *Resources for services*: resources / platforms to develop services; service content and resource performances; enterprise modelling; resource integration; channels / resources for service delivery; service resources management;

(**CA2.**) *Competencies for services*: processes for services; ERP; integration of processes and partners;

(**CA3.**) *Requirements for services*: market analysis and strategy, business process analysis, CRM, HCM;

(**CA4.**) The following curricular areas are defined in the business-oriented master programs: CRM, SCM, ERP, HCM, organizational innovation, business model innovation, demand innovation;

(**CA5.**) The following curricular areas are defined in the IT-oriented Master programs: new technologies for services; architectures for services; service analysis, design and optimization; technological innovation;

(**CA6.**) The curricular areas included in the undergraduate programs in *Service Engineering* and technology-oriented Master programs (including IT) are based on knowledge areas related to Services Computing [18];

(**CA7.**) The following curricular areas are defined in the general Master programs: ICT; operations, management and marketing (OMM); psychology, sociology and arts (PSA);

(**CA8.**) The curricular areas defined in the service sectors oriented Master programs: (1) generically substantiate the service, its modelling, architecture and flow of automated processes, development IT technologies, service analysis and optimization, and (2) associate and integrate resources, provide competences and manage operations and partners;

(**CA9.**) The following curricular areas are defined by the undergraduate program *Service Engineering*: basic concepts of services (service systems, value, resources, participants); basic concepts of IT and service computation (SOC); service design; service development and delivery; service integration and management; human resources management in services; service oriented enterprise architecture; business service consultancy.

## 5   Lifelong Learning Education Support in the SSME Model

The continuous adaptation and improvement of knowledge and competencies provided on different levels of SSME initial education is sustained by including sub-programs for lifelong education in services. These modules are dedicated to staff training and knowledge upgrading in services in public institutions and private business. The share of training components in each of service sector is stated as follows (Fig. 2): a) **SS_MSRP**: 25% basic concepts for services; 62.5% technology; 12.5% management; b) **SS_SBE**: 25% basic concepts for services; 37.5% technology; 37.5% management; c) **SS_GOV**: 25% basic concepts for services; 25% technology; 50% management.

Transposition of the specific elements in sets of disciplines for the defined curricular areas is realized through the association between (Fig. 2): A) the *resources for services* level and *sets of disciplines* for technologies (platforms / resources for service development), shared information (service content, client data), and human staff (resources exploitation); B) the *competences for services* level and *sets of disciplines* for *organization, competitor* and *provider*; and C) the *requirements for services* level and *sets of disciplines* for stakeholder and governance authority. The way occupations / professions in different service sectors are positioned is determined by the transposition of the key factors associated to resources-, competencies- and requirements for services in curricular areas and sets of disciplines that generate competencies in the three specified categories.

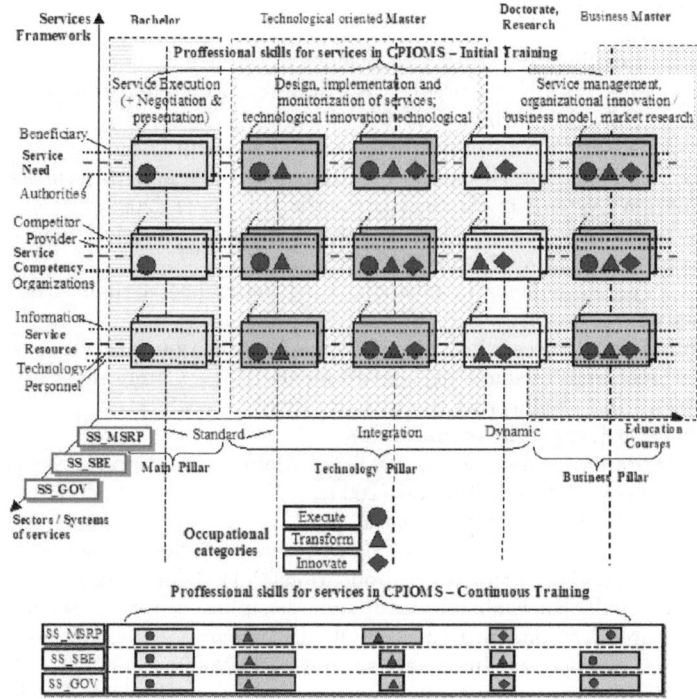

**Fig. 2.** Possible occupations in services in the SSME model

# 6    Conclusions

The whole education model proposed here strives to support the new *engineering perspective on service*: the *service* becomes a *commodity* that has to be conceptualized, designed, implemented and offered for consumption according to certain rules (the SLAs). The development of an educational program at the extent and vision of the **SSME model** should take into consideration that the components of a service are dynamic while including the human factor whose preferences are modelled and included in the outcome - the service. So, the **SSME model** proposed here should include a set of elements dedicated to the business organization, communication between service providers and consumers, formulation of preferences and value propositions and value co-creation. The SSME perspective on education for service innovation is undertaken in the **SSME model** and further developed in a novel perspective, with a global opening.

**Acknowledgments.** This work was supported by INSEED - Strategic Grant POSDRU/107/ 1.5/S/76903, Project ID 76903 (2011), co-financed by the European Social Fund – Investing in People, within the Sectoral Operational Programme Human Resource Development 2007 – 2013.

# References

1. Spohrer, J., Maglio, P.P.: Toward a Science of Service Systems - Value and Symbols. In: Maglio, P.P., Kielszewski, C.A., Spohrer, J.C. (eds.) Handbook of Service Science, pp. 157–193. Springer (2010)
2. Spohrer, J., Kwan, S.K.: Service Science, Management, Engineering, and Design (SSMED): An Emerging Discipline - Outline and References. International Journal of Information Systems in the Service Sector 1(3), 1–31 (2009)
3. Chesbrough, H., Spohrer, J.: A Research Manifesto for Services Science. Communications of the ACM 49(7), 35–40 (2006)
4. Lyons, K.: Service Science in iSchools. In: iConference, Urbana-Champaign, IL, USA, February 3-6 (2010)
5. IBM White Paper: Succeeding through Service Innovation: a service perspective for education, research, business and government. IBM - Cambridge Service Science, Management and Engineering Symposium (2007), http://www.ifm.eng.cam.ac.uk/ssme/
6. IBM White Paper: Making Service Science Mainstream. Service Science Summit, Aalto University, Helsinki, Finland (2009), http://www.servicefactory.aalto.fi/fi/
7. Cai, H., Chung, J.Y., Su, H.: Relooking at services science and services innovation. Service Oriented Computing and Applications 2(1), 1–14 (2008)
8. Ng, I.C.L., Maull, R.: Embedding the new discipline of service science: A service science research agenda. In: EEE/INFORMS International Conference on Service Operations, Logistics and Informatics, pp. 68–73 (2009)
9. Pinhanez, C., Kontogiorgis, P.: A Proposal for a Service Science Discipline Classification System. IBM Corporation (2008)
10. Glushko, R.J.: Designing a service science discipline with discipline. IBM Systems Journal 47(1), 15–27 (2008)
11. Kontogiorgis, P.: IT Services Curriculum - Cultivating in demand skills for an on demand world. IBM Corporation (2010)
12. Wang, K.M., Shin Sheu, T.: Developing Service Science Curricula for Industrial Engineering and Management Education in Taiwan. In: Asia Pacific Industrial Engineering and Management Systems Conference, APIEMS 2009, pp. 94–100 (2009)
13. Zhang, L.J., Chen, Z., Luo, M., Zhang, J., Hung, P.C.K.: A Reference Model for Master of Science Program in Services Computing. In: IEEE 6th World Congress on Services (2010)
14. Falcão e Cunha, J., Patricio, L., Camanho, A., Fisk, R.: A Master Program in Services Engineering and Management at the University of Porto. In: Service Science, Management and Engineering Education for the 21st Century. Service Science: Research and Innovations in the Service Economy Series, pp. 181–190 (2008)
15. Sorathia, V., Pires, L.F., van Sinderen, M., Wijnhoven, F.: Developing a Services Science Graduation Programme at the University of Twente. In: IEEE Transforming Engineering Education: Creating Interdisciplinary Skills for Complex Global Environments, pp. 1–18. IEEE Press (2010)
16. The DELLIISS project - DEsigning Lifelong Learning for Innovation in Information Services Science, http://www.delliiss.eu/home
17. INSEED: Strategic program fostering innovation in services through open, continuous education (2012), http://www.inseed.cimr.pub.ro/
18. Zhang, L.J.: Introduction to the Body of Knowledge Areas of Services Computing. IEEE Transactions on Services Computing 1(2) (2008)

# Factors Influencing Purchase Intention
# of Private Label Products: The Case of Smartphones

Dany C. Coelho, Raquel F.Ch. Meneses, and Maria R.A. Moreira

Faculty of Economics, Universidade do Porto
R.Dr. Roberto Frias, s/n, 4200-464 Porto, Portugal
costadany@live.com.pt, {raquelm,mrosario}@fep.up.pt

**Abstract.** A growth of the market share of private label brands has been observed in developed countries. This growth was initially confirmed for food and drugstore categories, but it quickly expanded to new product categories, particularly technology products.

This study focus on a specific technology segment - the private label brands in smartphones, due to the growth observed in its demand, in recent years.

In this context, we analyzed and studied the smartphone market and consumer, and examine the factors influencing purchase intention of private label smartphones. The literature review on private label technological products proved to be scarce, which raised a challenge in exploring the main differences among factors influencing purchase intention for this specific product category.

In this study, through the development and application of an analytical model, we test a set of variables that resulted from the literature review, which could potentially influence the purchase intention of smartphones. We applied a questionnaire to a study population, and recorded 339 valid answers. The results were estimated in accordance with the Structural Equation Model. Our analysis highlights the importance given to technology by consumers, as well as price and quality. This study also revealed the importance of private label brands in a market which has as yet been underexplored.

**Keywords:** Owned Brands; Store Brands, Private Label Brands, Smartphones, PLS.

## 1    Introduction

As a result of constant product quality improvement, lower prices than manufacturer brands and the growing concentration and development of the retail sector [1], a growth of the market share of private label brands (PLBs) has been observed in developed countries [2].

According to Nielsen (2008) *cit. in* [3], PLBs were associated to food and drugstore products until recently, but they are now also associated to durable goods, such as technological products or home appliances, which are dynamic categories. The assumptions of this study were based on the growth of PLBs in different product categories and their implications on the purchase decision process, particularly for technology product categories.

The main aim of this research is to determine which factors influence the purchase intention of PLB smartphones. Therefore, we will study the following factors that

J.F. e Cunha, M. Snene, and H. Nóvoa (Eds.): IESS 2013, LNBIP 143, pp. 313–321, 2013.

potentially influence the purchase intention of PLB smartphones: price consciousness, quality perception, technology perception, functional risk, social risk, brand awareness and country of origin.

Following the introduction, this paper is divided in three sections. The first section portrays the main theories and concepts of PLBs. This theoretical approach starts by explaining the theme of PLBs, highlighting the importance of "brand", and the importance of "private label brands". In this section, we also describe the purchase decision process and the factors influencing it. Then, the next section describes the study design and the methodology employed. Next, an analysis of the results and the model estimation are performed. Finally, we present the conclusions of this study and the respective implications.

## 2      Theoretical Framework

Brands were designed to identify and distinguish specific products, so that they are visible and distinct in the market. "A brand is a name, term, sign, symbol or design, or a combination of all these elements, with the aim of identifying goods or services of one seller and to differentiate them from the competitors" ([4], p.418 ).

The term "private label brand - PLBs" will be used in this study, based on the property rights and exclusivity of these products, which are owned and marketed by companies operating in distribution, rather than held by companies operating in production [6]. In other words, PLBs are owned, controlled and marketed exclusively by distributors [7].   This definition also suggests that the distributor has exclusive rights over the brand, given that, unlike when they sell manufacturer brands, retailers do not sell the same PLBs [8].

The purpose of PLBs is to allow the distributor to improve its position, in purchases and sales, while trying to retain consumers [10]. Consumers also have benefits from PLBs [11], due to the value they represent, because the budget available for the purchase of PLB goods is more elastic than the budget for buying national brands and, therefore, the same budget enables more quantity, variety and sometimes more quality. Several studies have shown that the market share of PLBs rises in periods of economic recession ([2], [12-13]), justified by greater price awareness by consumers resulting from a drop in income.

### 2.1      Purchase Decision Process and Smartphone Features

"The attitude is based on a set of information about the object evaluated and progressively accumulated by the individual (cognitive component), the attitude is oriented since it expresses a positive or negative evaluation in relation to the object (affective component), the attitude is dynamic and is a predisposition to action, and as such is a prediction of the behavior (behavioral component)" ([14], p.195).

Studying and consequently understanding the consumer's purchase intention is the key to winning market share within the respective market segment, it is necessary to understand which factors influence the purchase intention of smartphones.

Smartphones, a mobile phone that offers a more advanced computing ability and connectivity than a basic mobile phone, emerge as a powerful tool because of their portability and location detection (can be located via satellite), able to provide highly personalized and localized services [16]. Smartphone manufacturers provide, along with their devices, an open operating platform, encouraging creators to develop new mobile applications. Wang *et al.* [17] reveal as such, not only do manufacturers create applications valued by users, but third parties can also develop different applications and deliver them directly to users through the purchased device. Consequently, today we are witnessing the "app world" phenomenon, with thousands of applications, whose goal is to provide a variety of information services.

### 2.2    Research Hypothesis

Regarding durable goods, several authors suggest that some variables which influence the purchase intention of durable goods differ when compared with the purchase intention of consumer goods ([3], [23], [24], [25], and [26]).

One of the main features of PLBs is that they are sold at a lower price than manufacturer goods ([15], [27]). However, not all consumers attach the same importance to the price variable; consumers may be more or less sensitive to price when they buy a product from one category over another, for example, due to the difference in perceived risk between the different product categories [28]. According to the literature reviewed, the main hypotheses to be tested are:

*H1.* Price consciousness positively influences the purchase intention of private label smartphones. ([15], [27-28])

*H2.* Quality perception of private label goods positively influences the purchase intention of private label smartphones. ([3], [5], [12], [20], [23], [29-30])

*H3.* Technology perception positively influences the purchase intention of private label smartphones. (Mohr and Nader (2003) cit. in [26], Cooper and Edgett (2009) cit. in [26], [31-33])

*H4.* Functional risk negatively influences the purchase intention of private label smartphones. ([19], [22], [24], [34-36])

*H5.* Social risk negatively influences the purchase intention of private label smartphones. (Harrell (1986), cit. in [24], [18], [24])

*H6.* Brand awareness positively influences the purchase intention of private label smartphones. ([37-38])

*H7.* The reputation of the country of origin negatively influences the purchase intention of private label smartphones. ([26], [39])

*H8.* The purchase intention of a private label smartphone positively influences the consumer's purchase decision. ([40-42])

## 3    Methodology

Based on hypothesis, we made a quantitative analysis by collecting a large number of information related to the target population, allowing us to validate or reject the research hypotheses.

## 3.1    Questionnaire

A questionnaire was designed for this study, aimed at empirically testing our research model which resulted from the literature review and then draw conclusions about the factors that influence the purchase intention of PLB smartphones. The questionnaire's questions were extracted from the theoretical framework, although some were specifically formulated for the purpose (table 1). In order to assess the degree of agreement or disagreement for each statement in this block, we used the Likert scale of 1-7 (1-Strongly Disagree; 7-Strongly Agree).The other block aimed to collect demographic data on the respondents, so as to characterize the study population.

The entire questionnaire was processed via Web ("Facebook", "LinkedIn" and "Twitter", technology blogs, as well as personal and professional contacts).

**Table 1.** Representation of rating scales

| Scale | Nr of items | Source |
|---|---|---|
| Price Consciousness | 4 | [27] (*Price Consciousness Scale*) |
| Perceived Quality | 4 | [27] (*Quality Consciousness Scale*) |
| Perceived Technology | 4 | [26] (*Technology Scale*) |
| Functional Risk | 4 | Authors |
| Social Risk | 4 | Authors |
| Brand Awareness | 4 | [26] (*Brand Reputation Scale*) |
| Country of origin | 4 | [26] (*Country of Origin Scale*) |
| Purchase Intention | 4 | [42] (*Purchase Intention*) |
| Effective Purchase | 3 | [27] (*Store Brand Usage Scale*) |

## 3.2    Model Estimation

The PLS was chosen based on its estimation algorithm, to analyze a latent variable at each time, serving to minimize the residual variance of all the dependent variables of the model by applying multiple linear regressions to the estimated latent variables, and subsequently, be able to compare our study results with those of [3] and [26].

# 4    Main Results

## 4.1    Model Validation

The questionnaire was available between 12th May to 16th June 2012 and 339 responses were recorded.

The first step consisted in validating the model in terms of measures of reliability and construct validity. The scale's consistency, measured by Cronbach's Alpha is greater than or equal to 0.70 for all the scales used in our study, what means, according to [43] that all are acceptable.  All scales have acceptable reliability because composite reliability (CR), which varies between 0.80 and 0.96, fall within the range of recommended values by [44] and [45]. High values of the average variance extracted (AVE) occur when the indicators are truly representative of the latent variable. The values of AVE should exceed 0.50 [44], which also holds for the variables studied. For the correlation coefficients, [44] indicate that the correlations between all the variables should be less than 0.90. The correlation coefficients have values ranging from -0.13 to 0.77. A measure of a variable has discriminant validity when it is not significantly correlated with measures of other variables that theoretically should not be highly correlated with this variable [46]. We compared the square of the correlation coefficients with the AVE for each pair of variables and found that the AVE of all pairs of variables was higher than the square of the correlation coefficient between the respective variables, confirming the existence of discriminant validity.

The following table reveals the tests of significance, in order to understand which variables are statistically relevant.

**Table 2.** Parameter estimation results via *Bootstrapping*

| Variables | Original Sample (O) | Standard Error (STERR) | T Statistics (|O/STERR|) |
|---|---|---|---|
| **Purchase intention -> Effective purchase** | 0.7766 | 0.0238 | 32.6587 |
| **Brand -> Purchase intention** | 0.1503 | 0.0398 | 3.7745 |
| **Country of origin -> Purchase intention** | -0.1257 | 0.1054 | 1.1925 |
| **Price -> Purchase intention** | 0.2582 | 0.0427 | 6.0533 |
| **Quality -> Purchase intention** | 0.1893 | 0.0508 | 3.7235 |
| **Functional risk -> Purchase intention** | 0.1752 | 0.0462 | 3.7939 |
| **Social risk -> Purchase intention** | 0.0877 | 0.0443 | 1.9769 |
| **Technology -> Purchase intention** | 0.2977 | 0.0547 | 5.4400 |

## 4.2    Analysis and Discussions

This study identifies seven variables that potentially influence the purchase intention of PLB smartphones: price consciousness, quality perception, technology perception, functional risk, social risk, brand awareness and country of origin reputation; however, the "country of origin" variable cannot be validated because it is not statistically relevant (statistic T<1.96).

We can accept hypothesis H1, H2, H3, and H6. Regarding hypothesis H4 and H5, they have an opposite sign (positive) than expected. Consequently, we confirmed that these six variables directly influence the purchase intention of PLB smartphones. The $R^2$ value associated to the "purchase intention" variable is 0.39.

The variable with the greatest influence on purchase intention is "technology perception", yielding an estimated parameter value of 0.30, followed by "price consciousness" (0.26), "quality perception" (0.19), "functional risk" (0.18), "brand awareness" (0.15), and "social risk" (0.09).

The "technology perception" variable is the variable with the greatest influence on the purchase intention of PLB smartphones, mainly due to its importance in this product category. [26] found in his study that technology, as well as product characteristics influence the purchase intention of technological products.

With regard to the "price consciousness" variable, contradicting the results obtained in our study, [3] did not observe any significant relation between the "price consciousness" variable and the purchase intention of durable PLB goods. This lack of impact was highlighted by Jin and Suh (2005) *cit. in* [3], who also found that price consciousness does not influence the consumer's attitude regarding durable PLB goods, contrary to the case of PLB consumer goods ([15], [24], [28]).

However, the level of price consciousness is greater in users with low income ([47]; Lumpkin *et al.* 1986, *cit. in* [24]), which may explain the positive influence found for the "price consciousness" variable, since the annual net earnings of 49% of the respondents ranges from 0 to 15.000€.

As for the "quality perception" variable, [3] revealed in their study that differences in quality perception between two brands and satisfaction with PLBs in general, determines the purchase intention of PLB durable goods. It should be noted that it is difficult for the consumer to perceive differences between manufacturer smartphones and PLB smartphones because both apply the same technology, are manufactured in the same factories and provide the same applications. Thus, and according to [3] and [12], as the difference in quality perception among the manufacturer brand and the PLBs narrows, (when it is lower or zero) the consumer is more likely to buy PLBs.

The "functional risk" variable, contrary to what was defined in our research hypothesis, positively influences the purchase intention of PLB smartphones. We can assume that this effect is due to the knowledge and information consumers have on these products, allowing them to evaluate the complexity of the product category, that is, the know-how that is necessary to manufacture such a device and evaluate the product lifecycle, that is, the time elapsing from product acquisition to product abandonment.

We also found a positive relation between the distributor's brand awareness and purchase intention of PLB smartphones, which can be explained on the basis of familiarity consumers already have of the operator's products and services, which according to [38] can lead to the purchase decision.

The final determinant of purchase intention, the "social risk" variable, positively influences purchase intention, contrary to what was defined as a research hypothesis.

According to [26], society and the influence of groups play an important role in consumer behavior when considering purchase intention of technological products. The author found a relation between the influence of groups and product design, and states that consumers prefer to buy products with an advanced design, due to the influence of groups, and a second relation between society and brand awareness, explained as the consumers' preference in buying national brand products in order to get recognition from society. Although this value is non-significant (the estimated parameter value is 0.09), we assume that consumers believe they are judged if they buy a smartphone instead of a basic mobile phone, and believe that a smartphone gives them status, regardless of the brand.

Finally, hypothesis H8 is validated, confirming that the intention of a person to act (or not) in a certain way, is an immediate determinant that person's present behavior.

## 5    Conclusion

From the variables listed, only six appear to be direct influencers of the intention to purchase PLB smartphones: the price awareness, quality perception, technology perception, social and functional risk, and brand awareness. The "technology perception" variable is the variable that has the greatest influence on purchase intention of PLB smartphones, due to the importance it represents in this product category (it brings together essential components for excellent product performance).

The "price awareness" variable, overlooked by some researchers ([3]; Jin and Suh, 2005, *cit. in* [3]) in studies on durable goods, was considered relevant for our study and proved to be influential on the purchase intention of PLB smartphones. We believe that this relationship is justified on the basis of the socio-demographic data of our respondents, the net annual earnings.

Regarding the "quality perception" variable, [3] and [12] suggest that the consumer feels more likely to opt for PLBs when the difference in perceived quality between the manufacturer brand and the PLB is very small. The results for this variable provided support to this statement, which is justified by the difficulty that consumers have in perceiving differences in quality in this particular category.

We also found that brand awareness influences the purchase intention of PLB smartphones, which is justified by the consumer's relation with their telecommunications provider built over time. The "functional risk" and "social risk" variables took the opposite sign to the parameter estimated initially, which made this study even more interesting. We can assume that users of PLB smartphones are familiar with this type of device, being sufficiently knowledgeable about these products, allowing them to evaluate the complexity of the category and define the functional risk inherent to the purchase. As for the social risk, we know that users believe they are judged according to their purchase option (Harrell, 1986, *cit. in* [24]); however, this reversal sign may be due to the fact that when they buy a smartphone instead of a more basic mobile phone, they believe it gives them status, regardless of the brand.

Telecommunication operators can deduce from these findings that their customers or potential customers value technology, price and quality as the most distinctive elements in differentiating their offer, as well as perceived risk and brand awareness.

This study found some limitations that should be mentioned, related to the fact that it used an unrepresentative convenience sample. A second limitation relates to the choice of variables in the theoretical framework. Future studies should also explore the significance and importance of other variables that may influence the purchasing behavior of PLB technological products. For example, analyzing the influence of store image, the variety of products and brands, the importance of added value services, after-sales service, as well as assistance and return period.

**Acknowledgement.** This work is funded by the ERDF through the Programme COMPETE and by the Portuguese Government through FCT - Foundation for Science and Technology, project PTDC/EGE-GES/099741/2008.

# References

1. Steenkamp, J.-B., Hofstede, F., Wedel, M.: A cross-national investigation into the individual and national cultural antecedents of consumer innovativeness. J. Mark. 63(2), 55–69 (1999)

2. Lamey, L., et al.: How business cycles contribute to private-label success: evidence from the United States and Europe. J. Mark. 71(1), 1–15 (2007)
3. Caplliure, E.M., Miquel, M.J., Pérez, C.: La elección de la marca del distribuidor en productos duraderos: factores de influencia. Cuadernos de Gestión 10, 125–147 (2010)
4. Kotler, P.: Marketing Management, 11th edn. Prentice Hall, New Jersey (2003)
5. Cardoso, A., Alves, P.: Atitude dos consumidores relativamente à marca dos distribuidores. Revista da Faculdade de Ciências Humanas e Sociais – UFP 5, 38–55 (2008)
6. Schutte, T.E.: The Semantics of Branding. J. of Mark. 33, 5–11 (1969)
7. Batlas, G.: Determinants of store brand choice: a behavioral analysis. J. Product & Brand Management 6(5), 315–324 (1997)
8. Joshi, M.A., Pandya, A.R.: A Comparative Study on Consumers' Attitude Towards Private Labels: A Special Focus on Ahmedabad and Surat. The IUP J. Brand Manage. VIII(1), 36–47 (2011)
9. Ailawadi, K.L., et al.: Private-label use and store loyalty. J. Mark. 72, 19–30 (2008)
10. Rousseau, J.A.: Uma visão global e estruturante da moderna distribuição. Manual de Distribuição. Linda-a-Velha: Control Jornal Editora (1997)
11. Goldsmith, R.E., et al.: Consumer attitudes and loyalty towards private brands. Int. J. Consumer Studies 34, 339–348 (2010)
12. Hoch, S.J., Banerji, S.: When do private labels succeed? Sloan Manage. Rev. 34, 57–67 (1993)
13. Quelch, J.A., Harding, D.: Brands versus private labels: fighting to win. Harvard Bus. Rev. 74(1), 99–109 (1996)
14. Lambin, J.J.: Marketing Estratégico, 4th edn. Macgrow Hill, Lisboa (2000)
15. Burton, S., et al.: A Scale for Measuring attitude toward Private label Products and an Examination of Its Psychological and Behavioral Correlates. J. of the Academy Mark. Science 26(4), 293–306 (1998)
16. Charlesworth, A.: The ascent of smartphone. Engineering & Technology 4(3), 32–33 (2009)
17. Wang, D., Park, S., Fesenmaier, D.R.: An examination of information services and smartphone applications. University of Massachusetts, Amherst (2011)
18. Livesey, F., Lennon, P.: Factors Affecting Consumers' Choice Between Manufacturer Brands and Retailer Own Brands. European J. Mark. 12(2), 158–170 (1978)
19. Dunn, M.G., et al.: The Influence of Perceived Risk on Brand Preference for Supermarket Products. J. Retailing 62(2), 204–217 (1986)
20. Richardson, P., Jain, A.K., Dick, A.S.: The influence of store aesthetics on evaluation of private label brands. J. Product Brand Manage. 5(2), 19–28 (1996)
21. Dhar, S.K., Hoch, S.J.: Why store brand penetration varies by retailer. Marke. Sc. 16, 208–227 (1997)
22. Narasimhan, C., Wilcox, R.T.: Private labels and the channel relationship: a cross-category analysis. J. Business 71(4), 573–600 (1998)
23. Sethuraman, R., Cole, C.: Why do consumers pay more for national brands than for store brands? Marketing Science Institute Working Paper, Cambridge, 97–126 (1997)
24. Batra, R., Sinha, I.: Consumer-Level Factors Moderating: The Success of Private Label Brands. J. Retailing 76(2), 175–191 (2000)
25. Mohr, J., Sengupta, S., Slater, S.: Marketing of High Technology Products and Innovations. Prentice Hall, NewJersey (2004)
26. Sakkthivel, A.M.: Modelling of determinants influence consumer behaviour towards different technology products. International J. Electronic Finance 5(1) (2011)

27. Ailawadi, K.L., Neslin, S.A., Gedenk, K.: Pursuing the value-conscious consumer: store brands versus national brand promotions. J. Mark. 65(1), 71–89 (2001)
28. Batra, R., Sinha, I.: The effect of consumer price consciousness on private label purchase. International J. Res. Mark. 16, 237–251 (1999)
29. Bettman, J.R.: Perceived Risk and Its Components: A Model and Empirical Test. J. Mark. Res. 10(2), 184–190 (1973)
30. Shannon, R., Mandhachitara, R.: Private label grocery shopping attitudes and behavior: A cross-cultural study. Brand Manage. 12(6), 461–474 (2005)
31. Ziamou, P.L., Ratneshwar, S.: Promoting Consumer Adoption of High-Technology Products: Is More Information always better? J. Consumer Psychology 12, 341–351 (2002)
32. Brown, S.A., Venkatesh, V.: Model of Adoption of Technology in Households: A Baseline Model Test and Extension Incorporating Household Life Cycle. MIS Quarterly 29(3), 399–426 (2005)
33. Sriram, S., Chintigunta, K.P., Neelamegham, R.: Effects of brand preference, product attributes, and marketing mix variables in technology products markets. Mark. Sc. 25(5), 440–456 (2006)
34. Dowling, G.R., Staelin, R.: A model of perceived risk and intended risk-handling activity. J. Consumer Research 21, 119–134 (1994)
35. Sweeney, J.C., Soutar, G.N., Johnson, L.W.: The Role of Perceived Risk in the Quality-Value Relationship: A study in a Retail Environment. J. Retailing 75(1), 77–105 (1999)
36. Delvecchio, D.: Consumer perceptions of private label quality: the role of product category characteristics and consumer use of heuristics. J. Retailing Consumer Services 8, 239–249 (2001)
37. Aaker, D.A.: Building Strong Brands. The Free Press, New York (1996)
38. Keller, K.L.: Conceptualizing, Measuring, and Managing Costumer-Based Brand Equity. J. Mark. 57, 1–22 (1993)
39. Schweiger, G., et al.: The influence of country of origin and brand on product evaluation and the Implications thereof for location decisions. Vienna Univ. of Econ. and Business Administration (1995)
40. Mendes, M.: Processo de decisão de compra e estratégias de publicidade. Revista Eletróncia de Administração 8(4), 1–17 (1998)
41. Sheppard, B.H., et al.: The Theory of Reasoned Action: A Meta-Analysis of Past Research with Recommendations for Modifications and Future Research. J. of Consumer Res. 15(3), 325–343 (1988)
42. Coyle, J.R., Thorson, E.: The Effects of Progressive Levels of Interactivity and Vividness in Web Marketing Sites. J. of Advertising 30(3), 65–77 (2001)
43. Hill, M.M., Hill, A.: Investigação por questionário, 2nd edn. Edições Sílabo, Lisboa (2005)
44. Hair, J., et al.: Multivariate Data Analysis, 5th edn. Prentice Hall, Upper Saddle River (2006)
45. Anderson, J.C., Gerbing, D.W.: Structural equation modeling in practice: a review and recommended two-step approach. Psychological Bulletin 13(5), 411–423 (1988)
46. Fornell, C., Larcker, D.: Evaluating structural equation models with unobservable variables and measurement errors. J. Mark. Res. 18, 39–50 (1981)
47. Gabor, A., Granger, C.W.: Price Sensitivity of the Consumer. Manage. Dec. 17(8), 569–575 (1979)

# Media Sharing in Situated Displays: Service Design Lessons from Existing Practices with Paper Leaflets

Ana Melro, Bruno Silva, and Rui José

Centro Algoritmi, University of Minho
Campus de Azurém, Guimarães, Portugal
{amelro,bruno.silva,rui}@dsi.uminho.pt

**Abstract.** Digital public displays have an enormous potential as a collaborative technology to socialize in public venues, especially when they are open to the participation of visitors. However, user-generated content is a form of control sharing that requires safeguards against the publication of content deemed inappropriate. In this work, we study the perceptions of Café owners in regard to their acceptance of user-generated content displayed on their venue screens. Our goal is to inform the design of new media sharing services for public displays by uncovering how existing practices with paper leaflets could be leveraged as a conceptual framework for dealing with content appropriateness. Based on interviews with 10 café owners, we identify important insights into some of practices surrounding the distribution of paper leaflets and their implications for the design of media sharing services for public displays.

**Keywords:** public displays, user-generated content, social computing, situated computing.

## 1 Introduction

Situated services have a strong connection with the immediate physical environment in which they are deployed [1]. An interactive public display that accepts content from people in its vicinity is a representative example of a situated service. When interactive or in some other way reactive to the presence of people, public displays can have an enormous potential as focal points for social coordination, helping to create a shared sense of place, inviting people to action and setting behaviour expectations in public venues [2]. While situated displays have existed for quite some time, their wide deployment has been severely limited by the lack of appropriate and usable solutions for trust and control sharing. These solutions need to be able to combine the easy and spontaneous participation of people with safeguards against abuses.

In our research, we intend to uncover the key elements that could compose trust models for media sharing services for public displays. Since these elements may vary considerably, depending on the nature of the places, in this work we are specifically addressing cafés, bars, community centres, and other similar places where people go to mingle with others. More specifically, we study the perceptions of café owners about the appropriateness of content that could be published on their screens in scenarios where content was, at least partially, generated from café visitors.

J.F. e Cunha, M. Snene, and H. Nóvoa (Eds.): IESS 2013, LNBIP 143, pp. 322–328, 2013.
© Springer-Verlag Berlin Heidelberg 2013

The study is based on existing practices with the distribution of paper leaflets at these cafés. This is a very common practice that is grounded on well-established forms of social negotiation, making it an interesting source for informing the design of situated services. Based on interviews with 10 café owners we identify some of the key practices surrounding the distribution of paper leaflets and analyse the respective implications for service design according to three specific themes: content appropriateness, moderation strategies and connections between places. Together, these results constitute a novel contribution to inform the design of new media sharing services for public displays that reflect realistic practices around content publication.

## 2    Related Work

Strategies for content publication on public displays have been extensively studied in the context of specific display systems [3-7]. These studies involve the issue of moderation and access control, but they also identify less obvious challenges, such as the need for flexibility with regard to content creation, content expiration, and clean-up procedures [4]. While providing a fundamental background for our work, these studies are not focused on the role of social practices in the publication process.

The role of the social setting around the display and how it affects engagement has been addressed in the work by Brignull et al. [8] that has shown how the attention of passers-by (viewers) can be achieved through the honey-pot effect. This work has also shown that since the persons interacting with the display could easily be identified, thus allowing everyone to know who said what, this would lead to a form of social pressure that is not enjoyed by everyone, and was even compared by some people to the public shame felt when going to blackboard at school.

Other studies about user engagement have also shown that social embarrassment can be a huge barrier to use public displays for social interaction [9, 10]. This can change significantly when the interaction is based on mobile phones. This possibility is important as mobile phone is the everyday gadget, one that users do not need to learn how to work with (they are familiar with it) and at the same time contributes to diminish social embarrassment, as users do not need to be seen interacting with the display [8]. Together these studies highlight the importance of the social context in content publication practices, and how content publication policies for public displays should be strongly anchored on practices that are aligned with that social context.

Alt et al. [5] address the issue of the motivations venue owner can have to share their public boards and also their practices for controlling that content. They studied Public Notice Areas (PNAs) to understand what type of content is left there, how the control of content is made and the ways used to entice the publication of new content. Our focus is on the design of digital media sharing services in which the same content can be left at multiple locations.

## 3    Methodology

This study was focused on cafés and the existing practices for leaflet distribution. We selected 10 locations in the city of Guimarães and conducted semi-structured interviews with the respective owners, addressing the research questions of the study. A key challenge in our research is that the target audience of our study, the Café owners, still do not have any practices of publication in public displays. Their screens are merely used for TV viewing and therefore there is no such thing as someone asking permission to post their own content in there. Rather than asking venue managers about futuristic scenarios for which they have no practices and that they will always have some difficulties in envisioning in their entirety, we chose to explore the practices associated with paper leaflets as a relevant background for framing the emergence of practices associated with user-generated content on the public displays.

The distribution of paper leaflets is very common in these cafés, which often have a small corner, where they can be left. They are mainly used to promote events (parties, exhibitions, concerts, etc.), causes, or small local businesses (house selling, support in studies, etc.). The interesting point about these leaflets is that their distribution is grounded on a broad range of well-established practices surrounding the creation, placement, maintenance and appropriation of places as a display location. These practices are strongly embedded in implicit social behaviours, reflecting the various forms of negotiation around the design and use of those leaflets. Despite the differences in the medium, the essence of the social negotiation involved in leaflet distribution is probably the best approximation one could have to the complex social negotiation processes that may emerge in public displays. Their distribution is preceded by an informal authorization request, in which a distributor will approach the venue manager and show him or her the leaflet that is meant to be distributed. These requests are almost always accepted, in good part because there is an established understanding about what might be reasonable to ask.

### 3.1    Interviews

To prepare the interviews, we collected multiple leaflets and made a selection of 20 to be used in the interviews. This selection was carefully made to isolate the effect of particular content properties on the venue manager's decisions. Regarding the type of content, we have made an informal categorization of the various leaflets that had been collected, and then we made sure that those categories were properly represented in the 20 leaflets selected for the interviews. Regarding the type of location, we used mainly leaflets collected in cafés, but we also introduced 5 leaflets collected at the University. Finally, we also introduced 7 leaflets collected from cafés, but from a different town located 20 Km away.

Interviews started with the 20 leaflets being placed on a table. Participants were asked to indicate 5 leaflets that they would like to see on their display and 5 others that they would prefer not to be shown. The use of physical leaflets that are part of the daily reality of the participants was meant to provide some well-known context for specific questions, but worked well as a catalyst for the whole interview. The interview itself had 9 questions, distributed by 3 main topics: type of content that place owners would like and dislike to see on their public display; moderation issues; and content publication as a service that allows places to keep in touch and interact with each other. The interviews were recorded with the permission of the participants, lasted approximately 30 minutes and were all made in-situ, so that the interviewees could feel in the right context to answer. Participants were also told that questions were meant to be open, and they should not restrain themselves to direct answers.

## 3.2    Results

Table 1 summarises the number of leaflets in each category and the number of acceptances and refusals that occurred in the 10 interviews.

**Table 1.** Leaflets categories and number of times a leaflet category was selected or rejected

| Content type | Location where leaflet was collected | Number of leaflets used | Number of acceptances | Number of refusals |
|---|---|---|---|---|
| Announcing an event | Cafés (other location) | 1 | 7 | 0 |
| | Cafés Guimarães | 3 | 21 | 0 |
| | University Guimarães | 3 | 9 | 2 |
| Advertising a service | Cafés (other location) | 6 | 5 | 18 |
| | Cafés Guimarães | 5 | 2 | 14 |
| | University Guimarães | 2 | 2 | 1 |

These results are complemented with the analysis of the reasons indicated in the interviews for accepting or rejecting the leaflets. We have analysed those answers and classified them according to the categories presented in Table 2, which shows the reasons indicated to accept or reject leaflets and the qualitative view of the overall attitude towards each of those leaflet types.

**Table 2.** Main reasons indicated by place owners for accepting or refusing leaflets

| | Reason for accepting | Reason for refusing | Overall attitude |
|---|---|---|---|
| Leaflet is from a similar type of place | 6 | 3 | Mixed |
| Leaflet promotes cultural event | 3 | 0 | Positive |
| Leaflet is about local services (same town) | 7 | 0 | Positive |
| Leaflet is commercial advertising | 1 | 6 | Negative |

Acceptance motivations were mainly associated with a sense of community, and the promotion of the city, especially cultural events. Rejection motivations were primarily associated with competition. If the leaflet was from a competitor place that would be a strong reason for refusing it. We will now analyse the answers according to three specific themes: content appropriateness, moderation strategies and connections between places.

### Content Appropriateness

In regard to content appropriateness, we intended to uncover the main elements that drive the perception of venue owners about which content could be appropriate for presentation on their public display. By avoiding the noise that would potentially be introduced by obviously offending content, we tried to focus on less obvious values that venue owners could have in regard to the content and particularly on differences of perception between different places. Also, for the same reasons, this could indicate us any differences of perception caused by the fact that the medium is a digital display rather than a conventional non-digital medium. The leaflets that were most often se-lected as suitable for presentation were mainly related with cultural events in the city, with the justification being that it would be interesting information to visitors:

> [Leaflet nr. 1 was select for presentation] *because it's part of Guimarães culture and people need to know what's going to happen during the week.* [ER]

The reasons for possible rejection of some leaflets were varied. The notion of compe-tition was indicated by 4 of the interviewees as very important as many of those re-jected leaflets were announcing events at competing venues.

> *First, because they sell everything I sell.* [TB]

3 participants have identified the source of some leaflets as being from a different city (Braga) and for that reason considered those leaflets not appropriate. This clearly confirms the strongly locative nature of some of these leaflets, but also another di-mension of the social role in the appropriateness of content, in this case localism:

> *Would you reject any leaflet from Braga? Yes, I would, anything!* [Mu]

**Moderation Practices**
In regard to possible moderation practices, it was also clear that different participants chose to take very different perspectives on the moderation issue. While some seemed to struggle on what should be acceptable, other took a much more pragmatic approach by simply not rejecting any leaflets.

> *Why shouldn't I like?! There is nothing special in these leaflets; they don't have pornography or other content like that?! There is nothing here that would shock me.* [M]

> *I think there will be some moderation, even if a relaxed one, to avoid the possibil-ity of undesired publicity.* [TB]

> *No* [I wouldn't like to moderate], *I wouldn't have time for that, and I think that the interest of such a platform is everyone being free to do whatever they want.* [M]

Participants have also had a very diverse perspective on sharing moderation with others. While some claimed they would not even trust their employees, others have indicated that they would be able to identify several regular visitors they would trust as additional moderators. These results seem to indicate that in regard to moderation techniques there may be a need for flexible approaches that can accommodate a very diverse set of social settings, each with its own needs in regard to the best way to establish moderation.

**The Role of Collaboration Between Places**
The final set of questions addressed the issue of connections between different loca-tions, more specifically how venue owners perceive the possible dissemination of content about their own place in other places, even if competitors and their possible

role in some form of collaborative moderation. Most venue managers indicated they would be available for either receiving information/leaflets about other places, and for disseminating information about their place. Leaflets from other cafés and bars were more controversial. 3 interviewees have explicitly mentioned not wishing to have information (in leaflets or on screen) about parties or events occurring in places that offer the same service as they do, at the same hours. Competition was indicated as a major obstacle:

> Yes [I think it's important to connect with other places], *but when it's not direct competition to my place, but I accept information from restaurants, hotels, pubs after closing mine, which are not my competition.* [ER]

> Yes [we would accept] *if it is advertising, parties, discos as of 2 a.m.* [C]

However, 6 other interviewees indicated they would not have a problem with competition, and pointed out that it would be an advantage, because it may bring more and different people to the city, and consequently to the places:

> *I would accept* [information from other places] *if there were information about my bar as well, I can't see why not.* [EB]

In fact, tacit connections already seem to exist that make them accept leaflets from other places. Even if not a formal relationship, place owners already ask each other to leave paper leaflets announcing a party or other events. Reciprocity seems to play an important role in these collaborations. While competition is understandably an issue, the interviews have shown how this perception of competition can be subjective and much more embedded with local knowledge that simply assuming that similar businesses would necessarily see themselves as competitors. Overall, however, participants seemed to be well aware of the high value of collaboration opportunities between different venues in regard to content moderation and exchange.

## 4    Conclusions

The overall results of this work confirm the importance of established content sharing practices in setting the expectations and the control mechanisms for new situated services. In particular, those practices should be essential in establishing appropriate control sharing policies for user-generated content in public displays. A second important conclusion is the diversity of perspectives that place owners can have on the same issues, and particularly how the concept of appropriateness can depend more on personal values and culture than on content itself. This suggests that situated services should be designed with flexible control mechanisms that may accommodate a broad range of social settings and control practices. The results in regard to moderation also point in the same direction, highlighting the need to accommodate a very broad range of expectations in regard to how it is done, the guarantees provided and the people involved. In regard to connections between places and the role they may have in content publication procedures, most place owners recognised some value in those collaborations. However, it was also evident that many of them had a very subtle understanding about the nature of those connections. A solution to integrate them into content publication procedures for situated services should be able to capture these subtleties and allow place owners to be in full control of their engagement with others.

**Acknowledgements.** The research leading to these results has received funding from FCT under the Carnegie Mellon - Portugal agreement: Web Security and Privacy (CMU-PT/SE/028/2008).

# References

1. Kostakos, V., Oakley, I.: Designing trustworthy situated services: an implicit and explicit assessment of locative images-effect on trust. In: Proceedings of the SIGCHI Conference on Human Factors in Computing Systems, pp. 329–332. ACM, Boston (2009)
2. O'Hara, K., et al.: Introduction to public and situated displyas (2003)
3. Davies, N., et al.: Challenges in Developing an App Store for Public Displays – A Position Paper. In: Research in the Large: Using App Stores, Markets and other Wide Distribution Channels in UbiComp Research Workshop, UbiComp 2010, Copenhagen (2010)
4. Alt, F., et al.: Digifieds: Evaluating Suitable Interaction Techniques for Shared Public Notice Areas Digifieds. In: Pervasive (1) (2011)
5. Alt, F., Memarovic, N., Elhart, I., Bial, D., Schmidt, A., Langheinrich, M., Harboe, G., Huang, E., Scipioni, M.P.: Designing Shared Public Display Networks – Implications from Today's Paper-Based Notice Areas. In: Lyons, K., Hightower, J., Huang, E.M. (eds.) Pervasive 2011. LNCS, vol. 6696, pp. 258–275. Springer, Heidelberg (2011)
6. Langheinrich, M., et al.: Autopoiesic Content: A Conceptual Model for Enabling Situated Self-generative Content for Public Displays. In: First Workshop on Pervasive Urban Applications, San Francisco (2011)
7. McCarthy, J.F., Costa, T.J., Liongosari, E.S.: UniCast, OutCast & GroupCast: Three Steps Toward Ubiquitous, Peripheral Displays. In: Abowd, G.D., Brumitt, B., Shafer, S. (eds.) UbiComp 2001. LNCS, vol. 2201, pp. 332–345. Springer, Heidelberg (2001)
8. Brignull, H., Rogers, Y.: Enticing People to Interact with Large Public Displays in Public Spaces. In: INTERACT 2003. IOS Press (2003)
9. Finke, M., et al.: Lessons Learned: Game Design for Large Public Displays. In: 3rd International Conference on Digital Interactive Media in Entertainment and Arts, New York, NY, USA (2008)
10. Koppel, M., et al.: Chained displays: configurations of public displays can be used to influence actor-, audience-, and passer-by behavior. In: 2012 ACM Annual Conference on Human Factors in Computing Systems (CHI 2012), ACM, New York (2012)

# Towards a Personal Relationship-Based Assignment of Client Representatives to Accounts

Johannes Kunze von Bischhoffshausen[1] and Jeffrey T. Becker[2]

[1] Karlsruhe Institute of Technology, Karlsruhe Service Research Institute,
Englerstr. 11, 76131 Karlsruhe, Germany
johannes.kunze@kit.edu
[2] IBM Corporation, 1 North Castle Drive, Armonk, NY 10504, United States,
jtbecker@us.ibm.com

**Abstract.** Business-to-Business (B2B) companies are evolving from selling products towards engaging in long-lasting relationships to co-create value. This shift changes the role of the client rep from being a sales representative to being a value creator and manager of the relationship between both firms. The quality of the established personal relationship between the client rep and the account firms is thereby a critical determinant of future business success for B2B companies. Therefore, leveraging these established relationships is a crucial task in sales management – but can constitute a complex organizational challenge.

This paper provides an optimization approach to addresses this organizational complexity in B2B sales organization. We propose an integer programming model for assigning the right client rep to the right account based on the established personal relationships between client reps and accounts in order to maximize future revenue.

**Keywords:** Sales Force Management, Sales Force Optimization, Customer Relationship Management, Solution Selling, Service Marketing, Relationship Marketing, B2B Marketing.

## 1 Introduction

In the past decades, B2B companies in several industries transformed their business from selling products to engaging in long-term relationships to co-create value [1]. This requires B2B providers to integrate internal and external resources to create their value proposition to their customer accounts. Particularly in mature markets, which are characterized by fierce competition and limited growth, this transformation is perceived as a means to improve the competitive position. This development incorporates several concepts developed by marketing and management scholars, such as relationship marketing [2], the service dominant logic [3, 4], customer intimacy [5], one-to-one marketing [6], and solution selling [1].

For B2B companies, personal selling takes a strategic role and personal selling and sales management emerge as major subtopic in current B2B marketing literature D.

J.F. e Cunha, M. Snene, and H. Nóvoa (Eds.): IESS 2013, LNBIP 143, pp. 329–335, 2013.

The shift towards relational co-creation of value significantly impacts the role of the client rep: "The role of a salesperson in the emerging era will be more than that of a general manager. Salespersons will be responsible for marshaling internal and external resources to satisfy customer needs and wants." [7]. A similar role description for sales reps has been proposed in the context of selling complex services: "Salespeople involved in the marketing of complex services often perform the role of relationship managers" [8].

Therefore, salespeople play a key role in the development of the relationship between the B2B provider and the customer [7], as they are the primary link between both firms [9]. Indeed, Biong and Selnes [9] state that salespeople have a high influence on the account's perception of the reliability of the provider, the perceived value of the provider's services, and finally the buyer's likelihood to continue the relationship. Furthermore, previous empirical research suggests that future sales opportunities of complex service offerings depend mostly on the relationship quality between sales representatives and accounts [8]. Finally, current literature states that these days successful client reps develop a different relationship with their accounts. Instead of being a reactive problem solver, successful client reps are proactive partners to their accounts, maintaining and leveraging relationships with several account stakeholders [10].

Regarding the fact that established personal relationships between client reps and their accounts determine the future success of B2B companies, it may be surprising that, as the literature review in Section 2 indicates, personal relationships received little attention in the field of sales force optimization. Although there is a lot of research conducted in this field, little attention is given to the question how a provider should set up the sales organization in order to leverage the established relationships of client reps in the best possible way. As organizational complexity is a key challenge for sales organizations within the shift from selling products to engaging in long-term relationships to co-create value [1], there is a need to close this gap.

This paper introduces an approach to address this problem. The proposed integer programming model enables service providers to optimally leverage relationships of client reps based on the assessment of prospect revenue, personal established relationships, and the impact of personal established relationships on turning prospect revenue into sales. A brief literature review on current models for sales force optimization is outlined in Section 2. The proposed assignment model is introduced in Section 3. Section 4 elaborates on the managerial implication of this work, and proposes future research directions.

## 2    Literature Review

Sales force optimization, in particular sales force deployment has attracted much analytical study from management science in the past [11], while still "the volume of research on sales force topics in the leading marketing journals has not matched its importance in the marketing mix" [12].

In our literature review, we reviewed four sub problems of sales force optimization, proposed by Drexl and Haase [11]: sales force sizing (selecting the appropriate number of client reps), salesman location (locating client reps to set of accounts within one sales territory), sales territory alignment (clustering sets of accounts into territories) and sales resource allocation (aligning time of client reps per account), while.

Although there is such a diversity, most models for the assignment on a client rep to account level cluster accounts a-priori into a set of "Sales Coverage Units" [11] for keeping models where response functions need to be estimated on an appropriate size (e.g. [13]). This a-priori clustering limits the capability to model personal established relationships. The only research conducted on the client rep to distinct account level assignment we identified is proposed in the early work of Lodish [14], who proposes an assignment problem based on relative efficiency assumptions on each client-rep account pair. However, the proposed model is not dedicated to personal established relationships between client reps and accounts.

To summarize our findings, although a wide range of research has been conducted in the field of sales force optimization, none of the reviewed literature proposes an approach with takes established personal relationships of client reps to distinct accounts into consideration.

# 3   Model

The objective of the model is to find the optimal assignment of client reps to accounts in order to maximize the expected revenue. In this section, we elaborate on the assumptions of this model before we develop the integer programming model. Finally, we illustrate the application of our approach in a fictive scenario.

## 3.1   Model Assumptions

In this model, exactly one client rep has to be assigned to each account, while one rep can be assigned to a distinct maximum of accounts. Apart from established personal relationships, no other variable is taken into account in this model (such as travel distance or industry expertise). This model is therefore applicable in settings, where a homogenous set of client reps is already assigned to a specific set of customers (sales territory), and no other variables than personal relationships play a role for the assignment. This is especially the case for geographical small sales territories containing a homogeneous set of customers.

Furthermore, this model assumes that the prospect revenue for each account is estimated (which is common practice in sales force deployment), the relationship quality between client reps and accounts can be assessed (e.g. through questionnaire-based self-assessment), and the influence of personal relationships on turning prospect revenue into sales can be estimated (e.g. based on the sales history). The last assumption in the model is that the result of turning prospect revenue into sales is binary: either the account buys from the provider or the entire prospect revenue for this customer is generated by a competitor.

## 3.2     Integer Programming Model Formulation

The decision to be made in this model is whether to assign client rep $i$ to account $j$.

$$Let\ x_{ij} = \begin{cases} 1\ if\ client\ rep\ i\ is\ assigned\ to\ account\ j \\ 0\ else \end{cases}$$

Crosby et. al (1990) showed that future sales opportunities depend mostly on the relationship quality between client reps and the account. In line with these findings, we propose the probability $q_{ij}$ as the probability of turning prospect account revenue $V_j$ into sales in case of a distinct assignment. $q_{ij}$ is modeled as a function of the relationship quality $r_{ij}$ between client rep $i$ and account $j$, and additional noise $e$, which are effects not related to the relationship quality.

$$q_{ij} = P(Turning\ V_j\ into\ sales\ |\ x_{ij} = 1) = f(r_{ij}) + e. \tag{1}$$

Based on Formula 1, an integer programming problem with a set of constraints can be formulated. The first constraint is to assign each account $j = 1...m$ to exactly one client rep $i = 1...n$.

$$\sum_{i=1}^{n} x_{ij} = 1\ for\ j = 1, ..., n. \tag{2}$$

The second constraint is to assign a maximum number of $W_i$ accounts of $j = 1...m$ to each client rep $i = 1...n$.

$$\sum_{j=1}^{m} x_{ij} \le W_i\ for\ i = 1, ..., m. \tag{3}$$

One can now formally state the integer programming model in order to maximize revenue. As $q_{ij}$ as the probability of turning prospect account revenue $V_j$ into sales in case of a distinct assignment, we iterate through all possible assignments for each account. In case of an assignment, $q_{ij}^{x_{ij}} = q_{ij}$, else $q_{ij}^{x_{ij}} = 1$. The product is multiplied by the prospect account revenue $V_j$. The overall sum for all accounts is to be maximized.

$$max \sum_{j=1}^{n} \left( V_j \prod_{i=1}^{m} q_{ij}^{x_{ij}} \right) \tag{4}$$

subject to constraints (2) and (3).

## 3.3     Implementation Scenario

Consider a simple fictive scenario of a distinct sales territory of a B2B service provider, containing eight accounts $j = \{A,B,C,D,E,F,G,H\}$. Client rep X has previously been assigned to A,C,E,G and client rep Y has previously been assigned to B,D,F,H resulting in a very good relationship of the client reps to their previous accounts. Junior client rep Z established a good relationship with the accounts B,C,D,E during supporting X and Y in sales activities with these accounts. The growing market led to a growth in account size and workload. This requires changes in the assignment for the next period. Therefore, the sales resource allocation plan assigns three client reps to this account the next period, including client rep Z who will work on accounts on his own. Furthermore, in order to balance workload, the maximum number of accounts assigned to one rep increased to three. The decision to be made in this scenario is which of the accounts $j$ should be assigned to which of the client reps i = {X,Y,Z}. Therefore, the client reps rate their relationship with the eight accounts. The results are clustered into no relationship ($r_{ij} = 0$), good relationship ($r_{ij} = 1$), and very good relationship ($r_{ij} = 2$), resulting in the following relationship matrix R.

$$R = \begin{pmatrix} 2 & 0 & 2 & 0 & 2 & 0 & 2 & 0 \\ 0 & 2 & 0 & 2 & 0 & 2 & 0 & 2 \\ 0 & 0 & 1 & 1 & 1 & 1 & 0 & 0 \end{pmatrix}$$

The prospect revenue $V_j$ for each account is estimated resulting in the vector V.

$$V = (130 \quad 130 \quad 100 \quad 90 \quad 85 \quad 80 \quad 75 \quad 75)$$

Empirical evidence from previous sales activities shows that the probability of turning the prospect revenue into sales is 0.3. The probability increases to 0.35 if the client rep has a good relationship and 0.4 if the client rep has a very good relationship with the account. Hence, $q_{ij}$ can be modeled as a function of relationship (including noise).

$$q_{ij} = 0.3 + 0.05 * r_{ij}$$

Inserted into the optimization problem results in

$$max \sum_{j=1}^{n} \left( V_j \prod_{i=1}^{m} (0.3 + 0.1 * r_{ij})^{x_{ij}} \right)$$

subject to constraints (2) and (3).

Assuming each client rep should not be assigned to more than three accounts ($W_i = 3$ for each $i$), the optimal solution of the in Section 3.2 proposed assignment approach is compared to other assignment approaches in Table 1. Assignment $A_i$ is the set of accounts assigned to client rep $i$. The worst case scenario demonstrates what could happen in the worst case, if personal relationships are not considered for the assignment. The second scenario shows the result of a revenue balancing approach, which is usually applied by practitioners [13]. The third scenario is calculated by a greedy assignment approach, while the last one is the result of the proposed optimal assignment approach.

**Table 1.** Comparison of different assignment approaches.

| Approach | Approach Description | Assignment | Revenue |
|---|---|---|---|
| Worst Case | Minimize instead of maximize proposed assignment approach | $A_x = \{C, E, G\}, A_y$ $= \{D, F, H\}, A_z = \{A, B\}$ | 229.50 |
| Fair Balanced | Start with largest account to first rep, second largest to second rep, ... | $A_x = \{A, D, G\}, A_y$ $= \{B, E, H\}, A_z = \{C, F\}$ | 272.00 |
| Greedy | Calculate $V_j * q_{ij}$ values for each $ij$-pair, pick assignment starting with largest value, then assign second largest value, ... | $A_x = \{A, B, C\}, A_y$ $= \{E, F, G\}, A_z = \{D, G\}$ | 291.00 |
| Optimal | Proposed assignment approach | $A_x = \{A, B, D\}, A_y$ $= \{E, F, H\}, A_z = \{C, G\}$ | 297.75 |

## 4    Conclusion and Outlook

In this paper, we propose an approach for leveraging established personal relationships in the best possible way. This is done through assigning client reps based on their established relationships with the accounts. Therefore, this work proposes an integer programming model for finding the best possible assignment, which can have significant impact on future sales.

The optimal assignment is relevant for B2B service providers, as the relationship quality between client reps and accounts are a major determinant for future selling success. As it addresses the key challenge organizational complexity, the contribution is particularly relevant for large B2B service providers.

Furthermore, the proposed approach provides additional value for service providers which already have analytical solutions for sales force optimization in place. A major barrier for sales managers to dynamically adjust sales organization is the fear of losing the relationship with their accounts through restructuring, often resulting in static past-oriented sales structures instead of a sales organization prepared for the future [15]. Hence, the proposed approach provides additional value in highly dynamic markets. Combined with other optimization solutions, the sales organization can be dynamically adjusted while still the best possible utilization of established relationships is ensured.

The limitation of the proposed approach is mainly related to the strong model assumptions. Especially the binary modeling on turning prospect revenue into sales has to be refined.

The proposed contribution lays the foundation for our future research. This paper focused on the integer programming model. Our future research will focus on implementing this model in a real case scenario. Therefore, we first need to develop a predictive model in the form proposed in Formula 2, based on real-world data of a

B2B service provider. Afterwards, we will implement our suggested approach, including the predictive model, in an analytical application. This application will support sales managers in assigning their client reps to accounts.

**Acknowledgments.** This research was supported with funding by the Karlsruhe House of Young Scientists.

# References

1. Tuli, K.R., Kohli, A.K., Bharadwaj, S.G.: Rethinking Customer Solutions: From Product Bundles to Relational Processes. Journal of Marketing 71, 1–17 (2007)
2. Berry, L., Upah, G.: Emerging perspectives on services marketing. American Marketing Association (1983)
3. Vargo, S., Lusch, R.: Evolving to a New Dominant Logic for Marketing. Journal of Marketing 68, 1–17 (2004)
4. Vargo, S., Lusch, R.: Service-dominant logic: continuing the evolution. Journal of the Academy of Marketing Science 36, 1–10 (2007)
5. Treacy, M., Wiersema, F.: Customer Intimacy and Other Value Disciplines. Harvard Business Review, 84–93 (1993)
6. Peppers, D., Rogers, M., Dorf, B.: Is your company ready for one-to-one marketing? Harvard Business Review 77, 151–160 (1999)
7. Sheth, J.N., Sharma, A.: The impact of the product to service shift in industrial markets and the evolution of the sales organization. Industrial Marketing Management 37, 260–269 (2008)
8. Crosby, L., Evans, K., Cowles, D.: Relationship quality in services selling: an interpersonal influence perspective. The Journal of Marketing 54, 68–81 (1990)
9. Biong, H., Selnes, F.: The Strategic Role of the Salesperson in Established Buyer-Seller Relationships. Journal of Business-to-Business Marketing 3(3), 39–78 (1997)
10. Adamson, B., Dixon, M., Toman, N.: The End of Solution Sales. Harvard Business Review 4, 61–68 (2012)
11. Drexl, A., Haase, K.: Fast approximation methods for sales force deployment. Management Science 45, 1307–1323 (1999)
12. Mantrala, M.K., Albers, S., Caldieraro, F., Jensen, O., Joseph, K., Krafft, M., Narasimhan, C., Gopalakrishna, S., Zoltners, A., Lal, R., Lodish, L.: Sales force modeling: State of the field and research agenda. Marketing Letters 21, 255–272 (2010)
13. Skiera, B., Albers, S.: COSTA: Contribution Optimizing Sales Territory Alignment. Marketing Science 17, 196–213 (1998)
14. Lodish, L.: Assigning salesmen to accounts to maximize profit. Journal of Marketing Research 13, 440–444 (1976)
15. Rangaswamy, A., Sinha, P., Zoltners, A.: An integrated model-based approach for sales force structuring. Marketing Science 9, 279–298 (1990)

# Future Deployment of Technology
# in Healthcare Services - A Delphi Approach

Benedikt Brenken, Arno Schmitz-Urban, and Gerhard Gudergan

Department Service Management
FIR at the RWTH Aachen University
Pontdriesch 14/16, 52062 Aachen, Germany
{brenken,schmitz-urban,gudergan}@fir.rwth-aachen.de

**Abstract.** In an economy with a fast growing demand for services, productivity and innovation become crucial for the survival of service companies. In order to keep up with the change, these companies have to adopt new technologies in the service deployment. Also the healthcare industry is faced with a shift towards modern technology usage and personal services. However, due to budget restrictions, investments in new technologies have to be well considered and guarantee a swift return of investment and increase in productivity. In this paper, empirical results from different industries are presented. A Delphi study is used to get an outlook of the technology usage in the health and care provision industry. Therefore hypotheses are analyzed in detail to show possible impacts for the future. The results provide information about the significance of technology deployment for services and the potentials and barriers which go along with it in the healthcare business.

**Keywords:** Technology management, technology deployment, innovative ability, services, productivity, innovation.

## 1    Introduction

It is beyond question that services as well as the economic performance are important challenges for companies in Europe. According to a survey by Roland Berger the importance of services will increase in the future. In addition, efficiency of industrial services will be increased by optimizing the deployment [1]. This is especially shown in the labor-intensive healthcare industry. According to a study on assisted care of the future by the German Ministry of Education and Research, there exist at least three central challenges in the care sector, namely "shortage of skilled labor", "cost pressure" and the "growing number of people dependent on support and care".

In order to meet these challenges, a new range of both, efficient and patient-friendly, medical support is needed: innovative solutions based on modern technologies [2]. For instance, experts consider the concept of telemedicine as appropriate approach to meet central future challenges in the care sector, if its design is built around user´s needs [3].

J.F. e Cunha, M. Snene, and H. Nóvoa (Eds.): IESS 2013, LNBIP 143, pp. 336–342, 2013.
© Springer-Verlag Berlin Heidelberg 2013

On the one hand, the use of new technologies in healthcare can support the efficiency of service provision. On the other hand, innovative services can often only be enabled by the use of new technologies. It needs to be considered, that decisions for or against the use of technology in healthcare can have severe consequences for healthcare personal, insurance companies and of course patients. These decisions do not only entail costs in the short term, they can shape the healthcare system in the long term as well. Therefore, the use of new technologies in the healthcare sector should be well considered. Thus different challenges in the healthcare sector need to be addressed.

## 2     Objectives

As the usage of technologies in the healthcare sector is seen as suitable approach by experts to overcome future challenges in this industry, this paper attempts to identify future trends of personal services through a detailed analysis of hypotheses, which are based on a Delphi study.

From an organizational perspective neglected elements in service research of an integrated frame for personal services are systematically being developed by scenario technics. Based on that, potential visions of personal and also of technological-integrated service systems are developed in the form of hypotheses. The development and valuation of these hypotheses is carried out by a Delphi study. Besides the creation of a sound scientific and methodic basis the aim of the survey is to involve experts with new backgrounds, other than common expertise's or case studies. All hypotheses are tested along a given timeline of five till fifteen years. In addition, through the conducted Delphi study an exploration of so far gained findings is enabled for other fields of services. The results of the Delphi study will be supplemented by the development of cause-and-effect-models about system contexts.

## 3     Theoretical Background

The focus on this paper is on the question of future developments of personal services. Besides the question of the realization of technical-supported medicinal services there is also the question on the organizational level of the generation of services.

For the purpose of a process-orientated approach some requirements can be deducted for an organization of service processes from a service production model. These models are crucial to explain the circumstances of personal services and also to point out relevant factors of influence. The literature in this field offers various models of description for the production of services. Some basic models of various authors of service production are considered. In this paper the following model, which is illustrated in figure 1, is used to explain the influencing factors of the future organization of personal services. This model consists of several production models of specialized literature and combines essential components of the service production.

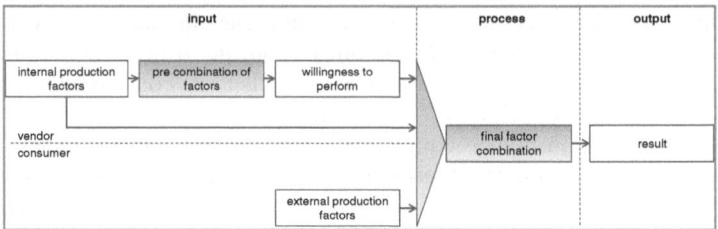

**Fig. 1.** The service production model for Tech4P

In an *input-orientated perspective* of service production internal production factors in the form of employees, technology and resources are pre-combined. This pre-combination as a granting of all internal production factors serves the creation of commitment.

In a *process-orientated perspective* the human being/patient is integrated as an external production factor. The service is delivered to human beings within an end-combination. The labor within personal services is shared among various production factors of several parties.

The *output-driven perspective* on the other hand focusses on the result of the interaction between the potential and the process of performance. From an organizational viewpoint the best result for a service can only be achieved, if both, the process and the potential are planned and controlled simultaneously with each other. Both factors interact closely with each other.

# 4    Research Question and Methodology

Based on the research's background and the outlined challenges, the following research question will be answered in this paper: *"Can future deployment of modern technologies enhance healthcare services?"* To determine the status quo as well as the future usage of technology deployment in healthcare services a Delphi study concerning expectations of experts was conducted. The Delphi study, developed in the 1940th, is a method to solve complex problems [4], [5], [6]. In practice it is often used for the development of forecasts [4], [6]. The Delphi methodology uses positions of various experts, which are obtained in several waves in order to give a short feedback in between. The feedback consists of an anonymous general view on the questions so far, which should help participants to gather more information for a qualified comment [6], [7], [8].

Referring to Häder [6], in reality a rating of existing Delphi studies is assigned, based on their purposes *(Generation of ideas, consensus-building, forecasting or awareness and sensitization of trends and future developments)*. Because there have been tremendous differences in the use of Delphi studies over time, the following part lists the characteristics of the classical Delphi study. Subsequently it is shown, which modifications of these characteristics have to be made for the present *TeleDelphi* [9]. There are some characteristics of a classical Delphi study in the literature [4], [6], [10]. The conducted Delphi study in this paper is matching in most characteristics with the classical version. One modification can be seen in the design of the online based questionnaire, which replaces delivery by mail. This has influences on the participants as well as on the analysis of the data. The data being present digitally on an external server is leading to the fact that there is no data exchange on the postal way between participants and the monitoring group. Because of the novelty of this web-based method, there are no clear statements of the workload, time-saving or the quality of the results yet. However, few studies show that a use of web-based forms is not superior to the classical version, because of unpredictable complications and differences in replying [9].

# 5   Results

## 5.1   Systematization of the Analysis and Participants of the Study

In the section below some of the results and analysis of the conducted Delphi study are shown. The conducted analysis of each hypothesis follows the same systematic: First, an introduction of the hypothesis is given, in which environmental aspects concerning the research question are described. Hereafter, the health and care provision is examined shortly. In the end basic findings are summarized and presented in form of a prospect. From this method a valuation arises into "critical" and "uncritical" descriptors'.

The composition of the group is split into a first and a second wave of surveys. This attribute is inherent to the characteristics of the Delphi study. As in previous case, a selected number of experts is contacted to participate in the survey. Because it is an invitation, it is not usual that the share of participants is identical in both waves. In total, 73 participants took part in the first wave and 47 experts participated in the second wave. Especially the share of expertise plays a significant role for the analysis of the study. A distinction was made between three main kinds of expertise: Development of technology and trends; organization of efforts in technology; acceptance of technology. Multiple answers were allowed in this matter. All three fields of expertise are represented equally well. In both waves there is a majority of experts with knowledge in "development of technology and trends".

A homogenous distribution of the composition of the three criteria disables the possibility of a specialization in certain areas and ensures high-quality results. The requirements on homogeneity of the distribution are mostly satisfied, but it should be noted that there is a dominant distribution of experts, who work in scientific fields. Also a analysis among these three groups did not show any significant differences, thus the main focus remains on the overall results of all participants.

## 5.2   Delphi Study

**Hypothesis 1:** In the future an increase in productivity in the sector of health and care provision can only be achieved by usage of additional technology.

The mean value for the 5-year range ($x;^- = 3,98$) is in the mid-range. However, the mean value for the 15-year range is valued in a very high range ($x;^- = 5,02$). The deviation of $\Delta = 1,04$ is an average value.

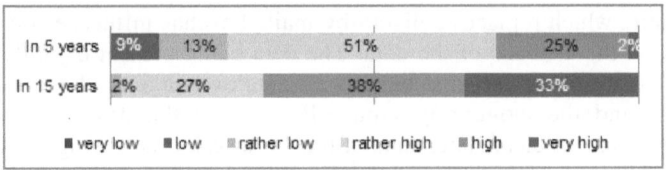

**Fig. 2.** Graphical display of the poll rating (Hyp. 1)

While in terms of the 5-year-forecast 22 % argue against the hypothesis, this fraction diminishes to 2 % in terms of the 15-year-forecast. One third of all experts rate with the highest affirmation "very high".

The usage of new technologies might increase the productivity and also efficiency in the area of health and care provision. These technologies are often summarized under the term eHealth and will optimize informational processes. Basic condition for implementing these technologies is a suitable IT infrastructure, which must fulfill technical and legal requirements and also interfaces, which are compatible to the healthcare industry.

**Hypothesis 2:** In the future the usage of technology in the area of health and care provision will increase the quality of services significantly.

The mean value of the 5-year-forecast $(x;^- = 3,69)$ is situated in a medium range, while the rate of approval for the hypothesis is above average $(x;^- = 4,80)$ in the 15-year-period. The increase of affirmation of the hypothesis is thereby to be considered as high ($\Delta = 1,11$).

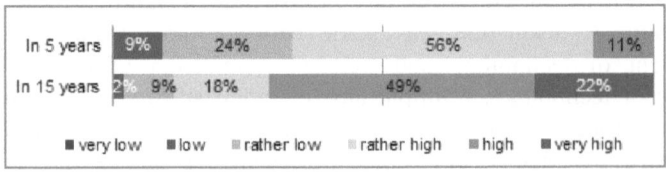

**Fig. 3.** Graphical display of the poll rating (Hyp. 2)

The hypothesis is validated by 67 % for the period of 5 years. None of the experts evaluate the scenario as "very high". In the context of the long term prediction the general affirmation of the hypothesis increases to 89 %, whereas already 22 % give the highest rating.

Tremendous potentials in increasing efficiency and quality, which are shown by the usage of service-supportive technologies, will enhance the usage in medicinal areas in the future. However, a major impediment is represented by heterogeneous (or none) IT infrastructure in healthcare [11].

**Hypothesis 3:** In the future the upcoming integration of technologies of all participants requires the ability to work together in networks in the health and care provision.

The survey displays mean values for the 5 years stretch at a high range (x;⁻ = 4,02) and for the 15 years stretch at a very high range (x;⁻ = 5,09). The increase of affirmation of the hypothesis is thereby to be considered as average (Δ = 1,07).

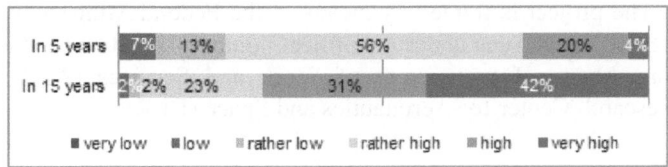

**Fig. 4.** Graphical display of the poll rating (Hyp. 3)

While in terms of the 5-year-forecast 20 % argue against the hypothesis, this fraction diminishes to 4 % in terms of the 15-year-forecast. Noticeable is the strong proportion of very high affirmation.

To furthermore allow the economical use of modern technology, networks between service-providers should be understood as establishments that obtain cost advantages and open up new markets. Additionally the quality of care can be improved by involving the patient in the networks, which than feature a holistic, patient-oriented and integrative character. In this way traditional barriers of the care system can be overcome, loss of information can be reduced and it allows reacting to increasing demands of the patients as well as to the dynamics and developments in healthcare.

# 6    Discussion

Due to the shown challenges, all stakeholders in healthcare sector have to develop their strategy for more integrated, interconnected and multidisciplinary service provision. As a consequence, the ability to use new technologies in service production is considered a success factor and becomes more and more important for companies in healthcare sector – also with regard to the strategic alignment. The results of the research verify the views of the companies: the use of technologies has a lot of potentials for the service input, the service process and the service output.

Generally, the results show that future deployment of modern technologies can enhance healthcare services. This could be achieved by the usage of additional technology, to higher the profitability and quality, usage of new media, to force the ability to work together in networks and working together with partners, to synchronize resources. For this all three perspectives of service provision in healthcare, "organization", "technology" and "people" must be considered.

# 7    Conclusion

From the results of this paper, a road map should be developed to define future strategies for research and innovation fields for the use of technology in personal services. This contributes the discussion of further development of the research area "service science" and is especially helpful to the evolution of the research area. This aim should be achieved by the integration of relevant stakeholders and the distribution of publications which will particularly be created for this purpose.

**Acknowledgment.** The results of this paper are worked out in the research project "Tech4P". The project is funded by means of the Federal Ministry of Education and Research (BMBF) and runs under the project number 01FG10002. It is supervised by the Funding Agency Development of Work and Services (AuD) in Germany's National Research Center for Aeronautics and Space (DLR).

# References

1. Berger, R.: Industrieservices in Deutschland (2010) (study)
2. Schavan, A.: Grusswort. In: Bröckerhoff, H.-P., Schlötelburg, C. (Hrsg.) Ehealth Compendium 2010/2011, p. 2. Health-Care-Com GmbH, Frankfurt (2011)
3. Schaar, A.K., Ziefle, M.: Technikakzpetanz und Nutzungsbewertungen im Kontext neuartiger medizintechnischer Anwendungen. In: Groß, D., Gründer, G., Simonovic, V. (hrsg.) Akzeptanz, Nutzungsbarrieren und Ethische Implikationen Neuer Medizintechnologien. Band 8 Studien des Aachener Kompetenzzentrums für Wissenschaftsgeschichte, pp. 83–87. University Press, Kassel (2010)
4. Linstone, H., Turoff, M.: The Delphi Method: Techniques and Applications. Addison-Wesley, Reading (1975)
5. Linstone, H., Turoff, M.: The Delphi Method: Techniques and Applications (2002)
6. Häder, M.: Delphi-Befragungen – Ein Arbeitsbuch.2. Auflage. VS Verlag für Sozialwissenschaften, Wiesbaden (2009)
7. Häder, M., Häder, S.: Die Delphi-Methode als Gegenstand der methodischen Forschung. In: Häder, M., Häder, S. (eds.) Die Delphi-Technik in den Sozialwissenschaften – Methodische Forschungen und Innovative Anwendungen, pp. 11–32. Westdeutscher Verlag, Wiesbaden (2000)
8. Bortz, J., Döring, N.: Forschungsmethoden und Evaluation 2, Auflage. Springer, Heidelberg (1995)
9. Florian, M.: Das Ladenburger "TeleDelphi " – Nutzung des Internets für eine Expertenbefragung. In: Häder/Häder, pp.195–215 (2000)
10. Wechsler, W.: Delphi-Methode – Gestaltung und Potential für betriebliche Prognoseprozesse. Verlag V. Florentz, München (1978)
11. Rohrweber, J.: Informationstechnik bringt neue Services ins Gesundheitswesen in: ZDNet, http://www.zdnet.de/magazin/41559129/informationstechnik-bringt-neue-services-ins-gesundheitswesen.htm (last accessed on September 30, 2012)

# Author Index

Almeida, Mário    292
Almeida, Rafael    186
Alves, Rui    215
Antunes, Gonçalo    29

Bajić-Bizumić, Biljana    200
Becker, Jeffrey T.    329
Berghoff, Florian    170
Borangiu, Theodor    306
Borbinha, José    29
Brenken, Benedikt    336
Brito e Abreu, Fernando    230
Bucur, Laurenţiu    14

Cardoso, Jorge    114, 141, 155
Castaño, Julian D.M.    58
Castro, Andre F.G.    299
Chi Huynh, Hieu    200
Coelho, Dany C.    313

De Leenheer, Pieter    141, 155
De Smet, Dieter    1
Dias, Teresa Galvão    263
Drăgoicea, Monica    14, 306
Dubois, Eric    100

Feldmann, Niels    73
Ferreira, Marta Campos    263
Fromm, Hansjörg    73, 170

Gama, Nelson    86
Gudergan, Gerhard    336

Henkel, Martin    43

Iacob, Iulia    306

Jardim Nunes, Nuno    215
José, Rui    322

Kieninger, Axel    170
Kimbrough, Steven O.    73

Kohler, Marc    73
Kunze von Bischhoffshausen, Johannes    329

Lemey, Elisah    285
Lillrank, Paul    279

Maia, Miguel A.S.    246
Melro, Ana    322
Mendes, Carlos    292
Meneses, Raquel F.Ch.    58, 246, 299, 313
Mira da Silva, Miguel    86, 129, 186, 292
Molnar, Wolfgang    1
Moreira, Maria R.A.    58, 246, 299, 313

Nóvoa, Maria Henriqueta    263
Nunes, Diogo    129

Oltean, Ecaterina    306

Pătraşcu, Monica    14
Pedrinaci, Carlos    141, 155
Pereira, Rúben    186
Perjons, Erik    43
Petitpierre, Claude    200
Poels, Geert    285

Roque, Marco    230
Rosa, Isabel    129
Rousseau, Anne    100

Satzger, Gerhard    170
Schmitz-Urban, Arno    336
Silva, Bruno    322
Sousa, Paulo S.A.    58, 246

Thelemyr, Anders    43
Torkki, Paulus    279

Van Der Vurst, Griet    285
Vicente, Marco    86

Wegmann, Alain    200